Accounting for Managers

LUBS 1225 and LUBS 2120

Compiled by Alice Shepherd and Peter Wood

Leeds University Business School

University of Leeds

Pearson Education Limited
Edinburgh Gate
Harlow
Essex CM20 2JE

And associated companies throughout the world

Visit us on the World Wide Web at:
www.pearson.com/uk

ISBN 978 1 78016 446 5

Printed and bound in Great Britain by Clays Ltd, Bungay, Suffolk.

Contents

INTRODUCTION TO ACCOUNTING AND FINANCE

INTRODUCTION

Welcome to the world of accounting and finance! In this opening chapter we seek to provide a broad outline of these subjects. We begin by considering the roles of accounting and finance and then go on to identify the main users of financial information. We shall see how both areas can be valuable tools in helping these users improve the quality of their decisions. In subsequent chapters, we develop this decision-making theme by examining in some detail the kinds of financial reports and methods used to aid decision making.

For many of you, accounting and finance are not the main focus of your studies and you may well be asking 'Why do I need to study these subjects?' So, after we have considered the key features of accounting and finance, we shall go on to discuss why some understanding of them is likely to be crucial to you.

Learning outcomes

When you have completed this chapter, you should be able to:

■ explain the nature and roles of accounting and finance;

■ identify the main users of financial information and discuss their needs;

■ distinguish between financial accounting and management accounting;

■ explain why an understanding of accounting and finance is likely to be relevant to your needs.

MyAccountingLab Visit www.myaccountinglab.com for practice and revision opportunities

From Chapter 1 of *Accounting and Finance for Non-Specialists*, 8/e. Peter Atrill and Eddie McLaney. © Pearson Education Limited 2013. All rights reserved.

WHAT ARE ACCOUNTING AND FINANCE?

Let us start by trying to understand the purpose of each. **Accounting** is concerned with *collecting, analysing* and *communicating* financial information. The ultimate aim is to help those using this information to make more informed decisions. If the financial information that is communicated is not capable of improving the quality of decisions made, there would be no point in producing it.

Sometimes the impression is given that the purpose of accounting is simply to prepare financial (accounting) reports on a regular basis. While it is true that accountants under-take this kind of work, it does not represent an end in itself. As already mentioned, the ultimate aim of the accountant's work is to give people better financial information on which to base their decisions. This decision-making perspective of accounting fits in with the theme of this book and shapes the way in which we deal with each topic.

Finance (or financial management), like accounting, exists to help decision makers. It is concerned with the ways in which funds for a business are raised and invested. This lies at the very heart of what business is about. In essence, a business exists to raise funds from investors (owners and lenders) and then to use those funds to make investments (in equipment, premises, inventories and so on) in order to create wealth. The way in which funds are raised must fit with the particular needs of the business. An understanding of finance should help in identifying:

■ the main forms of finance available;
■ the costs, benefits and risks of each form of finance;
■ the risks associated with each form of finance; and
■ the role of financial markets in supplying finance.

Once the funds are raised, they must be invested in a way that will provide the business with a worthwhile return. An understanding of finance should help in evaluating:

■ the returns from that investment; and
■ the risks associated with that investment.

Businesses tend to raise and invest funds in large amounts for long periods of time. The quality of the financing and investment decisions made can, therefore, have a profound impact on the fortunes of the business.

There is little point in trying to make a sharp distinction between accounting and finance. We have already seen that both are concerned with the financial aspects of decision making. There is considerable overlap between the two subjects: for example, accounting reports are a major source of information for financing and investment decision making. In this book, we shall not emphasise the distinctions between accounting and finance.

WHO ARE THE USERS OF ACCOUNTING INFORMATION?

For accounting information to be useful, the accountant must be clear *for whom* the information is being prepared and *for what purpose* the information will be used. There are likely to be various groups of people (known as 'user groups') with an interest in a particular organisation, in the sense of needing to make decisions about it. For the typical private sector business, the more important of these groups are shown in Figure 1.1. Take a look at this figure and then try Activity 1.1.

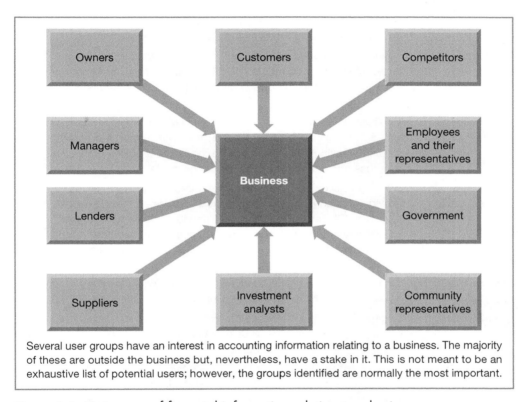

Several user groups have an interest in accounting information relating to a business. The majority of these are outside the business but, nevertheless, have a stake in it. This is not meant to be an exhaustive list of potential users; however, the groups identified are normally the most important.

Figure 1.1 Main users of financial information relating to a business

Activity 1.1

Ptarmigan Insurance plc (PI) is a large motor insurance business. Taking the user groups identified in Figure 1.1, suggest, for each group, the sorts of decisions likely to be made about PI and the factors to be taken into account when making these decisions.

Your answer may be along the following lines:

User group	Decision
Customers	Whether to take further motor policies with PI. This might involve an assessment of PI's ability to continue in business and to meet their needs, particularly in respect of any insurance claims made.

→

User group	Decision
Competitors	How best to compete against PI or, perhaps, whether to leave the market on the grounds that it is not possible to compete profitably with PI. This might involve competitors using PI's performance in various respects as a 'benchmark' when evaluating their own performance. They might also try to assess PI's financial strength and to identify significant changes that may signal PI's future actions (for example, raising funds as a prelude to market expansion).
Employees	Whether to continue working for PI and, if so, whether to demand higher rewards for doing so. The future plans, profits and financial strength of the business are likely to be of particular interest when making these decisions.
Government	Whether PI should pay tax and, if so, how much; whether it complies with agreed pricing policies; whether financial support is needed and so on. In making these decisions an assessment of PI's profits, sales revenues and financial strength would be made.
Community representatives	Whether to allow PI to expand its premises and/or whether to provide economic support for the business. When making such decisions, PI's ability to continue to provide employment for the community and its willingness to use community resources and to fund environmental improvements are likely to be important considerations.
Investment analysts	Whether to advise clients to invest in PI. This would involve an assessment of the likely risks and future returns associated with PI.
Suppliers	Whether to continue to supply PI and, if so, whether to supply on credit. This would involve an assessment of PI's ability to pay for any goods and services supplied.
Lenders	Whether to lend money to PI and/or whether to require repayment of any existing loans. PI's ability to pay the interest and to repay the principal sum would be important factors in such decisions.
Managers	Whether the performance of the business needs to be improved. Performance to date would be compared with earlier plans or some other 'benchmark' to decide whether action needs to be taken. Managers may also wish to decide whether there should be a change in PI's future direction. This would involve looking at PI's ability to perform and at the opportunities available to it.
Owners	Whether to invest more in PI or to sell all, or part, of the investment currently held. This would involve an assessment of the likely risks and returns associated with PI. Owners may also be involved with decisions on rewarding senior managers. The financial performance of the business would normally be considered when making such a decision.

Although this answer covers many of the key points, you may have identified other decisions and/or other factors to be taken into account by each group.

PROVIDING A SERVICE

One way of viewing accounting is as a form of service. The user groups identified in Figure 1.1 can be seen as the 'clients' and the accounting (financial) information produced can be seen as the service provided. The value of this service to the various 'clients' can be judged according to whether the accounting information meets their needs.

To be useful to users, the information provided must possess certain qualities. In particular, it must be relevant and it must faithfully represent what it is supposed to represent. These qualities are now explained:

- **Relevance.** Accounting information should make a difference. That is, it should be capable of influencing user decisions. To do this, it must help to *predict future events* (such as predicting next year's profit), or help to *confirm past events* (such as establishing last year's profit), or do both. By confirming past events, users can check on the accuracy of their earlier predictions. This can, in turn, help them to improve the ways in which they make predictions in the future.
- To be relevant, accounting information must cross a threshold of **materiality**. An item of information is considered material, or significant, if its omission or misstatement would alter the decisions that users make. If the information is not material, it should not be included within the accounting reports. It will merely clutter them up and, perhaps, interfere with the users' ability to interpret them.
- **Faithful representation.** Accounting information should represent what it is supposed to represent. This means that it should be *complete*, by providing all of the information needed to understand what is being portrayed. It should also be *neutral*, which means that the information should be presented and selected without bias. Finally, it should be *free from error*. This is not the same as saying that it must always be perfectly accurate; this is not really possible. Estimates may have to be made which eventually turn out to be inaccurate. It does mean, however, that there should be no errors in the way in which these estimates have been prepared and described. In practice, a piece of accounting information may not reflect perfectly these three aspects of faithful representation. It should try to do so, however, as far as possible.

Accounting information must contain these fundamental qualities if it is to be useful. There is little point in producing information that is relevant, but which lacks faithful representation, or producing information that is irrelevant, but which is faithfully represented.

Activity 1.2

Do you think that what is material for one business will also be material for all other businesses?

No, it will normally vary from one business to the next. What is material will depend on factors such as the size of the business, the nature of the information and the amounts involved.

Further qualities

Where accounting information is both relevant and faithfully represented, there are other qualities that, if present, can enhance its usefulness. These are comparability, verifiability, timeliness and understandability. Each of these qualities is now considered.

- **Comparability.** Users of accounting information often want to make comparisons. They may want to compare performance of the business over time (such as, profit this year compared to last year). They may also want to compare certain aspects of business performance to those of similar businesses (such as the level of sales achieved during the year). Better comparisons can be made where the accounting system treats items that are basically the same in the same way and where policies for measuring and presenting accounting information are made clear.
- **Verifiability.** This quality provides assurance to users that the accounting information provided faithfully represents what it is supposed to represent. Accounting information is verifiable where different, independent experts would be able to agree that it provides a faithful portrayal. Verifiable information tends to be supported by evidence.
- **Timeliness.** Accounting information should be produced in time for users to make their decisions. A lack of timeliness will undermine the usefulness of the information. Normally, the later accounting information is produced, the less useful it becomes.
- **Understandability.** Accounting information should be set out as clearly and concisely as possible. It should also be understood by those at whom the information is aimed.

Activity 1.3

Do you think that accounting reports should be understandable to those who have not studied accounting?

It would be very useful if accounting reports could be understood by everyone. This, however, is unrealistic as complex financial events and transactions cannot normally be expressed in simple terms. It is probably best that we regard accounting reports in the same way that we regard a report written in a foreign language. To understand either of these, we need to have had some preparation. When producing accounting reports, it is normally assumed that the user not only has a reasonable knowledge of business and accounting but is also prepared to invest some time in studying the reports.

Despite the answer to Activity 1.3, the onus is clearly on accountants to provide information in a way that makes it as understandable as possible to non-accountants.

It is worth emphasising that the four qualities just discussed cannot make accounting information useful. They can only enhance the usefulness of information that is already relevant and faithfully represented.

WEIGHING UP THE COSTS AND BENEFITS

Having read the previous sections you may feel that, when considering a piece of accounting information, provided the main qualities identified are present and it is material it should be gathered and made available to users. Unfortunately, there is one more hurdle to jump. Something may still exclude a piece of accounting information from the reports even when it is considered to be useful.

Activity 1.4

Suppose an item of information is capable of being provided. It is relevant to a particular decision and can be faithfully represented. It is also comparable, verifiable, timely and can be understood by the decision maker.

Can you think of the reason why, in practice, you might choose not to produce, or discover, the information?

The reason is that you judge the cost of doing so to be greater than the potential benefit of having the information. This cost–benefit issue will limit the amount of accounting information provided.

In theory, a particular item of accounting information should only be produced if the costs of providing it are less than the benefits, or value, to be derived from its use. In practice, however, these costs and benefits are difficult to assess.

To illustrate the practical problems of establishing the value of information, let us assume that someone has collided with our car in a car park, dented one of the doors and scraped the paintwork. We want to have the dent taken out and the door resprayed at a local garage. We know that the nearest garage would charge £350 but we believe that other local garages may offer to do the job for a lower price. The only way of finding out the prices at other garages is to visit them, so that they can see the extent of the damage. Visiting the garages will involve using some petrol and will take up some of our time. Is it worth the cost of finding out the price for the job at the various local garages? The answer, as we have seen, is that if the cost of discovering the price is less than the potential benefit, it is worth having that information.

To identify the various prices for the job, there are several points to be considered, including:

■ How many garages shall we visit?
■ What is the cost of petrol to visit each garage?
■ How long will it take to make all the garage visits?
■ At what price do we value our time?

The economic benefit of having the information on the price of the job is probably even harder to assess. The following points need to be considered:

■ What is the cheapest price that we might be quoted for the job?
■ How likely is it that we shall be quoted a price cheaper than £350?

As we can imagine, the answers to these questions may be far from clear – remember that we have only contacted the local garage so far. When assessing the value of accounting information we are confronted with similar problems.

Producing accounting information can be very costly. The costs, however, are often difficult to quantify. Direct, out-of-pocket costs, such as salaries of accounting staff, are not usually a problem, but these are only part of the total costs involved. There are other costs such as the cost of user's time spent on analysing and interpreting the information provided.

Activity 1.5

What about the economic benefits of producing accounting information? Do you think it is easier, or harder, to assess the economic benefits of accounting information than to assess the costs of producing it?

It is normally much harder to assess the benefits. Even if we could accurately measure the economic benefits arising from a particular decision we must bear in mind that accounting information will be only one factor influencing that decision. Other factors will also be taken into account. The precise weight that has been attached to accounting information by the decision maker is often impossible to establish.

There are no easy answers to the problem of weighing costs and benefits. Although it is possible to apply some 'science' to the problem, a lot of subjective judgement is normally involved.

The qualities, or characteristics, influencing the usefulness of accounting information, which have been discussed above, are summarised in Figure 1.2.

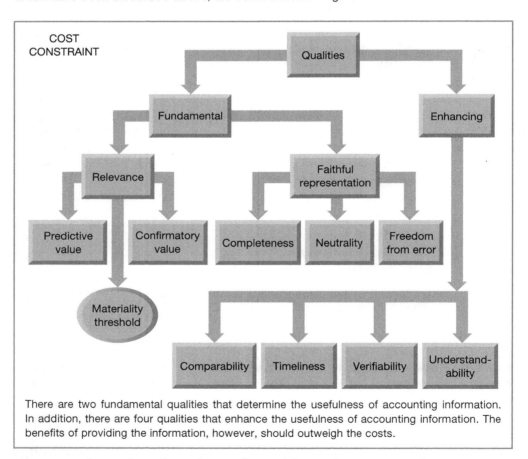

There are two fundamental qualities that determine the usefulness of accounting information. In addition, there are four qualities that enhance the usefulness of accounting information. The benefits of providing the information, however, should outweigh the costs.

Figure 1.2 The qualities that influence the usefulness of accounting information

ACCOUNTING AS AN INFORMATION SYSTEM

We have already noted that accounting can be seen as the provision of a service to 'clients'. Another way of viewing accounting is as a part of the business's total information system. Users, both inside and outside the business, have to make decisions concerning the allocation of scarce resources. To ensure that these resources are efficiently allocated, users often need financial information on which to base decisions. It is the role of the accounting system to provide this information.

The **accounting information system** should have certain features that are common to all information systems within a business. These are:

- identifying and capturing relevant information (in this case financial information);
- recording, in a systematic way, the information collected;
- analysing and interpreting the information collected; and
- reporting the information in a manner that suits the needs of users.

The relationship between these features is set out in Figure 1.3.

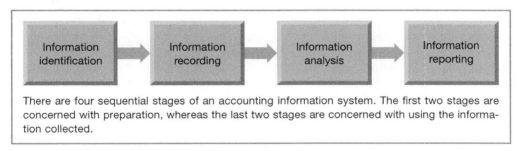

There are four sequential stages of an accounting information system. The first two stages are concerned with preparation, whereas the last two stages are concerned with using the information collected.

Figure 1.3 The accounting information system

Given the decision-making emphasis of this book, we shall be concerned primarily with the final two elements of the process: the analysis and reporting of financial information. We shall consider the way in which information is used by, and is useful to, users rather than the way in which it is identified and recorded.

Efficient accounting systems are an essential ingredient of an efficient business. When the accounting systems fail, the results can be disastrous. **Real World 1.1** provides an example of a systems failure when two businesses combined and then attempted to integrate their respective systems.

As a footnote to Real World 1.1, though Morrison had its problems, these were quickly overcome and the Safeway takeover has proved to be a success.

REAL WORLD 1.1

Blaming the system

When Sir Ken Morrison bought Safeway for £3.35 billion in March 2004, he almost doubled the size of his supermarket chain overnight and went from being a regional operator to a national force. His plan was simple enough. He had to sell off some Safeway stores – Morrison has to date sold off 184 stores for an estimated £1.3 billion – and convert the remaining 230 Safeway stores into Morrison's. Sir Ken has about another 50 to sell. But, nearly fifteen months on, and the integration process is proving harder in practice than it looked on paper. Morrison, once known for its robust performance, has issued four profit warnings in the past ten months. Each time the retailer has blamed Safeway. Last July, it was because of a faster-than-expected sales decline in Safeway stores. In March – there were two warnings that month – it was the fault of Safeway's accounting systems, which left Morrison with lower supplier incomes. This month's warning was put down to higher-than-expected costs from running parallel store systems. At the time of the first warning last July, Simon Procter, of the stockbrokers Charles Stanley, noted that the news 'has blown all profit forecasts out of the water and visibility is very poor from here on out'. But if it was difficult then to predict where Morrison's profits were heading, it is impossible now. Morrison itself cannot give guidance. 'No one envisaged this,' says Mr Procter. 'When I made that comment about visibility last July, I was thinking on a twelve-month time frame, not a two-year one.' Morrison says the complexity of the Safeway deal has put a 'significant strain' on its ability to cope with managing internal accounts. 'This is impacting the ability of the board to forecast likely trends in profitability and the directors are therefore not currently in a position to provide reliable guidance on the level of profitability as a whole,' admits the retailer.

 Source: Rigby, Elizabeth, 'Morrison in uphill battle to integrate Safeway', *Financial Times*, 26 May. 2005.

MANAGEMENT ACCOUNTING AND FINANCIAL ACCOUNTING

Accounting is usually seen as having two distinct strands. These are:

■ **management accounting**, which seeks to meet the accounting needs of managers; and
■ **financial accounting**, which seeks to meet those of all of the users identified earlier in the chapter, except for managers (see Figure 1.1).

The difference in their targeted user groups has led to each strand of accounting developing along different lines. The main areas of difference are as follows.

■ *Nature of the reports produced*. Financial accounting reports tend to be general-purpose. Although they are aimed primarily at providers of finance such as owners and lenders, they contain financial information that will be useful for a broad range of users and decisions. Management accounting reports, on the other hand, are often specific-purpose reports. They are designed with a particular decision in mind and/or for a particular manager.

■ *Level of detail*. Financial accounting reports provide users with a broad overview of the performance and position of the business for a period. As a result, information is aggregated and detail is often lost. Management accounting reports, however, often provide managers with considerable detail to help them with a particular operational decision.

■ *Regulations. Financial accounting reports*, for many businesses, are subject to accounting regulations that try to ensure that they are produced with standard content and in a standard format. The law and accounting rule makers impose these regulations. As management accounting reports are for internal use only, there are no regulations from external sources concerning the form and content of the reports. They can be designed to meet the needs of particular managers.

■ *Reporting interval. For most businesses*, financial accounting reports are produced on an annual basis, though some large businesses produce half-yearly reports and a few produce quarterly ones. Management accounting reports may be produced as frequently as required by managers. In many businesses, managers are provided with certain reports on a daily, weekly or monthly basis, which allows them to check progress frequently. In addition, special-purpose reports will be prepared when required (for example, to evaluate a proposal to purchase a piece of equipment).

■ *Time orientation*. Financial accounting reports reflect the performance and position of the business for the past period. In essence, they are backward-looking. Management accounting reports, on the other hand, often provide information concerning future performance as well as past performance. It is an oversimplification, however, to suggest that financial accounting reports never incorporate expectations concerning the future. Occasionally, businesses will release projected information to other users in an attempt to raise capital or to fight off unwanted takeover bids. Even preparation of the routine financial accounting reports typically requires making some judgements about the future, as we shall see in Chapter 3.

■ *Range and quality of information*. Financial accounting reports concentrate on information that can be quantified in monetary terms. Management accounting also produces such reports, but is also more likely to produce reports that contain information of a non-financial nature, such as physical volume of inventories, number of sales orders received, number of new products launched, physical output per employee and so on. Financial accounting places greater emphasis on the use of objective, verifiable evidence when preparing reports. Management accounting reports may use information that is less objective and verifiable, but nevertheless provide managers with the information they need.

We can see from this that management accounting is less constrained than financial accounting. It may draw from a variety of sources and use information that has varying degrees of reliability. The only real test to be applied when assessing the value of the information produced for managers is whether or not it improves the quality of the decisions made.

The main differences between financial accounting and management accounting are summarised in Figure 1.4.

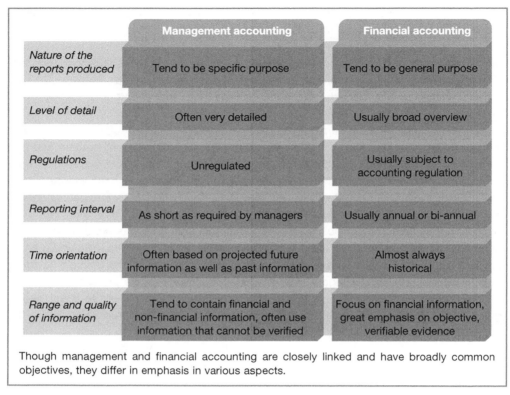

	Management accounting	Financial accounting
Nature of the reports produced	Tend to be specific purpose	Tend to be general purpose
Level of detail	Often very detailed	Usually broad overview
Regulations	Unregulated	Usually subject to accounting regulation
Reporting interval	As short as required by managers	Usually annual or bi-annual
Time orientation	Often based on projected future information as well as past information	Almost always historical
Range and quality of information	Tend to contain financial and non-financial information, often use information that cannot be verified	Focus on financial information, great emphasis on objective, verifiable evidence

Though management and financial accounting are closely linked and have broadly common objectives, they differ in emphasis in various aspects.

Figure 1.4 Management and financial accounting compared

The differences between management accounting and financial accounting suggest that there are differences in the information needs of managers and those of other users. While differences undoubtedly exist, there is also a good deal of overlap between these needs.

Activity 1.6

Can you think of any areas of overlap between the information needs of managers and those of other users? (*Hint*: Think about the time orientation and the level of detail of accounting information.)

Two points that spring to mind are:

- Managers will, at times, be interested in receiving a historical overview of business operations of the sort provided to other users.
- Other users would be interested in receiving detailed information relating to the future, such as the planned level of profits, and non-financial information, such as the state of the sales order book and the extent of product innovations.

To some extent, differences between the two strands of accounting reflect differences in access to financial information. Managers have much more control over the form and content of the information that they receive. Other users have to rely on what managers are prepared to provide or what financial reporting regulations state must be provided. Although the scope of financial accounting reports has increased over time, fears concerning loss of competitive advantage and user ignorance about the reliability of forecast data have resulted in other users not receiving the same detailed and wide-ranging information as that available to managers.

SCOPE OF THIS BOOK

This book covers both financial accounting and management accounting topics. Broadly speaking, the next five chapters (Part 1, Chapters 2 to 6) are concerned with financial accounting topics and the following three (Part 2, Chapters 7 to 9) with management accounting topics. The final part of the book (Part 3, Chapters 10 to 12) is concerned with financial management topics, that is, with issues relating to the financing and investing activities of the business. As mentioned earlier, accounting information is often vitally important for these kinds of decisions.

THE CHANGING FACE OF ACCOUNTING

Over the past four decades, the environment within which businesses operate has become increasingly turbulent and competitive. Various reasons have been identified to explain these changes, including:

- the increasing sophistication of customers;
- the development of a global economy where national frontiers become less important;
- rapid changes in technology;
- the deregulation of domestic markets (for example, electricity, water and gas);
- increasing pressure from owners (shareholders) for competitive economic returns; and
- the increasing volatility of financial markets.

This new, more complex, environment has brought new challenges for managers and other users of accounting information. Their needs have changed and both financial accounting and management accounting have had to respond. To meet the changing needs of users there has been a radical review of the kind of information to be reported.

The changing business environment has given added impetus to the search for a clear framework and principles upon which to base financial accounting reports. Various attempts have been made to clarify their purpose and to provide a more solid foundation for the development of accounting rules. The frameworks and principles that have been developed try to address fundamental questions such as:

- Who are the users of financial accounting information?
- What kinds of financial accounting reports should be prepared and what should they contain?
- How should items such as profit and asset values be measured?

In response to criticisms that the financial reports of some businesses are not clear enough to users, accounting rule makers have tried to improve reporting rules to ensure that the accounting policies of businesses are more comparable and more transparent and that they portray economic reality more faithfully.

The internationalisation of businesses has created a need for accounting rules to have an international reach. It can no longer be assumed that users of accounting information relating to a particular business are based in the country in which the business operates or are familiar with the accounting rules of that country. Thus, there has been increasing harmonisation of accounting rules across national frontiers.

Activity 1.7

How should the harmonisation of accounting rules benefit:

(a) An international investor?
(b) An international business?

An international investor should benefit because accounting definitions and policies that are used in preparing financial accounting reports will not vary across countries. This should make the comparison of performance between businesses operating in different countries much easier.

An international business should benefit because the cost of producing accounting reports in order to comply with the rules of different countries can be expensive. Harmonisation can, therefore, lead to significant cost savings.

Management accounting has also changed by becoming more outward-looking in its focus. In the past, information provided to managers has been largely restricted to that collected within the business. However, the attitude and behaviour of customers and rival businesses have now become the object of much information-gathering. Increasingly, successful businesses are those that are able to secure and maintain competitive advantage over their rivals.

To obtain this advantage, businesses have become more 'customer driven' (that is, concerned with satisfying customer needs). This has led to the production of management accounting information that provides details of customers and the market, such as customer evaluation of services provided and market share. In addition, information about the costs and profits of rival businesses, which can be used as 'benchmarks' by which to gauge competitiveness, is gathered and reported.

To compete successfully, businesses must also find ways of managing costs. The cost base of modern businesses is under continual review and this, in turn, has led to the development of more sophisticated methods of measuring and controlling costs.

WHY DO I NEED TO KNOW ANYTHING ABOUT ACCOUNTING AND FINANCE?

At this point you may be asking yourself 'Why do I need to study accounting and finance? I don't intend to become an accountant!' Well, from our discussion of what accounting and finance is about, it should be clear that the accounting/finance function within a business is a central part of its management information system. On the basis of information provided by the system, managers make decisions concerning the allocation of resources. These decisions may concern whether to:

- continue with certain business operations;
- invest in particular projects; or
- sell particular products.

Such decisions can have a profound effect on all those connected with the business. It is important, therefore, that *all* those who intend to work in a business should have a fairly clear idea of certain important aspects of accounting and finance. These aspects include:

- how accounting reports should be read and interpreted;
- how financial plans are made;
- how investment decisions are made; and
- how businesses are financed.

Many students have a career goal of being a manager within a business – perhaps a personnel manager, production manager, marketing manager or IT manager. If you are one of these students, an understanding of accounting and finance is very important. When you become a manager, even a junior one, it is almost certain that you will have to use accounting reports to help you to carry out your management tasks. It is equally certain that it is largely on the basis of accounting information and reports that your performance as a manager will be judged.

As a manager, it is likely that you will be expected to help in forward planning for the business. This will often involve the preparation of projected accounting reports and setting of financial targets. If you do not understand what the accounting reports really mean and the extent to which the financial information is reliable, you will find yourself at a distinct disadvantage to others who know their way round the system. As a manager, you will also be expected to help decide how the limited resources available to the business should be allocated between competing options. This will require an ability to evaluate the costs and benefits of the different options available. Once again, an understanding of accounting and finance is important to carrying out this management task.

This is not to say that you cannot be an effective and successful personnel, production, marketing or IT manager unless you are also a qualified accountant. It does mean, however, that you need to become a bit 'streetwise' in accounting and finance in order to succeed. This book aims to give you that street wisdom.

WHAT IS THE FINANCIAL OBJECTIVE OF A BUSINESS?

A business is normally created to enhance the wealth of its owners. Throughout this book we shall assume that this is its main objective. This may come as a surprise, as there are other objectives that a business may pursue that are related to the needs of others associated with the business. For example, a business may seek to provide good working conditions for its employees, or it may seek to conserve the environment for the local community. While a business may pursue these objectives, it is normally set up primarily with a view to increasing the wealth of its owners. In practice, the behaviour of businesses over time appears to be consistent with this objective.

Within a market economy there are strong competitive forces at work that ensure that failure to enhance owners' wealth will not be tolerated for long. Competition for the funds provided by the owners and competition for managers' jobs will normally mean that the owners' interests will prevail. If the managers do not provide the expected increase in ownership wealth, the owners have the power to replace the existing management team with a new team that is more responsive to owners' needs. Does this mean that the needs of other groups associated with the business (employees, customers, suppliers, the community and so on) are not really important? The answer to this question is certainly no, if the business wishes to survive and prosper over the longer term.

Satisfying the needs of other groups is usually consistent with increasing the wealth of the owners over the longer term. A business with disaffected customers, for example, may find that they turn to another supplier, resulting in a loss of shareholder wealth. **Real World 1.2** reveals how satisfying the needs of customer as a means to increase shareholder wealth is regarded by some businesses as their central purpose.

REAL WORLD 1.2

Standard practice

Standard Life, a leading long-term savings and investment business, states its purpose a follows:

> We will continue to drive shareholder value through being a leading, customer-centric business, focused on long-term savings and investment propositions. This means finding, acquiring and retaining valuable customers for mutual and sustained financial benefit.

On a mission

Elektron Technology plc, which operates in the fast-moving engineered products sector, states:

> Our mission is to deliver a highly competitive return to shareholders by using our technologies to create innovative solutions for our customers.

Sources: Standard Life plc, www.standardlife.com, accessed 25 January 2012. Elektron Technology plc, www.elektron-technology.com, accessed 21 August 2011.

A dissatisfied workforce may result in low productivity, strikes and so forth, which will in turn have an adverse effect on owners' wealth. Similarly, a business that upsets the local community by unacceptable behaviour, such as polluting the environment, may attract bad publicity, resulting in a loss of customers and heavy fines. **Real World 1.3** provides an example of how two businesses responded to potentially damaging allegations.

REAL WORLD 1.3

The price of clothes

US clothing and sportswear manufacturers Gap and Nike have many of their clothes produced in Asia where labour tends to be cheap. However, some of the contractors that produce clothes on behalf of the two companies have been accused of unacceptable practices. Campaigners visited the factories and came up with damaging allegations. The factories were employing minors, they said, and managers were harassing female employees.

Nike and Gap reacted by allowing independent inspectors into the factories. They promised to ensure their contractors obeyed minimum standards of employment. Earlier this year, Nike took the extraordinary step of publishing the names and addresses of all its contractors' factories on the internet. The company said it could not be sure all the abuse had stopped. It said that if campaigners visited its contractors' factories and found examples of continued malpractice, it would take action.

Nike and Gap said the approach made business sense. They needed society's approval if they were to prosper. Nike said it was concerned about the reaction of potential US recruits to the campaigners' allegations. They would not want to work for a company that was constantly in the news because of the allegedly cruel treatment of those who made its products.

 Source: Skapinker, M., 'Fair shares?', *Financial Times*, 11 June 2005.
Copyright © The Financial Times Ltd.

We should be clear that generating wealth for the owners is not the same as seeking to maximise the current year's profit. Wealth creation is concerned with the longer term. It relates not only to this year's profit but to that of future years as well. In the short term, corners can be cut and risks taken that improve current profit at the expense of future profit. **Real World 1.4** provides some examples of how emphasis on short-term profit can be damaging.

REAL WORLD 1.4

Short-term gains, long-term problems

For many years, under the guise of defending capitalism, we have been allowing ourselves to degrade it. We have been poisoning the well from which we have drawn wealth. We have misunderstood the importance of values to capitalism. We have surrendered to the idea that success is pursued by making as much money as the law allowed without regard to how it was made.

Thirty years ago, retailers would be quite content to source the shoes they wanted to sell as cheaply as possible. The working conditions of those who produced them was not their concern. Then headlines and protests developed. Society started to hold them responsible for previously invisible working conditions. Companies like Nike went through a transformation. They realised they were polluting their brand. Global sourcing became visible. It was no longer viable to define success simply in terms of buying at the lowest price and selling at the highest.

Financial services and investment are today where footwear was thirty years ago. Public anger at the crisis will make visible what was previously hidden. Take the building up of huge portfolios of loans to poor people on US trailer parks. These loans were authorised without proper scrutiny of the circumstances of the borrowers. Somebody else then deemed them fit to be securitised and so on through credit default swaps and the rest without anyone seeing the transaction in terms of its ultimate human origin.

Each of the decision makers thought it okay to act like the thoughtless footwear buyer of the 1970s. The price was attractive. There was money to make on the deal. Was it responsible? Irrelevant. It was legal, and others were making money that way. And the consequences for the banking system if everybody did it? Not our problem.

The consumer has had a profound shock. Surely we could have expected the clever and wise people who invested our money to be better at risk management than they have shown themselves to be in the present crisis? How could they have been so gullible in not challenging the bankers whose lending proved so flaky? How could they have believed that the levels of bonuses that were, at least in part, coming out of their savings could have been justified in 'incentivising' a better performance? How could they have believed that a 'better' performance would be one that is achieved for one bank without regard to its effect on the whole banking system? Where was the stewardship from those exercising investment on their behalf?

The answer has been that very few of them do exercise that stewardship. Most have stood back and said it doesn't really pay them to do so. The failure of stewardship comes from the same mindset that created the irresponsible lending in the first place. We are back to the mindset that has allowed us to poison the well: never mind the health of the system as a whole, I'm making money out of it at the moment. Responsibility means awareness for the system consequences of our actions. It is not a luxury. It is the cornerstone of prudence.

 Source: Goyder, M., 'How we've poisoned the well of wealth', *Financial Times,* 15 February 2009.

BALANCING RISK AND RETURN

All decision making involves the future. Business decision making is no exception. The only thing certain about the future, however, is that we cannot be sure what will happen. Things may not turn out as planned and this risk should be carefully considered when making financial decisions.

As in other aspects of life, risk and return tend to be related. Evidence shows that returns relate to risk in something like the way shown in Figure 1.5.

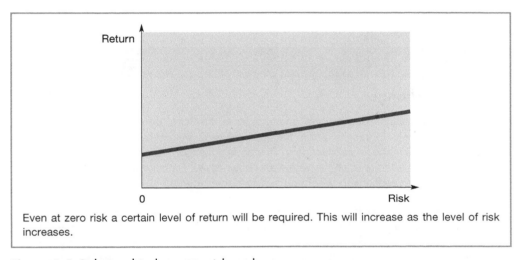

Even at zero risk a certain level of return will be required. This will increase as the level of risk increases.

Figure 1.5 Relationship between risk and return

Activity 1.8

Look at Figure 1.5 above and state, in broad terms, where an investment in:

(a) a government savings account, and
(b) a lottery ticket

should be placed on the risk-return line.

A government savings account is normally a very safe investment. Even if a government is in financial difficulties, it can always print more money to repay investors. Returns from this form of investment, however, are normally very low. Investing in a lottery ticket runs a very high risk of losing the whole amount invested. This is because the probability of winning is normally very low. However, a winning ticket can produce enormous returns.

Thus, the government savings account should be placed towards the far left of the risk-return line and the lottery ticket towards the far right.

This relationship between risk and return has important implications for setting financial objectives for a business. The owners will require a minimum return to induce them to invest at all, but will require an additional return to compensate for taking risks; the higher the risk, the higher the required return. Managers must be aware of this and must strike the appropriate balance between risk and return when setting objectives and pursuing particular courses of action.

The recent turmoil in the banking sector has shown, however, that the right balance is not always struck. Some banks have taken excessive risks in pursuit of higher returns and, as a consequence, have incurred massive losses. They are now being kept afloat with taxpayers' money. **Real World 1.5** discusses the collapse of one leading bank, in which the UK government took a majority stake, and argues that the risk appetite of banks must now change.

REAL WORLD 1.5

Banking on change

The taxpayer has become the majority shareholder in the Royal Bank of Scotland (RBS). This change in ownership, resulting from the huge losses sustained by the bank, will shape the future decisions made by its managers. This does not simply mean that it will affect the amount that the bank lends to homeowners and businesses. Rather it is about the amount of risk that it will be prepared to take in pursuit of higher returns.

In the past, those managing banks such as RBS saw themselves as producers of financial products that enabled banks to grow faster than the economy as a whole. They did not want to be seen as simply part of the infrastructure of the economy. It was too dull. It was far more exciting to be seen as creators of financial products that created huge profits and, at the same time, benefited us all through unlimited credit at low rates of interest. These financial products, with exotic names such as 'collateralised debt obligations' and 'credit default swaps', ultimately led to huge losses that taxpayers had to absorb in order to prevent the banks from collapse.

Now that many banks throughout the world are in taxpayers' hands, they are destined to lead a much quieter life. They will have to focus more on the basics such as taking deposits, transferring funds and making simple loans to customers. Is that such a bad thing?

The history of banking has reflected a tension between carrying out their core functions and the quest for high returns through high risk strategies. It seems, however, that for some time to come they will have to concentrate on the former and will be unable to speculate with depositors' cash.

Source: Peston, Robert, 'We own Royal Bank', 28 November 2008, BBC News, www.bbc.co.uk.

NOT-FOR-PROFIT ORGANISATIONS

Though the focus of this book is accounting as it relates to private sector businesses, there are many organisations that do not exist mainly for the pursuit of profit.

Activity 1.9

Can you think of at least four types of organisation that are not primarily concerned with making profits?

We thought of the following:

- charities
- clubs and associations
- universities
- local government authorities
- national government departments
- churches
- trade unions.

All of these organisations need to produce accounting information for decision-making purposes. Once again, various user groups need this information to help them to make decisions. These user groups are often the same as, or similar to, those identified for private sector businesses. They may have a stake in the future viability of the organisation and may use accounting information to check that the wealth of the organisation is being properly controlled and used in a way that is consistent with its objectives.

Real World 1.6 provides an example of the importance of accounting to relief agencies, which are, of course, not-for-profit organisations.

REAL WORLD 1.6

Accounting for disasters

In the aftermath of the Asian tsunami more than £400 million was raised from charitable donations. It was important that this huge amount of money for aid and reconstruction was used as efficiently and effectively as possible. That did not just mean medical staff and engineers. It also meant accountants.

The charity that exerts financial control over aid donations is Mango: Management Accounting for Non-Governmental Organisations (NGOs). It provides accountants in the field and it provides the back-up, such as financial training and all the other services that should result in really robust financial management in a disaster area.

The world of aid has changed completely as a result of the tsunami. According to Mango's director, Alex Jacobs, 'Accounting is just as important as blankets. Agencies have been aware of this for years. But when you move on to a bigger scale there is more pressure to show the donations are being used appropriately.'

More recently, the earthquake in Haiti led to a call from Mango for French-speaking accountants to help support the relief programme and to help in the longer-term rebuilding of Haiti.

Source: Adapted from Bruce, R., 'Tsunami: finding the right figures for disaster relief', FT.com, 7 March 2005; Bruce, R., 'The work of Mango: coping with generous donations', FT.com, 27 February 2006; and Grant, P., 'Accountants needed in Haiti', *Accountancy Age*, 5 February 2010.

SUMMARY

The main points of this chapter may be summarised as follows.

What are accounting and finance?

- Accounting provides financial information to help various user groups make better judgements and decisions.
- Finance is concerned with the financing and investing activities of the business and is also concerned with improving the quality of user decisions.

Accounting and user needs

- For accounting to be useful, there must be a clear understanding of *for whom* and *for what purpose* the information will be used.
- Owners, managers and lenders are important user groups, but there are several others.

Providing a service

- Accounting can be viewed as a form of service as it involves providing financial information required by the various users.
- To provide a useful service, accounting must possess certain qualities, or characteristics. The fundamental qualities are relevance and faithful representation. Other qualities that enhance the usefulness of accounting information are comparability, verifiability, timeliness and understandability.
- Providing a service to users can be costly and financial information should be produced only if the cost of providing the information is less than the benefits gained.

Accounting information

- Accounting is part of the total information system within a business. It shares the features that are common to all information systems within a business, which are the identification, recording, analysis and reporting of information.

Management accounting and financial accounting

- Accounting has two main strands – management accounting and financial accounting.
- Management accounting seeks to meet the needs of the business's managers, and financial accounting seeks to meet the needs of providers of finance but will also be of use to other user groups.
- These two strands differ in terms of the types of reports produced, the level of reporting detail, the time horizon, the degree of regulation and the range and quality of information provided.

The changing face of accounting

- Changes in the economic environment have led to changes in the nature and scope of accounting.

- Financial accounting has improved its framework of rules and there has been greater international harmonisation of accounting rules.

- Management accounting has become more outward-looking, and new methods for managing costs have emerged.

Why study accounting?

- Everyone connected with business should be a little 'streetwise' about accounting and finance because they exert such an enormous influence over business operations.

What is the financial objective of a business?

- The key financial objective is to enhance the wealth of the owners. To achieve this objective, the needs of other groups connected with the business, such as employees, cannot be ignored.

- When setting financial objectives, the right balance must be struck between risk and return.

MyAccountingLab

Go to www.myaccountinglab.com to check your understanding of the chapter, create a personalised study plan, and maximise your revision time

KEY TERMS

accounting p. 2
finance p. 2
relevance p. 5
materiality p. 5
faithful representation p. 5
comparability p. 6

verifiability p. 6
timeliness p. 6
understandability p. 6
accounting information system p. 9
management accounting p. 10
financial accounting p. 10

FURTHER READING

If you would like to explore the topics covered in this chapter in more depth, we recommend the following books:

Atrill, P. *Financial Management for Decision Makers*, 6th edn, Financial Times Prentice Hall, 2012, Chapter 1.

Drury C., *Management and Cost Accounting*, 8th edn, Cengage Learning, 2012, Chapter 1.

Elliot, B. and Elliot, J., *Financial Accounting and Reporting*, 15th edn, Financial Times Prentice Hall, 2012, Chapter 9.

McLaney, E., *Business Finance: Theory and Practice*, 9th edn, Prentice Hall, 2012, Chapters 1 and 2.

? REVIEW QUESTIONS

Solutions to these questions can be found at the back of the book, in Appendix C.

1.1 What is the purpose of providing accounting information?

1.2 Identify the main users of accounting information for a university. For what purposes would different user groups need information? Is there a major difference in the ways in which accounting information for a university would be used compared with that of a private-sector business?

1.3 Management accounting has been described as 'the eyes and ears of management'. What do you think this expression means?

1.4 Financial accounting statements tend to reflect past events. In view of this, how can they be of any assistance to a user in making a decision when decisions, by their very nature, can only be made about future actions?

MEASURING AND REPORTING FINANCIAL POSITION

INTRODUCTION

We saw in Chapter 1 that accounting has two distinct strands: financial accounting and management accounting. This chapter, along with Chapters 3, 4 and 5, examines the three major financial statements that form the core of financial accounting. We start by taking an overview of these statements to see how each contributes towards an assessment of the overall financial position and performance of a business.

Following this overview, we begin a more detailed examination by turning our attention towards one of these financial statements: the statement of financial position. We shall see how it is prepared and examine the principles underpinning it. We shall also consider its value for decision-making purposes.

Learning outcomes

When you have completed this chapter, you should be able to:

- explain the nature and purpose of the three major financial statements;
- prepare a simple statement of financial position and interpret the information that it contains;
- discuss the accounting conventions underpinning the statement of financial position;
- discuss the uses and limitations of the statement of financial position for decision-making purposes.

MyAccountingLab   Visit www.myaccountinglab.com for practice and revision opportunities

THE MAJOR FINANCIAL STATEMENTS – AN OVERVIEW

The major financial accounting statements aim to provide a picture of the financial position and performance of a business. To achieve this, a business's accounting system will normally produce three financial statements on a regular, recurring basis. These three statements are concerned with answering the following questions relating to a particular period:

■ What cash movements took place?
■ How much wealth was generated?
■ What is the accumulated wealth of the business at the end of the period and what form does it take?

To address each of the above questions, there is a separate financial statement. The financial statements are:

■ the **statement of cash flows**;
■ the **income statement** (also known as the profit and loss account);
■ the **statement of financial position** (also known as the balance sheet).

Together they provide an overall picture of the financial health of the business.

Perhaps the best way to introduce these financial statements is to look at an example of a very simple business. From this we shall be able to see the sort of information that each of the statements can usefully provide. It is, however, worth pointing out that, while a simple business is our starting point, the principles for preparing the financial statements apply equally to the largest and most complex businesses. Thus, we shall frequently encounter these principles again in later chapters.

Example 2.1

Paul was unemployed and unable to find a job. He therefore decided to embark on a business venture. With Christmas approaching, he decided to buy gift wrapping paper from a local supplier and to sell it on the corner of his local high street. He felt that the price of wrapping paper in the high street shops was too high. This provided him with a useful business opportunity.

He began the venture with £40 of his own money, in cash. On Monday, Paul's first day of trading, he bought wrapping paper for £40 and sold three-quarters of it for £45 cash.

What cash movements took place in Paul's business during Monday?
For Monday, a *statement of cash flows* showing the cash movements (that is, cash in and cash out) for the day can be prepared as follows:

Statement of cash flows for Monday

	£
Cash introduced (by Paul)	40
Cash from sales of wrapping paper	45
Cash paid to buy wrapping paper	(40)
Closing balance of cash	45

→

The statement shows that Paul placed £40 cash into the business. The business received £45 cash from customers, but paid £40 cash to buy the wrapping paper. This left £45 of cash by Monday evening. Note that we are taking the standard approach found in the financial statements of showing figures to be deducted (in this case the £40 paid out) in brackets. We shall take this approach consistently throughout the chapters dealing with financial statements.

How much wealth (that is, profit) was generated by the business during Monday?
An *income statement* can be prepared to show the wealth (profit) generated on Monday. The wealth generated arises from trading and will be the difference between the value of the sales made and the cost of the goods (that is, wrapping paper) sold:

Income statement for Monday

	£
Sales revenue	45
Cost of goods sold ($^3/_4$ of £40)	(30)
Profit	15

Note that it is only the cost of the wrapping paper *sold* that is matched against (and deducted from) the sales revenue in order to find the profit, not the whole of the cost of wrapping paper acquired. Any unsold inventories (also known as *stock*) will be charged against the future sales revenue that it generates. In this case the cost of the unsold inventories it is $^1/_4$ of £40 = £10.

What is the accumulated wealth on Monday evening and what form does it take?
To establish the accumulated wealth at the end of Monday's trading, we can draw up a *statement of financial position* for Paul's business. This statement will also list the forms of wealth held at the end of that day:

Statement of financial position as at Monday evening

	£
Cash (closing balance)	45
Inventories of goods for resale ($^1/_4$ of £40)	10
Total assets	55
Equity	55

Note the terms 'assets' and 'equity' that appear in this statement. 'Assets' are business resources (things of value to the business) and include cash and inventories. 'Equity' is the word used in accounting to describe the investment, or stake, of the owner(s) – in this case Paul – in the business. Both of these terms will be discussed in some detail a little later in this chapter.

We can see from the financial statements in Example 2.1 that each statement provides part of a picture of the financial performance and position of the business. We begin by showing the cash movements. Cash is a vital resource that is necessary for any business to function effectively. It is required to meet debts that become due and to acquire other resources (such as inventories). Cash has been described as the 'lifeblood' of a business.

Reporting cash movements alone, however, is not enough to portray the financial health of the business. To find out how much profit was generated, we need an income statement. It is important to recognise that cash and profits rarely move in unison. During Monday, for example, the cash balance increased by £5, but the profit generated, as shown in the income statement, was £15. The cash balance did not increase in line with profit because part of the wealth generated (£10) was held in the form of inventories.

The statement of financial position that was drawn up as at the end of Monday's trading, provides an insight to the total wealth of the business. This wealth can be held in various forms. For Paul's business, wealth is held in the form of cash and inventories. Hence, when drawing up the statement of financial position, both forms will be listed. For a large business, many other forms of wealth may be held, such as property, equipment, motor vehicles and so on.

Let us now continue with our example.

Example 2.1 (continued)

On Tuesday, Paul bought more wrapping paper for £20 cash. He managed to sell all of the new inventories and all of the earlier inventories, for a total of £48.

The statement of cash flows for Tuesday will be as follows:

Statement of cash flows for Tuesday

	£
Opening balance (from Monday evening)	45
Cash from sales of wrapping paper	48
Cash paid to buy wrapping paper	(20)
Closing balance	73

The income statement for Tuesday will be as follows:

Income statement for Tuesday

	£
Sales revenue	48
Cost of goods sold (£20 + £10)	(30)
Profit	18

The statement of financial position as at Tuesday evening will be:

Statement of financial position as at Tuesday evening

	£
Cash (closing balance)	73
Inventories	–
Total assets	73
Equity	73

We can see that the total business wealth increased to £73 by Tuesday evening. This represents an increase of £18 (that is, £73 – £55) over Monday's figure – which, of course, is the amount of profit made during Tuesday as shown on the income statement.

Activity 2.1

On Wednesday, Paul bought more wrapping paper for £46 cash. However, it was raining hard for much of the day and sales were slow. After Paul had sold half of his total inventories for £32, he decided to stop trading until Thursday morning.

Have a go at drawing up the three financial statements for Paul's business for Wednesday.

Statement of cash flows for Wednesday

	£
Opening balance (from the Tuesday evening)	73
Cash from sales of wrapping paper	32
Cash paid to buy wrapping paper	(46)
Closing balance	59

Income statement for Wednesday

	£
Sales revenue	32
Cost of goods sold ($1/2$ of £46)	(23)
Profit	9

Statement of financial position as at Wednesday evening

ASSETS

	£
Cash (closing balance)	59
Inventories ($1/2$ of £46)	23
Total assets	82
Equity	82

Note that the total business wealth has increased by £9 (that is, the amount of Wednesday's profit) even though the cash balance has declined. This is because the business is holding more of its wealth in the form of inventories rather than cash, compared with the position on Tuesday evening.   *Paul had invested 82 into the business*

By Wednesday evening, the equity stood at £82. This arose from Paul's initial investment of £40, plus his profits for Monday (£15), Tuesday (£18) and Wednesday (£9). This represents Paul's total investment in his business at that time. The equity of most businesses will similarly be made up of injections of funds by the owner plus any accumulated profits.

We can see that the income statement and statement of cash flows are both concerned with measuring flows (of wealth and cash respectively) during a particular period. The statement of financial position, however, is concerned with the financial position at a particular moment in time. Figure 2.1 illustrates this point.

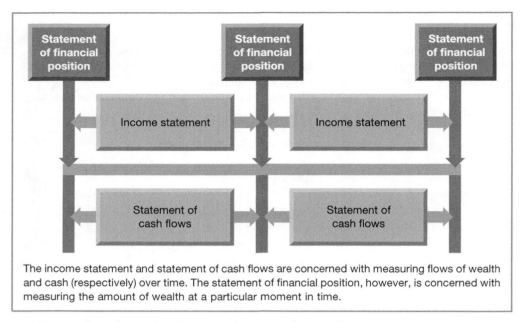

The income statement and statement of cash flows are concerned with measuring flows of wealth and cash (respectively) over time. The statement of financial position, however, is concerned with measuring the amount of wealth at a particular moment in time.

Figure 2.1 The relationship between the major financial statements

The three financial statements discussed are often referred to as the **final accounts** of the business.

For external users (that is virtually all users except the managers of the business concerned), these statements are normally backward looking because they are based on information concerning past events and transactions. This can be useful in providing feedback on past performance and in identifying trends that provide clues to future performance. However, the statements can also be prepared using projected data to help assess likely future profits, cash flows and so on. Normally, this is done only for management decision-making purposes.

Now that we have an overview of the financial statements, we shall consider each one in detail. The remainder of this chapter is devoted to the statement of financial position.

THE STATEMENT OF FINANCIAL POSITION

We saw a little earlier that this statement shows the forms in which the wealth of a business is held and how much wealth is held in each form. We can, however, be more specific about the nature of this statement by saying that it sets out the **assets** of a business, on the one hand, and the **claims** against the business, on the other. Before looking at the statement of financial position in more detail, we need to be clear about what these terms mean.

Assets

An asset is essentially a resource held by a business. For a particular item to be treated as an asset, for accounting purposes, it should have the following characteristics:

- *A probable future economic benefit must exist.* This simply means that the item must be expected to have some future monetary value. This value can arise through the asset's use within the business or through its hire or sale. Thus, an obsolete piece of equipment that will be sold for scrap would still be considered an asset, whereas an obsolete piece of equipment that has no scrap value would not be regarded as one.

- *The benefit must arise from some past transaction or event.* This means that the transaction (or other event), giving rise to a business's right to the benefit, must have already occurred and will not arise at some future date. Thus an agreement by a business to buy a piece of equipment at some future date would not mean the item is currently an asset of the business.

- *The business must have the right to control the resource.* Unless the business controls the resource, it cannot be regarded as an asset for accounting purposes. Thus, for a business offering holidays on barges, the canal system may be a very valuable resource, but as the business will not be able to control the access of others to the canal system, it cannot be regarded as an asset of the business. (However, any barges owned by the business would be regarded as assets.)

- *The asset must be capable of measurement in monetary terms.* Unless the item can be measured in monetary terms, with a reasonable degree of reliability, it will not be regarded as an asset for inclusion on the statement of financial position. Thus, the title of a magazine (for example *Hello!* or *Vogue*) that was created by its publisher may be extremely valuable to that publishing business, but this value is usually difficult to quantify. It will not, therefore, be treated as an asset.

Note that all four of these conditions must apply. If one of them is missing, the item will not be treated as an asset, for accounting purposes, and will not, therefore, appear on the statement of financial position. Figure 2.2 summarises the above discussion in the form of a decision chart.

We can see that these conditions will strictly limit the kind of resources that may be referred to as 'assets' in the statement of financial position. Some resources, like the canal system or the magazine title *Hello!*, may well be assets in a broader sense, but not for accounting purposes. Once an asset has been acquired by a business, it will continue to be considered an asset until the benefits are exhausted or the business disposes of it.

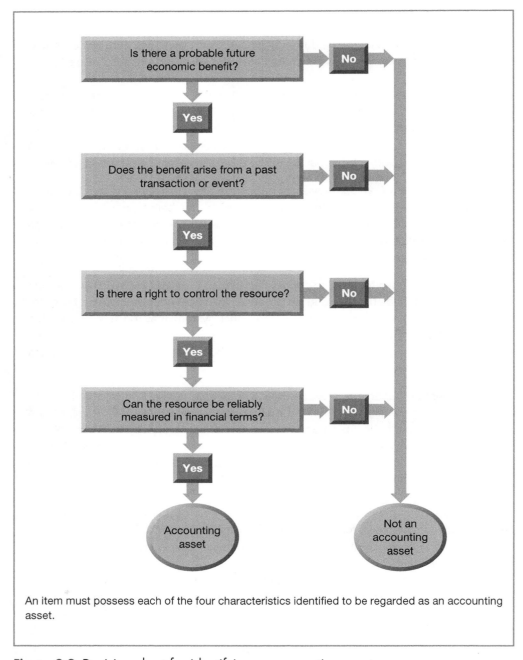

An item must possess each of the four characteristics identified to be regarded as an accounting asset.

Figure 2.2 Decision chart for identifying an accounting asset

Activity 2.2

Indicate which of the following items could appear as an asset on the statement of financial position of a business. Explain your reasoning in each case.

1 £1,000 owed to the business by a credit customer who is unable to pay.

2 A patent, bought from an inventor, that gives the business the right to produce a new product. Production of the new product is expected to increase profits over the period during which the patent is held.

3 A recently hired, new marketing director who is confidently expected to increase profits by over 30 per cent during the next three years.

4 A recently purchased machine that will save the business £10,000 each year. It is already being used by the business but it has been acquired on credit and is not yet paid for.

Your answer should be along the following lines.

1 Under normal circumstances, a business would expect a customer to pay the amount owed. Such an amount is therefore typically shown as an asset under the heading 'trade receivables' (or 'debtors'). However, in this particular case the customer is unable to pay. As a result, the item is incapable of providing future economic benefits and the £1,000 owing would not be regarded as an asset. Debts that are not paid are referred to as 'bad debts'.

2 The patent would meet all of the conditions set out above and would therefore be regarded as an asset.

3 The new marketing director would not be considered as an asset. One argument for this is that the business does not have exclusive rights of control over the director. (It may have an exclusive right to the services that the director provides, however.) Perhaps a stronger argument is that the value of the director cannot be measured in monetary terms with any degree of reliability.

4 The machine would be considered an asset even though it is not yet paid for. Once the business has agreed to buy the machine, and has accepted it, the machine represents an asset even though payment is still outstanding. (The amount outstanding would be shown as a claim, as we shall see shortly.)

The sorts of items that often appear as assets in the statement of financial position of a business include:

- property
- plant and equipment
- fixtures and fittings — *furniture*
- patents and trademarks
- trade receivables (debtors)
- investments outside the business.

Activity 2.3

Can you think of two additional items that might appear as assets in the statement of financial position of a typical business?

You may be able to think of a number of other items. Two that we have met so far, because they were held by Paul's wrapping paper business (in Example 2.1), are inventories and cash.

Note that an asset does not have to be a physical item – it may be a non-physical one that gives a right to certain benefits. Assets that have a physical substance and can be touched (such as inventories) are referred to as **tangible assets**. Assets that have no physical substance but which, nevertheless, provide expected future benefits (such as patents) are referred to as **intangible assets**.

Claims

A claim is an obligation of the business to provide cash, or some other form of benefit, to an outside party. It will normally arise as a result of the outside party providing assets for use by the business. There are essentially two types of claim against a business:

- **Equity**. This represents the claim of the owner(s) against the business. This claim is sometimes referred to as the *owner's capital*. Some find it hard to understand how the owner can have a claim against the business, particularly when we consider the example of a sole-proprietor-type business, like Paul's, where the owner *is*, in effect, the business. For accounting purposes, however, a clear distinction is made between the business and the owner(s). The business is viewed as being quite separate from the owner. It is seen as a separate entity with its own separate existence. Thus, when financial statements are prepared, they relate to the business rather than to the owner(s). Viewed from this perspective, any funds contributed by the owner will be seen as coming from outside the business and will appear as a claim against the business in its statement of financial position.
- **Liabilities**. Liabilities represent the claims of all individuals and organisations, apart from the owner(s). They arise from past transactions or events such as supplying goods or lending money to the business. A liability will be settled through an outflow of assets (usually cash).

Once a claim from the owners or outsiders has been incurred by a business, it will remain as an obligation until it is settled.

Now that the meaning of the terms *assets*, *equity* and *liabilities* has been established, we can consider the relationship between them. This relationship is quite straightforward. If a business wishes to acquire assets, it must raise the necessary funds from somewhere. It may raise these funds from the owner(s), or from other outside parties, or from both. Example 2.2 illustrates this relationship.

Example 2.2

Jerry and Company is a new business that was created by depositing £20,000 in a bank account on 1 March. This amount was raised partly from the owner (£6,000) and partly from borrowing (£14,000). Raising funds in this way will give rise to a claim on the business by both the owner (equity) and the lender (liability). If a statement of financial position of Jerry and Company is prepared following the above transactions, it will appear as follows:

Jerry and Company
Statement of financial position as at 1 March

	£
ASSETS	
Cash at bank	20,000
Total assets	20,000
EQUITY AND LIABILITIES	
Equity	6,000
Liabilities – borrowing	14,000
Total equity and liabilities	20,000

We can see from the statement of financial position that the total claims (equity and liabilities) are the same as the total assets. Thus:

Assets = Equity + Liabilities

This equation – which we shall refer to as the *accounting equation* – will always hold true. Whatever changes may occur to the assets of the business or the claims against it, there will be compensating changes elsewhere that will ensure that the statement of financial position always 'balances'. By way of illustration, consider the following transactions for Jerry and Company:

2 March	Bought a motor van for £5,000, paying by cheque.
3 March	Bought inventories (that is, goods to be sold) on one month's credit for £3,000. (This means that the inventories were bought on 3 March, but payment will not be made to the supplier until 3 April.)
4 March	Repaid £2,000 of the amount borrowed to the lender, by cheque.
6 March	Owner introduced another £4,000 into the business bank account.

A statement of financial position may be drawn up after each day in which transactions have taken place. In this way, we can see the effect of each transaction on the assets and claims of the business. The statement of financial position as at 2 March will be:

Jerry and Company
Statement of financial position as at 2 March

	£
ASSETS	
Cash at bank (20,000 – 5,000)	15,000
Motor van	5,000
Total assets	20,000
EQUITY AND LIABILITIES	
Equity	6,000
Liabilities – borrowing	14,000
Total equity and liabilities	20,000

As we can see, the effect of buying the motor van is to decrease the balance at the bank by £5,000 and to introduce a new asset – a motor van – to the statement of financial position. The total assets remain unchanged. It is only the 'mix' of assets that has changed. The claims against the business remain the same because there has been no change in the way in which the business has been funded.

The statement of financial position as at 3 March, following the purchase of inventories, will be:

Jerry and Company
Statement of financial position as at 3 March

	£
ASSETS	
Cash at bank	15,000
Motor van	5,000
Inventories	3,000
Total assets	23,000
EQUITY AND LIABILITIES	
Equity	6,000
Liabilities – borrowing	14,000
Liabilities – trade payable	3,000
Total equity and liabilities	23,000

The effect of buying inventories has been to introduce another new asset (inventories) to the statement of financial position. Furthermore, the fact that the goods have not yet been paid for means that the claims against the business will be increased by the £3,000 owed to the supplier, who is referred to as a *trade payable* (or trade creditor) on the statement of financial position.

Activity 2.4

Try drawing up a statement of financial position for Jerry and Company as at 4 March.

The statement of financial postion as at 4 March, following the repayment of part of the borrowing, will be:

Jerry and Company
Statement of financial position as at 4 March

	£
ASSETS	
Cash at bank (15,000 – 2,000)	13,000
Motor van	5,000
Inventories	3,000
Total assets	21,000
EQUITY AND LIABILITIES	
Equity	6,000
Liabilities – borrowing (14,000 – 2,000)	12,000
Liabilities – trade payable	3,000
Total equity and liabilities	21,000

The repayment of £2,000 of the borrowing will result in a decrease in the balance at the bank of £2,000 and a decrease in the lender's claim against the business by the same amount.

Activity 2.5

Try drawing up a statement of financial position as at 6 March for Jerry and Company.

The statement of financial position as at 6 March, following the introduction of more funds, will be:

Jerry and Company
Statement of financial position as at 6 March

	£
ASSETS	
Cash at bank (13,000 + 4,000)	17,000
Motor van	5,000
Inventories	3,000
Total assets	25,000
EQUITY AND LIABILITIES	
Equity (6,000 + 4,000)	10,000
Liabilities – borrowing	12,000
Liabilities – trade payable	3,000
Total equity and liabilities	25,000

The introduction of more funds by the owner will result in an increase in the equity of £4,000 and an increase in the cash at bank by the same amount.

This example (Jerry and Company) illustrates the point that the accounting equation (assets equals equity plus liabilities) will always hold true, because it reflects the fact that, if a business wishes to acquire more assets, it must raise funds equal to the cost of those assets. The funds raised must be provided by the owners (equity), or by others (liabilities) or by a combination of the two. Hence the total cost of assets acquired should always equal the total equity plus liabilities.

It is worth pointing out that businesses do not normally draw up a statement of financial position after each day, as shown in the example. We have done this to illustrate the effect on the statement of financial position of each transaction. In practice, a statement of financial position for a business is usually prepared at the end of a defined reporting period.

Determining the length of the reporting period will involve weighing up the costs of producing the information against the perceived benefits of having that information for decision-making purposes. In practice, the reporting period will vary between businesses; it could be monthly, quarterly, half-yearly or annually. For external reporting purposes, an annual reporting period is the norm (although certain businesses, typically larger ones, report more frequently than this). For internal reporting purposes to managers, however, more frequent (perhaps monthly) financial statements may be prepared.

THE EFFECT OF TRADING TRANSACTIONS

In the example (Jerry and Company), we showed how various types of transactions affected the statement of financial position. However, one very important type of transaction – trading transactions – has yet to be considered. To show how this type of transaction affects the statement of financial position, let us return to Jerry and Company.

Example 2.2 (continued)

The statement of financial position that we drew up for Jerry and Company as at 6 March was as follows:

Jerry and Company
Statement of financial position as at 6 March

	£
ASSETS	
Cash at bank	17,000
Motor van	5,000
Inventories	3,000
Total assets	25,000
EQUITY AND LIABILITIES	
Equity	10,000
Liabilities – borrowing	12,000
Liabilities – trade payable	3,000
Total equity and liabilities	25,000

On 7 March, the business managed to sell all of the inventories for £5,000 and received a cheque immediately from the customer for this amount. The statement of financial position on 7 March, after this transaction has taken place, will be:

38

Jerry and Company
Statement of financial position as at 7 March

	£
ASSETS	
Cash at bank (17,000 + 5,000)	22,000
Motor van	5,000
Inventories (3,000 – 3,000)	–
Total assets	27,000
EQUITY AND LIABILITIES	
Equity (10,000 + (5,000 – 3,000))	12,000
Liabilities – borrowing	12,000
Liabilities – trade payable	3,000
Total equity and liabilities	27,000

We can see that the inventories (£3,000) have now disappeared from the statement of financial position, but the cash at bank has increased by the selling price of the inventories (£5,000). The net effect has therefore been to increase assets by £2,000 (that is, £5,000 less £3,000). This increase represents the net increase in wealth (the profit) that has arisen from trading. Also note that the equity of the business has increased by £2,000, in line with the increase in assets. This increase in equity reflects the fact that wealth generated, as a result of trading or other operations, will be to the benefit of the owners and will increase their stake in the business.

Activity 2.6

What would have been the effect on the statement of financial position if the inventories had been sold on 7 March for £1,000 rather than £5,000?

The statement of financial position on 7 March would then have been:

Jerry and Company
Statement of financial position as at 7 March

	£
ASSETS	
Cash at bank (17,000 + 1,000)	18,000
Motor van	5,000
Inventories (3,000 – 3,000)	–
Total assets	23,000
EQUITY AND LIABILITIES	
Equity (10,000 + (1,000 – 3,000))	8,000
Liabilities – borrowing	12,000
Liabilities – trade payable	3,000
Total equity and liabilities	23,000

As we can see, the inventories (£3,000) will disappear from the statement of financial position but the cash at bank will rise by only £1,000. This will mean a net reduction in assets of £2,000. This reduction represents a loss arising from trading and will be reflected in a reduction in the equity of the owners.

What we have just seen means that the accounting equation can be extended as follows:

Assets (at the end of the period) = Equity (amount at the start of the period
+ Profit (or – Loss) for the period)
+ Liabilities (at the end of the period)

(This is assuming that the owner makes no injections or withdrawals of equity during the period.)

Any funds introduced or withdrawn by the owners also affect equity. If the owners withdrew £1,500 for their own use, the equity of the owners would be reduced by £1,500. If these drawings were in cash, the cash balance would decrease by £1,500 in the statement of financial position.

Like all items in the statement of financial position, the amount of equity is cumulative. This means that any profit not taken out as drawings by the owner(s) remains in the business. These retained (or 'ploughed-back') earnings have the effect of expanding the business.

CLASSIFYING ASSETS

On the statement of financial position, assets and claims are usually grouped into categories. This is designed to help users, as a haphazard listing of these items could be confusing. Assets may be categorised as being either current or non-current.

Current assets

Current assets are basically assets that are held for the short term. To be more precise, they are assets that meet any of the following conditions:

- they are held for sale or consumption during the business's normal operating cycle;
- they are expected to be sold within the next year;
- they are held principally for trading;
- they are cash, or near cash such as easily marketable, short-term investments.

The operating cycle of a business, mentioned above, is the time between buying and/or creating a product or service and receiving the cash on its sale. For most businesses, this will be less than a year. (It is worth mentioning that sales made by many businesses are made on credit. The customer pays some time after the goods are received or the service is rendered.)

The most common current assets are inventories, trade receivables (customers who owe amounts for goods or services supplied on credit) and cash. For businesses that sell goods, rather than render a service, the current assets of inventories, trade receivables and cash are interrelated. They circulate within a business as shown in Figure 2.3. We can see that cash can be used to buy inventories, which are then sold on credit. When the credit customers (trade receivables) pay, the business receives an injection of cash and so on.

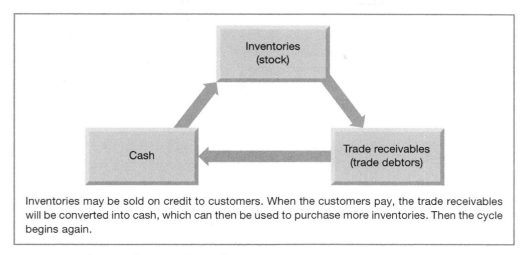

Inventories may be sold on credit to customers. When the customers pay, the trade receivables will be converted into cash, which can then be used to purchase more inventories. Then the cycle begins again.

Figure 2.3 The circulating nature of current assets

For purely service businesses, the situation is similar, except that inventories are not involved.

Non-current assets

Non-current assets (also called fixed assets) are simply assets that do not meet the definition of current assets. They tend to be held for long-term operations. Non-current assets may be either tangible or intangible. Tangible non-current assets normally consist of **property, plant and equipment**. We shall refer to them in this way from now on. This is a rather broad term that includes items such as land and buildings, motor vehicles and fixtures and fittings.

The distinction between assets that are continuously circulating within the business (current) and assets used for long-term operations (non-current) may be helpful when trying to assess the appropriateness of the mix of assets held. Most businesses will need a certain amount of both types of asset to operate effectively.

Activity 2.7

Can you think of two examples of assets that may be classified as non-current assets for an insurance business?

Examples of assets that may be defined as being non-current are:

- property
- furniture
- motor vehicles
- computers
- computer software
- reference books.

This is not an exhaustive list. You may have thought of others.

It is important to appreciate that how a particular asset is classified (that is, between current and non-current) may vary according to the nature of the business. This is because the *purpose* for which a particular type of asset is held may differ from business to business. For example, a motor vehicle manufacturer will normally hold inventories of the finished motor vehicles produced for resale; it would, therefore, classify them as part of the current assets. On the other hand, a business that uses motor vehicles for delivering its goods to customers (that is, as part of its long-term operations) would classify them as non-current assets.

Activity 2.8

The assets of Kunalun and Co., a large advertising agency, are as follows:

- cash at bank
- fixtures and fittings
- office equipment
- motor vehicles
- property
- computer equipment
- work in progress (that is, partly completed work for clients).

Which of these do you think should be defined as non-current assets and which should be defined as current assets?

Your answer should be as follows:

Non-current assets	*Current assets*
Fixtures and fittings	Cash at bank
Office equipment	Work in progress
Motor vehicles	
Property	
Computer equipment	

CLASSIFYING CLAIMS

As we have already seen, claims are normally classified into equity (owner's claim) and liabilities (claims of outsiders). Liabilities are further classified as either current or non-current:

Current liabilities

Current liabilities are basically amounts due for settlement in the short term. To be more precise, they are liabilities that meet any of the following conditions:

- they are expected to be settled within the business's normal operating cycle;
- they are held principally for trading purposes;
- they are due to be settled within a year after the date of the relevant statement of financial position;
- there is no right to defer settlement beyond a year after the date of the relevant statement of financial position.

Non-current liabilities

Non-current liabilities represent amounts due that do not meet the definition of current liabilities and so represent longer-term liabilities.

Activity 2.9

Can you think of one example of a current liability and one of a non-current liability?

An example of a current liability would be amounts owing to suppliers for goods supplied on credit (trade payables) or a bank overdraft (a form of short-term bank borrowing that is repayable on demand). An example of a non-current liability would be long-term borrowings.

It is quite common for non-current liabilities to become current liabilities. For example, borrowings to be repaid 18 months after the date of a particular statement of financial position will normally appear as a non-current liability, but will appear as a current liability in the statement of financial position in the following year.

This classification of liabilities between current and non-current helps to highlight those financial obligations that must shortly be met. The amount of current liabilities can be compared with the amount of current assets (that is, the assets that are either cash or will turn into cash within the normal operating cycle). This should reveal whether a business can cover its maturing obligations.

The classification of liabilities between current and non-current also helps to reveal the proportion of total long-term finance that is raised through borrowings rather than equity. Where a business relies on long-term borrowings, rather than relying solely on funds provided by the owner(s), the financial risks increase. This is because borrowing brings a commitment to make periodic interest payments and capital repayments. The business may be forced to stop trading if this commitment cannot be fulfilled. Thus, when raising long-term finance, the right balance must be struck between long-term borrowings and owner's equity. We shall consider this issue in more detail in Chapter 11.

STATEMENT LAYOUTS

Having looked at the classification of assets and liabilities, we shall now consider the layout of the statement of financial position. Although there is an almost infinite number of ways in which the same information on assets and claims could be presented, we shall consider two basic layouts. The first of these follows the style that we adopted with Jerry and Company earlier (see pages 36 to 40). A more comprehensive example of this style is shown in Example 2.3.

Example 2.3

Brie Manufacturing
Statement of financial position as at 31 December 2012

	£000
ASSETS	
Non-current assets	
Property	45
Plant and equipment	30
Motor vans	19
	94
Current assets	
Inventories	23
Trade receivables	18
Cash at bank	12
	53
Total assets	147
EQUITY AND LIABILITIES	
Equity	60
Non-current liabilities	
Long-term borrowings	50
Current liabilities	
Trade payables	37
Total equity and liabilities	147

The non-current assets have a total of £94,000, which together with the current assets total of £53,000 gives a total of £147,000 for assets. Similarly, the equity totals £60,000, which together with the £50,000 for non-current liabilities and £37,000 for current liabilities gives a total for equity and liabilities of £147,000.

Within each category of asset (non-current and current) shown in Example 2.3, the items are listed in reverse order of liquidity (nearness to cash). Thus, the assets that are furthest from cash come first and the assets that are closest to cash come last. In the case of non-current assets, property is listed first as this asset is usually the most difficult to turn into cash, and motor vans are listed last as there is usually a ready market for them. In the case of current assets, we have already seen that inventories are converted to trade receivables and then trade receivables are converted to cash. Hence, under the heading of current assets, inventories are listed first, followed by trade receivables and finally cash itself. This ordering of assets will occur irrespective of the layout used.

Note that, in addition to a grand total for assets held, subtotals for non-current assets and current assets are shown. Subtotals are also used for non-current liabilities and current liabilities when more than one item appears within these categories.

A slight variation from the standard layout illustrated in Example 2.3 is as shown in Example 2.4.

Example 2.4

Brie Manufacturing
Statement of financial position as at 31 December 2012

	£000
ASSETS	
Non-current assets	
Property	45
Plant and equipment	30
Motor vans	19
	94
Current assets	
Inventories	23
Trade receivables	18
Cash at bank	12
	53
Total assets	147
LIABILITIES	
Non-current liabilities	
Long-term borrowings	(50)
Current liabilities	
Trade payables	(37)
Total liabilities	(87)
Net assets	60
EQUITY	60

We can see that the total liabilities are deducted from the total assets. This derives a figure for net assets – which is equal to equity. Using this format, the basic accounting equation is rearranged so that:

Assets – Liabilities = Equity

This re-arranged equation highlights the fact that equity represents the residual interest of the owner(s) after deducting all liabilities of the business.

The layout shown in Example 2.3 is the most popular in practice in the UK and will be used throughout the book.

CAPTURING A MOMENT IN TIME

As we have already seen, the statement of financial position reflects the assets, equity and liabilities of a business at *a specified point in time*. It has been compared to a photograph. A photograph 'freezes' a particular moment in time and will represent the situation only at that moment. Hence, events may be quite different immediately before and immediately after the photograph was taken. When examining a statement of financial position, therefore, it is important to establish the date for which it has been drawn up. This information should be prominently displayed in the heading to the statement, as shown above in Example 2.4. When we are trying to assess current financial position, the more recent the statement of financial position date, the better.

A business will normally prepare a statement of financial position as at the close of business on the last day of its annual reporting period. In the UK, businesses are free to choose their reporting period. When making a decision on which year-end date to choose, commercial convenience can often be a deciding factor. For example, a business operating in the retail trade may choose to have a year-end date early in the calendar year (for example, 31 January) because trade tends to be slack during that period and more staff time is available to help with the tasks involved in the preparation of the annual financial statements (such as checking the amount of inventories held). Since trade is slack, it is also a time when the amount of inventories held by the retail business is likely to be unusually low as compared with other times of the year. Thus the statement of financial position, though showing a fair view of what it purports to show, may not show a picture of what is more typically the position of the business over the rest of the year.

THE ROLE OF ACCOUNTING CONVENTIONS

Accounting has a number of rules or conventions that have evolved over time. They have evolved as attempts to deal with practical problems experienced by preparers and users of financial statements, rather than to reflect some theoretical ideal. In preparing the statements of financial position earlier, we have followed various **accounting conventions**, though they have not been explicitly mentioned. We shall now identify and discuss the major conventions that we have applied.

Business entity convention

For accounting purposes, the business and its owner(s) are treated as being quite separate and distinct. This is why owners are treated as being claimants against their own business in respect of their investment. The **business entity convention** must be distinguished from the legal position that may exist between businesses and their owners. For sole proprietorships and partnerships, the law does not make any distinction between the business and its owner(s). For limited companies, on the other hand, there is a clear legal distinction between the business and its owners. (As we shall see in Chapter 4, the limited company is regarded as having a separate legal existence.) For accounting purposes, these legal distinctions are irrelevant and the business entity convention applies to all businesses.

Historic cost convention

The **historic cost convention** holds that the value of assets shown on the statement of financial position should be based on their acquisition cost (that is, historic cost). Many argue, however, that historic costs soon become outdated and so are unlikely to help in the assessment of current financial position. Recording assets at their current value would provide a more realistic view of financial position and would be relevant for a wide range of decisions. A system of measurement based on current values can, however, present a number of problems.

The term 'current value' can be defined in different ways. It can be defined broadly as either the current replacement cost or the current realisable value (selling price) of an asset. These two types of valuation may result in quite different figures being produced to represent the current value of an item. Furthermore, the broad terms 'replacement cost' and 'realisable value' can be defined in different ways. We must therefore be clear about what kind of current value accounting we wish to use.

Current values, however defined, are often difficult to establish with any real degree of objectivity. Activity 2.10 illustrates the practical problems associated with current value accounting.

Activity 2.10

Plumber and Company has some motor vans that are used by staff when visiting customers' premises to carry out work. If it were decided to show these vans on the statement of financial position at a current value (rather than a value based on their historic cost), how might the business arrive at a suitable value and how reliable would this figure be?

Two ways of deriving a current value are to find out:

- how much would have to be paid to buy vans of a similar type and condition (current replacement cost);
- how much a motor van dealer would pay for the vans, were the business to sell them (current realisable value).

Both options will normally rely on opinion and so a range of possible values could be produced for each. For example, both the cost to replace the vans and the proceeds of selling them is likely to vary from one dealer to another. Moreover, the range of values for each option could be significantly different from one option to the other. (The selling prices of the vans are likely to be lower than the amount required to replace them.) Thus, any value finally decided upon could arouse some debate.

Figures based on current values may be heavily dependent on the opinion of managers. Some form of independent verification is, therefore, normally required to ensure that the financial statements retain their credibility among users. The motor vans discussed in Activity 2.10 are less of a problem than many types of asset. There is a ready market for motor vans, which means that a value can be obtained by contacting a dealer. For a custom-built piece of equipment, however, identifying a replacement cost, or worse still a selling price, could be very difficult.

By reporting assets at their historic cost, more reliable information is provided. Subjective judgement is reduced as the amount paid for a particular asset is usually a matter of demonstrable fact. Information based on past costs, however, may not always be relevant to user needs.

Later in the chapter, we shall see that the historic cost convention is not always rigidly adhered to. Moreover, departures from this convention are becoming more frequent.

Prudence convention

The **prudence convention** holds that caution should be exercised when making accounting judgements. The application of this convention normally involves recording all losses at once and in full; this refers to both actual losses and expected losses. Profits, on the other hand, are recognised only when they actually arise. Greater emphasis is, therefore, placed on expected losses than on expected profits. To illustrate the application of this convention, let us assume that certain inventories held by a business prove unpopular with customers and so a decision is made to sell them below their original cost. The prudence convention requires that the expected loss from future sales be recognised immediately rather than when the goods are eventually sold. If, however, these inventories could have been sold above their original cost, profit would only be recognised at the time of sale.

The prudence convention evolved to counteract the excessive optimism of some managers and is designed to prevent an overstatement of financial position and performance. Applying this convention, however, requires judgement. This means that the way in which it is applied by preparers of financial statements may differ over time and between businesses. Where excessive prudence is applied, it will lead to an understatement of profits and financial position. This will mean a consistent bias in the reporting of both financial performance and position.

Activity 2.11

What might be the effect of applying excessive prudence on the quality of decisions made by the owners of a business who are considering selling their share of the business?

Being excessively prudent will tend to obscure the underlying financial reality and may lead to poor decisions being made. The owners may sell their stake in the business at a lower price than they would have received if a more balanced view of the financial health of the business had been presented.

In recent years, the prudence convention has weakened its grip on accounting and has become a less dominant force. Nevertheless, it remains an important convention.

Going concern convention

The **going concern convention** holds that the financial statements should be prepared on the assumption that a business will continue operations for the foreseeable future, unless there is evidence to the contrary. In other words, it is assumed that there is no intention, or need, to sell off the non-current assets of the business.

Where a business is in financial difficulties, however, non-current assets may have to be sold to repay those with claims against the business. The realisable (sale) value of many non-current assets is often much lower than the values reported in the statement of financial position. This is because the value to the business of the assets, were it to continue operating, is higher than their realisable value. In the event of a forced sale of assets, therefore, significant losses would arise. These losses must be anticipated and fully reported when a business's going concern status is called into question.

Dual aspect convention

The **dual aspect convention** asserts that each transaction has two aspects, both of which will affect the statement of financial position. Thus, the purchase of a motor car for cash results in an increase in one asset (motor car) and a decrease in another (cash). The repayment of borrowings results in the decrease in a liability (borrowings) and the decrease in an asset (cash).

Activity 2.12

What are the two aspects of each of the following transactions?

1　Purchasing £1,000 of inventories on credit.
2　Owner withdrawing £2,000 in cash.
3　Paying a supplier for £1,000 of inventories bought on credit a few weeks earlier.

Your answer should be as follows:

1　Inventories increase by £1,000, trade payables increase by £1,000.
2　Equity reduces by £2,000, cash reduces by £2,000.
3　Trade payables reduce by £1,000, cash reduces by £1,000.

Recording the dual aspect of each transaction ensures that the statement of financial position will continue to balance.

Figure 2.4 summarises the main accounting conventions that exert an influence on the construction of the statement of financial position.

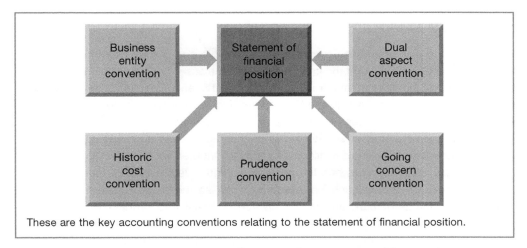

These are the key accounting conventions relating to the statement of financial position.

Figure 2.4 Accounting conventions influencing the statement of financial position

MONEY MEASUREMENT

We saw earlier that a resource will only be regarded as an asset and included on the statement of financial position if it can be measured in monetary terms, with a reasonable degree of reliability. Some resources of a business, however, do not meet this criterion and so are excluded from the statement of financial position. As a result, the scope of the statement of financial position is limited.

Activity 2.13

Can you think of resources of a business that cannot usually be measured reliably in monetary terms?

In answering this activity you may have thought of the following:

■ the quality of the human resources of the business;
■ the reputation of the business's products;
■ the location of the business;
■ the relationship the business enjoys with its customers.

There have been occasional attempts to measure and report resources of a business that are normally excluded from the statement of financial position so as to provide a more complete picture of its financial position. These attempts, however, invariably fail the test of reliability. Unreliable measurement can lead to inconsistency in reporting and can create uncertainty among users of the financial statements. This, in turn, undermines the credibility of financial statements.

We shall now discuss some key resources of a business that normally defy reliable measurement.

Goodwill and brands

Some intangible non-current assets are similar to tangible non-current assets: they have a clear and separate identity and the cost of acquiring the asset can be reliably measured. Examples normally include patents, trademarks, copyrights and licences. Other intangible non-current assets, however, are quite different. They lack a clear and separate identity and reflect a hotchpotch of attributes, which are part of the essence of the business. Goodwill and product brands are often examples of assets that lack a clear and separate identity.

The term 'goodwill' is often used to cover various attributes such as the quality of the products, the skill of employees and the relationship with customers. The term 'product brands' is also used to cover various attributes, such as the brand image, the quality of the product, the trademark and so on. Where goodwill and product brands have been generated internally by the business, it is often difficult to determine their cost or to measure their current market value or even to be clear that they really exist. They are, therefore, excluded from the statement of financial position.

When they are acquired through an 'arm's-length transaction', however, the problems of uncertainty about their existence and measurement are resolved. (An arm's-length transaction is one that is undertaken between two unconnected parties.) If goodwill is acquired when taking over another business, or if a business acquires a particular product brand from another business, these items will be separately identified and a price agreed for them. Under these circumstances, they can be regarded as assets (for accounting purposes) by the business that acquired them and included on the statement of financial position.

To agree a price for acquiring goodwill or product brands means that some form of valuation must take place and this raises the question as to how it is done. Usually, the valuation will be based on estimates of future earnings from holding the asset – a process that is fraught with difficulties. Nevertheless, a number of specialist businesses now exist that are prepared to take on this challenge. **Real World 2.1** shows how one specialist business ranked and valued the top ten brands in the world for 2011.

REAL WORLD 2.1

Brand leaders

Millward Brown Optimor, part of WPP marketing services group, produces an annual report which ranks and values the top world brands. For 2011, the top ten brands are as follows.

Ranking	Brand	Value ($m)
1	Apple	153,285
2	Google	111,498
3	IBM	100,849
4	McDonalds	81,016
5	Microsoft	78,243
6	Coca-Cola	73,752
7	AT&T	69,916
8	Marlboro	67,522
9	China Mobile	57,326
10	General Electric	50,318

We can see that the valuations placed on the brands owned are quite staggering.

Source: Brandz Top 100 Most Valuable Global Brands 2011, Millward Brown Optimor, 2011, www.millwardbrown.com.

Human resources

Attempts have been made to place a monetary measurement on the human resources of a business, but without any real success. There are, however, certain limited circumstances in which human resources are measured and reported in the statement of financial position. Professional football clubs provide an example of where these circumstances normally arise. While football clubs cannot own players, they can own the rights to the players' services. Where these rights are acquired by compensating other clubs for releasing the players from their contracts, an arm's-length transaction arises and the amounts paid provide a reliable basis for measurement. This means that the rights to services can be regarded as an asset of the club for accounting purposes (assuming, of course, the player will also bring benefits to the club).

Real World 2.2 describes how one leading club reports its investment in players on the statement of financial position.

REAL WORLD 2.2

Spurs players appear on the pitch and on the statement of financial position

Tottenham Hotspur Football Club (Spurs) has acquired several key players as a result of paying transfer fees to other clubs. In common with most UK football clubs, Spurs reports the cost of acquiring the rights to the players' services on its statement of financial position. The club's statement as at 30 June 2011 shows the total cost of registering its squad of players at about £227 million. The club treats a proportion of each player's transfer fee as an expense each year. The exact proportion depends on the length of the particular player's contract.

The £227 million does not include 'home-grown' players such as Ledley King, because Spurs did not pay a transfer fee for them and so no clear-cut value can be placed on their services. During the year to 30 June 2011, the club was active in the transfer market and spent around £27.5 million on acquiring new players, including Rafael van der Vaart, William Gallas and Steven Pienaar. Some players also left the club during the year, including Jonathan Woodgate and Adel Taarabt.

The item of players' registrations is shown as an intangible asset in the statement of financial position as it is the rights to services, not the players, that are the assets. It is shown net of depreciation (or amortisation as it is usually termed for intangible non-current assets). The carrying amount at 30 June 2011 was £101 million and represented 35 per cent of Spurs' assets, as shown in the statement of financial position.

Source: Tottenham Hotspur plc Annual Report 2011.

Monetary stability

When using money as the unit of measurement, we normally fail to recognise the fact that it will change in value over time. In the UK and throughout much of the world, however, inflation has been a persistent problem. This has meant that the value of money has declined in relation to other assets. In past years, high rates of inflation have resulted in statements of financial position, which were prepared on a historic cost basis, reflecting figures for assets that were much lower than if current values were employed. Rates of inflation have been relatively low in recent years and so the disparity between historic cost values and current values has been less pronounced. Nevertheless, it can still be significant and has added fuel to the debate concerning how to measure asset values on the statement of financial position. It is to the issue of valuing assets that we now turn.

VALUING ASSETS

We saw earlier that, when preparing the statement of financial position, the historic cost convention is normally applied for the reporting of assets. This point requires further explanation as, in practice, things are a little more complex than this. Large businesses throughout much of the world adhere to asset valuation rules set out in International Financial Reporting Standards. (These reporting standards will be discussed in detail in Chapter 4.) The key valuation rules are considered below.

Non-current assets

Non-current assets have lives that are either *finite* or *indefinite*. Those with a finite life provide benefits to a business for a limited period of time, whereas those with an indefinite life provide benefits without a foreseeable time limit. The distinction between the two types of non-current assets applies to both tangible and intangible assets.

Initially non-current assets are recorded at their historic cost, which will include any amounts spent on getting them ready for use.

Non-current assets with finite lives

Benefits from assets with finite lives will be used up over time as a result of market changes, wear and tear and so on. The amount used up, which is referred to as *depreciation* (or *amortisation*, in the case of intangible non-current assets), must be measured for each reporting period for which the assets are held. Although we shall leave a detailed examination of depreciation until Chapter 3, we need to know that when an asset has been depreciated, this must be reflected in the statement of financial position.

The total depreciation that has accumulated over the period since the asset was acquired must be deducted from its cost. This net figure (that is, the cost of the asset less the total depreciation to date) is referred to as the *carrying amount*. It is sometimes also known as *net book value* or *written down value*. The procedure just described is not really a contravention of the historic cost convention. It is simply recognition of the fact that a proportion of the historic cost of the non-current asset has been consumed in the process of generating benefits for the business.

Activity 2.14

Can you think of a non-current asset that has a finite life and which can be classified as:

(a) tangible
(b) intangible?

Plant, equipment, motor vehicles and computers are examples of tangible assets that are normally considered to have a finite life. A patent, which gives the owner exclusive rights to use an invention, is an example of an intangible asset that has a finite life. (Many patents are granted for a period of 20 years.)

Non-current assets with indefinite lives

Benefits from assets with indefinite lives may, or may not, be used up over time. Property (real estate) is usually an example of a tangible non-current asset with an indefinite life. Purchased goodwill could be an example of an intangible one, though this is not always the case. These assets are not subject to routine annual depreciation over time.

Fair values

Although initially historic cost is the standard or 'benchmark' treatment for recording non-current assets of all types (tangible and intangible, finite or indefinite lives), an alternative is allowed. Non-current assets may be recorded using **fair values** provided that these values can be measured reliably. The fair values, in this case, are the current market values (that is, the exchange values in an arm's-length transaction). The use of fair values, rather than cost figures, whether depreciated or not, can provide users with more up-to-date information, which may well be more relevant to their needs. It may also place the business in a better light, as assets such as property may have increased significantly in value over time. Of course, increasing the statement of financial position value of an asset does not make that asset more valuable. Perceptions of the business, however, may be altered by such a move.

One consequence of upwardly revaluing non-current assets with finite lives is that the depreciation charge will be increased. This is because the depreciation charge is based on the new (increased) value of the asset.

Real World 2.3 shows the effect of the revaluation of non-current assets on the financial position of one large business.

REAL WORLD 2.3

Rising asset levels

During the year to 31 March 2010, Veolia Water UK plc, which owns Thames Water, changed its policy on the valuation of certain types of non-current assets. These assets included land and buildings, infrastructure assets and vehicles, plant and machinery. The business switched from the use of historic cost to the use of fair values and a revaluation exercise was carried out by independent qualified valuers. The effect of this policy change was to report a revaluation gain of more than £436 million during the year. There was a 40 per cent increase in owners' (shareholders') equity, which was largely due to this gain.

Source: Veolia Water UK plc, Annual Report 2009/10.

Activity 2.15

Refer to the statement of financial position of Brie Manufacturing shown earlier in Example 2.3 (page 45). What would be the effect of revaluing the property to a figure of £110,000 on the statement of financial position?

The effect on the statement of financial position would be to increase the property to £110,000 and the gain on revaluation (that is, £110,000 − £45,000 = £65,000) would be added to equity, as it is the owner(s) who will benefit from the gain. The revised statement of financial position would therefore be as follows:

Brie Manufacturing
Statement of financial position as at 31 December 2012

	£000
ASSETS	
Non-current assets (property, plant and equipment)	
Property	110
Plant and equipment	30
Motor vans	19
	159
Current assets	
Inventories	23
Trade receivables	18
Cash at bank	12
	53
Total Assets	212
EQUITY AND LIABILITIES	
Equity (60 + 65)	125
Non-current liabilities	
Long-term borrowings	50
Current liabilities	
Trade payables	37
Total equity and liabilities	212

Once assets are revalued, the frequency of revaluation then becomes an important issue as assets recorded at out-of-date revaluations can mislead users. Using such figures on the statement of financial position is the worst of both worlds. It lacks the objectivity and verifiability of historic cost; it also lacks the realism of current values. Where fair values are used, revaluations should therefore be frequent enough to ensure that the carrying amount of the revalued asset does not differ materially from its true fair value at the statement of financial position date.

When an item of property, plant or equipment (a tangible asset) is revalued on the basis of fair values, all assets within that particular group must be revalued. Thus, it is not acceptable to revalue some items of property but not others. Although this provides some degree of consistency within a particular group of assets, it does not prevent the statement of financial position from containing a mixture of valuations.

Intangible assets are not often revalued to fair values. This is because revaluations can only be used where there is an active market, thereby permitting fair values to be properly determined. Such markets, however, rarely exist for intangible assets.

The impairment of non-current assets

All types of non-current asset are at risk of suffering a significant fall in value. This may be caused by changes in market conditions, technological obsolescence and so on. In some cases, this fall in value may lead to the carrying amount of the asset being higher than the amount that could be recovered from the asset through its continued use or through its sale. When this occurs, the asset value is said to be impaired and the general rule is to reduce the value on the statement of financial position to the recoverable amount. Unless this is done, the asset value will be overstated. (This type of impairment in value should not be confused with routine depreciation of assets with finite lives.)

Activity 2.16

With which one of the accounting conventions that we discussed earlier is this accounting treatment of impaired assets consistent?

The answer is the prudence convention, which states that actual or anticipated losses should be recognised in full.

Real World 2.4 provides an example of where impairment charges for one large business had a dramatic effect on profits and led to huge write-downs in the value of goodwill.

REAL WORLD 2.4

Making the wrong call

Swisscom said on Wednesday that earnings for this year would be hit by a €1.3 billion impairment charge on Fastweb, its ailing Italian business. The charge, which the Swiss telecommunications group attributed partly to the eurozone crisis, will lower net profits by SFr1.2 billion this year ($1.3 billion). Analysts had long expected a reduction in the goodwill carried for the Italian internet and telecommunications business. But Swisscom had always defended the valuation.

Swisscom bought Fastweb in stages, starting in early 2007, paying a total of €4.6 billion in what it described as a high growth, high technology business in a big and flourishing market. Swisscom said the company had lived up to expectations in the corporate sector, with strong growth and earnings. 'With a market share of 20 per cent, Fastweb is the clear number two in the segment devoted to corporate customers, and is growing steadily,' it said. But sales to private customers had 'come under pressure in the last few quarters' after an initial growth phase because of intense and rising competition, pricing pressures and overall weakness in Italian private consumption.

Carsten Schloter, Swisscom chief executive, defended the Fastweb purchase price, which he said was in line with valuations of the time, although he recognised it appeared excessive in retrospect.

FT *Source*: Extracts from Simonian, H., 'Swisscom takes €1.3bn charge on Fastweb', FT.com, 14 December 2011.

We should bear in mind that impairment reviews involve making judgements about the appropriate value to place on assets. Employing independent valuers to make these judgements will normally give users greater confidence in the information reported. There is always a risk that managers will manipulate impairment values to portray a picture that they would like users to see.

Inventories

It is not only non-current assets that run the risk of a significant fall in value. The inventories of a business could also suffer this fate as a result of changes in market taste, obsolescence, deterioration, damage and so on. Where a fall in value means that the amount likely to be recovered from the sale of the inventories will be lower than their cost, this loss must be reflected in the statement of financial position. Thus, if the net realisable value (that is, selling price less any selling costs) falls below the historic cost of inventories held, the former should be used as the basis of valuation. This reflects, once again, the influence of the prudence convention on the statement of financial position.

Real World 2.5 reveals how one well-known business wrote down the inventories of one of its products following a sharp reduction in selling prices.

REAL WORLD 2.5

You're fired!

'You're fired!' Is what some investors might like to tell Amstrad, run by Apprentice star Sir Alan Sugar. Shares in the company fell nearly 10 per cent as it revealed that sales of its much-vaunted videophone have failed to take off.

Amstrad launched the E3, a phone allowing users to hold video calls with each other, in a blaze of publicity last year. But, after cutting the price from £99 to £49, Amstrad sold just 61,000 E3s in the year to June and has taken a £5.7m stock (inventories) write down.

Source: Amstrad (AMT), *Investors Chronicle*, 7 October 2005.

The published financial statements of large businesses will normally show the basis on which inventories are valued. **Real World 2.6** shows how one business reports this information.

REAL WORLD 2.6

Reporting inventories

The 2010/11 annual report of Ted Baker plc, a leading designer clothes brand, includes the following explanation concerning inventories:

> Inventories and work in progress are stated at the lower of cost and net realisable value. Cost includes materials, direct labour and inward transportation costs. Net realisable value is based on estimated selling price, less further costs expected to be incurred to completion and disposal. Provision is made for obsolete, slow moving or defective items where appropriate.

Source: Ted Baker plc, Report and Accounts 2010/11, p. 51.

MEETING USER NEEDS

The statement of financial position is the oldest of the three main financial statements and may help users in the following ways:

- *It provides insights about how the business is financed and how its funds are deployed.* The statement of financial position shows how much finance is contributed by the owners and how much is contributed by outside lenders. It also shows the different kinds of assets acquired and how much is invested in each kind.
- *It can provide a basis for assessing the value of the business.* Since the statement of financial position lists, and places a value on, the various assets and claims, it can provide a starting point for assessing the value of the business. We have seen earlier, however, that accounting rules may result in assets being shown at their historic cost and that the restrictive definition of assets may exclude certain business resources from the statement of financial position.
- *Relationships between assets and claims can be assessed.* It can be useful to look at relationships between various statement of financial position items, for example the relationship between how much wealth is tied up in current assets and how much is owed in the short term (current liabilities). From this relationship, we can see whether the business has sufficient short-term assets to cover its maturing obligations. We shall look at this and other relationships between statement of financial position items in some detail in Chapter 6.
- *Performance can be assessed.* The effectiveness of a business in generating wealth can usefully be assessed against the amount of investment that was involved. Thus, the relationship between profit earned during a period and the value of the net assets invested can be helpful to many users, particularly owners and managers. This and similar relationships will also be explored in detail in Chapter 6.

Once armed with the insights that a statement of financial position can provide, users are better placed to make investment and other decisions. **Real World 2.7** reveals how a small business was able to obtain a loan because its bank was impressed by its strong statement of financial position.

REAL WORLD 2.7

A sound education

Sandeep Sud is a qualified solicitor who also runs a school uniform business based in Hounslow, in partnership with his parents. The business, which has four full-time employees, uses its statement of financial position to gauge how it is progressing. It has also been a key factor in securing a bank loan for the improvement and expansion of the business premises.
According to Sandeep:

Having a strong statement of financial position helped when it came to borrowing. When we first applied for a refurbishment loan we couldn't provide up-to-date accounts to the bank manager. This could have been a problem, but we quickly got our accounts in order and the loan was approved straight away. Because our statement of financial position was strong, the bank thought we were a good risk. Although we decided not to draw down on the loan – because we used cashflow instead – it did open our eyes to the importance of a strong statement of financial position.

Source: Adapted from: 'Balance sheets: the basics', www.businesslink.gov.uk, accessed 14 April 2010.

? SELF-ASSESSMENT QUESTION 2.1

The following information relates to Simonson Engineering as at 30 September 2012:

	£
Plant and equipment NCA	25,000
Trade payables CL	18,000
Short-term borrowing CL	26,000
Inventories CA	45,000
Property NCA	72,000
Long-term borrowing NCL	51,000
Trade receivables CA	48,000
Equity at 1 October 2011 E	117,500
Cash in hand CA	1,500
Motor vehicles NCA	15,000
Fixtures and fittings NCA	9,000
Profit for the year to 30 September 2012 E	18,000
Drawings for the year to 30 September 2012	15,000

Required:
(a) Prepare a statement of financial position for the business as at 30 September 2012 using the standard layout illustrated in Example 2.3.
(b) Comment on the financial position of the business based on the statement prepared in (a) above.
(c) Show the effect on the statement of financial position shown in (a) above of a decision to revalue the property to £115,000 and to recognise that the net realisable value of inventories at the year end is £38,000.

The solution to this question can be found at the back of the book, in Appendix B.

SUMMARY

The main points of this chapter may be summarised as follows.

The major financial statements

- There are three major financial statements: the statement of cash flows, the income statement and the statement of financial position.
- The statement of cash flows shows the cash movements over a particular period.
- The income statement shows the wealth (profit) generated over a particular period.
- The statement of financial position shows the accumulated wealth at a particular point in time.

The statement of financial position

- This sets out the assets of the business, on the one hand, and the claims against those assets, on the other.
- Assets are resources of the business that have certain characteristics, such as the ability to provide future economic benefits.
- Claims are obligations on the part of the business to provide cash, or some other benefit, to outside parties.
- Claims are of two types: equity and liabilities.
- Equity represents the claim(s) of the owner(s) and liabilities represent the claims of others.
- The statement of financial position reflects the accounting equation:

$$\text{Assets} = \text{Equity} + \text{Liabilities}$$

Classification of assets and liabilities

- Assets are normally categorised as being current or non-current.
- Current assets are cash or near cash or are held for sale or consumption in the normal course of business, or for trading, or for the short term.
- Non-current assets are assets that are not current assets. They are normally held for the long-term operations of the business.
- Liabilities are normally categorised as being current or non-current liabilities.
- Current liabilities represent amounts due in the normal course of the business's operating cycle, or are held for trading, or are to be settled within a year of, or cannot be deferred for at least a year after, the end of the reporting period.
- Non-current liabilities represent amounts due that are not current liabilities.

Statement of financial position layouts

- The standard layout begins with assets at the top of the statement of financial position and places equity and liabilities underneath.

- A variation of the standard layout begins with the assets at the top of the statement of financial position. From the total assets figure are deducted the non-current and current liabilities to arrive at a net assets figure. Equity is placed underneath.

Accounting conventions

- Accounting conventions are the rules of accounting that have evolved to deal with practical problems experienced by those preparing financial statements.
- The main conventions relating to the statement of financial position include business entity, historic cost, prudence, going concern and dual aspect.

Money measurement

- Using money as the unit of measurement limits the scope of the statement of financial position.
- Certain resources such as goodwill, product brands and human resources are difficult to measure. An 'arm's-length transaction' is normally required before such assets can be reliably measured and reported on the statement of financial position.
- Money is not a stable unit of measurement – it changes in value over time.

Asset valuation

- The 'benchmark treatment' is to show non-current assets at historic cost.
- Fair values may be used rather than historic cost, provided that they can be reliably obtained. This is rarely possible, however, for intangible non-current assets.
- Non-current assets with finite lives should be shown at cost (or fair value) less any accumulated depreciation (amortisation).
- Where the value of a non-current asset is impaired, it should be written down to its recoverable amount.
- Inventories are shown at the lower of cost or net realisable value.

The usefulness of the statement of financial position

- It shows how finance has been raised and how it has been been deployed.
- It provides a basis for valuing the business, though it can only be a starting point.
- Relationships between various statement of financial position items can usefully be explored.
- Relationships between wealth generated and wealth invested can be helpful indicators of business effectiveness.

MyAccountingLab

Go to www.myaccountinglab.com to check your understanding of the chapter, create a personalised study plan, and maximise your revision time

KEY TERMS

FURTHER READING

If you would like to explore the topics covered in this chapter in more depth, we recommend the following books:

Elliott, B. and Elliott, J., *Financial Accounting and Reporting*, 15th edn, Financial Times Prentice Hall, 2012, Chapters 17 and 19.

International Accounting Standards Board, *2011 International Financial Reporting Standards IFRS* (2-volume set) 2011.

KPMG, *Insights into IFRS*, 7th edn, 2010/11, 2011, Sections 3.1, 3.2, 3.3, 3.10 and 3.13. A summarised version of this is available free at www.kpmg.com.

Melville, A., *International Financial Reporting: A Practical Guide*, 3rd edn, Financial Times Prentice Hall, 2011, Chapters 5 to 8.

? REVIEW QUESTIONS

Solutions to these questions can be found at the back of the book, in Appendix C.

2.1 An accountant prepared a statement of financial position for a business. In this statement, the equity of the owner was shown next to the liabilities. This confused the owner, who argued: 'My equity is my major asset and so should be shown as an asset on the statement of financial position.' How would you explain this misunderstanding to the owner?

2.2 'The statement of financial position shows how much a business is worth.' Do you agree with this statement? Explain the reasons for your response.

2.3 What is meant by the accounting equation? How does the form of this equation differ between the two statement of financial position layouts mentioned in the chapter?

2.4 In recent years there have been attempts to place a value on the 'human assets' of a business in order to derive a figure that can be included on the statement of financial position. Do you think humans should be treated as assets? Would 'human assets' meet the conventional definition of an asset for inclusion on the statement of financial position?

✳ EXERCISES

*Exercises 2.1 and 2.2 are basic level. Exercise 2.3 is intermediate level and Exercises 2.4 and 2.5 are advanced level. Those with **coloured numbers** have answers at the back of the book, in Appendix D.*

> If you wish to try more exercises, visit the website at www.myaccountinglab.com.

2.1 On Thursday, the fourth day of his business venture, Paul, the street trader in wrapping paper (see earlier in the chapter, pages 27 to 30), bought more inventories for £53 cash. During the day he sold inventories that had cost £33 for a total of £47.

Required:
Draw up the three financial statements for Paul's business venture for Thursday.

2.2 While on holiday in Bridlington, Helen had her credit cards and purse stolen from the beach while she was swimming. She was left with only £40, which she had kept in her hotel room, but she had three days of her holiday remaining. She was determined to continue her holiday and decided to make some money to enable her to do so. She decided to sell orange juice to holidaymakers using the local beach. On the first day she bought 80 cartons of orange juice at £0.50 each for cash and sold 70 of these at £0.80 each. On the following day she bought 60 cartons at £0.50 each for cash and sold 65 at £0.80 each. On the third and final day she bought another 60 cartons at £0.50 each for cash. However, it rained and, as a result, business was poor. She managed to sell 20 at £0.80 each but sold off the rest of her inventories at £0.40 each.

Required:
Prepare an income statement and statement of cash flows for each day's trading and prepare a statement of financial position at the end of each day's trading.

2.3 On 1 March, Joe Conday started a new business. During March he carried out the following transactions:

1 March	Deposited £20,000 in a newly opened bank account.
2 March	Bought fixtures and fittings for £6,000 cash and inventories £8,000 on credit.
3 March	Borrowed £5,000 from a relative and deposited it in the bank.
4 March	Bought a motor car for £7,000 cash and withdrew £200 in cash for his own use.
5 March	A further motor car costing £9,000 was bought. The motor car bought on 4 March was given in part exchange at a value of £6,500. The balance of purchase price for the new car was paid in cash.
6 March	Conday won £2,000 in a lottery and paid the amount into the business bank account. He also repaid £1,000 of the borrowings.

Required:
Draw up a statement of financial position for the business at the end of each day.

2.4 The following is a list of the assets and claims of Crafty Engineering Ltd at 30 June last year:

	£000
Trade payables	86
Motor vehicles	38
Long-term borrowing from Industrial Finance Co.	260
Equipment and tools	207
Short-term borrowings	116
Inventories	153
Property	320
Trade receivables	185

Required:

(a) Prepare the statement of financial position of the business as at 30 June last year from the above information using the standard layout. (*Hint*: There is a missing item that needs to be deduced and inserted.)

(b) Discuss the significant features revealed by this financial statement.

2.5 The statement of financial position of a business at the start of the week is as follows:

	£
ASSETS	
Property	145,000
Furniture and fittings	63,000
Inventories	28,000
Trade receivables	33,000
Total assets	269,000
EQUITY AND LIABILITIES	
Equity	203,000
Short-term borrowing (bank overdraft)	43,000
Trade payables	23,000
Total equity and liabilities	269,000

During the week the following transactions take place:

(a) Sold inventories for £11,000 cash; these inventories had cost £8,000.
(b) Sold inventories for £23,000 on credit; these inventories had cost £17,000.
(c) Received cash from trade receivables totalling £18,000.
(d) The owners of the business introduced £100,000 of their own money, which was placed in the business bank account.
(e) The owners brought a motor van, valued at £10,000, into the business.
(f) Bought inventories on credit for £14,000.
(g) Paid trade payables £13,000.

Required:

Show the statement of financial position after all of these transactions have been reflected.

MEASURING AND REPORTING FINANCIAL PERFORMANCE

INTRODUCTION

In this chapter, we continue our examination of the major financial statements by looking at the income statement. This statement was briefly considered in Chapter 2, but we shall now look at it in some detail. We shall see how it is prepared and how it links with the statement of financial position. We shall also consider some of the key measurement problems to be faced when preparing the income statement.

Learning outcomes

When you have completed this chapter, you should be able to:

■ discuss the nature and purpose of the income statement;

■ prepare an income statement from relevant financial information and interpret the information that it contains;

■ discuss the main recognition and measurement issues that must be considered when preparing the income statement;

■ explain the main accounting conventions underpinning the income statement.

MyAccountingLab Visit www.myaccountinglab.com for practice and revision opportunities

THE INCOME STATEMENT

Businesses exist for the primary purpose of generating wealth, or profit, and it is the profit generated *during a period* that is the concern of many users. The main purpose of the income statement – or profit and loss account, as it is sometimes called – is to measure and report how much **profit** (wealth) the business has generated over a period.

To measure profit, the total revenue generated during a particular period must be identified. **Revenue** is simply a measure of the inflow of economic benefits arising from the ordinary operations of a business. These benefits will result in either an increase in assets (such as cash or amounts owed to the business by its customers) or a decrease in liabilities. Different forms of business enterprise will generate different forms of revenue. Some examples of the different forms that revenue can take are as follows:

- sales of goods (for example, by a manufacturer);
- fees for services (for example, of a solicitor);
- subscriptions (for example, of a club);
- interest received (for example, on an investment fund).

Real World 3.1 shows the various forms of revenue generated by a leading football club.

REAL WORLD 3.1

Gunning for revenue

Arsenal Football Club generated total revenue of almost £256 million for the year ended 31 May 2011. Like other leading clubs, it relies on various forms of revenue to sustain its success. Figure 3.1 below shows the contribution of each form of revenue for the year.

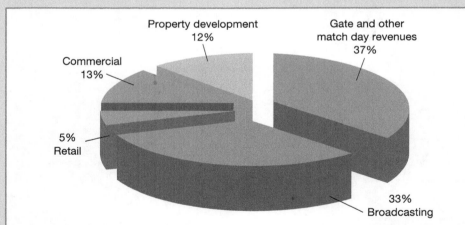

Gate receipts and broadcasting tend to be Arsenal's main forms of revenue, although commercial activities (including sponsorship and events) and property development are also significant. Revenue from player trading was negligible for 2011.

Figure 3.1 Arsenal's revenue for the year ended 31 May 2011

Source: Based on information in Arsenal Holdings plc Annual Report 2011, p. 44.

The total expenses relating to each period must also be identified. **Expense** is really the opposite of revenue. It represents the outflow of economic benefits arising from the ordinary operations of a business. This loss of benefits will result in either a decrease in assets (such as cash) or an increase in liabilities (such as amounts owed to suppliers). Expenses are incurred in the process of generating, or attempting to generate, revenue. The nature of the business will again determine the type of expenses that will be incurred. Examples of some of the more common types of expense are:

- the cost of buying or making the goods that are sold during the period concerned – known as *cost of sales* or *cost of goods sold*;
- salaries and wages;
- rent and rates;
- motor vehicle running expenses;
- insurance;
- printing and stationery;
- heat and light;
- telephone and postage.

The income statement simply shows the total revenue generated during a particular period and deducts from this the total expenses incurred in generating that revenue. The difference between the total revenue and total expenses will represent either profit (if revenue exceeds expenses) or loss (if expenses exceed revenue). Thus, we have:

> **Profit (or loss) for the period = Total revenue for the period – Total expenses incurred in generating that revenue**

The period over which profit or loss is normally measured is usually known as the **reporting period**, but it is sometimes called the 'accounting period' or 'financial period'.

DIFFERENT ROLES

The income statement and the statement of financial position are not substitutes for one another. Rather, they perform different roles. The statement of financial position sets out the wealth held by the business at a single moment in time, whereas the income statement is concerned with the *flow* of wealth over a period of time. The two statements are, however, closely related.

The income statement links the statements of financial position at the beginning and the end of a reporting period. At the start of a new reporting period, the statement of financial position shows the opening wealth position of the business. After an appropriate period, an income statement is prepared to show the wealth generated over that period. A statement of financial position is then prepared to reveal the new wealth position at the end of the period. It will reflect changes in wealth that have occurred since the previous statement of financial position was drawn up.

We saw in Chapter 2 (page 41) that the effect on the statement of financial position of making a profit (or loss) means that the accounting equation can be extended as follows:

> **Assets (at the end of the period) = Equity (amount at the start of the period**
> **+ Profit (or – Loss) for the period)**
> **+ Liabilities (at the end of the period)**

(This is assuming that the owner makes no injections or withdrawals of equity during the period.)

Activity 3.1

Can you recall from Chapter 2 how a profit, or loss, for a period is shown in the statement of financial position?

It is shown as an adjustment to owners' equity. Profit is added and a loss is subtracted.

The equation above can be extended to:

> **Assets (at the end of the period) = Equity (amount at the start of the period)**
> **+ (Sales revenue – Expenses) (for the period)**
> **+ Liabilities (at the end of the period)**

In theory, it is possible to calculate the profit (or loss) for the period by making all adjustments for revenue and expenses through the equity section of the statement of financial position. However, this would be rather cumbersome. A better solution is to have an 'appendix' to the equity section, in the form of an income statement. By deducting expenses from revenue for the period, the income statement derives the profit (or loss) by which the equity figure in the statement of financial position needs to be adjusted. This profit (or loss) figure represents the net effect of trading for the period. By providing this 'appendix', users are presented with a detailed and more informative view of performance.

INCOME STATEMENT LAYOUT

The layout of the income statement will vary according to the type of business to which it relates. To illustrate an income statement, let us consider the case of a retail business (that is, a business that buys goods in their completed state and resells them).

Example 3.1 sets out a typical layout for the income statement of a retail business.

Example 3.1

Better-Price Stores
Income statement for the year ended 31 October 2012

	£
Sales revenue	232,000
Cost of sales	(154,000)
Gross profit	78,000
Salaries and wages	(24,500)
Rent and rates	(14,200)
Heat and light	(7,500)
Telephone and postage	(1,200)
Insurance	(1,000)
Motor vehicle running expenses	(3,400)
Depreciation – fixtures and fittings	(1,000)
Depreciation – motor van	(600)
Operating profit	24,600
Interest received from investments	2,000
Interest on borrowings	(1,100)
Profit for the period	25,500

We saw in Chapter 2 that brackets are used to denote when an item is to be deducted. This convention is used by accountants in preference to + or − signs and will be used throughout the text.

Gross profit

The first part of the income statement is concerned with calculating the **gross profit** for the period. We can see that revenue, which arises from selling the goods, is the first item to appear. Deducted from this item is the cost of sales (also called cost of goods sold) during the period. This gives the gross profit, which represents the profit from buying and selling goods, without taking into account any other revenues or expenses associated with the business.

Operating profit

From the gross profit, operating expenses (overheads) incurred in running the business (salaries and wages, rent and rates and so on) are deducted. The resulting figure is known as the **operating profit**. This represents the wealth generated during the period from the normal activities of the business. It does not take account of income from other activities. Better-Price Stores in Example 3.1 is a retailer, so interest received on some spare cash that the business has invested is not part of its operating profit. Costs of financing the business are also ignored in the calculation of the operating profit.

Profit for the period

Having established the operating profit, we add any non-operating income (such as interest receivable) and deduct any interest payable on borrowings to arrive at the **profit for the period** (or net profit). This final measure of wealth generated represents the amount attributable to the owner(s) and will be added to the equity figure in the statement of financial position. It is a residual: that is, the amount remaining after deducting all expenses incurred in generating the sales revenue and taking account of non-operating income.

FURTHER ISSUES

Having set out the main principles involved in preparing an income statement, we need to consider some further points.

Cost of sales

The **cost of sales** (or cost of goods sold) for a period can be identified in different ways. In some businesses, the cost of sales for each individual sale is identified at the time of the transaction. Each item of sales revenue is matched with the relevant cost of that sale. Many large retailers (for example, supermarkets) have point-of-sale (checkout) devices that not only record each sale but also simultaneously pick up the cost of the goods that are the subject of the particular sale. Businesses that sell a relatively small number of high-value items (for example, an engineering business that produces custom-made equipment) also tend to match sales revenue with the cost of the goods sold, at the time of sale. However, some businesses (for example, small retailers) may not find it practical to do this. Instead, they identify the cost of sales after the end of the reporting period.

To understand how this is done, we must remember that the cost of sales represents the cost of goods that were *sold* during the period rather than the cost of goods that were *bought* during the period. Part of the goods bought during the period may remain, as inventories, at the end of the period. These will normally be sold in the next period. To derive the cost of sales, we need to know the amount of opening and closing inventories for the period and the cost of goods bought during the period. Example 3.2 illustrates how the cost of sales is derived.

Example 3.2

Better-Price Stores, which we considered in Example 3.1 above, began the year with unsold inventories of £40,000 and during that year bought inventories at a cost of £189,000. At the end of the year, unsold inventories of £75,000 were still held by the business.

→

The opening inventories at the beginning of the year *plus* the goods bought during the year will represent the total goods available for resale. Thus:

	£
Opening inventories	40,000
Purchases (goods bought)	189,000
Goods available for resale	229,000

The closing inventories will represent that portion of the total goods available for resale that remains unsold at the end of the year. Thus, the cost of goods actually sold during the year must be the total goods available for resale *less* the inventories remaining at the end of the year. That is:

	£
Goods available for resale	229,000
Closing inventories	(75,000)
Cost of sales (or cost of goods sold)	154,000

These calculations are sometimes shown on the face of the income statement as in Example 3.3.

Example 3.3

	£	£
Sales revenue		232,000
Cost of sales:		
Opening inventories	40,000	
Purchases (goods bought)	189,000	
Closing inventories	(75,000)	(154,000)
Gross profit		78,000

This is just an expanded version of the first section of the income statement for Better-Price Stores, as set out in Example 3.1. We have simply included the additional information concerning inventories balances and purchases for the year provided in Example 3.2.

Classifying expenses

The classification of expense items is often a matter of judgement. Thus, the income statement set out in Example 3.1 could have included the insurance expense with the telephone and postage expense under a single heading – say, 'general expenses'. Such decisions are normally based on how useful a particular classification will be to users. This will usually mean that expense items of material size will be shown separately. For businesses that trade as limited companies, however, rules dictate the classification of expense items for external reporting purposes. These rules will be discussed in Chapter 4.

Activity 3.2

The following information relates to the activities of H & S Retailers for the year ended 30 April 2012:

	£
Motor vehicle running expenses	1,200
Closing inventories	3,000
Rent and rates payable	5,000
Motor vans – cost less depreciation	6,300
Annual depreciation – motor vans	1,500
Heat and light	900
Telephone and postage	450
Sales revenue	97,400
Goods purchased	68,350
Insurance	750
Loan interest payable	620
Balance at bank	4,780
Salaries and wages	10,400
Opening inventories	4,000

Prepare an income statement for the year ended 30 April 2012. (*Hint*: Not all items listed should appear on this statement.)

Your answer to this activity should be as follows:

H & S Retailers
Income statement for the year ended 30 April 2012

	£	£
Sales revenue		97,400
Cost of sales:		
Opening inventories	4,000	
Purchases	68,350	
Closing inventories	(3,000)	(69,350)
Gross profit		28,050
Salaries and wages		(10,400)
Rent and rates		(5,000)
Heat and light		(900)
Telephone and postage		(450)
Insurance		(750)
Motor vehicle running expenses		(1,200)
Depreciation – motor vans		(1,500)
Operating profit		7,850
Loan interest		(620)
Profit for the period		7,230

Note that neither the motor vans nor the bank balance are included in this statement, because they are both assets and so neither revenues nor expenses.

Figure 3.2 shows the layout of the income statement.

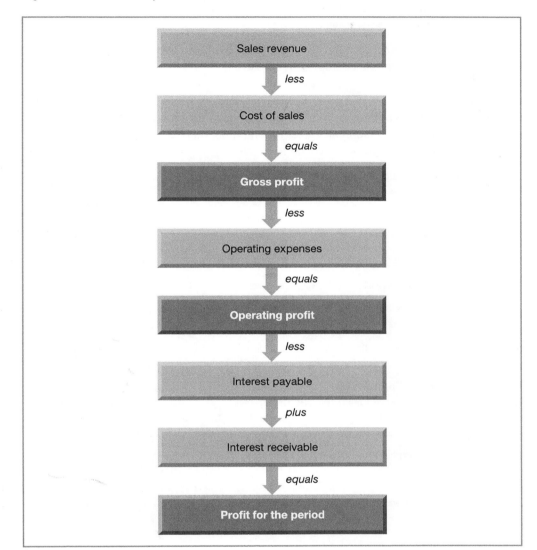

Figure 3.2 The layout of the income statement

RECOGNISING REVENUE

A key issue in the measurement of profit concerns the point at which revenue is recognised. Revenue arising from the sale of goods or provision of a service could be recognised at various points. Where, for example, a motor car dealer receives an order for a new car from one of its customers, the associated revenue could be recognised by the dealer:

- at the time that the order is placed by the customer;
- at the time that the car is collected by the customer; or
- at the time that the customer pays the dealer.

These three points could be quite far apart, particularly where the order relates to a specialist car that is sold to the customer on credit.

The point chosen can have a profound impact on the total revenues reported for the reporting period. This, in turn, can have a profound effect on profit. If the sale transaction straddled the end of a reporting period, the point chosen for recognising revenue could determine whether it is included in an earlier reporting period or a later one.

The main criteria for recognising revenue from the sale of goods or services are that:

- the amount of revenue can be measured reliably; and
- it is probable that the economic benefits will be received.

An additional criterion, however, must be applied where the revenue comes from the sale of goods, which is that:

- ownership and control of the items should pass to the buyer.

Activity 3.3 provides an opportunity to apply these criteria to a practical problem.

Activity 3.3

A manufacturing business sells goods on credit. Below are four points in the production/ selling cycle at which revenue might be recognised:

1 when the goods are produced;
2 when an order is received from the customer;
3 when the goods are delivered to, and accepted by, the customer;
4 when the cash is received from the customer.

At what point do you think the business should recognise revenue?

All of the three criteria mentioned above will usually be fulfilled at point 3: when the goods are passed to, and accepted by, the customer. This is because:

- the selling price and the settlement terms will have been agreed and, therefore, the amount of revenue can be reliably measured;
- delivery and acceptance of the goods leads to ownership and control passing to the buyer;
- transferring ownership gives the seller legally enforceable rights that makes it probable that the buyer will pay.

We can see that the effect of applying these criteria is that a sale on credit is usually recognised *before* the cash is received. This means that the total sales revenue shown in the income statement may include sales transactions for which the cash has yet to be received. The total sales revenue will often, therefore, be different from the total cash received from sales during the period. For cash sales (that is, sales where cash is paid at the same time as the goods are transferred), there will be no difference in timing between reporting sales revenue and cash received.

Long-term contracts

Some contracts for goods or services may take more than one reporting period to complete. A misleading impression may be given, however, if a business waits until the completion of a long-term contract before recognising revenue. This is because all the revenue would be shown in the final reporting period and none in the preceding reporting periods when work was also carried out.

Construction contracts

Construction contracts often extend over a long period of time. Suppose that a customer enters into a contract with a builder to have a new factory built that will take three years to complete. In such a situation, it is possible to recognise revenue *before* the factory is completed provided that the building work can be broken down into a number of stages and each stage can be measured reliably. Let us assume that building the factory could be broken down into the following stages:

Stage 1 – clearing and levelling the land and putting in the foundations.
Stage 2 – building the walls.
Stage 3 – putting on the roof.
Stage 4 – putting in the windows and completing all the interior work.

Each stage can be awarded a separate price with the total for all the stages being equal to the total contract price for the factory. This means that, as each stage is completed, the builder can recognise the price for that stage as revenue and bill the customer accordingly. This is provided that the outcome of the contract as a whole can be estimated reliably.

Real World 3.2 sets out the revenue recognition criteria for one large business.

REAL WORLD 3.2

Subject to contract

AMEC plc is an international business offering consultancy, engineering and project management services. The point at which revenue on long-term contracts is recognised by the business is as follows:

> As soon as the outcome of a long-term contract can be estimated reliably, contract revenue and expenses are recognised in the income statement in proportion to the stage of completion of the contract. The stage of completion is assessed by reference to surveys of work performed. When the outcome of a contract cannot be estimated reliably, revenue is recognised only to the extent of contract costs incurred that it is probable will be recoverable, and contract costs are expensed as incurred. An expected loss on a contract is recognised immediately in the income statement.

Source: AMEC plc, Annual Report and Accounts 2010, Notes to Consolidated Accounts, p. 69.

Services

There are certain kinds of service that may take years to complete. One example is where a consultancy business installs a new computer system for the government.

Activity 3.4

From what we discussed earlier, can you suggest how revenue might be recognised for this kind of service?

If the contract can be broken down into stages, and each stage of completion measured reliably, a similar approach to that taken for construction contracts can be adopted. This would allow revenue to be recognised at each stage of completion.

In some cases, a continuous service may be provided to a customer. For example, a telecommunications business may provide open access to the internet for subscribers. Here, the benefits from providing the service are usually assumed to arise evenly over time and so revenue is recognised evenly over the subscription period.

Where it is not possible to break down a service into particular stages of completion, or to assume that benefits from providing the service accrue evenly over time, revenue is normally recognised after the service is completed. An example might be the work done by a solicitor on a house purchase for a client. **Real World 3.3** provides an example of how one major business recognises revenue from providing services.

REAL WORLD 3.3

Sky-high broadcasting revenue

British Sky Broadcasting Group plc is a major satellite broadcaster that generates various forms of revenue. Here are the ways in which some of its revenues are recognised:

- pay-per-view revenues – when the event (movie or football match) is viewed;
- subscription services, including Sky TV and Sky Broadband – as the services are provided;
- advertising revenues – when the advertising is broadcast;
- installation, hardware and service revenue – when the goods and services are activated.

Source: Based on information in British Sky Broadcasting Group plc Annual Report and Accounts 2011, p. 69.

Revenue for providing services is often recognised *before* the cash is received. There are occasions, however, when the business demands payment before providing the service.

Activity 3.5

Can you think of any examples where cash may be demanded in advance of a service being provided? (*Hint*: Try to think of services that you may use.)

Examples of cash being received in advance of the service being provided may include:

- rent received from letting premises;
- telephone line rental charges;
- TV licence (BBC) or subscription fees (for example, Sky);
- subscriptions received for the use of health clubs or golf clubs.

You may have thought of others.

RECOGNISING EXPENSES

Having considered the recognition of revenue, let us now turn to the recognition of expenses. The **matching convention** provides guidance on this. This convention states that expenses should be matched to the revenue that they helped to generate. In other words, the expenses associated with a particular item of revenue must be taken into account in the same reporting period as that in which the item of revenue is included. Applying this convention often means that an expense reported in the income statement for a period may not be the same as the cash paid for that item during the period. The expense reported might be either more or less than the cash paid during the period. Let us consider two examples that illustrate this point.

When the expense for the period is more than the cash paid during the period

Example 3.4

Domestic Ltd, a retailer, sells household electrical appliances. It pays its sales staff a commission of 2 per cent of sales revenue generated. Total sales revenue for last year amounted to £300,000. Thus, the commission to be paid on sales for the year will be £6,000. However, by the end of the year, the amount of sales commission actually paid was only £5,000. If the business reported this amount, it would mean that the income statement would not reflect the full expense for the year. This would contravene the *matching convention* because not all of the expenses associated with the revenue of the year would have been matched in the income statement. This will be remedied as follows:

- Sales commission expense in the income statement will include the amount paid plus the amount outstanding (that is, £6,000 = £5,000 + £1,000).
- The amount outstanding (£1,000) represents an outstanding liability at the end of the year and will be included under the heading **accrued expenses**, or 'accruals', in the statement of financial position. As this item will have to be paid within twelve months of the year end, it will be treated as a current liability.
- The cash will already have been reduced to reflect the commission paid (£5,000) during the period.

These points are illustrated in Figure 3.3.

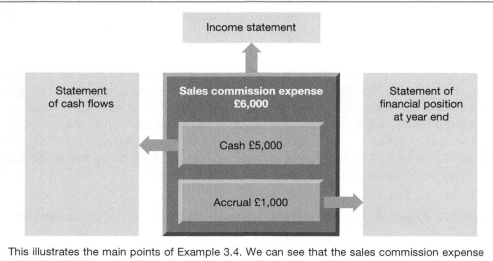

This illustrates the main points of Example 3.4. We can see that the sales commission expense of £6,000 (which appears in the income statement) is made up of a cash element of £5,000 and an accrued element of £1,000. The cash element appears in the statement of cash flows and the accrued element will appear as a year-end liability in the statement of financial position.

Figure 3.3 Accounting for sales commission

In principle, all expenses should be matched to the period in which the sales revenue to which they relate is reported. It is sometimes difficult, however, to match certain expenses to sales revenue in the same precise way that we have matched sales commission to sales revenue. For example, electricity charges incurred often cannot be linked directly to particular sales in this way. As a result, the electricity charges incurred by, say, a retailer would be matched to the *period* to which they relate. Example 3.5 illustrates this.

Example 3.5

Domestic Ltd has reached the end of its reporting period and has only paid for electricity for the first three quarters of the year (amounting to £1,900). This is simply because the electricity company has yet to send out bills for the quarter that ends on the same date as Domestic Ltd's year end. The amount of Domestic Ltd's bill for the last quarter of the year is £500. In this situation, the amount of the electricity expense outstanding is dealt with as follows:

■ Electricity expense in the income statement will include the amount paid, plus the amount of the bill for the last quarter of the year (that is, £1,900 + £500 = £2,400) in order to cover the whole year.

■ The amount of the outstanding bill (£500) represents a liability at the end of the year and will be included under the heading 'accruals' or 'accrued expenses' in the statement of financial position. This item would normally have to be paid within twelve months of the year end and will, therefore, be treated as a current liability.

■ The cash will already have been reduced to reflect the amount (£1,900) paid for electricity during the period.

This treatment will mean that the correct figure for the electricity expense for the year will be included in the income statement. It will also have the effect of showing that, at the end of the reporting period, Domestic Ltd owed the amount of the last quarter's electricity bill. Dealing with the outstanding amount in this way reflects the dual aspect of the item and will ensure that the accounting equation is maintained.

Domestic Ltd may wish to draw up its income statement before it is able to discover how much it owes for the last quarter's electricity. In this case it is quite normal to make an estimate of the amount of the bill and to use this amount as described above.

Activity 3.6

How will the payment of the outstanding sales commission (Example 3.4) and the electricity bill for the last quarter (Example 3.5) be dealt with in the accounting records of Domestic Ltd?

When these amounts are eventually paid, they will be dealt with as follows:

■ Reduce cash by the amounts paid.
■ Reduce the amount of the accrued expense as shown on the statement of financial position by the same amounts.

Other expenses, apart from electricity charges, may also be matched to the period to which they relate.

Activity 3.7

Can you think of other expenses for a retailer that cannot be linked directly to sales revenue and for which matching will therefore be done on a time basis?

You may have thought of the following examples:

■ rent and rates
■ insurance
■ interest payments
■ license fees payable.

This is not an exhaustive list. You may have thought of others.

When the amount paid during the period is more than the full expense for the period

It is not unusual for a business to be in a situation where it has paid more during the year than the full expense for that year. Example 3.6 illustrates how we deal with this.

Example 3.6

Images Ltd, an advertising agency, normally pays rent for its premises quarterly in advance (on 1 January, 1 April, 1 July and 1 October). On the last day of the last reporting period (31 December), it paid the next quarter's rent (£4,000) to the following 31 March, which was a day earlier than required. This would mean that a total of five quarters' rent was paid during the year. If Images Ltd reports all of the cash paid as an expense in the income statement, this would be more than the full expense for the year. This would contravene the matching convention because a higher figure than the expenses associated with the revenue of the year would appear in the income statement.

The problem is overcome by dealing with the rental payment as follows:

- Show the rent for four quarters as the appropriate expense in the income statement (that is, 4 × £4,000 = £16,000).
- The cash (that is, 5 × £4,000 = £20,000) would already have been paid during the year.
- Show the quarter's rent paid in advance (£4,000) as a prepaid expense under assets in the statement of financial position. (The rent paid in advance will appear as a current asset in the statement of financial position, under the heading **prepaid expenses** or 'prepayments'.)

In the next reporting period, this prepayment will cease to be an asset and will become an expense in the income statement of that period. This is because the rent prepaid relates to the next period and will be 'used up' during it.

These points are illustrated in Figure 3.4.

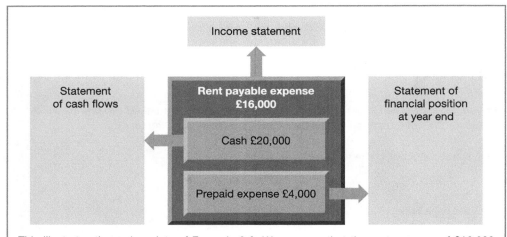

This illustrates the main points of Example 3.6. We can see that the rent expense of £16,000 (which appears in the income statement) is made up of four quarters' rent at £4,000 per quarter. This is the amount that relates to the period and is 'used up' during the period. The cash paid of £20,000 (which appears in the statement of cash flows) is made up of the cash paid during the period, which is five quarters at £4,000 per quarter. Finally, the prepayment of £4,000 (which appears on the statement of financial position) represents the payment made on 31 December and relates to the next reporting period.

Figure 3.4 Accounting for rent payable

In practice, the treatment of accruals and prepayments will be subject to the **materiality convention**. This convention states that, where the amounts involved are immaterial, we should consider only what is expedient. This will usually mean treating an item as an expense in the period in which it is acquired, rather than strictly matching it to the revenue to which it relates. For example, a business may find that, at the end of a reporting period, it holds £2 worth of unused stationery. The time and effort taken to record this as a prepayment would outweigh the negligible effect on the measurement of profit or financial position. Thus, it would be treated as an expense of the current period and ignored in the following period.

Profit, cash and accruals accounting

We have seen that it is normally the case that, for a particular reporting period, total revenue is not the same as total cash received, and total expenses are not the same as total cash paid. As a result, the profit for the period (that is, total revenue minus total expenses) will not normally represent the net cash generated during that period. This reflects the difference between profit and liquidity. Profit is a measure of achievement, or productive effort, rather than a measure of cash generated. Although making a profit increases wealth, cash is only one possible form in which that wealth may be held.

These points are reflected in the **accruals convention**, which asserts that profit is the excess of revenue over expenses for a period, not the excess of cash receipts over cash payments. Leading on from this, the approach to accounting that is based on the accruals convention is frequently referred to as **accruals accounting**. The statement of financial position and the income statement are both prepared on the basis of accruals accounting.

Activity 3.8

What about the statement of cash flows? Is it prepared on an accruals accounting basis?

No. The statement of cash flows simply deals with cash receipts and payments.

DEPRECIATION

The expense of **depreciation**, which we have already come across, requires further examination. Most non-current assets do not have a perpetual existence, but have finite, or limited, lives. They are eventually 'used up' in the process of generating revenue for the business. This 'using up' may relate to physical deterioration (as with a motor vehicle). It may however be linked to obsolescence (as with some IT software that is no longer useful) or the mere passage of time (as with a purchased patent, which has a limited period of validity).

In essence, depreciation is an attempt to measure that portion of the cost (or fair value) of a non-current asset that has been depleted in generating the revenue recognised during a particular period. In the case of intangibles, we usually refer to the expense as **amortisation**, rather than *depreciation*. In the interests of brevity, we shall use the word depreciation for both tangibles and intangibles.

Calculating the depreciation expense

To calculate a depreciation expense for a period, four factors have to be considered:

- the cost (or fair value) of the asset;
- the useful life of the asset;
- the residual value of the asset; and
- the depreciation method.

The cost (or fair value) of the asset

The cost of an asset will include all costs incurred by the business to bring the asset to its required location and to make it ready for use. Thus, in addition to the cost of acquiring the asset, any delivery costs, installation costs (for example, setting up a new machine) and legal costs incurred in the transfer of legal title (for example, in purchasing a lease on property) will be included as part of the total cost of the asset. Similarly, any costs incurred in improving or altering an asset to make it suitable for use will also be included as part of the total cost.

Activity 3.9

Andrew Wu (Engineering) Ltd bought a new motor car for its marketing director. The invoice received from the motor car supplier showed the following:

	£
New BMW 325i	26,350
Delivery charge	80
Alloy wheels	660
Sun roof	200
Petrol	30
Number plates	130
Road fund licence	120
	27,570
Part exchange – Reliant Robin	(1,000)
Amount outstanding	26,570

What is the total cost of the new car to be treated as part of the business's property, plant and equipment?

The cost of the new car will be as follows:

	£
New BMW 325i	26,350
Delivery charge	80
Alloy wheels	660
Sun roof	200
Number plates	130
	27,420

This cost includes delivery charges, which are necessary to bring the asset into use, and it includes number plates, as they are a necessary and integral part of the asset. Improvements (alloy wheels and sun roof) are also regarded as part of the total cost of the motor car. The petrol and road fund license, however, are costs of operating the asset: hence these amounts will be treated as an expense in the period incurred (although part of the cost of the license may be regarded as a prepaid expense in the period incurred).

The part-exchange figure shown is part payment of the total amount outstanding and so is not relevant to a consideration of the total cost.

The fair value of an asset was defined in Chapter 2 as the exchange value that could be obtained in an arm's-length transaction. As we saw, assets may be revalued to fair value only if this can be measured reliably. Where fair values have been applied, the depreciation expense should be based on those fair values, rather than on the historic costs.

The useful life of the asset

A non-current asset has both a *physical life* and an *economic life*. The physical life will be exhausted through the effects of wear and tear and/or the passage of time. The economic life is decided by the effects of technological progress, by changes in demand or changes in the way that the business operates. The benefits provided by the asset are eventually outweighed by the costs as it becomes unable to compete with newer assets, or becomes irrelevant to the needs of the business. The economic life of an asset may be much shorter than its physical life. For example, a computer may have a physical life of eight years and an economic life of three years.

The economic life determines the expected useful life of an asset for depreciation purposes. It is often difficult, however, to estimate as technological progress and shifts in consumer tastes can be swift and unpredictable.

Residual value (disposal value)

When a business disposes of a non-current asset that may still be of value to others, some payment may be received. This payment will represent the **residual value**, or *disposal value*, of the asset. To calculate the total amount to be depreciated, the residual value must be deducted from the cost (or fair value) of the asset. The likely amount to be received on disposal can, once again, be difficult to predict. The best guide is often past experience of similar assets sold.

Depreciation method

Once the amount to be depreciated (that is, the cost, or fair value, of the asset less any residual value) has been estimated, the business must select a method of allocating this depreciable amount between the reporting periods covering the asset's useful life. Although there are various ways in which this may be done, there are really only two methods that are commonly used in practice.

The first of these is known as the **straight-line method**. This method simply allocates the amount to be depreciated evenly over the useful life of the asset. In other words, there is an equal depreciation expense for each year that the asset is held.

Example 3.7

To illustrate this method, consider the following information:

Cost of machine	£78,124
Estimated residual value at the end of its useful life	£2,000
Estimated useful life	4 years

To calculate the depreciation expense for each year, the total amount to be depreciated must be calculated. This will be the total cost less the estimated residual value: that is, £78,124 − £2,000 = £76,124. Having done this, the annual depreciation expense can be derived by dividing the amount to be depreciated by the estimated useful life of the asset of four years. The calculation is therefore:

$$\frac{£76,124}{4} = £19,031$$

Thus, the annual depreciation expense that appears in the income statement in relation to this asset will be £19,031 for each of the four years of the asset's life.

The amount of depreciation relating to the asset will be accumulated for as long as the asset continues to be owned by the business or until the accumulated depreciation amounts to the cost less residual value. This accumulated depreciation figure will increase each year as a result of the annual depreciation expense in the income statement. This accumulated amount will be deducted from the cost of the asset on the statement of financial position. At the end of the second year, for example, the accumulated depreciation will be £19,031 × 2 = £38,062. The asset details will appear on the statement of financial position as follows:

	£
Machine at cost	78,124
Accumulated depreciation	(38,062)
	40,062

As we saw in Chapter 2, this balance of £40,062 is referred to as the **carrying amount** (sometimes also known as the **written-down value** or **net book value**) of the asset. It represents that portion of the cost (or fair value) of the asset that has still to be treated as an expense (written off) in future years plus the residual value. This carrying-amount figure does not, except by coincidence, represent the current market value, which may be quite different. The only point at which the carrying amount is intended to represent the market value of the asset is immediately before its disposal. Thus, in Example 3.7, at the end of the four-year life of the machine, the carrying amount would be £2,000 – its estimated disposal value.

The straight-line method derives its name from the fact that the carrying amount of the asset at the end of each year, when plotted against time, will result in a straight line, as shown in Figure 3.5.

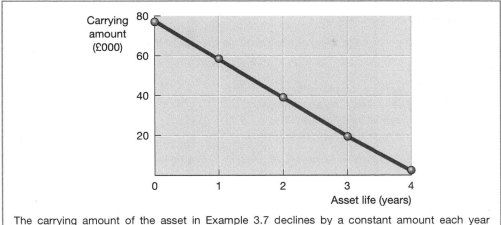

The carrying amount of the asset in Example 3.7 declines by a constant amount each year (£19,031). This is because the straight-line method provides a constant depreciation expense each year. The result, when plotted on a graph, is a straight line.

Figure 3.5 Graph of carrying amount against time using the straight-line method

The second approach to calculating the depreciation expense for a period is referred to as the **reducing-balance method**. This method applies a fixed percentage rate of depreciation to the carrying amount of the asset each year. The effect of this will be high annual depreciation expenses in the early years and lower expenses in the later years. To illustrate this method, let us take the same information that was used in Example 3.7. By using a fixed percentage of 60 per cent of the carrying amount to determine the annual depreciation expense, the effect will be to reduce the carrying amount to £2,000 after four years.

The calculations will be as follows:

	£
Cost of machine	78,124
Year 1 depreciation expense (60%* of cost)	(46,874)
Carrying amount	31,250
Year 2 depreciation expense (60% of carrying amount)	(18,750)
Carrying amount	12,500
Year 3 depreciation expense (60% of carrying amount)	(7,500)
Carrying amount	5,000
Year 4 depreciation expense (60% of carrying amount)	(3,000)
Residual value	2,000

* See the box below for an explanation of how to derive the fixed percentage.

Deriving the fixed percentage

Deriving the fixed percentage to be applied requires the use of the following formula:

$$P = (1 - \sqrt[n]{R/C} \times 100\%)$$

where: P = the depreciation percentage
   n = the useful life of the asset (in years)
   R = the residual value of the asset
   C = the cost, or fair value, of the asset.

The fixed percentage rate will, however, be given in all examples used in this text.

We can see that the pattern of depreciation is quite different between the two methods. If we plot the carrying amount of the asset, which has been derived using the reducing-balance method, against time, the result will be as shown in Figure 3.6.

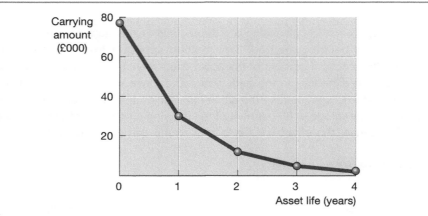

Under the reducing-balance method, the carrying amount of the asset in Example 3.7 falls by a larger amount in the earlier years than in the later years. This is because the depreciation expense is based on a fixed-rate percentage of the carrying amount.

Figure 3.6 Graph of carrying amount against time using the reducing-balance method

Activity 3.10

Assume that the machine used in Example 3.7 was owned by a business that made a profit before depreciation of £40,000 for each of the four years in which the asset was held.

Calculate the profit for the business for each year under each depreciation method, and comment on your findings.

$\rightarrow$

Your answer should be as follows:

Straight-line method

	(a) Profit before depreciation £	(b) Depreciation £	(a – b) Profit £
Year 1	40,000	19,031	20,969
Year 2	40,000	19,031	20,969
Year 3	40,000	19,031	20,969
Year 4	40,000	19,031	20,969

Reducing-balance method

	(a) Profit before depreciation £	(b) Depreciation £	(a – b) Profit/(loss) £
Year 1	40,000	46,874	(6,874)
Year 2	40,000	18,750	21,250
Year 3	40,000	7,500	32,500
Year 4	40,000	3,000	37,000

The straight-line method of depreciation results in the same profit figure for each year of the four-year period. This is because both the profit before depreciation and the depreciation expense are constant over the period. The reducing-balance method, however, results in very different profit figures for the four years, despite the fact that in this example the pre-depreciation profit is the same each year. In the first year a loss is reported and, thereafter, a rising profit.

Although the *pattern* of profit over the four-year period will be quite different, depending on the depreciation method used, the *total* profit for the period (£83,876) will remain the same. This is because both methods of depreciating will allocate the same amount of total depreciation (£76,124) over the four-year period. It is only the amount allocated *between years* that will differ.

In practice, the use of different depreciation methods may not have such a dramatic effect on profits as suggested in Activity 3.10. This is because businesses typically have more than one depreciating non-current asset. Where a business replaces some of its assets each year, the total depreciation expense calculated under the reducing-balance method will reflect a range of expenses (from high through to low), as assets will be at different points in the replacement cycle. This could mean that each year's total depreciation expense may not be significantly different from that which would have been derived under the straight-line method.

Selecting a depreciation method

The appropriate depreciation method to choose is the one that best matches the depreciation expense to the pattern of economic benefits that the asset provides. Where these benefits are provided evenly over time (buildings, for example), the straight-line method is usually appropriate. Where assets lose their efficiency (as with certain types of machinery), the benefits provided will decline over time and so the reducing-balance method may be more appropriate. Where the pattern of economic benefits provided by the asset is uncertain, the straight-line method is normally chosen.

There is an international financial reporting standard (or international accounting standard) to deal with the depreciation of property, plant and equipment. (As we shall see in Chapter 4, the purpose of accounting standards is to narrow areas of accounting difference and to try to ensure that information provided to users is transparent and comparable.) The relevant standard endorses the view that the depreciation method chosen should reflect the pattern of economic benefits provided but does not specify particular methods to be used. It states that the useful life, depreciation method and residual values of non-current assets should be reviewed at least annually and adjustments made where appropriate.

Real World 3.4 sets out the depreciation policies of Carphone Warehouse Group plc, the mobile 'phone and PC retailer.

REAL WORLD 3.4

Some text about depreciation policies

Carphone Warehouse Group plc uses the straight-line method to depreciate all its property, plant and equipment, other than land and assets in the course of construction. The financial statements for the year ended 31 March 2011 show the annual rate at which different classes of assets are depreciated as follows:

Investment properties	2 per cent
Short leasehold costs	10 per cent or the lease term if less
Network equipment and computer hardware	12.5 to 50 per cent
Fixtures and fittings	20 to 25 per cent
Motor vehicles	25 per cent
Software and licences	At least 12.5 per cent

We can see that there are wide variations in the expected useful lives of the various assets held.

Source: Carphone Warehouse Group plc Annual Report 2011, p. 53.

Carphone Warehouse is typical of most UK businesses in that it uses the straight-line method. The reducing-balance method is much less popular.

The approach taken to calculating depreciation is summarised in Figure 3.7.

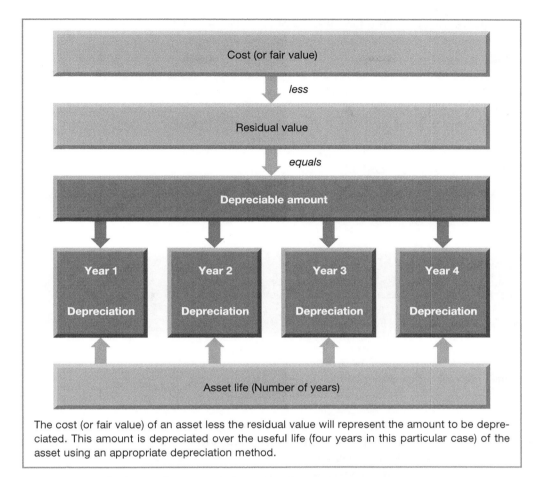

Figure 3.7 Calculating the annual depreciation expense

Impairment and depreciation

We saw in Chapter 2 that all non-current assets could be subjected to an impairment test. Where a non-current asset with a finite life has its carrying amount reduced as a result of an impairment test, depreciation expenses for future reporting periods should be based on the impaired value of that asset.

Depreciation and asset replacement

Some people appear to believe that the purpose of depreciation is to provide the funds for the replacement of a non-current asset when it reaches the end of its useful life. However, this is not the case. It was mentioned earlier that depreciation represents an attempt to allocate the cost or fair value (less any residual value) of a non-current asset over its expected useful life. The depreciation expense for a particular reporting period is used in calculating profit for that period. If a depreciation charge is excluded from the income statement, we will not have a fair measure of financial performance. Whether or not the business intends to replace the asset in the future is irrelevant.

Where an asset is to be replaced, the depreciation expense in the income statement will not ensure that liquid funds are set aside specifically for this purpose. Although the depreciation expense will reduce profit, and therefore reduce the amount that the owners may decide to withdraw, the amounts retained within the business as a result may be invested in ways that are unrelated to the replacement of the asset.

Depreciation and judgement

From our discussions about depreciation, it is clear that accounting is not as precise and objective as it is sometimes portrayed. There are areas where subjective judgement is required.

Activity 3.11

What kinds of judgements must be made to calculate a depreciation expense for a period?

You may have thought of the following:

■ the expected residual or disposal value of the asset;
■ the expected useful life of the asset;
■ the choice of depreciation method.

Making different judgements on these matters would result in a different pattern of depreciation expenses over the life of the asset and, therefore, in a different pattern of reported profits. However, underestimations or overestimations that are made in relation to the above will be adjusted for in the final year of an asset's life. As a result, the total depreciation expense (and total profit) over the asset's life will not be affected by estimation errors.

Real World 3.5 describes the effect on annual performance of extending the useful life of a non-current asset held by a well-known business.

REAL WORLD 3.5

Engineering an improvement?

BA reported a loss of £358 million for the 2008/09 financial year. This loss, however, would have been significantly higher had the business not changed its depreciation policies. The 2008/09 annual report of the business states:

> During the prior year, the Group changed the depreciation period for the RB211 engine, used on Boeing 747 and 767 fleets, from 54 months to 78 months. The change resulted in a £33 million decrease in the annual depreciation charge for this engine type.

Source: British Airways Annual Report and Accounts 2008/09, Note 15, www.britishairways.com.

COSTING INVENTORIES

The cost of inventories is important in determining financial performance and position. The cost of inventories sold during a reporting period will affect the calculation of profit, and the cost of inventories held at the end of the reporting period will affect the portrayal of assets held.

To calculate the cost of inventories, an assumption must be made about the physical flow of inventories through the business. This assumption need not have anything to do with how inventories *actually* flow through the business. It is concerned only with providing useful measures of performance and position.

Three common assumptions used are:

- **first in, first out (FIFO)**, in which it is assumed that the earliest acquired inventories held are the first to be used;
- **last in, first out (LIFO)**, in which it is assumed that the latest acquired inventories held are the first to be used; and
- **weighted average cost (AVCO)**, in which it is assumed that inventories acquired lose their separate identity and go into a 'pool'. Any issues of inventories from this pool will reflect the weighted average cost of inventories held.

During a period of changing prices, the choice of assumption used in costing inventories can be important. Example 3.8 provides an illustration of how each assumption is applied and the effect of each on financial performance and position.

Example 3.8

A business commenced on 1 May to supply oil to factories. During the first month, the following transactions took place:

	Tonnes	Cost per tonne
May 2 Purchased	10,000	£10
May 10 Purchased	20,000	£13
May 18 Sold	9,000	

First in, first out (FIFO)

Using the first in, first out assumption, 9,000 tonnes of the 10,000 tonnes bought on 2 May are treated as if these are the ones to be sold. The remaining inventories bought on 2 May (1,000 tonnes) and the inventories bought on 10 May (20,000 tonnes) will become the closing inventories. Thus we have:

		£
Cost of sales	(9,000 @ £10 per tonne)	90,000
Closing inventories	(1,000 @ £10 per tonne)	10,000
	(20,000 @ £13 per tonne)	260,000
		270,000

Last in, first out (LIFO)

Using the last in, first out assumption, 9,000 tonnes of the inventories bought on 10 May will be treated as if these are the first to be sold. The earlier inventories bought on 2 May (10,000 tonnes) and the remainder of the inventories bought on 10 May (11,000 tonnes) will become the closing inventories. Thus we have:

		£
Cost of sales	(9,000 @ £13 per tonne)	117,000
Closing inventories	(11,000 @ £13 per tonne)	143,000
	(10,000 @ £10 per tonne)	100,000
		243,000

Figure 3.8 below contrasts LIFO and FIFO.

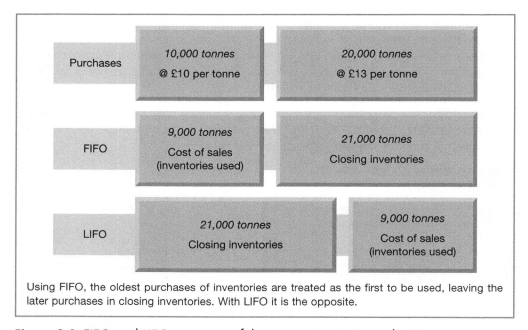

Using FIFO, the oldest purchases of inventories are treated as the first to be used, leaving the later purchases in closing inventories. With LIFO it is the opposite.

Figure 3.8 FIFO and LIFO treatment of the inventories in Example 3.8

Weighted average cost (AVCO)

Under this assumption, newly acquired inventories are treated as if they lose their separate identity. A weighted average cost, based on the quantities of each batch purchased, is calculated. The weighted average cost is then used to derive both the cost of goods sold and the cost of remaining inventories held. This simply means that the cost of the inventories bought on 2 May and 10 May are added together and then divided by the total number of tonnes to obtain the weighted average cost per tonne. That is:

Average cost = ((10,000 × £10) + (20,000 × £13))/(10,000 + 20,000) = £12 per tonne

Both the cost of sales and the value of the closing inventories are then based on this average cost per tonne. Thus we have:

Cost of sales	(9,000 @ £12 per tonne)	£108,000
Closing inventories	(21,000 @ £12 per tonne)	£252,000

Activity 3.12

Suppose that the 9,000 tonnes of inventories in Example 3.8 were sold for £15 a tonne.

(a) Calculate the gross profit for the period under each of the three costing assumptions.
(b) What do you note about the different profit and closing inventories valuations when using each method, when prices are rising?

Your answer should be along the following lines:

(a) Gross profit calculation:

	FIFO £000	LIFO £000	AVCO £000
Sales revenue (9,000 @ £15)	135	135	135
Cost of sales	(90)	(117)	(108)
Gross profit	45	18	27
Closing inventories figure	270	243	252

(b) These figures show that FIFO will give the highest gross profit during a period of rising prices. This is because sales revenue is matched with the earlier (and cheaper) purchases. LIFO will give the lowest gross profit because sales revenue is matched against the more recent (and dearer) purchases. The AVCO assumption will normally give a figure that is between these two extremes.

The closing inventories figure in the statement of financial position will be highest with the FIFO assumption. This is because the cost of oil still held will be based on the more recent (and dearer) purchases. LIFO will give the lowest closing inventories figure, as the oil held will be based on the earlier (and cheaper) purchases. Once again, the AVCO assumption will normally give a figure that is between these two extremes. During a period of falling prices, the position of FIFO and LIFO is reversed.

The different costing assumptions only have an effect on reported profit from one reporting period to the next. The figure derived for closing inventories will be carried forward and matched with sales revenue in a later period. Thus, if the cheaper purchases of inventories are matched to sales revenue in the current period, it will mean that the dearer purchases will be matched to sales revenue in a later period. Over the life of the business, therefore, total profit will be the same either way.

Inventories – some further issues

We saw in Chapter 2 that the convention of prudence requires that inventories be valued at the lower of cost and net realisable value. (The net realisable value of inventories is the estimated selling price less any further costs necessary to complete the goods and any costs involved in selling and distributing them.) In theory, this means that the valuation method applied to inventories could switch each year, depending on which of cost and net realisable value is the lower. In practice, however, the cost of the inventories held is usually below the current net realisable value – particularly during a period of rising prices. It is, therefore, the cost figure that will normally appear in the statement of financial position.

Activity 3.13

Can you think of any circumstances where the net realisable value will be lower than the cost of inventories held, even during a period of generally rising prices?

The net realisable value may be lower where:

- goods have deteriorated or become obsolete;
- there has been a fall in the market price of the goods;
- the goods are being used as a 'loss leader';
- bad buying decisions have been made.

There is an International Financial Reporting Standard that deals with inventories. It states that, when preparing financial statements for external reporting, the cost of inventories should normally be determined using either FIFO or AVCO. The LIFO assumption is not acceptable for external reporting. The standard also requires the 'lower of cost and net realisable value' rule to be used and so endorses the application of the prudence convention.

Real World 3.6 sets out the inventories costing approach of one well-known high street retail business.

REAL WORLD 3.6

Costing inventories at leisure

Blacks Leisure Group plc, the leisure clothes and accessories business (Blacks, Millets, O'Neill and so on), uses the weighted average basis of inventories valuation. The business reports:

> Inventories are stated at the lower of cost and net realisable value. The cost includes all costs in bringing each product into the business. Inventories are valued on a weighted average basis and this is not deemed to be materially different to that which would be calculated on a 'first in, first out' basis. Net realisable value is defined as the estimated selling price less any direct costs of disposal

Source: Blacks Leisure Group plc, Annual Report 2011, p. 39.

Costing inventories and depreciation provide two examples where the **consistency convention** must be applied. This convention holds that once a particular method of accounting is selected, it should be applied consistently over time. Thus, it would not be acceptable to switch from, say, FIFO to AVCO between periods (unless exceptional circumstances make it appropriate). The purpose of this convention is to help users make valid comparisons of performance and position from one period to the next.

Activity 3.14

Reporting inventories in the financial statements provides a further example of the need to apply subjective judgement. For the inventories of a retail business, what are the main areas where judgement is required?

The main areas are:

- the choice of cost method (FIFO, LIFO, AVCO);
- deducing the net realisable value figure for inventories held.

TRADE RECEIVABLES PROBLEMS

We have seen that, when businesses sell goods or services on credit, revenue will usually be recognised before the customer pays the amounts owing. Recording the dual aspect of a credit sale will involve increasing sales revenue and increasing trade receivables by the amount of the revenue from the credit sale.

With this type of sale there is always the risk that the customer will not pay the amount due. Where it becomes reasonably certain that the customer will not pay, the amount owed is considered to be a **bad debt**, which must be taken into account when preparing the financial statements.

Activity 3.15

What would be the effect on the income statement, and on the statement of financial position, of not taking into account the fact that a debt is bad?

The effect would be to overstate the assets (trade receivables) on the statement of financial position and to overstate profit in the income statement, as the revenue that has been recognised will not result in any future benefit.

To provide a more realistic picture of financial performance and position, the bad debt must be 'written off'. This will involve reducing the trade receivables and increasing expenses (by creating an expense known as 'bad debts written off') by the amount of the bad debt. The matching convention requires that the bad debt is written off in the same period as the sale that gave rise to the debt is recognised.

Note that, when a debt is bad, the accounting response is not simply to cancel the original sale. If this were done, the income statement would not be so informative. Reporting the bad debts as an expense can be extremely useful in assessing management performance.

Activity 3.16

The treatment of bad debts represents a further example where judgement is needed to derive an appropriate expense figure. What will be the effect of different judgements concerning the appropriate amount of bad debts expense on the profit for a particular period and on the total profit reported over the life of the business?

The judgement concerning whether to write off a bad debt will affect the expenses for the period and, therefore, the reported profit. Over the life of the business, however, total reported profit would not be affected, as incorrect judgements made in one period will be adjusted for in a later period.

Suppose that a debt of £100 was written off in a period and that, in a later period, the amount owing was actually received. The increase in expenses of £100 in the period in which the bad debt was written off would be compensated for by an increase in revenue of £100 when the amount outstanding was finally received (bad debt recovered). If, on the other hand, the amount owing of £100 was never written off in the first place, the profit for the two periods would not be affected by the bad debt adjustment and would, therefore, be different – but the total profit for the two periods would be the same.

Real World 3.7 describes the level of bad debts in different industry sectors.

REAL WORLD 3.7

Bad debts getting worse

A survey of almost 6,000 businesses across Europe shows significant differences in how industry sectors are hit by bad debt and late payments. Businesses in professional services (lawyers, accountants and so on) on average have to write off 4.5 per cent of all transactions whilst businesses in utilities (gas, water, electricity and so on) only write off 1.5 per cent. The survey was undertaken by credit management services group, Intrum Justitia, which believes the situation will worsen in 2012. Key findings are as follows:

Industry sector	Written off percentage 2011	Development 2010–11 percentage change
Professional services	4.5	12.5
Real Estate	3.8	–5
Education	3.7	5.7
Construction and building	3.6	5.8
Financial services	3.1	3.3
Health industry	2.9	7.4
Telecom	2.7	0
Media	2.6	4
Manufacturing	2.5	4.2
Wholesale and retail	2.4	–4
Business services	2.3	4.5
Transport	2.3	9.5
Utilities	1.5	0

Lars Wollung, the chief executive officer of Intrum Justitia states:

> Our survey indicates that things will start turning worse before they turn for the better . . . Although the picture painted in our report may seem grim, there are measures companies can take to protect themselves. . . . We see that businesses that know their customers and implement efficient credit policies get paid earlier and have to write off a smaller percentage of sales.

Source: EPI 2011 Industry White Paper, www.intrum.com, accessed 3 February 2012.

USES AND USEFULNESS OF THE INCOME STATEMENT

The income statement may help in providing information on:

- *How effective the business has been in generating wealth.* Since wealth generation is the primary reason for most businesses to exist, assessing how much wealth has been created is an important issue. The income statement reveals the profit for the period, or bottom line as it is sometimes called. This provides a measure of the wealth created for the owners. Gross profit and operating profit are also useful measures of wealth creation.
- *How profit was derived.* In addition to providing various measures of profit, the income statement provides other information needed for a proper understanding of business performance. It reveals the level of sales revenue and the nature and amount of expenses incurred, which can help in understanding how profit was derived. The analysis of financial performance will be considered in detail in Chapter 6.

? SELF-ASSESSMENT QUESTION 3.1

TT and Co. is a new business that started trading on 1 January 2011. The following is a summary of transactions that occurred during the first year of trading:

1 The owners introduced £50,000 of equity, which was paid into a bank account opened in the name of the business.
2 Premises were rented from 1 January 2011 at an annual rental of £20,000. During the year, rent of £25,000 was paid to the owner of the premises.
3 Rates (a tax on business premises) were paid during the year as follows:

       For the period 1 January 2011 to 31 March 2011   £ 500
       For the period 1 April 2011 to 31 March 2012   £1,200

4 A delivery van was bought on 1 January 2011 for £12,000. This is expected to be used in the business for four years and then to be sold for £2,000.
5 Wages totalling £33,500 were paid during the year. At the end of the year, the business owed £630 of wages for the last week of the year.
6 Electricity bills for the first three quarters of the year were paid totalling £1,650. After 31 December 2011, but before the financial statements had been finalised for the year, the bill for the last quarter arrived showing a charge of £620.
7 Inventories totalling £143,000 were bought on credit.
8 Inventories totalling £12,000 were bought for cash.
9 Sales revenue on credit totalled £152,000 (cost of sales £74,000).
10 Cash sales revenue totalled £35,000 (cost of sales £16,000).
11 Receipts from trade receivables totalled £132,000.
12 Payments to trade payables totalled £121,000.
13 Van running expenses paid totalled £9,400.

At the end of the year it was clear that a credit customer (trade receivable) who owed £400 would not be able to pay any part of the debt. All of the other trade payables were expected to settle in full.

The business uses the straight-line method for depreciating non-current assets.

Required:

Prepare a statement of financial position as at 31 December 2011 and an income statement for the year to that date.

The solution to this question can be found at the back of the book, in Appendix B.

SUMMARY

The main points of this chapter may be summarised as follows:

The income statement (profit and loss account)

- The income statement reveals how much profit (or loss) has been generated over a period and links the statements of financial position at the beginning and end of a reporting period.

- Profit (or loss) is the difference between total revenue and total expenses for a period.

- There are three main measures of profit.

- Gross profit – which is calculated by deducting the cost of sales from the sales revenue.

- Operating profit – which is calculated by deducting overheads from the gross profit.

- Profit for the period – which is calculated by adding non-operating income and deducting finance costs from the operating profit.

Expenses and revenue

- Cost of sales may be identified by matching the cost of each sale to the particular sale or by adjusting the goods bought during a period by the opening and closing inventories.

- Classifying expenses is often a matter of judgement, although there are rules for businesses that trade as limited companies.

- Revenue is recognised when the amount of revenue can be measured reliably and it is probable that the economic benefits will be received.

- Where there is a sale of goods, there is an additional criterion that ownership and control must pass to the buyer before revenue can be recognised.

- Revenue can be recognised after partial completion provided that a particular stage of completion can be measured reliably.

- The matching convention states that expenses should be matched to the revenue that they help generate.

- A particular expense reported in the income statement may not be the same as the cash paid. This will result in accruals or prepayments appearing in the statement of financial position.
- The materiality convention states that where the amounts are immaterial, we should consider only what is expedient.
- The accruals convention states that profit = revenue − expenses (not cash receipts − cash payments).

Depreciation of non-current assets

- Depreciation requires a consideration of the cost (or fair value), useful life and residual value of an asset. It also requires a consideration of the method of depreciation.
- The straight-line method of depreciation allocates the amount to be depreciated evenly over the useful life of the asset.
- The reducing-balance method applies a fixed percentage rate of depreciation to the carrying amount of an asset each year.
- The depreciation method chosen should reflect the pattern of benefits associated with the asset.
- Depreciation is an attempt to allocate the cost (or fair value), less the residual value, of an asset over its useful life. It does not provide funds for replacement of the asset.

Costing inventories

- The way in which we derive the cost of inventories is important in the calculation of profit and the presentation of financial position.
- The first in, first out (FIFO) assumption is that the earliest inventories held are the first to be used.
- The last in, first out (LIFO) assumption is that the latest inventories are the first to be used.
- The weighted average cost (AVCO) assumption applies an average cost to all inventories used.
- When prices are rising, FIFO gives the lowest cost of sales figure and highest closing inventories figure and for LIFO it is the other way around. AVCO gives figures for cost of sales and closing inventories that lie between FIFO and LIFO.
- When prices are falling, the positions of FIFO and LIFO are reversed.
- Inventories are shown at the lower of cost and net realisable value.
- When a particular method of accounting, such as a depreciation method, is selected, it should be applied consistently over time.

Bad debts

- Where it is reasonably certain that a credit customer will not pay, the debt is regarded as 'bad' and written off.

Uses of the income statement

- It provides measures of profit generated during a period.
- It provides information on how the profit was derived.

MyAccountingLab

Go to www.myaccountinglab.com to check your understanding of the chapter, create a
personalised study plan, and maximise your revision time

KEY TERMS

profit p. 67
revenue p. 67
expense p. 68
reporting period p. 68
gross profit p. 70
operating profit p. 70
profit for the period p. 71
cost of sales p. 71
matching convention p. 78
accrued expenses p. 78
prepaid expenses p. 81
materiality convention p. 82
accruals convention p. 82
accruals accounting p. 82

depreciation p. 82
amortisation p. 82
residual value p. 84
straight-line method p. 84
carrying amount p. 85
written-down value p. 85
net book value p. 85
reducing-balance method p. 86
first in, first out (FIFO) p. 92
last in, first out (LIFO) p. 92
weighted average cost (AVCO)
    p. 92
consistency convention p. 95
bad debt p. 96

FURTHER READING

If you would like to explore the topics covered in this chapter in more depth, we recommend the following books:

Alexander, D. and Nobes, C., *Financial Accounting: An International Introduction*, 4th edn, Financial Times Prentice Hall, 2010, Chapters 2, 16, 19 and 20.

Elliott, B. and Elliott, J., *Financial Accounting and Reporting*, 15th edn, Financial Times Prentice Hall, 2012, Chapters 2, 20 and 21.

International Accounting Standards Board, *2011 International Financial Reporting Standards IFRS* (2-volume set), 2011.

KPMG, *Insights into IFRS*, 8th edn, Sweet and Maxwell, 2011, Sections 3.2, 3.3, 3.8, 3.10 and 4.2. A summarised version of this is available free at www.kpmg.com.

? REVIEW QUESTIONS

Solutions to these questions can be found at the back of the book, in Appendix C.

3.1 'Although the income statement is a record of past achievement, the calculations required for certain expenses involve estimates of the future.' What does this statement mean? Can you think of examples where estimates of the future are used?

3.2 'Depreciation is a process of allocation and not valuation.' What do you think is meant by this statement?

3.3 What is the convention of consistency? Does this convention help users in making a more valid comparison between businesses?

3.4 'An asset is similar to an expense.' Do you agree?

✳ EXERCISES

*Exercise 3.1 is basic level, Exercises 3.2 and 3.3 are intermediate level and Exercises 3.4 and 3.5 are advanced level. Exercises with **coloured numbers** have solutions at the back of the book, in Appendix D.*

> If you wish to try more exercises, visit the website at www.myaccountinglab.com.

3.1 You have heard the following statements made. Comment critically on them.

(a) 'Equity only increases or decreases as a result of the owners putting more cash into the business or taking some out.'
(b) 'An accrued expense is one that relates to next year.'
(c) 'Unless we depreciate this asset we shall be unable to provide for its replacement.'
(d) 'There is no point in depreciating the factory building. It is appreciating in value each year.'

3.2 Singh Enterprises, which started business on 1 January 2009, has a reporting period to 31 December and uses the straight-line method of depreciation. On 1 January 2009 the business bought a machine for £10,000. The machine had an expected useful life of four years and an estimated residual value of £2,000. On 1 January 2010 the business bought another machine for £15,000. This machine had an expected useful life of five years and an estimated residual value of £2,500. On 31 December 2011 the business sold the first machine bought for £3,000.

Required:
Show the relevant income statement extracts and statement of financial position extracts for the years 2009, 2010 and 2011.

3.3 Fill in the values (a) to (f) in the following table on the assumption that there were no opening balances involved.

	Relating to period		At end of period	
	Paid/Received	Expense/revenue for period	Prepaid	Accruals/deferred revenues
	£	£	£	£
Rent payable	10,000	(a)	1,000	
Rates and insurance	5,000	(b)		1,000
General expenses	(c)	6,000	1,000	
Interest payable on borrowings	3,000	2,500	(d)	
Salaries	(e)	9,000		3,000
Rent receivable	(f)	1,500		1,500

3.4 The following is the statement of financial position of TT and Co. (see Self-assessment question 3.1 on page 98) at the end of its first year of trading:

Statement of financial position as at 31 December 2011

	£
ASSETS	
Non-current assets	
Property, plant and equipment	
Delivery van at cost	12,000
Depreciation	(2,500)
	9,500
Current assets	
Inventories	65,000
Trade receivables	19,600
Prepaid expenses*	5,300
Cash	750
	90,650
Total assets	100,150
EQUITY AND LIABILITIES	
Equity	
Original	50,000
Retained earnings	26,900
	76,900
Current liabilities	
Trade payables	22,000
Accrued expenses†	1,250
	23,250
Total equity and liabilities	100,150

* The prepaid expenses consisted of rates (£300) and rent (£5,000).
† The accrued expenses consisted of wages (£630) and electricity (£620).

During 2012, the following transactions took place:

1 The owners withdrew equity in the form of cash of £20,000.
2 Premises continued to be rented at an annual rental of £20,000. During the year, rent of £15,000 was paid to the owner of the premises. →

3 Rates on the premises were paid during the year as follows: for the period 1 April 2012 to 31 March 2013 £1,300.

4 A second delivery van was bought on 1 January 2012 for £13,000. This is expected to be used in the business for four years and then to be sold for £3,000.

5 Wages totalling £36,700 were paid during the year. At the end of the year, the business owed £860 of wages for the last week of the year.

6 Electricity bills for the first three quarters of the year and £620 for the last quarter of the previous year were paid totalling £1,820. After 31 December 2012, but before the financial statements had been finalised for the year, the bill for the last quarter arrived showing a charge of £690.

7 Inventories totalling £67,000 were bought on credit.

8 Inventories totalling £8,000 were bought for cash.

9 Sales revenue on credit totalled £179,000 (cost £89,000).

10 Cash sales revenue totalled £54,000 (cost £25,000).

11 Receipts from trade receivables totalled £178,000.

12 Payments to trade payables totalled £71,000.

13 Van running expenses paid totalled £16,200.

The business uses the straight-line method for depreciating non-current assets.

Required:

Prepare a statement of financial position as at 31 December 2012 and an income statement for the year to that date.

3.5 The following is the statement of financial position of WW Associates as at 31 December 2011:

Statement of financial position as at 31 December 2011

	£
ASSETS	
Non-current assets	
Machinery	25,300
Current assets	
Inventories	12,200
Trade receivables	21,300
Prepaid expenses (rates)	400
Cash	8,300
	42,200
Total assets	67,500
EQUITY AND LIABILITIES	
Equity	
Original	25,000
Retained earnings	23,900
	48,900
Current liabilities	
Trade payables	16,900
Accrued expenses (wages)	1,700
	18,600
Total equity and liabilities	67,500

During 2012, the following transactions took place:

1 The owners withdrew equity in the form of cash of £23,000.
2 Premises were rented at an annual rental of £20,000. During the year, rent of £25,000 was paid to the owner of the premises.
3 Rates on the premises were paid during the year for the period 1 April 2012 to 31 March 2013 and amounted to £2,000.
4 Some machinery (a non-current asset), which was bought on 1 January 2011 for £13,000, has proved to be unsatisfactory. It was part-exchanged for some new machinery on 1 January 2012 and WW Associates paid a cash amount of £6,000. The new machinery would have cost £15,000 had the business bought it without the trade-in.
5 Wages totalling £23,800 were paid during the year. At the end of the year, the business owed £860 of wages.
6 Electricity bills for the four quarters of the year were paid totalling £2,700.
7 Inventories totalling £143,000 were bought on credit.
8 Inventories totalling £12,000 were bought for cash.
9 Sales revenue on credit totalled £211,000 (cost £127,000).
10 Cash sales revenue totalled £42,000 (cost £25,000).
11 Receipts from trade receivables totalled £198,000.
12 Payments to trade payables totalled £156,000.
13 Van running expenses paid totalled £17,500.

The business uses the reducing-balance method of depreciation for non-current assets at the rate of 30 per cent each year.

Required:
Prepare an income statement for the year ended 31 December 2012 and a statement of financial position as at that date.

ACCOUNTING FOR LIMITED COMPANIES

INTRODUCTION

Most businesses in the UK, including some of the very smallest, operate in the form of limited companies. About two and a half million limited companies now exist and they account for the majority of UK business activity and employment. The economic significance of this type of business is not confined to the UK; it can be seen in most of the world's developed countries.

In this chapter we consider the nature of limited companies and how they differ from sole proprietorship businesses and partnerships. We examine the ways in which the owners provide finance, as well as the rules governing the way in which limited companies must account to their owners and to other interested parties. We shall also see how the financial statements, which were discussed in the previous two chapters, are prepared for this type of business.

Learning outcomes

When you have completed this chapter, you should be able to:

- discuss the nature of the limited company;
- describe the main features of the equity (owners' claim) in a limited company;
- discuss the framework of rules designed to safeguard the interests of shareholders;
- explain how the income statement and statement of financial position of a limited company differ in detail from those of sole proprietorships and partnerships.

From Chapter 4 of *Accounting and Finance for Non-Specialists*, 8/e. Peter Atrill and Eddie McLaney. © Pearson Education Limited 2013. All rights reserved.

THE MAIN FEATURES OF LIMITED COMPANIES

Legal nature

Let us begin our examination of limited companies by discussing their legal nature. A **limited company** has been described as an artificial person that has been created by law. This means that a company has many of the rights and obligations that 'real' people have. It can, for example, sue or be sued by others and can enter into contracts in its own name. This contrasts sharply with other types of businesses, such as sole proprietorships and partnerships (that is, unincorporated businesses). Here it is the owner(s) rather than the business that must sue, enter into contracts and so on, because the business has no separate legal identity.

With the rare exceptions of those that are created by Act of Parliament or by Royal Charter, all UK companies are created (or *incorporated*) by registration. To create a company the person or persons wishing to create it (usually known as *promoters*) fill in a few simple forms and pay a modest registration fee. After having ensured that the necessary formalities have been met, the Registrar of Companies, a UK government official, enters the name of the new company on the Registry of Companies. Thus, in the UK, companies can be formed very easily and cheaply (for about £100).

A limited company may be owned by just one person, but most have more than one owner and some have many owners. The owners are usually known as *members* or *shareholders*. The ownership of a company is normally divided into a number of **shares**, each of equal size. Each owner, or shareholder, owns one or more shares in the company. Large companies typically have a very large number of shareholders. For example, at 31 March 2011, BT Group plc, the telecommunications business, had about 1.1 million different shareholders.

Since a limited company has its own legal identity, it is regarded as being quite separate from those who own and manage it. The legal separateness of owners and the company has no connection with the business entity convention, which we discussed in Chapter 2. This accounting convention applies to all business types, including sole proprietorships and partnerships where there is certainly no legal distinction between the owner(s) and the business.

The legal separateness of the limited company and its shareholders leads to two important features of the limited company: perpetual life and limited liability. These are now explained.

Perpetual life

A company is normally granted a perpetual existence and so will continue even where an owner of some, or even all, of the shares in the company dies. The shares of the deceased person will simply pass to the beneficiary of his or her estate. The granting of perpetual existence means that the life of a company is quite separate from the lives of those individuals who own or manage it. It is not, therefore, affected by changes in ownership that arise when individuals buy and sell shares in the company.

Though a company may be granted a perpetual existence when it is first formed, it is possible for either the shareholders or the courts to bring this existence to an end. When this is done, the assets of the company are usually sold to generate cash to meet the outstanding liabilities. Any surplus arising after all liabilities have been met will then be used to pay the shareholders. Shareholders may agree to end the life of a company where it has achieved the purpose for which it was formed or where they feel that the company has no real future. The courts may bring the life of a company to an end where creditors have applied to the courts for this to be done because they have not been paid amounts owing.

Where shareholders agree to end the life of a company, it is referred to as a 'voluntary liquidation'. **Real World 4.1** describes the demise of one company by this method.

REAL WORLD 4.1

Monotub Industries in a spin as founder gets Titan for £1

Monotub Industries, maker of the Titan washing machine, yesterday passed into corporate history with very little ceremony and with only a whimper of protest from minority shareholders.

At an extraordinary meeting held in a basement room of the group's West End headquarters, shareholders voted to put the company into voluntary liquidation and sell its assets and intellectual property to founder Martin Myerscough for £1. [The shares in the company were at one time worth 650p each.]

The only significant opposition came from Giuliano Gnagnatti who, along with other shareholders, has seen his investment shrink faster than a wool twin-set on a boil wash.

The not-so-proud owner of 100,000 Monotub shares, Mr Gnagnatti, the managing director of an online retailer, described the sale of Monotub as a 'free gift' to Mr Myerscough. This assessment was denied by Ian Green, the chairman of Monotub, who said the closest the beleaguered company had come to a sale was an offer for £60,000 that gave no guarantees against liabilities, which are thought to amount to £750,000.

The quiet passing of the washing machine, eventually dubbed the Titanic, was in strong contrast to its performance in many kitchens.

Originally touted as the 'great white goods hope' of the washing machine industry with its larger capacity and removable drum, the Titan ran into problems when it kept stopping during the spin cycle, causing it to emit a loud bang and leap into the air.

Summing up the demise of the Titan, Mr Green said: 'Clearly the machine had some revolutionary aspects, but you can't get away from the fact that the machine was faulty and should not have been launched with those defects.'

The usually-vocal Mr Myerscough, who has promised to pump £250,000 into the company and give Monotub shareholders £4 for every machine sold, refused to comment on his plans for the Titan or reveal who his backers were. But . . . he did say that he intended to 'take the Titan forward'.

Limited liability

Since the company is a legal person in its own right, it must take responsibility for its own debts and losses. This means that, once the shareholders have paid what they have agreed to pay for the shares, their obligation to the company, and to the company's creditors, is satisfied. Thus shareholders can limit their losses to the amount that they have paid, or agreed to pay, for their shares. Contrast this with the position of sole proprietors or partners. They cannot 'ring-fence' assets that they do not want to put into the business. If a sole proprietorship or partnership business finds itself in a position where liabilities exceed the business assets, the law gives unsatisfied creditors the right to demand payment out of what the sole proprietor or partner may have regarded as 'non-business' assets. Thus the sole proprietor or partner could lose everything – house, car, the lot. This is because the law sees Jill, the sole proprietor, as being the same as Jill the private individual.

Real World 4.2 gives an example of a well-known case where the shareholders of a particular company were able to avoid any liability to those that had lost money as a result of dealing with the company.

REAL WORLD 4.2

Carlton and Granada 1 – Nationwide Football League 0

Two television broadcasting companies, Carlton and Granada, each owned 50 per cent of a separate company, ITV Digital (formerly ON Digital). ITV Digital signed a contract to pay the Nationwide Football League (in effect the three divisions of English football below the Premiership) more than £89 million on both 1 August 2002 and 1 August 2003 for the rights to broadcast football matches over three seasons. ITV Digital was unable to sell enough subscriptions for the broadcasts and collapsed because it was unable to meet its liabilities. The Nationwide Football League tried to force Carlton and Granada (ITV Digital's only shareholders) to meet ITV Digital's contractual obligations. It was unable to do so because the shareholders could not be held legally liable for the amounts owing.

Carlton and Granada subsequently merged into one business, but at the time of ITV Digital were two independent companies.

Activity 4.1

The fact that shareholders can limit their losses to that which they have paid, or have agreed to pay, for their shares is of great practical importance to potential shareholders.
Can you think of any practical benefit to a private-sector economy, in general, of this ability of shareholders to limit losses?

Business is a risky venture – in some cases very risky. People will usually be happier to invest money when they know the limit of their liability. If investors are given limited liability, new businesses are more likely to be formed and existing ones are likely to find it easier to raise more finance. This is good for the private-sector economy and may ultimately lead to the generation of greater wealth for society as a whole.

Although **limited liability** benefits the shareholders it may not be to the advantage of others who have a stake in the business, as we saw in the case of the Nationwide Football League clubs (Real World 4.2). Limited liability is attractive to shareholders because they can, in effect, walk away from the unpaid debts of the company if their contribution has not been sufficient to meet those debts. This may make an individual, or another business, wary of entering into a contract with a limited company. This can be a particular problem for smaller, less established companies. Suppliers may insist on cash payment before delivery of goods or the rendering of a service. Alternatively, they may require a personal guarantee from a major shareholder that the debt will be paid before allowing trade credit. In the latter case, the supplier circumvents the company's limited liability status by demanding the personal liability of an individual. Larger, more established companies, however, tend to have built up the confidence of suppliers.

Legal safeguards

Various safeguards exist to protect individuals and businesses contemplating dealing with a limited company. These include the requirement to indicate limited liability status in the name of the company. By doing this, a warning is issued to prospective suppliers and lenders.

A further safeguard is the restrictions placed on the ability of shareholders to withdraw their equity from the company. These restrictions are designed to prevent shareholders from protecting their own investment and, as a result, leaving lenders and suppliers in an exposed position. We shall consider this point in more detail later in the chapter.

Finally, limited companies are required to produce annual financial statements (income statements, statements of financial position and statements of cash flows) and make these publicly available. This means that anyone interested can gain an impression of the financial performance and position of the company. The form and content of the first two of these statements are considered in some detail later in the chapter. Chapter 5 is devoted to the statement of cash flows.

Public and private companies

When a company is registered with the Registrar of Companies, it must be registered either as a public or as a private company. The main practical difference between these is that a **public limited company** can offer its shares for sale to the general public, but a **private limited company** is restricted from doing so. A public limited company must signal its status to all interested parties by having the words 'public limited company', or its abbreviation 'plc', in its name. For a private limited company, the word 'limited' or 'Ltd' must appear as part of its name.

Private limited companies tend to be smaller businesses where the ownership is divided among relatively few shareholders who are usually fairly close to one another – for example, a family company. Numerically, there are vastly more private limited companies in the UK than there are public ones. Of the 2.49 million UK limited companies now in existence, only 7,812 (representing 0.3 per cent of the total) are public limited companies.

Since individual public companies tend to be larger, they are often economically more important. In some industry sectors, such as banking, insurance, oil refining and grocery retailing, they are completely dominant. Although some large private limited companies exist, many private limited companies are little more than the vehicle through which one-person businesses operate.

Real World 4.3 shows the extent of the market dominance of public limited companies in one particular business sector.

REAL WORLD 4.3

A big slice of the market

The grocery sector is dominated by four large players: Tesco, Sainsbury, Morrison and Asda. The first three are public limited companies and the fourth, Asda, is owned by a large US public company, Wal-Mart. Figure 4.1 shows the share of the grocery market enjoyed by each during the twelve-week period to 2 October 2011.

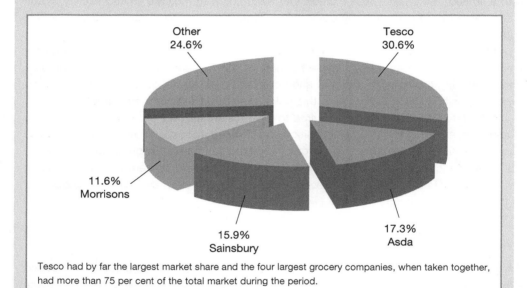

Other
24.6%

Tesco
30.6%

11.6%
Morrisons

15.9%
Sainsbury

17.3%
Asda

Tesco had by far the largest market share and the four largest grocery companies, when taken together, had more than 75 per cent of the total market during the period.

Figure 4.1 Market share of the four largest grocery companies: 12 weeks to 2 October 2011

Source: Compiled from information in 'William Morrison Supermarkets market share up', www.marketwatch.com, 11 October 2011.

Taxation

Another consequence of the legal separation of the limited company from its owners is that companies must be accountable to the tax authorities for tax on their profits and gains. This leads to the reporting of tax in the financial statements of limited companies. The charge for tax is shown in the income statement. The tax charge for a particular year is based on that year's profit. Since only 50 per cent of a company's tax liability is due for payment during the year concerned, the other 50 per cent will appear on the end-of-year statement of financial position as a current liability. This will be illustrated a little later in the chapter. The tax position of companies contrasts with that of sole proprietorships and partnerships, where tax is levied not on the business but on the owner(s). Thus tax does not impact on the financial statements of unincorporated businesses. It is an individual matter between the owner(s) and the tax authorities.

. Companies are charged **corporation tax** on their profits and gains. The percentage rates of tax tend to vary from year to year, but have recently been 26 per cent for larger companies and 20 per cent for smaller companies. These rates of tax are levied on the company's taxable profit, which is not necessarily the same as the profit shown on the income statement. This is because tax law does not, in every respect, follow the normal accounting rules. Generally, however, the taxable profit and the company's accounting profit are pretty close to one another.

Transferring share ownership: the role of the Stock Exchange

We have already seen that shares in a company may be transferred from one owner to another. The desire of some shareholders to sell their shares, coupled with the desire of others to buy those shares, has led to the existence of a formal market in which shares can be bought and sold. The London Stock Exchange and similar organisations around the world, provide a marketplace in which shares in public companies may be bought and sold. Share prices are determined by the laws of supply and demand, which are, in turn, determined by investors' perceptions of the future economic prospects of the companies concerned. Only the shares of certain companies (*listed* companies) may be traded on the London Stock Exchange. Just over 1,000 UK companies are listed. This represents only about 1 in 2,250 of all UK companies (public and private) and roughly one in seven public limited companies. However, many of these listed companies are massive. Nearly all of the 'household-name' UK businesses (for example, Tesco, Next, BT, Vodafone, BP and so on) are listed companies.

Activity 4.2

We saw earlier that changes in share ownership do not directly affect the particular company. In which case, why do many public companies actively seek to have their shares traded in a recognised market?

The main reason is that investors are generally reluctant to pledge their money unless they can see some way in which they can turn their investment back into cash. In theory, the shares of a particular company may be very valuable because the company has bright prospects. However, unless this value can be turned into cash, the benefit to the shareholders is dubious. After all, we cannot spend shares; we normally need cash.

This means that potential shareholders are much more likely to be prepared to buy new shares from the company (thereby providing the company with new investment finance) where they can see a way of liquidating their investment (turning it into cash) as and when they wish. Stock Exchanges provide the means of liquidation.

Although the buying and selling of 'second-hand' shares does not provide the company with cash, the fact that a market for shares exists can make it easier for the company to raise new share capital when it needs to do so.

MANAGING A COMPANY

A limited company may have legal personality, but it is not a human being capable of making decisions and plans about the business and exercising control over it. People must undertake these management tasks. The most senior level of management of a company is the board of directors.

The shareholders elect **directors** to manage the company on a day-to-day basis on behalf of those shareholders. By law there must be at least one director for a private limited company and two for a public limited company. Although directors are often shareholders, they do not have to be. In a small company, the board of directors may be the only level of management and may consist of all of the shareholders. In larger companies, the board may consist of ten or so directors. Below the board of directors of the typical large company could be several levels of management.

In recent years, the issue of **corporate governance** has generated much debate. The term is used to describe the ways in which companies are directed and controlled. Corporate governance is important because, with larger companies, those who own the company (that is, the shareholders) are usually divorced from the day-to-day control of the business. The shareholders employ directors to manage the company for them. Although the directors should act in the best interests of shareholders, this may not always be the case. They may be more concerned with pursuing their own interests, such as increasing their pay and 'perks' (buying expensive motor cars, overseas visits and so on) and improving their job security and status. As a result, a conflict can arise between the interests of shareholders and the interests of directors.

Where directors pursue their own interests at the expense of the shareholders, there is clearly a problem for the shareholders. However, it may also be a problem for society as a whole. If shareholders feel that their funds are likely to be mismanaged, they will be reluctant to invest. A shortage of funds will mean that companies can make fewer investments. Furthermore, the costs of finance will increase as businesses compete for what little funds are available. Thus, a lack of concern for shareholders can have a profound effect on the performance of individual companies and, with this, the health of the economy.

To avoid these problems, most competitive market economies have a framework of rules to help monitor and control the behaviour of directors. These rules are usually based around three guiding principles:

- *Disclosure*. This lies at the heart of good corporate governance. Adequate and timely disclosure can help shareholders to judge the performance of the directors. Where performance is considered unsatisfactory this will be reflected in the price of shares. Changes should then be made to ensure the directors regain the confidence of shareholders.
- *Accountability*. This involves setting out the duties of the directors and establishing an adequate monitoring process. In the UK, company law requires that the directors act in the best interests of the shareholders. This means, among other things, that they must not try to use their position and knowledge to make gains at the expense of the shareholders. The law also requires larger companies to have their annual financial statements independently audited. The purpose of an independent audit is to lend credibility to the financial statements prepared by the directors. We shall consider this point in more detail later in the chapter.
- *Fairness*. Directors should not be able to benefit from access to 'inside' information that is not available to shareholders. As a result, both the law and the Stock Exchange place restrictions on the ability of directors to buy and sell the shares of the company. This means, for example, that the directors cannot buy or sell shares immediately before the announcement of the annual profits or before the announcement of a significant event such as a planned merger.

These principles are set out in Figure 4.2.

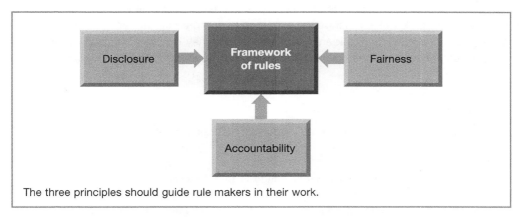

The three principles should guide rule makers in their work.

Figure 4.2 Principles underpinning a framework of rules

Strengthening the framework of rules

The number of rules designed to safeguard shareholders has increased considerably over the years. This has been in response to weaknesses in corporate governance procedures, which have been exposed through well-publicised business failures and frauds, excessive pay increases to directors and evidence that some financial reports were being 'massaged' so as to mislead shareholders.

Many believe, however, that the shareholders must shoulder some of the blame for any weaknesses. Not all shareholders in large companies are private individuals owning just a few shares each. In fact, ownership, by market value, of the shares listed on the London Stock Exchange is dominated by investing institutions such as insurance businesses, banks and pension funds. These are often massive operations, owning large quantities of the shares of the companies in which they invest. These institutional investors employ specialist staff to manage their portfolios of shares in various companies. It has been argued that the large institutional shareholders, despite their size and relative expertise, have not been very active in corporate governance matters. As a result there has been little monitoring of directors. However, things seem to be changing. There is increasing evidence that institutional investors are becoming more proactive in relation to the companies in which they hold shares.

THE UK CORPORATE GOVERNANCE CODE

In recent years there has been a real effort to address the problems of poor corporate governance. This has resulted in a code of best practice, known as the **UK Corporate Governance Code** (formerly known as the Combined Code). The Code sets out a number of principles relating to such matters as the role of the directors, their relations with shareholders and their accountability. **Real World 4.4** outlines some of the more important of these.

The Code has the backing of the London Stock Exchange. This means that companies listed on the London Stock Exchange are expected to comply with the requirements of the Code or must give their shareholders good reason why they do not. Failure to do one or other of these can lead to the company's shares being suspended from listing.

Activity 4.3

Why might being suspended be an important sanction against a non-compliant company?

A major advantage of a Stock Exchange listing is that it enables investors to sell their shares whenever they wish. A company that is suspended from listing would find it hard and, therefore, expensive to raise funds from investors because there would be no ready market for the shares.

The existence of the Code has improved the quality of information available to shareholders. It has also resulted in better checks on the powers of directors, and provided greater transparency in corporate affairs. However, rules can only be a partial answer. A balance must be struck between the need to protect shareholders and the need to encourage the entrepreneurial spirit of directors, which could be stifled under a welter of rules. This implies that rules should not be too tight, and so unscrupulous directors may still find ways around them.

REAL WORLD 4.4

The UK Corporate Governance Code

Key elements of the UK Code are as follows:

- Every listed company should have a board of directors that is collectively responsible for its success.
- There should be a clear division of responsibilities between the chairman and the chief executive officer of the company to try to ensure that a single person does not have unbridled power.
- As part of their role as members of a unitary board, non-executive directors should constructively challenge and help develop proposals on strategy.
- There should be an appropriate balance of skills, experience, independence and knowledge to enable the board to carry out its duties effectively.
- The board should receive timely information that is of sufficient quality to enable it to carry out its duties. All board members should refresh their skills regularly and new board members should receive induction.
- Appointments to the board should be the subject of rigorous, formal and transparent procedures and should be drawn from a broad talent pool.
- All directors should submit themselves for re-election at regular intervals, subject to satisfactory performance.
- Remuneration levels should be sufficient to attract, retain and motivate directors of the appropriate quality and should take account of both individual and company performance.
- There should be formal and transparent procedures for developing policy on directors' remuneration. No director should determine his or her own level of remuneration.
- The board should present a balanced and understandable assessment of the company's position and future prospects.
- The board should try to ensure that a satisfactory dialogue with shareholders occurs.
- Boards should use the annual general meeting to communicate with investors and encourage their participation.
- The board should define the company's risk appetite and tolerance and should maintain a sound risk management system.
- Formal and transparent arrangements for applying financial reporting and internal control principles and for maintaining an appropriate relationship with auditors should be in place.
- The board should undertake a formal and rigorous examination of its own performance each year, which will include its committees and individual directors.

Source: www.frc.org.uk.

FINANCING LIMITED COMPANIES

Equity (the owners' claim)

The equity of a sole proprietorship is normally encompassed in one figure on the statement of financial position. In the case of companies, things are a little more complicated, although the same broad principles apply. The equity of a company is divided between shares (for example, the original investment), on the one hand, and **reserves** (that is, profits and gains made but not as yet transferred to shareholders), on the other. Within this basic division of share capital and reserves, there might well be subdivisions. A company may have more than one type of shares and more than one type of reserves. This might seem complicated, but we shall shortly consider the reasons for these subdivisions and all should become clearer.

The basic division

When a company is first formed, those who take steps to form it (the promoters) will decide how much needs to be raised by the potential shareholders to set the company up with the necessary assets to operate. Example 4.1 illustrates this.

Example 4.1

Some friends decide to form a company to operate an office cleaning business. They estimate that the company will need £50,000 to obtain the necessary assets. Between them, they raise the cash, which they use to buy shares in the company, on 31 March 2011, with a **nominal value** (or **par value**) of £1 each.

At this point the statement of financial position of the company would be:

Statement of financial position as at 31 March 2011

	£
Net assets (all in cash)	50,000
Equity	
Share capital	
50,000 shares of £1 each	50,000

The company now buys the necessary non-current assets (vacuum cleaners and so on) and inventories (cleaning materials) and starts to trade. During the first year, the company makes a profit of £10,000. This, by definition, means that the equity expands by £10,000. During the year, the shareholders (owners) make no drawings of their equity, so at the end of the year the summarised statement of financial position looks like this:

Statement of financial position as at 31 March 2012

	£
Net assets (various assets less liabilities*)	60,000
Equity	
Share capital	
50,000 shares of £1 each	50,000
Reserves (revenue reserve)	10,000
Total equity	60,000

* We saw in Chapter 2 that Assets = Equity + Liabilities. We also saw that this can be rearranged so that Assets – Liabilities = Equity.

Note that the profits are shown in a reserve, known as a **revenue reserve**. This type of reserve arises from trading profits and gains from the disposal of non-current assets. In practice, the total of revenue reserves is rarely the total of all trading profits and gains on disposals of non-current assets that have been generated. This total will normally have been reduced by at least one of the following three factors:

■ corporation tax paid on those profits;
■ any **dividends** paid to shareholders or amounts paid to purchase the company's own shares;
■ any losses from trading and the disposal of non-current assets.

There is a legal restriction on the maximum that shareholders can withdraw (through dividends, for example) from their equity. This maximum is defined by the revenue reserves and so the law requires that revenue reserves be separated from the share capital for the sake of clarity.

Share capital

Ordinary shares

All companies issue **ordinary shares**, which are also known as *equities*. Ordinary shareholders are the primary risk-takers as they can only share in the residue of profits after other claims have been satisfied. This residue may range from zero to a very large amount: with no upper limits. The potential rewards reflect the risks that ordinary shareholders are prepared to take. Since they take most of the risks, power resides in their hands. Thus, only ordinary shareholders are normally able to vote on issues that affect the company, such as who the directors should be.

The nominal, or par, value of ordinary shares is at the discretion of the people who start up the company. For example, if the initial share capital is to be £50,000, this could be two shares of £25,000 each, 5 million shares of one penny each or any other combination that gives a total of £50,000. All shares must have equal value.

Activity 4.4

The initial financial requirement for a new company is £50,000. There are to be two equal shareholders. Would you advise them to issue two shares of £25,000 each? Why?

Such large-denomination shares tend to be unwieldy. Suppose that one of the shareholders wanted to sell her shareholding. She would have to find one buyer. If there were shares of smaller denomination, it would be possible to sell part of the shareholding to various potential buyers. Furthermore, it would be possible to sell just part of the holding and retain a part.

In practice, £1 is the normal maximum nominal value for shares. Shares of 25 pence each and 50 pence each are probably the most common.

Preference shares

In addition to ordinary shares, some companies issue other classes of shares; the most common being **preference shares**. Preference shares guarantee that *if a dividend is paid*, the preference shareholders will receive the first part of it up to a maximum value. This maximum is normally a fixed percentage of the nominal value of the shares. If, for example, a company issues one million preference shares of £1 each with a dividend rate of 6 per cent, this means that the preference shareholders are entitled to receive the first £60,000 (that is, 6 per cent of £1 million) of any dividend paid for a particular year. The excess over £60,000 goes to the ordinary shareholders.

Other classes of shares classes may be issued – with some perhaps having unusual and exotic conditions. In practice, however, only ordinary and preference shares are normally issued. (Even preference shares are not widely issued.) Although different classes of shares may confer different rights, all shares within a particular class must be treated equally. The rights of the various classes of shareholders, as well as other matters relating to the company, are contained in the company's set of rules, known as the '*memorandum and articles of association*'. A copy of these rules must be lodged with the Registrar of Companies, who makes it available for inspection by the general public.

Altering the nominal value of shares

As mentioned earlier, the promoters of a new company choose the nominal value of the shares. This value need not be permanent. At a later date, the shareholders can decide to change it.

Suppose that a company has 1 million ordinary shares of £1 each and a decision is made to change the nominal value of the shares from £1 to £0.50, in other words to halve the value. All of the shareholder would then be registered by the company as holding twice as many shares as their original holdings, with each share at half the nominal value of the original shares. As a result, each shareholder would still hold shares with the same *total* nominal value. This process is known, not surprisingly, as **splitting** the shares. The opposite, reducing the number of shares and increasing their nominal value per share to compensate, is known as **consolidating**. Since each shareholder would be left, after a split or consolidation, with exactly the same proportion of ownership of the company's assets as before, the process should not increase the value of the total shares held.

Splitting is fairly common whereas consolidating is relatively rare. Both may be used to help make the shares more marketable. Splitting may help avoid share prices becoming too high and consolidating may help avoid share prices becoming too low. It seems that investors do not like either extreme. In addition, certain Stock Exchanges do not allow shares to be traded at too low a price.

Real World 4.5 provides an example of a share split by one business.

REAL WORLD 4.5

Doing the splits

Premier Oil plc, the oil and gas exploration and production business, had a share split in May 2011, as announced by the business in a letter to its shareholders:

> The share split will result in shareholders holding four new ordinary shares of 12.5 pence each in the company for each existing ordinary share they held immediately prior to the share split. In recent months the price of the company's ordinary shares of 50 pence each has risen substantially to the point where the closing mid-market price on 1 April 2011 was £20.06. The board believes that the share split may improve the liquidity of the market in the company's shares and reduce the bid/offer spread of the company's shares.

Source: Premier Oil plc, Letter from the chairman, 15 April 2011, www.premier-oil.com.

Reserves

We have seen that reserves reflect profits and gains that a company has made.

Activity 4.5

Are reserves amounts of cash? Can you think of a reason why this is an odd question?

To deal with the second point first, it is an odd question because reserves are a claim, or part of one, on the assets of the company, whereas cash is an asset. So reserves cannot be cash.

Reserves are classified as either revenue reserves or **capital reserves**. In Example 4.1 we came across a revenue reserve. We should recall that this reserve represents the company's retained trading profits and gains on the disposal of non-current assets. Capital reserves arise for two main reasons:

- issuing shares at above their nominal value (for example, issuing £1 shares at £1.50);
- revaluing (upwards) non-current assets.

Where a company issues shares at above their nominal value, UK law requires that the excess of the issue price over the nominal value be shown separately.

Activity 4.6

Can you think why shares might be issued at above their nominal value? (*Hint*: This would not usually happen when a company is first formed and the initial shares are being issued.)

Once a company has traded successfully, its shares will normally be worth more than the nominal value at which they were issued. Where additional shares are to be issued to new shareholders to raise further finance, they should be issued at a value higher than the nominal value. Unless this is done, the new shareholders will gain at the expense of the original ones.

Example 4.2 shows how this works.

Example 4.2

Based on future prospects, the net assets of a company are worth £1.5 million. There are currently 1 million ordinary shares in the company, each with a nominal value of £1. The company wishes to raise an additional £0.6 million of cash for expansion and has decided to raise it by issuing new shares. If the shares are issued for £1 each (that is 600,000 shares), the total number of shares will be:

$$1.0m + 0.6m = 1.6m$$

and their total value will be the value of the existing net assets plus the new injection of cash:

$$£1.5m + £0.6m = £2.1m.$$

This means that the value of each share after the new issue will be:

$$£2.1m / 1.6m = £1.3125.$$

The current value of each share is:

$$£1.5m / 1.0m = £1.50$$

so the original shareholders will lose:

$$£1.50 - £1.3125 = £0.1875 \text{ a share}$$

and the new shareholders will gain:

$$£1.3125 - £1.0 = £0.3125 \text{ a share.}$$

The new shareholders will, no doubt, be delighted with this outcome; the original ones will not.

Things could be made fair between the two sets of shareholders described in Example 4.2 by issuing the new shares at £1.50 each. In this case it would be necessary to issue 400,000 shares to raise the necessary £0.6 million. £1 a share of the £1.50 is the nominal value and will be included with share capital in the statement of financial position (£400,000 in total). The remaining £0.50 is a share premium, which will be shown as a capital reserve known as the **share premium account** (£200,000 in total).

It is not clear why UK company law insists on the distinction between nominal share values and the premium. In some other countries (for example, the United States) with similar laws governing the corporate sector, there is not the necessity of distinguishing between share capital and share premium. Instead, the total value at which shares are issued is shown as one comprehensive figure on the company's statement of financial position.

Real World 4.6 shows the equity of one very well-known business.

REAL WORLD 4.6

Flying funds

Ryanair Holdings plc, the no-frills airline, had the following share capital and reserves as at 31 March 2011:

	€ million
Share capital (10p ordinary shares)	9.5
Share premium	659.3
Retained earnings	1,967.6
Other reserves	317.5
Total equity	2,953.9

Note how the nominal share capital figure is only a tiny fraction of the share premium account figure. This implies that Ryanair has issued shares at much higher prices than the 10p a share nominal value. This reflects its trading success since the company was first formed. In 2011, retained earnings (profits) made up two-thirds of the total for share capital and reserves.

Source: Ryanair Holdings plc Annual Report 2011, p. 128.

Bonus shares

It is always open to a company to take reserves of any kind (capital or revenue) and turn them into share capital. This will involve transferring the desired amount from the reserve concerned to share capital and then distributing the appropriate number of new shares to the existing shareholders. New shares arising from such a conversion are known as **bonus shares**. Issues of bonus shares used to be quite frequently encountered in practice, but more recently they are much less common. Example 4.3 illustrates this aspect of share issues.

Example 4.3

The summary statement of financial position of a company at a particular point in time is as follows:

Statement of financial position

	£
Net assets (various assets less liabilities)	128,000
Equity	
Share capital	
50,000 shares of £1 each	50,000
Reserves	78,000
Total equity	128,000

The directors decide that the company will issue existing shareholders with one new share for every share currently owned by each shareholder. The statement of financial position immediately following this will appear as follows:

Statement of financial position

	£
Net assets (various assets less liabilities)	128,000
Equity	
Share capital	
100,000 shares of £1 each (50,000 + 50,000)	100,000
Reserves (78,000 – 50,000)	28,000
Total equity	128,000

We can see that the reserves have decreased by £50,000 and share capital has increased by the same amount. Existing shareholders will be registered by the company as holding twice as many shares as before to complete the transaction.

Activity 4.7

A shareholder of the company in Example 4.3 owned 100 shares before the bonus issue. How will things change for this shareholder as regards the number of shares owned and the value of the shareholding?

The answer should be that the number of shares would double, from 100 to 200. Now the shareholder owns one five-hundredth of the company (that is, 200/100,000). Before the bonus issue, the shareholder also owned one five-hundredth of the company (that is, 100/50,000). The company's assets and liabilities have not changed as a result of the bonus issue and so, logically, one five-hundredth of the value of the company should be identical to what it was before. Thus, each share is worth half as much as it used to be.

A bonus issue simply takes one part of the equity (a reserve) and puts it into another part (share capital). The transaction has no effect on the company's assets or liabilities, so there is no effect on shareholders' wealth. Note that a bonus issue is not the same as a share split. A split does not affect the reserves.

Activity 4.8

Can you think of any reasons why a company might want to make a bonus issue if it has no economic consequence?

We think that there are three possible reasons:

- *Share price*. To lower the value of each share without reducing the shareholders' collective or individual wealth. This has a similar effect to share splitting.

→

■ *Shareholder confidence*. To provide the shareholders with a 'feel-good factor'. It is believed that shareholders like them because they seem to make them better off, although in practice bonus issues should not affect their wealth.

■ *Lender confidence*. Where reserves arising from operating profits and/or realised gains on the sale of non-current assets (revenue reserves) are used to make the bonus issue, it has the effect of taking part of that portion of the shareholders' equity, that could be withdrawn by the shareholders, and locking it up. The amount transferred becomes part of the permanent equity base of the company. An individual or business contemplating lending money to the company may insist that the extent that shareholders can withdraw their funds is restricted as a condition of making the loan.

Real World 4.7 provides an example of a bonus share issue.

REAL WORLD 4.7

Is it really a bonus?

Medusa Mining is a gold producer that is listed on various international stock markets. In 2010, it announced a one-for-ten bonus issue of shares to all shareholders of the company.

In a statement, the company said it had achieved several significant milestones in the last calendar year and the bonus issue is in recognition of the invaluable support the company has received from its shareholders. The bonus issue was also designed to encourage greater liquidity in Medusa shares.

Geoff Davis, managing director of Medusa, said: 'The board is extremely pleased to be in a position to reward shareholders as a result of the company having rapidly expanded its production over the last 12 months and having met all targets on time.'

Source: Adapted from 'Medusa Mining', www.proactiveinvestors co.uk, 8 March 2010.

Share capital jargon

Before leaving our detailed discussion of share capital, it might be helpful to clarify some of the jargon relating to shares that is used in company financial statements.

Share capital that has been issued to shareholders is known as the **issued share capital** (or **allotted share capital**). Sometimes, but not very often, a company may not require shareholders to pay the whole amount that is due to be paid for the shares at the time of issue. This may happen where the company does not need the money all at once. Some money would normally be paid at the time of issue and the company would 'call' for further instalments until the shares were **fully paid shares**. That part of the total issue price that has been called is known as the **called-up share capital**. That part that has been called and paid is known as the **paid-up share capital**.

BORROWINGS

Most companies borrow to supplement the funds raised from share issues and retained profits. Company borrowing is often on a long-term basis, perhaps on a ten-year contract. The loan contract normally sets out the rate of interest, the interest payment dates and the date of repayment of the loan. Usually, long-term loans are secured on assets of the company. This would give the lender the right to seize the assets concerned, sell them and satisfy the repayment obligation, should the company default on either its interest payments or the repayment of the loan.

A common form of borrowing is through the issue of **loan notes**. Where a large issue of loan notes is made, it can sometimes be taken up in small slices, by private investors, or in large slices, by investing institutions such as pension funds and insurance companies. These slices of loans can also, at times, be bought and sold through the Stock Exchange. This means that investors need not wait the full term of the loan to obtain repayment, but can sell their slice of it to another investor at any point. Loan notes are often known as *loan stock* or *debentures*.

The fact that loan notes may be traded on the Stock Exchange can lead to confusing loan notes with shares. They are, however, quite different. Holders of shares own the company and share in its losses and profits. Holders of loan notes simply lend money to the company under a legally binding contract.

Long-term financing of companies can be depicted as in Figure 4.3.

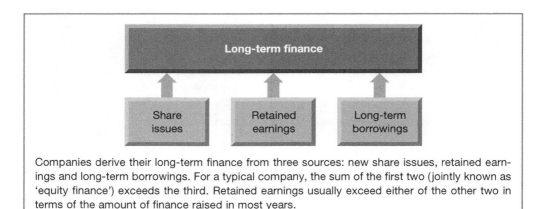

Companies derive their long-term finance from three sources: new share issues, retained earnings and long-term borrowings. For a typical company, the sum of the first two (jointly known as 'equity finance') exceeds the third. Retained earnings usually exceed either of the other two in terms of the amount of finance raised in most years.

Figure 4.3 Sources of long-term finance for a typical limited company

It is vital to the prosperity and stability of a company that a suitable balance is struck between finance provided by the shareholders (equity) and from borrowing. This topic will be explored in Chapters 6 and 11.

WITHDRAWING EQUITY

We have seen that a company must distinguish, on its statement of financial position, between that part of the shareholders' equity that may be withdrawn and that part which may not. The withdrawable part is represented by *revenue reserves*, which consist of profits arising from trading and from the disposal of non-current assets.

The non-withdrawable part is represented by *share capital* and *capital reserves*. Capital reserves consist of profits arising from shareholders buying shares in the company and from upward revaluations of assets still held. The law does not state how large the non-withdrawable part of a particular company's shareholders' equity should be. Prospective lenders and suppliers would no doubt prefer it to be as large as possible.

Figure 4.4 shows the important division between the part of the shareholders' equity that can be withdrawn and the part that cannot.

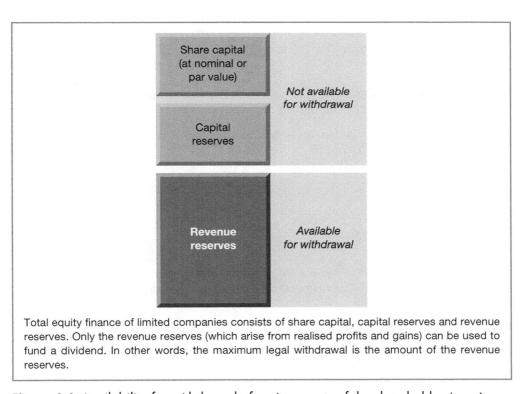

Total equity finance of limited companies consists of share capital, capital reserves and revenue reserves. Only the revenue reserves (which arise from realised profits and gains) can be used to fund a dividend. In other words, the maximum legal withdrawal is the amount of the revenue reserves.

Figure 4.4 Availability for withdrawal of various parts of the shareholders' equity

Activity 4.9

Why are limited companies required to distinguish different parts of their shareholders' equity, whereas sole proprietorship and partnership businesses are not?

The reason stems from the limited liability that company shareholders enjoy but which owners of unincorporated businesses do not. If a sole proprietor or partner withdraws all of the equity, or even an amount in excess of this, the position of the lenders and credit suppliers of the business is not weakened since they can legally enforce their claims against the sole proprietor or partner as an individual. With a limited company, the business and the owners are legally separated and such a right to enforce claims against individuals does not exist. To protect the company's lenders and credit suppliers, however, the law insists that the shareholders cannot normally withdraw a specific part of their equity.

Let us now look at an example that illustrates how this protection of lenders works.

Example 4.4

The summary statement of financial position of a company at a particular date is as follows:

Statement of financial position

	£
Total assets	43,000
Equity	
Share capital	
20,000 shares of £1 each	20,000
Reserves (revenue)	23,000
Total equity	43,000

A bank has been asked to make a £25,000 long-term loan to the company. If the loan were to be made, the statement of financial position immediately following would appear as follows:

Statement of financial position (after the loan)

	£
Total assets (£43,000 + £25,000)	68,000
Equity	
Share capital	
20,000 shares of £1 each	20,000
Reserves (revenue)	23,000
	43,000
Non-current liability	
Borrowings – loan	25,000
Total equity and liabilities	68,000

→

As things stand, there are assets with a total carrying amount of £68,000 to meet the bank's claim of £25,000. It would be possible and perfectly legal, however, for the company to withdraw part of the shareholders' equity (through a dividend or share repurchase) equal to the total revenue reserves (£23,000). The statement of financial position would then appear as follows:

Statement of financial position

	£
Total assets (£68,000 – £23,000)	45,000
Equity	
Share capital	
20,000 shares of £1 each	20,000
Reserves [revenue (£23,000 – £23,000)]	–
	20,000
Non-current liabilities	
Borrowings – bank loan	25,000
Total equity and liabilities	45,000

This leaves the bank in a very much weaker position as there are now total assets with a carrying amount of £45,000 to meet a claim of £25,000. Note that the difference between the amount of the borrowings (bank loan) and the total assets equals the equity (share capital and reserves) total. Thus, the equity represents a margin of safety for lenders and suppliers. The larger the amount of the equity withdrawable by the shareholders, the smaller is the potential margin of safety for lenders and suppliers.

Activity 4.10

Would you expect a company to pay all of its revenue reserves as a dividend? What factors might be involved with a dividend decision?

It would be rare for a company to pay all of its revenue reserves as a dividend: the fact that it is legally possible does not necessarily make it a good idea. Most companies see ploughed-back profits as a major – usually *the* major – source of new finance. The factors that tend most to influence the dividend decision are likely to include:

■ the availability of cash to pay a dividend: it would not be illegal to borrow to pay a dividend, but it would be unusual, and possibly imprudent;
■ the needs of the business for finance for new investment;
■ the expectations of shareholders concerning the amount of dividends to be paid.

You may have thought of others. We shall look again at dividend policy in Chapter 11.

THE MAIN FINANCIAL STATEMENTS

The financial statements of a limited company are, in essence, the same as those of a sole proprietor or partnership. There are, however, differences of detail, which we shall now consider. Example 4.5 sets out the income statement and statement of financial position of a limited company.

Example 4.5

Da Silva plc
Income statement for the year ended 31 December 2012

	£m
Revenue	840
Cost of sales	(520)
Gross profit	320
Wages and salaries	(98)
Heat and light	(18)
Rent and rates	(24)
Motor vehicle expenses	(20)
Insurance	(4)
Printing and stationery	(12)
Depreciation	(45)
Audit fee	(4)
Operating profit	95
Interest payable	(10)
Profit before taxation	85
Taxation	(24)
Profit for the year	61

Statement of financial position as at 31 December 2012

	£m
ASSETS	
Non-current assets	
Property, plant and equipment	203
Intangible assets	100
	303
Current assets	
Inventories	65
Trade receivables	112
Cash	36
	213
Total assets	516

→

EQUITY AND LIABILITIES	
Equity	
Ordinary shares of £0.50 each	200
Share premium account	30
Other reserves	50
Retained earnings	25
	305
Non-current liabilities	
Borrowings	100
Current liabilities	
Trade payables	99
Taxation	12
	111
Total equity and liabilities	516

Let us now go through these statements and pick up those aspects that are unique to limited companies.

The income statement

The main points for consideration in the income statement are as follows:

Profit

Following the calculation of operating profit, two further measures of profit are shown.

■ The first of these is the **profit before taxation**. Interest charges are deducted from the operating profit to derive this figure. In the case of a sole proprietor or partnership business, the income statement would end here.

■ The second measure of profit is the **profit for the period** (usually a year). As the company is a separate legal entity, it is liable to pay tax (known as corporation tax) on the profits generated. This measure of profit represents the amount that is available for the shareholders, after corporation tax has been paid.

Audit fee

Companies beyond a certain size are required to have their financial statements audited by an independent firm of accountants, for which a fee is charged. As mentioned earlier, the purpose of the audit is to lend credibility to the financial statements. Although sole proprietorships and partnerships could also have their financial statements audited, relatively few choose to do so. It is, therefore, an expense most often seen in the income statement of a company.

Figure 4.5 shows an outline of the income statement for a limited company.

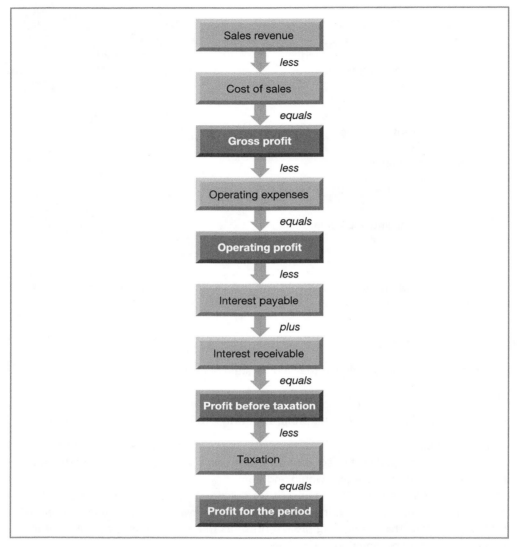

Figure 4.5 Outline of the income statement of a limited company

The statement of financial position

The main points for consideration in the statement of financial position are as follows:

Taxation

The amount that appears as part of the current liabilities represents 50 per cent of the tax on the profit for the year 2011. It is, therefore, 50 per cent (£12 million) of the charge that appears in the income statement (£24 million); the other 50 per cent (£12 million) will already have been paid. The unpaid 50 per cent will be paid shortly after the statement of financial position date. These payment dates are set down by law.

Other reserves

This will include any reserves that are not separately identified on the face of the statement of financial position. It may include a *general reserve*, which normally consists of trading profits that have been transferred to this separate reserve for reinvestment ('ploughing back') into the operations of the company. It is not at all necessary to set up a separate reserve for this purpose. The trading profits could remain unallocated and still swell the retained earnings of the company. It is not entirely clear why directors make transfers to general reserves, since the profits concerned remain part of the revenue reserves, and as such remain available for dividend. The most plausible explanation seems to be that directors feel that placing profits in a separate reserve indicates an intention to invest the funds, represented by the reserve, permanently in the company rather than use them to pay a dividend or to fund a share repurchase. Of course, the retained earnings appearing on the statement of financial position are also a reserve, but that fact is not indicated in its title.

DIVIDENDS

Dividends represent drawings by the shareholders of the company. They are paid out of revenue reserves and should be deducted from these reserves (usually retained earnings) when preparing the statement of financial position. Shareholders are often paid an annual dividend, perhaps in two parts. An 'interim' dividend may be paid part way through the year and a 'final' dividend by that date shortly after the year end.

Dividends declared by the directors during the year but still unpaid at the year end *may* appear as a liability in the statement of financial position. To be recognised as a liability, however, they must be properly authorised before the year-end date. This normally means that the shareholders must approve the dividend.

ADDITIONAL FINANCIAL STATEMENTS

In the sections below, we turn our attention to two new financial statements that must be provided by those companies that are subject to International Financial Reporting Standards. We shall consider the nature and role of these standards a little later in the chapter.

Statement of comprehensive income

The **statement of comprehensive income** extends the conventional income statement to include certain other gains and losses that affect shareholders' equity. It may be presented either in the form of a single statement or as two separate statements, comprising an income statement (like the one shown in Example 4.5) and a statement of comprehensive income.

This new statement attempts to overcome the perceived weaknesses of the conventional income statement. In broad terms, the conventional income statement shows all *realised* gains and losses for the period. It also shows some unrealised losses. However, gains, and some losses, that remain *unrealised* (because the asset is still held) tend not to pass through the income statement, but will go, instead, directly to a reserve. We saw, in an earlier chapter, an example of such an unrealised gain.

Activity 4.11

Can you think of this example?

The example that we met earlier is where a business revalues its land and buildings. The gain arising is not shown in the conventional income statement, but is transferred to a revaluation reserve, which forms part of the equity. (See example in Activity 2.15 on page 55.) Land and buildings are not the only assets to which this rule relates, but revaluations of these types of asset are, in practice, the most common examples of unrealised gains.

An example of an unrealised gain, or loss, that has not been mentioned so far, arises from exchange differences when the results of foreign operations are translated into UK currency. Any gain, or loss, bypasses the income statement and is taken directly to a currency translation reserve.

A weakness of conventional accounting is that there is no robust principle that we can apply to determine precisely what should, and what should not, be included in the income statement. Thus, on the one hand, losses arising from the impairment of non-current assets normally appear in the income statement. On the other hand, losses arising from translating the carrying value of assets expressed in an overseas currency (because they are owned by an overseas branch) do not. This difference in treatment, which is ingrained in conventional accounting, is difficult to justify.

The statement of comprehensive income ensures that all gains and losses, both realised and unrealised, are reported within a single statement. To do this, it extends the conventional income statement by including unrealised gains, as well as any unrealised losses not yet reported, immediately below the measure of profit for the year. An illustration of this statement is shown in Example 4.6.

Example 4.6

Malik plc
Statement of comprehensive income for the year ended 31 July 2012

	£m
Revenue	97.2
Cost of sales	(59.1)
Gross profit	38.1
Other income	3.5
Distribution expenses	(16.5)
Administration expenses	(11.2)
Other expenses	(2.4)
Operating profit	11.5
Finance charges	(1.8)
Profit before tax	9.7
Tax	(2.4)
Profit for the year	7.3
Other comprehensive income	
Revaluation of property, plant and equipment	6.6
Foreign currency translation differences for foreign operations	4.0
Tax on other comprehensive income	(2.6)
Other comprehensive income for the year, net of tax	8.0
Total comprehensive income for the year	15.3

This example adopts a single-statement approach to presenting comprehensive income. The alternative two-statement approach simply divides the information shown above into two separate parts. The income statement, which is the first statement, begins with the revenue for the year and ends with the profit for the year. The statement of comprehensive income, which is the second statement, begins with the profit for the year and ends with the total comprehensive income for the year.

Statement of changes in equity

The **statement of changes in equity** aims to help users to understand the changes in share capital and reserves that took place during the period. It reconciles the figures for these items at the beginning of the period with those at the end. This is achieved by showing the effect on the share capital and reserves of total comprehensive income as well as the effect of share issues and purchases during the period. The effect of dividends during the period may also be shown in this statement, although dividends can be shown in the notes instead.

To see how a statement of changes in equity may be prepared, let us consider Example 4.7.

Example 4.7

At 1 January 2012, Miro plc had the following equity:

Miro plc

	£m
Share capital (£1 ordinary shares)	100
Revaluation reserve	20
Translation reserve	40
Retained earnings	150
Total equity	310

During 2012, the company made a profit for the year from normal business operations of £42 million and reported an upward revaluation of property, plant and equipment of £120 million (net of any tax that would be payable were the unrealised gains to be realised). The company also reported a £10 million loss on exchange differences on translating the results of foreign operations. To strengthen its financial position, the company issued 50 million ordinary shares during the year at a premium of £0.40. Dividends for the year were £27 million.

This information for 2012 can be set out in a statement of changes in equity as follows:

Statement of changes in equity for the year ended 31 December 2012

	Share capital £m	Share premium £m	Revaluation reserve £m	Translation reserve £m	Retained earnings £m	Total £m
Balance as at 1 January 2012	100	–	20	40	150	310
Changes in equity for 2012						
Issue of ordinary shares (Note 1)	50	20	–	–	–	70
Dividends (Note 2)	–	–	–	–	(27)	(27)
Total comprehensive income for the year (Note 3)	–	–	120	(10)	42	152
Balance at 31 December 2012	150	20	140	30	165	505

Notes

1 The premium on the share price is transferred to a specific reserve.
2 Dividends are shown in the statement of changes in equity. They are deducted from retained earnings. An alternative would be to show them as a note to the financial statements.
3 The effect of each component of comprehensive income on the various components of shareholders' equity must be separately disclosed. The revaluation gain and the loss on translating foreign operations are each allocated to a specific reserve. The profit for the year is added to retained earnings.

THE DIRECTORS' DUTY TO ACCOUNT

With many companies, there is a separation of ownership from day-to-day control. This creates the need for directors to be accountable for their stewardship (management) of the company's assets. Thus, the law requires that directors:

- maintain appropriate accounting records;
- prepare annual financial statements and a directors' report and make these available to shareholders and lenders.

The financial statements must also be made available to the public by submitting a copy to the Registrar of Companies (The Department for Business, Enterprise and Regulatory Reform), who allows any interested person to inspect them. In addition, Stock Exchange listed companies must publish their financial statements on their website.

Activity 4.12

What are the possible consequences of failing to make financial statements available to shareholders, lenders and suppliers on the ability of the business to operate?

If shareholders do not receive information about the performance and position of their investment, they will have problems in appraising their investment. Under these circumstances, they would probably be reluctant to invest. Furthermore, individuals and organisations would be reluctant to engage in commercial relationships, such as supplying goods or lending money, where a company does not provide information about its financial health.

THE NEED FOR ACCOUNTING RULES

If we accept the need for directors to prepare and publish financial statements, we should also accept the need for rules about how they are prepared and presented. Without rules, there is a much greater risk that unscrupulous directors will adopt accounting policies and practices that portray an unrealistic view of financial health. There is also a much greater risk that the financial statements will not be comparable over time or with those of other businesses. Accounting rules can narrow areas of differences and reduce the variety of accounting methods. This should help ensure that similar transactions are treated in a similar way.

Although accounting rules should help to provide confidence in the integrity of financial statements, users must be realistic about what can be achieved. Problems of manipulation and of concealment can still occur even within a highly regulated environment. The scale of these problems, however, should be reduced where there is a practical set of rules. Problems of comparability can also still occur as judgements and estimates must be made when preparing financial statements. There is also the problem that no two companies are identical and so accounting policies may vary between companies for entirely valid reasons.

SOURCES OF ACCOUNTING RULES

In recent years there have been increasing trends towards the internationalisation of business and the integration of financial markets. These trends have helped to strengthen the case for the international harmonisation of accounting rules. By adopting a common set of rules, users of financial statements should be better placed to compare the financial health of companies based in different countries. It should also relieve international companies of some of the burden of preparing financial statements as different financial statements would no longer be required to comply with the rules of different countries in which a particular company operates.

The International Accounting Standards Board (IASB) is an independent body that is dedicated to developing a single set of high-quality, global accounting rules. These rules are known as **International Financial Reporting Standards** (IFRSs) or **International Accounting Standards** (IASs) and deal with key issues such as:

- what information should be disclosed;
- how information should be presented;
- how assets should be valued; and
- how profit should be measured.

Activity 4.13

We have already come across some IASs and IFRSs in earlier chapters. Try to recall at least two topics where they were mentioned.

We came across financial reporting standards when considering:

- the valuation and impairment of assets (Chapter 2);
- depreciation (Chapter 3);
- the valuation of inventories (Chapter 3).

Over the years, the IASB has greatly extended its influence and authority. The point has now been reached where all major economies adopt IFRSs or have set time lines to adopt, or to converge with, IFRSs. Although, in the UK, the authority of the IASB extends only to listed companies, non-listed UK companies have the option to adopt IFRSs.

Company law also imposes rules on UK companies. These rules relate to corporate governance issues and go beyond anything required by IFRSs. There is, for example, a requirement to disclose details of directors' remuneration in the published financial statements. Furthermore, the Financial Services Authority (FSA), in its role as the UK (Stock Exchange) listing authority, imposes rules on Stock Exchange listed companies. These include the requirement to publish a condensed set of interim (half-year) financial statements in addition to the annual financial statements.

Figure 4.6 sets out the main sources of accounting rules for Stock Exchange listed companies discussed above.

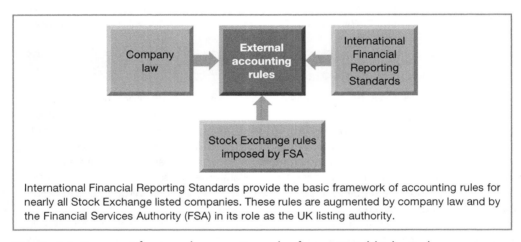

International Financial Reporting Standards provide the basic framework of accounting rules for nearly all Stock Exchange listed companies. These rules are augmented by company law and by the Financial Services Authority (FSA) in its role as the UK listing authority.

Figure 4.6 Sources of external accounting rules for a UK public limited company listed on the London Stock Exchange

THE AUDITORS' ROLE

Shareholders are required to elect a qualified and independent person or, more usually, a firm to act as **auditors**. The auditors' main duty is to report whether, in their opinion, the financial statements do what they are supposed to do, namely to show a true and fair view of the financial performance, position and cash flows of the company. To form such an opinion, auditors must carefully scrutinise the annual financial statements and the underlying evidence upon which they are based. They must examine the accounting principles followed, the accounting estimates made and the robustness of the company's internal control systems. The auditors' opinion will be included with the financial statements sent to the shareholders and to the Registrar of Companies.

The relationship between the shareholders, the directors and the auditors is illustrated in Figure 4.7. This shows that the shareholders elect the directors to act on their behalf, in the day-to-day running of the company. The directors are then required to 'account' to the shareholders on the performance, position and cash flows of the company, on an annual basis. The shareholders also elect auditors, whose role it is to give the shareholders an independent view of the truth and fairness of the financial statements prepared by the directors.

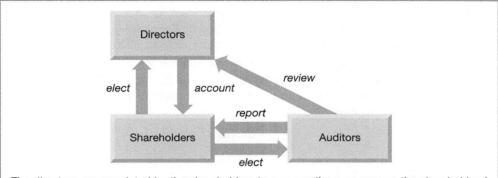

The directors are appointed by the shareholders to manage the company on the shareholders' behalf. The directors are required to report each year to the shareholders, principally by means of financial statements, on the company's performance, position and cash flows. To give greater confidence in the statements, the shareholders also appoint auditors to investigate the reports and to express an opinion on their reliability.

Figure 4.7 The relationship between the shareholders, the directors and the auditors

THE DIRECTORS' REPORT

In addition to preparing the financial statements, UK law requires the directors to prepare an annual report to shareholders and other interested parties. The **directors' report** will contain both financial and non-financial information, which goes beyond that contained in the financial statements. The information to be disclosed is diverse and will include the names of those who were directors during the year, the principal activities of the company and any recommended dividend. The most important element of the report, however, is probably the **business review**. This is aimed at helping shareholders to assess how well the directors have performed. It should provide an analysis of financial performance and position and should also set out the principal risks and uncertainties facing the business.

In addition to disclosing the above information, the directors' report must contain a declaration that the directors are not aware of any other information that the auditors might need in preparing their audit report. Furthermore, the report must declare that the directors have taken steps to ensure that the auditors are aware of all relevant information. The auditors do not carry out an audit of the directors' report. However, they will check to see that the information in the report is consistent with that contained in the audited financial statements.

For companies listed on the Stock Exchange, the law also requires the publication of an annual directors' remuneration report. This should help shareholders to assess whether the rewards received by directors are appropriate.

CREATIVE ACCOUNTING

Despite the proliferation of accounting rules and the independent checks that are imposed, concerns over the quality of published financial statements surface from time to time. There are occasions when directors apply particular accounting policies, or structure particular transactions, in such a way as to portray a picture of financial health that is in line with what they want users to see, rather than what is a true and fair view of financial position and performance. Misrepresenting the performance and position of a business in this way is referred to as **creative accounting** and it poses a major problem for accounting rule makers and for society generally.

Activity 4.14

Why might the directors of a company engage in creative accounting?

There are many reasons including:

■ to get around restrictions (for example, to report sufficient profit to pay a dividend);
■ to avoid government action (for example, the taxation of excessive profits);
■ to hide poor management decisions;
■ to achieve sales revenue or profit targets, thereby ensuring that performance bonuses are paid to the directors;
■ to attract new share capital or long-term borrowing by showing an apparently healthy financial position; and
■ to satisfy the demands of major investors concerning levels of return.

Creative accounting methods

The ways in which unscrupulous directors can manipulate the financial statements are many and varied. However, they usually involve adopting novel or unorthodox practices for reporting key elements of the financial statements such as revenue, expenses, assets and liabilities. They may also involve the use of complicated or obscure transactions in an attempt to hide the underlying economic reality. The manipulation carried out may be designed either to bend the rules or to break them.

Many creative accounting methods are designed to overstate the revenue for a period. These methods often involve the early recognition of sales revenue or the reporting of sales transactions that have no real substance. **Real World 4.8** provides examples of both types of revenue manipulation.

REAL WORLD 4.8

Overstating revenue

Channel stuffing: A business, usually with considerable market power, may pressurise its distributors to accept more goods than is needed to meet normal sales demand. In this way, the business can record additional sales for a period even though there has effectively been only a transfer of inventories from the business to its distributors. This method of artificially increasing sales is also known as 'trade loading'.

Pre-dispatching: Normally, revenue for credit sales is recognised when goods have been passed to, and accepted by, the customer. To boost sales and profits for a period, however, some businesses have been known to recognise revenue as soon as the order for goods has been received.

Hollow swaps: Telecom businesses may agree to sell unused fibre optic capacity to each other – usually at the same price. Although this will not increase profits, it will increase revenues and give an impression that the business is growing.

Round tripping: Energy businesses may agree to buy and sell energy between each other. Again this is normally for the same price and so no additional profits will be made. It will, however, boost revenues to give a false impression of business growth. This method is also known as 'in and out trading'.

Source: Based on information in 'Dirty laundry: how companies fudge the numbers', *The Times*, Business Section, 22 September 2002.

Some years ago there was a wave of creative accounting scandals, particularly in the US but also in Europe. It seems, however, that this wave has now subsided. As a result of the actions taken by various regulatory bodies, creative accounting has become a more risky and difficult process. However, it will never disappear completely and a further wave of creative accounting scandals may occur in the future. The most recent wave coincided with a period of strong economic growth and, during good economic times, investors and auditors become less vigilant. The temptation to manipulate the figures, therefore becomes greater.

? SELF-ASSESSMENT QUESTION 4.1

This question requires you to correct some figures on a set of company financial statements. It should prove useful practice for the material that you covered in Chapters 2 and 3, as well as helping you to become familiar with the financial statements of a company.

Presented below is a draft set of simplified financial statements for Pear Limited for the year ended 30 September 2012.

Income statement for the year ended 30 September 2012

	£000
Revenue	1,456
Cost of sales	(768)
Gross profit	688
Salaries	(220)
Depreciation	(249)
Other operating costs	(131)
Operating profit	88
Interest payable	(15)
Profit before taxation	73
Taxation at 30%	(22)
Profit for the year	51

Statement of financial position as at 30 September 2012

ASSETS	£000
Non-current assets	
Property, plant and equipment	
Cost	1,570
Depreciation	(690)
	880
Current assets	
Inventories	207
Trade receivables	182
Cash at bank	21
	410
Total assets	1,290
EQUITY AND LIABILITIES	
	Equity
Share capital	300
Share premium account	300
Retained earnings at beginning of year	104
Profit for year	51
	755
Non-current liabilities	
Borrowings (10% loan notes repayable 2015)	300
Current liabilities	
Trade payables	88
Other payables	20
Taxation	22
Borrowings (bank overdraft)	105
	235
Total equity and liabilities	1,290

→

The following information is available:

1 Depreciation has not been charged on office equipment with a carrying amount of £100,000. This class of assets is depreciated at 12 per cent a year using the reducing-balance method.
2 A new machine was purchased, on credit, for £30,000 and delivered on 29 September 2012 but has not been included in the financial statements. (Ignore depreciation.)
3 A sales invoice to the value of £18,000 for September 2012 has been omitted from the financial statements. (The cost of sales figure is stated correctly.)
4 A dividend of £25,000 had been approved by the shareholders before 30 September 2012, but was unpaid at that date. This is not reflected in the financial statements.
5 The interest payable on the loan notes for the second half-year was not paid until 1 October 2012 and has not been included in the financial statements.
6 An allowance for trade receivables is to be made at the level of 2 per cent of trade receivables.
7 An invoice for electricity to the value of £2,000 for the quarter ended 30 September 2012 arrived on 4 October and has not been included in the financial statements.
8 The charge for taxation will have to be amended to take account of the above information. Make the simplifying assumption that tax is payable shortly after the end of the year, at the rate of 30 per cent of the profit before tax.

Required:
Prepare a revised set of financial statements for the year ended 30 September 2012 incorporating the additional information in 1 to 8 above. (Work to the nearest £1,000.)

The solution to this question can be found at the back of the book, in Appendix B.

SUMMARY

The main points of this chapter may be summarised as follows.

Main features of a limited company

- It is an artificial person that has been created by law.
- It has a separate life to its owners and is granted a perpetual existence.
- It must take responsibility for its own debts and losses but its owners are granted limited liability.
- A public company can offer its shares for sale to the public; a private company cannot.
- It is governed by a board of directors, which is elected by the shareholders.
- Corporate governance is a major issue.

Financing the limited company

- The share capital of a company can be of two main types: ordinary shares and preference shares.

- Holders of ordinary shares (equities) are the main risk takers and are given voting rights; they form the backbone of the company.

- Holders of preference shares are given a right to a fixed dividend before ordinary shareholders receive a dividend.

- Reserves are profits and gains made by the company and form part of the ordinary shareholders' equity.

- Borrowings provide another major source of finance.

Share issues

- Bonus shares are issued to existing shareholders when part of the reserves of the company is converted into share capital. No funds are raised.

- The shares of public companies may be bought and sold on a recognised Stock Exchange.

Reserves

- Reserves are of two types: revenue reserves and capital reserves.

- Revenue reserves arise from trading profits and from gains on the sale of non-current assets.

- Capital reserves arise from the issue of shares above their nominal value or from the upward revaluation of non-current assets.

- Revenue reserves can be withdrawn as dividends by the shareholders whereas capital reserves normally cannot.

Financial statements of limited companies

- The financial statements of limited companies are based on the same principles as those of sole proprietorship and partnership businesses. However, there are some differences in detail.

- The income statement has two measures of profit displayed after the operating profit figure: profit before taxation and profit for the period, usually a year.

- The income statement also shows audit fees and tax on profits for the period.

- Any unpaid tax will appear in the statement of financial position as current liabilities.

- The statement of comprehensive income extends the income statement to include all gains and losses, both realised and unrealised.

- The statement of changes in equity reconciles the equity figure at the beginning of a reporting period with that at the end.

Directors' duty

- The directors have a duty to:
  - maintain appropriate accounting records;
  - prepare and publish financial statements and a directors' report.

→

The need for accounting rules

- Accounting rules are necessary to:
  - avoid unacceptable accounting practices;
  - improve the comparability of financial statements.

Accounting rules

- The International Accounting Standards Board (IASB) has become an important source of rules.

- Company law and the London Stock Exchange are also sources of rules for UK companies.

Other statutory reports

- The auditors' report provides an opinion by independent auditors concerning whether the financial statements provide a true and fair view of the financial health of a business.

- The directors' report contains information of a financial and a non-financial nature, which goes beyond that contained in the financial statements.

Creative accounting

- Despite the accounting rules in place there have been examples of creative accounting by directors.

- This involves using accounting practices to show what the directors would like users to see rather than what is a fair representation of reality.

MyAccountingLab

Go to www.myaccountinglab.com to check your understanding of the chapter, create a personalised study plan, and maximise your revision time

KEY TERMS

limited company p. 107	reserves p. 117
shares p. 107	nominal value p. 117
limited liability p. 110	par value p. 117
public limited company p. 110	revenue reserve p. 118
private limited company p. 110	dividends p. 118
corporation tax p. 112	ordinary shares p. 118
directors p. 113	preference shares p. 119
corporate governance p. 113	splitting p. 119
UK Corporate Governance Code p. 115	consolidating p. 119
	capital reserves p. 120

FURTHER READING

If you would like to explore the topics covered in this chapter in more depth, we recommend the following books:

Elliott, B. and Elliott, J., *Financial Accounting and Reporting*, 15th edn, Financial Times Prentice Hall, 2012, Chapters 9 and 12.

Financial Reporting Council, *UK Corporate Governance Code*, FRC 2010, available free at www.frc.org.uk.

Melville, A., *International Financial Reporting*, 3rd edn, Financial Times Prentice Hall, 2011, Chapters 1 and 18.

Thomas, A. and Ward, A. M., *Introduction to Financial Accounting*, 6th edn, McGraw Hill, 2009, Chapter 29.

❔ REVIEW QUESTIONS

Solutions to these questions can be found at the back of the book, in Appendix C.

4.1 How does the liability of a limited company differ from the liability of a real person, in respect of amounts owed to others?

4.2 Some people are about to form a company, as a vehicle through which to run a new business. What are the advantages to them of forming a private limited company rather than a public one?

4.3 What is a reserve? Distinguish between a revenue reserve and a capital reserve.

4.4 What is a preference share? Compare the main features of a preference share with those of:
  (a) an ordinary share; and
  (b) loan notes.

✳ EXERCISES

*Exercises 4.1 and 4.2 are basic level, Exercise 4.3 is intermediate level and Exercises 4.4 and 4.5 are advanced level. Exercises with **coloured numbers** have solutions at the back of the book, in Appendix D.*

> If you wish to try more exercises, visit the website at **www.myaccountinglab.com**.

4.1 Comment on the following quote:

> Limited companies can set a limit on the amount of debts that they will meet. They tend to have reserves of cash, as well as share capital and they can use these reserves to pay dividends to the shareholders. Many companies have preference as well as ordinary shares. The preference shares give a guaranteed dividend. The shares of many companies can be bought and sold on the Stock Exchange. Shareholders selling their shares can represent a useful source of new finance to the company.

4.2 Briefly explain each of the following expressions that you have seen in the financial statements of a limited company:

(a) dividend
(b) audit fee
(c) share premium account.

4.3 The following information was extracted from the financial statements of I. Ching (Booksellers) plc for the year to 31 December 2012:

	£m
Finance charges	40
Cost of sales	460
Distribution expenses	110
Revenue	943
Administration expenses	212
Other expenses	25
Gain on revaluation of property, plant and equipment	20
Loss on foreign currency translations on foreign operations	15
Tax on profit for the year	24
Tax on other components of comprehensive income	1

Required:
Prepare a statement of comprehensive income for the year ended 31 December 2012.

4.4 Presented below is a draft set of financial statements for Chips Limited.

Chips Limited
Income statement for the year ended 30 June 2012

	£000
Revenue	1,850
Cost of sales	(1,040)
Gross profit	810
Depreciation	(220)
Other operating costs	(375)
Operating profit	215
Interest payable	(35)
Profit before taxation	180
Taxation	(60)
Profit for the year	120

Statement of financial position as at 30 June 2012

	Cost £000	Depreciation £000	£000
ASSETS			
Non-current assets			
Property, plant and equipment			
Buildings	800	(112)	688
Plant and equipment	650	(367)	283
Motor vehicles	102	(53)	49
	(1,552)	(532)	1,020
Current assets			
Inventories			950
Trade receivables			420
Cash at bank			16
			1,386
Total assets			2,406
EQUITY AND LIABILITIES			
Equity			
Ordinary shares of £1, fully paid			800
Reserves at beginning of the year			248
Profit for the year			120
			1,168
Non-current liabilities			
Borrowings (secured 10% loan notes)			700
Current liabilities			
Trade payables			361
Other payables			117
Taxation			60
			538
Total equity and liabilities			2,406

→

Accounting for Limited Companies

The following additional information is available:

1. Purchase invoices for goods received on 29 June 2012 amounting to £23,000 have not been included. This means that the cost of sales figure in the income statement has been understated.
2. A motor vehicle costing £8,000 with depreciation amounting to £5,000 was sold on 30 June 2012 for £2,000, paid by cheque. This transaction has not been included in the company's records.
3. No depreciation on motor vehicles has been charged. The annual rate is 20 per cent of cost at the year end.
4. A sale on credit for £16,000 made on 1 July 2012 has been included in the financial statements in error. The cost of sales figure is correct in respect of this item.
5. A half-yearly payment of interest on the secured loan due on 30 June 2012 has not been paid.
6. The tax charge should be 30 per cent of the reported profit before taxation. Assume that it is payable, in full, shortly after the year end.

Required:

Prepare a revised set of financial statements incorporating the additional information in 1 to 6 above. (Work to the nearest £1,000.)

4.5 Rose Limited operates a small chain of retail shops that sell high-quality teas and coffees. Approximately half of sales are on credit. Abbreviated and unaudited financial statements are as follows:

Rose Limited
Income statement for the year ended 31 March 2012

	£000
Revenue	12,080
Cost of sales	(6,282)
Gross profit	5,798
Labour costs	(2,658)
Depreciation	(625)
Other operating costs	(1,003)
Operating profit	1,512
Interest payable	(66)
Profit before taxation	1,446
Taxation	(434)
Profit for the year	1,012

Statement of financial position as at 31 March 2012

	£000
ASSETS	
Non-current assets	2,728
Current assets	
Inventories	1,583
Trade receivables	996
Cash	26
	2,605
Total assets	5,333
EQUITY AND LIABILITIES	
Equity	
Share capital (50p shares, fully paid)	750
Share premium	250
Retained earnings	1,468
	2,468
Non-current liabilities	
Borrowings – secured loan notes (2014)	300
Current liabilities	
Trade payables	1,118
Other payables	417
Tax	434
Borrowings – overdraft	596
	2,565
Total equity and liabilities	5,333

Since the unaudited financial statements for Rose Limited were prepared, the following information has become available:

1 An additional £74,000 of depreciation should have been charged on fixtures and fittings.
2 Invoices for credit sales on 31 March 2012 amounting to £34,000 have not been included; cost of sales is not affected.
3 Trade receivables totalling £21,000 are recognised as having gone bad, but they have not yet been written off.
4 Inventories which had been purchased for £2,000 have been damaged and are unsaleable. This is not reflected in the financial statements.
5 Fixtures and fittings to the value of £16,000 were delivered just before 31 March 2012, but these assets were not included in the financial statements and the purchase invoice had not been processed.
6 Wages for Saturday-only staff, amounting to £1,000, have not been paid for the final Saturday of the year. This is not reflected in the financial statements.
7 Tax is payable at 30 per cent of profit before taxation. Assume that it is payable shortly after the year end.

Required:
Prepare revised financial statements for Rose Limited for the year ended 31 March 2012, incorporating the information in 1 to 7 above. (Work to the nearest £1,000.)

MEASURING AND REPORTING CASH FLOWS

INTRODUCTION

This chapter is devoted to the third major financial statement identified in Chapter 2: the statement of cash flows. This statement reports the movements of cash over a period and the effect of these movements on the cash position of the business. It is an important financial statement because cash is vital to the survival of a business. Without cash, a business cannot operate.

In this chapter, we shall see how the statement of cash flows is prepared and how the information that it contains may be interpreted. We shall also see why the deficiencies of the income statement, in identifying and explaining cash flows, make a separate statement necessary.

The statement of cash flows is being considered after the chapter on limited companies because the format of the statement requires an understanding of this type of business. Most limited companies are required to provide a statement of cash flows for shareholders and other users as part of their annual financial reports.

Learning outcomes

When you have completed this chapter, you should be able to:

- discuss the crucial importance of cash to a business;
- explain the nature of the statement of cash flows and discuss how it can be helpful in identifying cash flow problems;
- prepare a statement of cash flows;
- interpret a statement of cash flows.

MyAccountingLab   Visit www.myaccountinglab.com
for practice and revision opportunities

From Chapter 5 of *Accounting and Finance for Non-Specialists*, 8/e. Peter Atrill and Eddie McLaney. © Pearson Education Limited 2013. All rights reserved.

THE STATEMENT OF CASH FLOWS

The statement of cash flows is a fairly recent addition to the annual published financial statements. Companies used only to be required to publish an income statement and a statement of financial position. The prevailing view seems to have been that all of the financial information needed by users would be contained within these two statements. This view may have been based partly on the assumption that if a business were profitable, it would also have plenty of cash. Although in the long run this is likely to be true, it is not necessarily true in the short to medium term.

We saw in Chapter 3 that the income statement sets out the revenue and expenses, for the period, rather than the cash inflows and outflows. This means that the profit (or loss), which represents the difference between the revenue and expenses for the period, may have little or no relation to the cash generated for the period.

To illustrate this point, let us take the example of a business making a sale (generating revenue). This may well lead to an increase in wealth that will be reflected in the income statement. However, if the sale is made on credit, no cash changes hands – at least not at the time of sale. Instead, the increase in wealth is reflected in another asset: an increase in trade receivables. Furthermore, if an item of inventories is the subject of the sale, wealth is lost to the business through the reduction in inventories. This means that an expense is incurred in making the sale, which will also be shown in the income statement. Once again, however, no cash changes hands at the time of sale. For such reasons, the profit and the cash generated for a period will rarely go hand in hand.

Activity 5.1 should help to underline how profit and cash for a period may be affected differently by particular transactions or events.

Activity 5.1

The following is a list of business/accounting events. In each case, state the effect (increase, decrease or none) on both profit and cash:

	Effect	
	on profit	on cash
1 Repayment of borrowings	_____	_____
2 Making a profitable sale on credit	_____	_____
3 Buying a current asset on credit	_____	_____
4 Receiving cash from a credit customer (trade receivable)	_____	_____
5 Depreciating a non-current asset	_____	_____
6 Buying some inventories for cash	_____	_____
7 Making a share issue for cash	_____	_____

→

You should have come up with the following:

	Effect	
	on profit	on cash
1 Repayment of borrowings	none	decrease
2 Making a profitable sale on credit	increase	none
3 Buying a current asset on credit	none	none
4 Receiving cash from a credit customer (trade receivable)	none	increase
5 Depreciating a non-current asset	decrease	none
6 Buying some inventories for cash	none	decrease
7 Making a share issue for cash	none	increase

The reasons for these answers are as follows:

1 Repaying borrowings requires that cash be paid to the lender. This means that two figures in the statement of financial position will be affected, but none in the income statement.
2 Making a profitable sale on credit will increase the sales revenue and profit figures. No cash will change hands at this point, however.
3 Buying a current asset on credit affects neither the cash balance nor the profit figure.
4 Receiving cash from a credit customer increases the cash balance and reduces the credit customer's balance. Both of these figures are on the statement of financial position. The income statement is unaffected.
5 Depreciating a non-current asset means that an expense is recognised. This causes the carrying amount of the asset, as it is recorded on the statement of financial position, to fall by an amount equal to the amount of the expense. No cash is paid or received.
6 Buying some inventories for cash means that the value of the inventories will increase and the cash balance will decrease by a similar amount. Profit is not affected.
7 Making a share issue for cash increases the shareholders' equity and increases the cash balance; profit is unaffected.

It is clear from the above that if we are to gain insights about cash movements over time, the income statement is not the place to look. We need a separate statement of cash flows.

WHY IS CASH SO IMPORTANT?

It is worth asking why cash is so important. In one sense, it is just another asset that the business needs to enable it to function. Hence, it is no different from inventories or non-current assets.

The importance of cash lies in the fact that people will only normally accept cash in settlement of their claims. If a business wants to employ people, it must pay them in cash. If it wants to buy a new non-current asset, it must normally pay the seller in cash (perhaps after a short period of credit). When businesses fail, it is the lack of cash to pay amounts owed that really pushes them under. Cash generation is vital for businesses to survive and to be able to take advantage of commercial opportunities. These are the things that make cash the pre-eminent business asset.

During an economic downturn, the ability to generate cash takes on even greater importance. Banks become more cautious in their lending, and businesses with weak cash flows often find it difficult to obtain finance. **Real World 5.1** describes how the recent financial crisis has led banks in China to place greater emphasis on cash flows when considering loan applications.

REAL WORLD 5.1

Cash flow is in top three places

'The banks are tightening the screws,' says K. B. Chan, chairman of Surface Mount Technology, which supplies consumer electronics companies. 'A lot of companies are strapped for cash.'

Stanley Wong, business development director at Man Yue Electronics, the world's fifth largest maker of aluminium capacitors, says: 'Banks don't even trust each other. They are being a lot more careful.' Mr Wong says that companies such as his, with strong cash flows, will still get working capital and other loans but bankers who used to lend to Man Yue and other manufacturers sight unseen are now tramping out to their factories for a closer look.

'The banks only look at cash flow – number one is cash flow, number two is cash flow and number three is cash flow,' says Mr Chan. 'Profit is only an accounting statement.'

 Source: Mitchell, T. and Lau, J., 'Rations cut for army of buyers', *Financial Times*, 20 October 2008.

Real World 5.2 is taken from a column written by John Timpson, which appeared in *The Daily Telegraph*. He is the chief executive of the successful, high street shoe-repairing and key-cutting business that bears his name. In the column he highlights the importance of cash reporting in managing the business.

REAL WORLD 5.2

Cash is key

I look at our cash balance every day (not Saturdays and Sundays). It is the best way to test the financial temperature of our business. The trick is to compare with the same day last year, thus showing cash flow for the past 12 months.

It is not a perfect system (never forget that your finance department may secretly massage the cash by paying suppliers sooner or later than you anticipate) but a glance at the daily cash is more transparent than management accounts that are full of provisions and only appear once a month.

Finance and IT take a delight in producing a deluge of data. But being in possession of too many statistics is counterproductive. This daily cash report helps to clear the clutter created by computers – it's a simple report that helps you pose the right questions.

Why have things suddenly got worse? Are we in danger of breaking our bank borrowing limit? Why does the cash flow look so much better than in the management accounts? This cash report can also give you an early warning of changing financial circumstances.

It came to my rescue in 2004 when, through a major acquisition, the business doubled in size overnight and was going through a great deal of change. Our financial control suffered but I didn't realise how bad things were until I was waiting to board a plane to go on a Caribbean holiday. A quick look at my Blackberry (when my wife wasn't looking) showed an unexpected £500,000 deterioration in our overdraft. It wasn't a great start to the holiday and my wife was upset when I spent the first day on the telephone. However we were able to tackle the problem six weeks before it would have been revealed in the management accounts.

Source: Timpson, John, The Management Column, *The Daily Telegraph*, Business Section, 14 June 2010.

THE MAIN FEATURES OF THE STATEMENT OF CASH FLOWS

The statement of cash flows summarises the inflows and outflows of cash (and cash equivalents) for a business over a period. To aid user understanding, these cash flows are divided into categories (for example, those relating to investments in non-current assets). Cash inflows and outflows falling within each category are added together to provide a total for that category. These totals are shown on the statement of cash flows and, when added together, reveal the net increase or decrease in cash (and cash equivalents) over the period.

When describing in detail how this statement is prepared and presented, we shall follow the requirements of international accounting standard IAS 7 *Statement of Cash Flows*.

A DEFINITION OF CASH AND CASH EQUIVALENTS

IAS 7 defines cash as notes and coins in hand and deposits in banks and similar institutions that are accessible to the business on demand. Cash equivalents are short-term, highly liquid investments that are readily convertible to known amounts of cash and which are subject to an insignificant risk of changes of value. Figure 5.1 sets out this definition of cash equivalents in the form of a decision chart.

Activity 5.2 should clarify the types of items that fall within the definition of 'cash equivalents'.

Activity 5.2

At the end of its reporting period, Zeneb plc's statement of financial position included the following items:

1 A bank deposit account where one month's notice of withdrawal is required.
2 Ordinary shares in Jones plc (a Stock Exchange listed business).
3 A high-interest bank deposit account that requires six-months notice of withdrawal.
4 An overdraft on the business's bank current account.

Which (if any) of these four items would be included in the figure for cash and cash equivalents?

Your response should have been as follows:

1 A cash equivalent. It is readily withdrawable.
2 Not a cash equivalent. It can be converted into cash because it is Stock Exchange listed. There is, however, a significant risk that the amount expected (hoped for!) when the shares are sold may not actually be forthcoming.
3 Not a cash equivalent because it is not readily convertible into liquid cash.
4 This is cash itself, though a negative amount of it. The only exception to this classification would be where the business is financed in the longer term by an overdraft, when it would be part of the financing of the business, rather than negative cash.

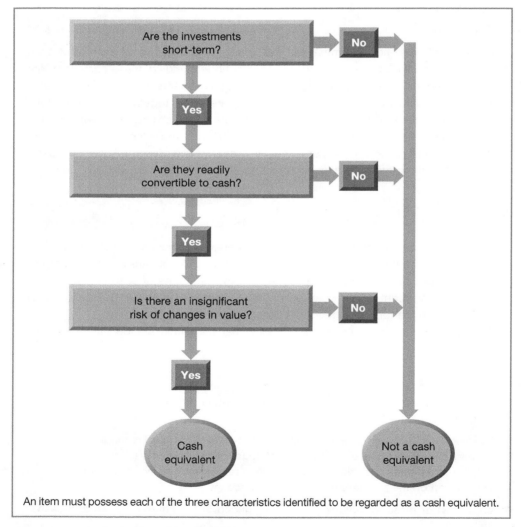

An item must possess each of the three characteristics identified to be regarded as a cash equivalent.

Figure 5.1 Decision chart for identifying cash equivalents

THE RELATIONSHIP BETWEEN THE MAIN FINANCIAL STATEMENTS

The statement of cash flows is now accepted, along with the income statement and the statement of financial position, as a major financial statement. The relationship between the three statements is shown in Figure 5.2. The statement of financial position reveals the various assets (including cash) and claims (including the shareholders' equity) of the business *at a particular point in time*. The statement of cash flows and the income statement explain the *changes over a period* to two of the items in the statement of financial position. The statement of cash flows explains the changes to cash. The income statement explains changes to equity, arising from trading operations.

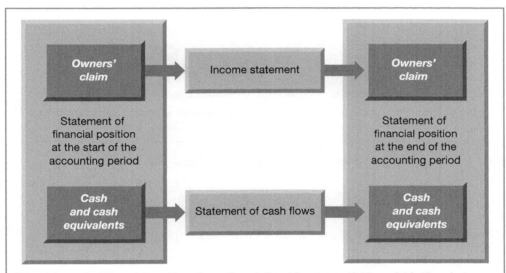

The statement of financial position shows the relationship, at a particular point in time, between the business's assets and claims. The income statement explains how, over a period between two statements of financial position, the equity figure in the first statement of financial position has altered as a result of trading operations. The statement of cash flows also looks at changes over the reporting period, but this statement explains the alteration in the cash (and cash equivalent) balances from the first to the second of the two consecutive statements of financial position.

Figure 5.2 The relationship between the statement of financial position, the income statement and the statement of cash flows

THE LAYOUT OF THE STATEMENT OF CASH FLOWS

As mentioned earlier, the cash flows of a business are divided into categories. The various categories and the way in which they are presented in the statement of cash flows are shown in Figure 5.3 below.

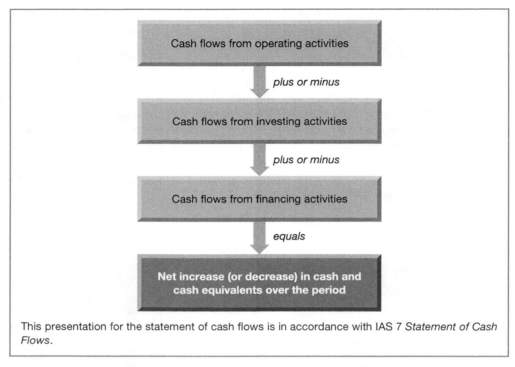

This presentation for the statement of cash flows is in accordance with IAS 7 *Statement of Cash Flows*.

Figure 5.3 Standard presentation for the statement of cash flows

Let us now consider each of the categories that has been identified.

Cash flows from operating activities

These represent the cash inflows and outflows arising from normal trading activities, after taking account of the tax paid and the financing costs (equity and borrowings) relating to these activities. Cash inflows are the amounts received from trade receivables and cash sales for the period. Cash outflows are the amounts paid for inventories, operating expenses (such as rent and wages), corporation tax, interest and dividends.

Note that it is cash inflows and outflows during a period that appear in the statement of cash flows, not revenue and expenses for that period. Similarly, tax and dividends that appear in the statement of cash flows are those actually paid in the period. Companies normally pay tax on their annual profits in four equal instalments. Two of these are paid during the year concerned and the other two are paid during the following year. Thus, by the end of each year, half of the tax will have been paid and the remaining half will still be outstanding, to be paid during the following year. This means that the tax payment during a year is normally equal to half of the previous year's tax charge and half of that of the current year.

Cash flows from investing activities

These include cash outflows to acquire non-current assets and cash inflows from the disposal of non-current assets. In addition to the normal items, such as buildings and machinery, non-current assets might include financial investments made in loans or shares in another company.

These cash flows also include cash inflows *arising from* financial investments (loans and shares). This means interest on loans made by the business and dividends from shares in other companies.

Cash flows from financing activities

These represent cash inflows and outflows relating to the long-term financing of the business. It, therefore, includes cash movements relating to the raising and redemption of long-term borrowings and to shares.

Under IAS 7, it is permissible to include dividend payments made by the business here, as an alternative to including them in 'Cash flows from operating activities' (above).

Net increase or decrease in cash and cash equivalents

The final total shown on the statement will be the net increase or decrease in cash and cash equivalents over the period. It will be deduced from the totals from each of the three categories mentioned above.

The effect on a business's cash and cash equivalents of activities relating to each catgory is shown in Figure 5.4. The arrows show the *normal* direction of cash flow for the typical, profitable, business in a typical reporting period.

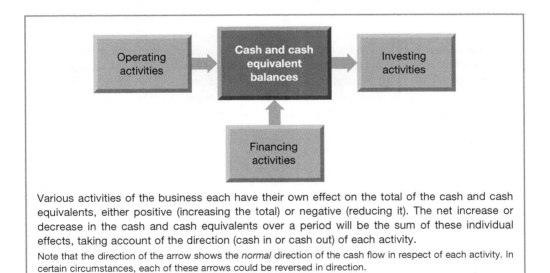

Various activities of the business each have their own effect on the total of the cash and cash equivalents, either positive (increasing the total) or negative (reducing it). The net increase or decrease in the cash and cash equivalents over a period will be the sum of these individual effects, taking account of the direction (cash in or cash out) of each activity.

Note that the direction of the arrow shows the *normal* direction of the cash flow in respect of each activity. In certain circumstances, each of these arrows could be reversed in direction.

Figure 5.4 Diagrammatical representation of the statement of cash flows

THE NORMAL DIRECTION OF CASH FLOWS

Normally, 'operating activities' provide positive cash flows and, therefore, increase the business's cash resources. For most UK businesses, cash generated from day-to-day trading, even after deducting tax, interest and dividends, is by far the most important source of new finance.

Activity 5.3

Last year's statement of cash flows for Angus plc showed a negative cash flow from operating activities. What could be the reason for this and should the business's management be alarmed by it? (*Hint*: We think that there are two broad possible reasons for a negative cash flow.)

The two reasons are:

1 The business is unprofitable. This leads to more cash being paid out to employees, to suppliers of goods and services, for interest and so on than is received from trade receivables in respect of sales. This would be alarming as a major expense for most businesses is depreciation. Since depreciation does not lead to a cash flow, it is not considered in 'net cash inflows from operating activities'. This means that a negative operating cash flow might well indicate a much larger trading loss – in other words, a significant loss of the business's wealth.

2 The business is expanding its activities (level of sales revenue). This may involve spending a lot of cash relative to the amount of cash coming in from sales. Cash will be spent on acquiring more assets (non-current and current) to accommodate the increased demand. For example, a business may need to have inventories in place before additional sales can be made. Similarly, staff will have to be employed and paid. Even when additional sales are made, they would normally be made on credit, with the cash inflow lagging behind the sales. This means that there would be no immediate cash benefit.

   Expansion often causes cash flow strains for new businesses, which may be expanding inventories and other assets from zero. They would also need to employ and pay staff. To add to this problem, increased profitability may encourage a feeling of optimism, leading to a lack of attention being paid to the cash flows.

Investing activities typically cause net negative cash flows. This is because many non-current assets either wear out or become obsolete and need to be replaced. Businesses may also expand their asset base. Non-current assets may, of course, be sold, which would give rise to positive cash flows. In net terms, however, the cash flows are normally negative with cash spent on new assets outweighing that received from the sale of old ones.

Financing can go in either direction, depending on the financing strategy at the time. Since businesses seek to expand, there is a general tendency for this area to lead to cash coming into the business rather than leaving it.

Real World 5.3 shows the summarised statement of cash flows of Tesco plc, the UK-based supermarket company.

REAL WORLD 5.3

Cashing in

Like many larger companies, Tesco produces summary versions of its financial statements for users who do not want all of the detail. The summary statement of cash flows for the business for the year ended 26 February 2011 shows the cash flows of the business under each of the headings described above.

Summary group statement of cash flows
52 weeks ended 26 February 2011

	£m
Cash generated from operations	5,366
Interest paid	(614)
Corporation tax paid	(760)
Net cash from operating activities	3,992
Net cash used in investing activities	(1,859)
Cash flows from financing activities	
Dividends paid to equity owners	(1,081)
Other net cash flows from financing activities	(1,955)
Net cash from financing activities	(3,036)
Net decrease in cash and cash equivalents	(903)

Source: Tesco Annual Review 2011, p. 35, www.tescocorporate.com.

As we shall see shortly, more detailed information under each of the main headings is provided in the statement of cash flows presented to shareholders and other users.

PREPARING THE STATEMENT OF CASH FLOWS

Deducing net cash flows from operating activities

As we have seen, the first category within the statement of cash flows is the 'cash flows from operating activities'. There are two approaches that can be taken to deriving this figure: the direct method and the indirect method.

The direct method

The **direct method** involves an analysis of the cash records of the business for the period, picking out all payments and receipts relating to operating activities. These are summarised to give the total figures for inclusion in the statement of cash flows. Done on a computer, this is a simple matter, but hardly any businesses adopt the direct method.

The indirect method

The **indirect method** is much the more popular method. It relies on the fact that, sooner or later, sales revenue gives rise to cash inflows and expenses give rise to outflows. This means that the figure for profit for the year will be closely linked to the net cash flows from operating activities. Since businesses have to produce an income statement in any case, information from it can be used as a starting point to deduce the cash flows from operating activities.

Of course, profit for the period will not normally equal the net cash inflows from operating activities. When sales are made on credit, the cash receipt occurs some time after the sale. This means that sales revenue made towards the end of a reporting period will be included in that reporting period's income statement. However, most of the cash from those sales will flow into the business, and should be included in the statement of cash flows, in the following period. Fortunately it is easy to deduce the cash inflows from sales if we have the relevant income statement and statements of financial position, as we shall see in Activity 5.4.

Activity 5.4

How can we deduce the cash inflows from sales using the income statement and statement of financial position for the business?

The statement of financial position will tell us how much was owed in respect of credit sales at the beginning and end of the reporting period (trade receivables). The income statement tells us the sales revenue figure. If we adjust the sales revenue figure by the increase or decrease in trade receivables over the period, we deduce the cash from sales for the period.

Example 5.1

The sales revenue figure for a business for the year was £34 million. The trade receivables totalled £4 million at the beginning of the year, but had increased to £5 million by the end of the year.

Basically, the trade receivables figure is dictated by sales revenue and cash receipts. It is increased when a sale is made and decreased when cash is received from a credit customer. If, over the year, the sales revenue and the cash receipts had been equal, the beginning-of-year and end-of-year trade receivables figures would have been equal. Since the trade receivables figure increased, it must mean that less cash was received than sales revenues were made. In fact, the cash receipts from sales must have been £33 million (that is, 34 − (5 − 4)).

Put slightly differently, we can say that as a result of sales, assets of £34 million flowed into the business. If £1 million of this went to increasing the asset of trade receivables, this leaves only £33 million that went to increase cash.

The same general point is true in respect of nearly all of the other items that are taken into account in deducing the operating profit figure. The main exception is depreciation. The depreciation expense for a reporting period is not necessarily associated with any movement in cash during that same period.

All of this means that we can take the profit before taxation (that is, the profit after interest but before taxation) for the year, add back the depreciation and interest expense charged in arriving at that profit, and adjust this total by movements in inventories, trade (and other) receivables and payables. If we then go on to deduct payments made during the reporting period for taxation, interest on borrowings and dividends, we have the net cash from operating activities.

Example 5.2

The relevant information from the financial statements of Dido plc for last year is as follows:

	£m
Profit before taxation (after interest)	122
Depreciation charged in arriving at profit before taxation	34
Interest expense	6
At the beginning of the year:	
Inventories	15
Trade receivables	24
Trade payables	18
At the end of the year:	
Inventories	17
Trade receivables	21
Trade payables	19

The following further information is available about payments during last year:

	£m
Taxation paid	32
Interest paid	5
Dividends paid	9

The cash flow from operating activities is derived as follows:

	£m
Profit before taxation (after interest)	122
Depreciation	34
Interest expense	6
Increase in inventories (17 – 15)	(2)
Decrease in trade receivables (21 – 24)	3
Increase in trade payables (19 – 18)	1
Cash generated from operations	164
Interest paid	(5)
Taxation paid	(32)
Dividends paid	(9)
Net cash from operating activities	118

As we can see, the net increase in **working capital*** (that is, current assets less current liabilities) as a result of trading was £162 million (that is, 122 + 34 + 6). Of this, £2 million went into increased inventories. More cash was received from trade receivables than sales revenue was made. Similarly, less cash was paid to trade payables than purchases of goods and services on credit. Both of these had a favourable effect on cash. Over the year, therefore, cash increased by £164 million. When account was taken of the payments for interest, tax and dividends, the net cash from operating activities was £118 million (inflow).

Note that we needed to adjust the profit before taxation (after interest) by the depreciation and interest expenses to derive the profit before depreciation, interest and taxation.

* Working capital is a term widely used in accounting and finance, not just in the context of the statement of cash flows. We shall encounter it several times in later chapters.

Activity 5.5

In deriving the cash generated from operations, we add the depreciation expense for the period to the profit before taxation. Does this mean that depreciation is a source of cash?

No, it does not mean that depreciation is a source of cash. The periodic depreciation expense is irrelevant to cash flow. Since the profit before taxation is derived *after* deducting the depreciation expense for the period, we need to eliminate the impact of depreciation by adding it back to the profit figure. This will give us the profit before tax *and before* depreciation, which is what we need.

We should be clear why we add back an amount for interest at the start of the derivation of cash flow from operating activities only to deduct an amount for interest further down. The reason is that the first is the interest expense for the reporting period, whereas the second is the amount of cash paid out for interest during that period. These may well be different amounts, as was the case in Example 5.2.

The indirect method of deducing the net cash flow from operating activities is summarised in Figure 5.5.

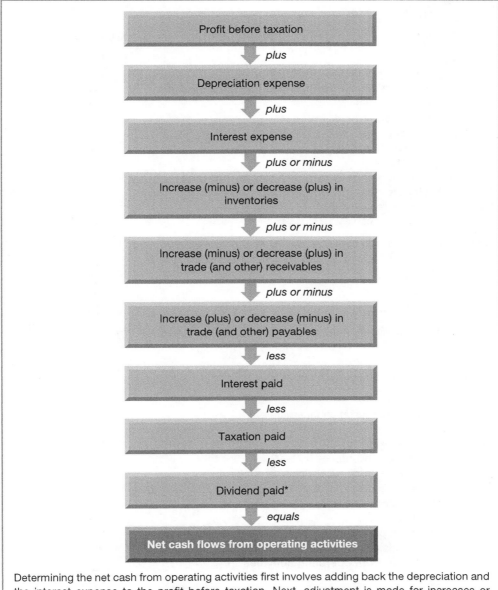

Determining the net cash from operating activities first involves adding back the depreciation and the interest expense to the profit before taxation. Next, adjustment is made for increases or decreases in inventories, receivables and payables. Lastly, cash paid for interest, taxation and dividends is deducted.

* Note that dividends could alternatively be included under the heading 'Cash flows from financing activities'.

Figure 5.5 The indirect method of deducing the net cash flows from operating activities

Activity 5.6

The relevant information from the financial statements of Pluto plc for last year is as follows:

	£m
Profit before taxation (after interest)	165
Depreciation charged in arriving at operating profit	41
Interest expense	21
At the beginning of the year:	
Inventories	22
Trade receivables	18
Trade payables	15
At the end of the year:	
Inventories	23
Trade receivables	21
Trade payables	17

The following further information is available about payments during last year:

	£m
Taxation paid	49
Interest paid	25
Dividends paid	28

What figure should appear in the statement of cash flows for 'Cash flows from operating activities'?

Net cash inflows from operating activities:

	£m
Profit before taxation (after interest)	165
Depreciation	41
Interest expense	21
Increase in inventories (23 − 22)	(1)
Increase in trade receivables (21 − 18)	(3)
Increase in trade payables (17 − 15)	2
Cash generated from operations	225
Interest paid	(25)
Taxation paid	(49)
Dividends paid	(28)
Net cash from operating activities	123

Deducing the other areas of the statement of cash flows

We can now go on to take a look at the preparation of a complete statement of cash flows through Example 5.3.

Example 5.3

Torbryan plc's income statement for the year ended 31 December 2012 and the statements of financial position as at 31 December 2011 and 2012 are as follows:

Income statement for the year ended 31 December 2012

	£m
Revenue	576
Cost of sales	(307)
Gross profit	269
Distribution expenses	(65)
Administrative expenses	(26)
	178
Other operating income	21
Operating profit	199
Interest receivable	17
Interest payable	(23)
Profit before taxation	193
Taxation	(46)
Profit for the year	147

Statements of financial position as at 31 December 2011 and 2012

	2010 £m	2011 £m
ASSETS		
Non-current assets		
Property, plant and equipment		
Land and buildings	241	241
Plant and machinery	309	325
	550	566
Current assets		
Inventories	44	41
Trade receivables	121	139
	165	180
Total assets	715	746
EQUITY AND LIABILITIES		
Equity		
Called-up ordinary share capital	150	200
Share premium account	–	40
Retained earnings	26	123
	176	363
Non-current liabilities		
Borrowings – loan notes	400	250
Current liabilities		
Borrowings (all bank overdraft)	68	56
Trade payables	55	54
Taxation	16	23
	139	133
Total equity and liabilities	715	746

During 2012, the business spent £95 million on additional plant and machinery. There were no other non-current-asset acquisitions or disposals. A dividend of £50 million was paid on ordinary shares during the year. The interest receivable revenue and the interest payable expense for the year were equal to the cash inflow and outflow respectively. £150,000 of loan notes were redeemed at their face (par) value.

The statement of cash flows would be as follows:

Torbryan plc
Statement of cash flows for the year ended 31 December 2012

	£m
Cash flows from operating activities	
Profit before taxation (after interest) (see Note 1 below)	193
Adjustments for:	
Depreciation (Note 2)	79
Interest receivable (Note 3)	(17)
Interest payable (Note 4)	23
Increase in trade receivables (139 – 121)	(18)
Decrease in trade payables (55 – 54)	(1)
Decrease in inventories (44 – 41)	3
Cash generated from operations	262
Interest paid	(23)
Taxation paid (Note 5)	(39)
Dividend paid	(50)
Net cash from operating activities	150
Cash flows from investing activities	
Payments to acquire tangible non-current assets	(95)
Interest received (Note 3)	17
Net cash used in investing activities	(78)
Cash flows from financing activities	
Repayments of loan notes	(150)
Issue of ordinary shares (Note 6)	90
Net cash used in financing activities	(60)
Net increase in cash and cash equivalents	12
Cash and cash equivalents at 1 January 2012 (Note 7)	(68)
Cash and cash equivalents at 31 December 2012	(56)

To see how this relates to the cash of the business at the beginning and end of the year it can be useful to provide a reconciliation as follows:

Analysis of cash and cash equivalents during the year ended 31 December 2012

	£m
Overdraft balance at 1 January 2012	(68)
Net cash inflow	12
Overdraft balance at 31 December 2012	(56)

Notes

1 This is simply taken from the income statement for the year.

2 Since there were no disposals, the depreciation charges must be the difference between the start and end of the year's plant and machinery (non-current assets) values, adjusted by the cost of any additions.

	£m
Carrying amount at 1 January 2012	309
Additions	95
	404
Depreciation (balancing figure)	(79)
Carrying amount at 31 December 2012	325

3 Interest receivable must be deducted to work towards what the profit would have been before it was added in the income statement, because it is not part of operations but of investing activities. The cash inflow from this source appears under the 'Cash flows from investing activities' heading.

4 The interest payable expense must be taken out, by adding it back to the profit figure. We subsequently deduct the cash paid for interest payable during the year. In this case the two figures are identical.

5 Taxation is paid by companies 50 per cent during their reporting year and 50 per cent in the following year. As a result the 2012 payment would have been half the tax on the 2011 profit (that is, the figure that would have appeared in the current liabilities at the end of 2011), plus half of the 2012 taxation charge (that is, $16 + (^1/_2 \times 46) = 39$). Probably the easiest way to deduce the amount paid during the year to 31 December 2012 is by following this approach:

	£m
Taxation owed at start of the year (from the statement of financial position as at 31 December 2011)	16
Taxation charge for the year (from the income statement)	46
	62
Taxation owed at the end of the year (from the statement of financial position as at 31 December 2012)	(23)
Taxation paid during the year	39

This follows the logic that if we start with what the business owed at the beginning of the year, add what was owed as a result of the current year's taxation charge and then deduct what was owed at the end, the resulting figure must be what was paid during the year.

6 The share issue raised £90 million, of which £50 million went into the share capital total on the statement of financial position and £40 million into share premium.

7 There were no 'cash equivalents', just cash (though negative).

WHAT DOES THE STATEMENT OF CASH FLOWS TELL US?

The statement of cash flows tells us how the business has generated cash during the period and where that cash has gone. This is potentially very useful information. Looking at the statement of cash flows for Torbryan plc, in Example 5.3, we can see the following:

■ Net cash flow from operations seems strong, much larger than the profit for the year, after taking account of the dividend paid. This might be expected as depreciation is deducted in arriving at profit. Working capital has absorbed some cash, which may indicate an expansion of activity (sales revenue) over the year. As we have only one year's income statement, however, we cannot tell whether this has occurred.

■ There were net outflows of cash for investing activities, but this would not be unusual. Many types of non-current assets have limited lives and need to be replaced. Expenditure during the year was not out of line with the depreciation expense for the year, which is to be expected for a business with a regular replacement programme for its non-current assets.

- There was a major outflow of cash to redeem borrowings, which was partly offset by the proceeds of a share issue. This may well represent a change of financing strategy. These financing changes, together with the retained profit for the year, have led to a significant shift in the equity/borrowings balance.

Real World 5.4 looks at the statement of cash flows of an emerging business, LiDCO Group plc, which is experiencing negative cash flows as it seeks to establish a profitable market for its products.

REAL WORLD 5.4

Not losing heart

LiDCO Group plc has its shares quoted on the Alternative Investment Market (AIM). AIM is a junior market of the London Stock Exchange that specialises in the shares of smaller, up-and-coming businesses.

LiDCO makes highly sophisticated equipment for monitoring the hearts of cardiac patients, typically in hospitals and clinics. The business was started by doctors and scientists. It has spent £6.8 million over ten years developing its products, obtaining registration for their use from both the UK and US authorities and creating manufacturing facilities.

LiDCO's statement of cash flows for the year to 31 January 2011 was:

	£000
Net cash outflow from operating activities	115
Cash flows from investing activities	
Purchase of property, plant and equipment	(127)
Purchase of intangible assets	(429)
Interest received	8
Net cash used in investing activities	(548)
Cash flows from financing activities	
Repayment of finance lease	(10)
Issue of ordinary share capital	1
Net cash (outflow)/inflow from financing activities	(9)
Net (decrease)/inflow in cash and cash equivalents	(442)

[Note that this was adapted from the statement that appeared in the business's annual report. Some more detail was supplied in the way of notes to the accounts.]

To put these figures into context, there was a loss before taxation for the year of £490,000 and the sales revenue for the year was £6.24 million. This means that the net cash inflow from operating activities was equal to 2 per cent of the revenue figure. This was an improvement, since it had been a negative (outflow) of 8 per cent in 2010, 27 per cent in 2009, 30 per cent in 2008, 40 per cent in 2007 and over 50 per cent in 2006.

2011 was the first year that the business had generated a positive net cash inflow from operating activities

Such cash flow profiles are fairly typical of 'high-tech' businesses that have enormous start-up costs to bring their products to the market in sufficient quantities to yield a profit. Of course, not all such businesses achieve this, but LiDCO seems to be turning into a profitable business.

Sources: LiDCO Group plc Annual Report 2011, and AIM company profile, www.londonstockexchange.com.

? SELF-ASSESSMENT QUESTION 5.1

Touchstone plc's income statements for the years ended 31 December 2011 and 2012 and statements of financial position as at 31 December 2011 and 2012 are as follows:

Income statements for the years ended 2011 and 2012

	2011	2012
	£m	£m
Revenue	173	207
Cost of sales	(96)	(101)
Gross profit	77	106
Distribution expenses	(18)	(20)
Administrative expenses	(24)	(26)
Other operating income	3	4
Operating profit	38	64
Interest payable	(2)	(4)
Profit before taxation	36	60
Taxation	(8)	(16)
Profit for the year	28	44

Statements of financial position as at 31 December 2011 and 2012

	2011	2012
	£m	£m
ASSETS		
Non-current assets		
Property, plant and equipment		
Land and buildings	94	110
Plant and machinery	53	62
	147	172
Current assets		
Inventories	25	24
Treasury bills (short-term investments)	–	15
Trade receivables	16	26
Cash at bank and in hand	4	4
	45	69
Total assets	192	241
EQUITY AND LIABILITIES		
Equity		
Called-up ordinary share capital	100	100
Retained earnings	30	56
	130	156
Non-current liabilities		
Borrowings – loan notes (10%)	20	40
Current liabilities		
Trade payables	38	37
Taxation	4	8
	42	45
Total equity and liabilities	192	241

Included in 'cost of sales', 'distribution expenses' and 'administrative expenses', depreciation was as follows:

	2011 £m	2012 £m
Land and buildings	5	6
Plant and machinery	6	10

There were no non-current asset disposals in either year.

The interest payable expense equalled the cash payment made during each of the years.

The business paid dividends on ordinary shares of £14 million during 2010 and £18 million during 2011.

The Treasury bills represent a short-term investment of funds that will be used shortly in operations. There is insignificant risk that this investment will lose value.

Required:

Prepare a statement of cash flows for the business for 2012.

The solution to this question can be found at the back of the book, in Appendix B.

SUMMARY

The main points of this chapter may be summarised as follows:

The need for a statement of cash flows

- Cash is important because no business can operate without it.
- The statement of cash flows is specifically designed to reveal movements in cash over a period.
- Cash movements cannot be readily detected from the income statement, which focuses on revenue and expenses rather than on cash inflows and outflows.
- Profit (or loss) and cash generated for the period are rarely equal.
- The statement of cash flows is a major financial statement, along with the income statement and the statement of financial position.

Preparing the statement of cash flows

- The statement of cash flows contains three major categories of cash flows: cash flows from operating activities, cash flows from investing activities, and cash flows from financing activities.
- The total of the cash movements under these three categories will provide the net increase or decrease in cash and cash equivalents for the period.
- A reconciliation can be undertaken to check that the opening balance of cash and cash equivalents plus the net increase (or decrease) for the period equals the closing balance.

→

Calculating the cash generated from operations

- The net cash flows from operating activities can be derived by either the direct method or the indirect method.

- The direct method is based on an analysis of the cash records for the period, whereas the indirect method uses information contained within the income statement and statements of financial position.

- The indirect method takes the operating profit for the period, adds back any depreciation charge and then adjusts for changes in inventories, receivables and payables during the period.

Interpreting the statement of cash flows

- The statement of cash flows shows the main sources and uses of cash.

- It provides an insight to the financing and investing activities of a business.

MyAccountingLab

Go to www.myaccountinglab.com to check your understanding of the chapter, create a personalised study plan, and maximise your revision time

KEY TERMS

direct method p. 160
indirect method p. 161

working capital p. 163

FURTHER READING

If you would like to explore the topics covered in this chapter in more depth, we recommend the following books:

Alexander, D. and Nobes, C., *Financial Accounting: An International Introduction*, 4th edn, Financial Times Prentice Hall, 2010, Chapter 13.

Elliott, B. and Elliott, J., *Financial Accounting and Reporting*, 15th edn, Financial Times Prentice Hall, 2012, Chapter 5.

International Accounting Standards Board, *2011 International Financial Reporting Standards IFRS* (2-volume set), 2011.

KPMG, *Insights into IFRS*, 8th edn, Sweet and Maxwell, KPMG, 2011, Section 2.3. A summary of this book is available free at www.kpmg.com.

? REVIEW QUESTIONS

Solutions to these questions can be found at the back of the book, in Appendix C.

5.1 The typical business outside the service sector has about 50 per cent more of its resources tied up in inventories than in cash, yet there is no call for a 'statement of inventories flows' to be prepared. Why is cash regarded as more important than inventories?

5.2 What is the difference between the direct and indirect methods of deducing cash generated from operations?

5.3 Taking each of the categories of the statement of cash flows in turn, in which direction would you normally expect the cash flow to be? Explain your answer.
(a) Cash flows from operating activities.
(b) Cash flows from investing activities.
(c) Cash flows from financing activities.

5.4 What causes the profit for the reporting period not to equal the net cash inflow?

✳ EXERCISES

*Exercises 5.1 and 5.2 are basic level, Exercise 5.3 is intermediate level and Exercises 5.4 and 5.5 are advanced level. Exercises with **coloured numbers** have solutions at the back of the book, in Appendix D.*

> If you wish to try more exercises, visit the website at www.myaccountinglab.com.

5.1 How will each of the following events ultimately affect the amount of cash?

(a) an increase in the level of inventories
(b) a rights issue of ordinary shares
(c) a bonus issue of ordinary shares
(d) writing off part of the value of some inventories
(e) the disposal of a large number of the business's shares by a major shareholder
(f) depreciating a non-current asset.

5.2 The following information has been taken from the financial statements of Juno plc for last year and the year before last:

	Year before last £m	Last year £m
Operating profit	156	187
Depreciation charged in arriving at operating profit	47	55
Inventories held at end of year	27	31
Trade receivables at end of year	24	23
Trade payables at end of year	15	17

Required:
What is the figure for cash generated from the operations for Juno plc for last year?

172

5.3 Torrent plc's income statement for the year ended 31 December 2011 and the statements of financial position as at 31 December 2010 and 2011 are as follows:

Income statement for the year ended 31 December 2011

	£m
Revenue	623
Cost of sales	(353)
Gross profit	270
Distribution expenses	(71)
Administrative expenses	(30)
Rental income	27
Operating profit	196
Interest payable	(26)
Profit before taxation	170
Taxation	(36)
Profit for the year	134

Statements of financial position as at 31 December 2010 and 2011

	2010 £m	2011 £m
ASSETS		
Non-current assets		
Property, plant and equipment		
Land and buildings	310	310
Plant and machinery	325	314
	635	624
Current assets		
Inventories	41	35
Trade receivables	139	145
	180	180
Total assets	815	804
EQUITY AND LIABILITIES		
Equity		
Called-up ordinary share capital	200	300
Share premium account	40	–
Revaluation reserve	69	9
Retained earnings	123	197
	432	506
Non-current liabilities		
Borrowings – loan notes	250	150
Current liabilities		
Borrowings (all bank overdraft)	56	89
Trade payables	54	41
Taxation	23	18
	133	148
Total equity and liabilities	815	804

During 2011, the business spent £67 million on additional plant and machinery. There were no other non-current asset acquisitions or disposals.

There was no share issue for cash during the year. The interest payable expense was equal in amount to the cash outflow. A dividend of £60 million was paid.

Required:

Set out the cash flows from operating activities for Torrent plc for the year ended 31 December 2011.

5.4 Chen plc's income statements for the years ended 31 December 2010 and 2011 and the statements of financial position as at 31 December 2010 and 2011 are as follows:

Income statements for the years ended 31 December 2010 and 2011

	2010 £m	2011 £m
Revenue	207	153
Cost of sales	(101)	(76)
Gross profit	106	77
Distribution expenses	(22)	(20)
Administrative expenses	(20)	(28)
Operating profit	64	29
Interest payable	(4)	(4)
Profit before taxation	60	25
Taxation	(16)	(6)
Profit for the year	44	19

Statements of financial position as at 31 December 2010 and 2011

	2010 £m	2011 £m
ASSETS		
Non-current assets		
Property, plant and equipment		
Land and buildings	110	130
Plant and machinery	62	56
	172	186
Current assets		
Inventories	24	25
Trade receivables	26	25
Cash at bank and in hand	19	–
	69	50
Total assets	241	236
EQUITY AND LIABILITIES		
Equity		
Called-up ordinary share capital	100	100
Retained earnings	56	57
	156	157
Non-current liabilities		
Borrowings – loan notes (10%)	40	40
Current liabilities		
Borrowings (all bank overdraft)	–	2
Trade payables	37	34
Taxation	8	3
	45	39
Total equity and liabilities	241	236

$\rightarrow$

Included in 'cost of sales', 'distribution expenses' and 'administrative expenses', depreciation was as follows:

	2010 £m	2011 £m
Land and buildings	6	10
Plant and machinery	10	12

There were no non-current asset disposals in either year. The amount of cash paid for interest equalled the expense in each years. Dividends were paid totalling £18 million in each year.

Required:
Prepare a statement of cash flows for the business for 2011.

5.5 The following financial statements for Blackstone plc are a slightly simplified set of published accounts. Blackstone plc is an engineering business that developed a new range of products four years ago. These products now account for 60 per cent of its turnover.

Income statement for the years ended 31 March

	Notes	2011 £m	2012 £m
Revenue		7,003	11,205
Cost of sales		(3,748)	(5,809)
Gross profit		3,255	5,396
Operating expenses		(2,205)	(3,087)
Operating profit		1,050	2,309
Interest payable	1	(216)	(456)
Profit before taxation		834	1,853
Taxation		(210)	(390)
Profit for the year		624	1,463

Statements of financial position as at 31 March

	Notes	2011 £m	2012 £m
ASSETS			
Non-current assets			
Property, plant and equipment	2	4,300	7,535
Intangible assets	3	–	700
		4,300	8,235
Current assets			
Inventories		1,209	2,410
Trade receivables		641	1,173
Cash at bank		123	–
		1,973	3,583
Total assets		6,273	11,818

	2011 £m	2012 £m
EQUITY AND LIABILITIES		
Equity		
Share capital	1,800	1,800
Share premium	600	600
Capital reserves	352	352
Retained earnings	685	1,748
	3,437	4,500
Non-current liabilities		
Borrowings – Bank loan (repayable 2015)	1,800	3,800
Current liabilities		
Trade payables	931	1,507
Taxation	105	195
Borrowings (all bank overdraft)	–	1,816
	1,036	3,518
Total equity and liabilities	6,273	11,818

Notes

1 The expense and the cash outflow for interest payable are equal for each year.

2 The movements in property, plant and equipment during the year are:

	Land and buildings £m	Plant and machinery £m	Fixtures and fittings £m	Total £m
Cost				
At 1 April 2011	4,500	3,850	2,120	10,470
Additions	–	2,970	1,608	4,578
Disposals	–	(365)	(216)	(581)
At 31 March 2012	4,500	6,455	3,512	14,467
Depreciation				
At 1 April 2011	1,275	3,080	1,815	6,170
Charge for year	225	745	281	1,251
Disposals	–	(305)	(184)	(489)
At 31 March 2012	1,500	3,520	1,912	6,932
Carrying amount				
At 31 March 2012	3,000	2,935	1,600	7,535

3 Intangible assets represent the amounts paid for the goodwill of another engineering business acquired during the year.

4 Proceeds from the sale of non-current assets in the year ended 31 March 2012 amounted to £54 million.

5 Dividends were paid on ordinary shares of £300 million in 2011 and £400 million in 2012.

Required:

Prepare a statement of cash flows for Blackstone plc for the year ended 31 March 2012. (*Hint*: A loss (deficit) on disposal of non-current assets is simply an additional amount of depreciation and should be dealt with as such in preparing the statement of cash flows.)

ANALYSING AND INTERPRETING FINANCIAL STATEMENTS

INTRODUCTION

In this chapter we shall consider the analysis and interpretation of the financial statements that we discussed in Chapters 2 and 3. We shall see how financial (or accounting) ratios can help in assessing the financial health of a business. We shall also consider the problems that are encountered when applying this technique.

Financial ratios can be used to examine various aspects of financial position and performance and are widely used for planning and control purposes. They can be very helpful to managers in a wide variety of decision areas, such as profit planning, pricing, working-capital management and financial structure.

Learning outcomes

When you have completed this chapter, you should be able to:

■ identify the major categories of ratios that can be used for analysis purposes;

■ calculate key ratios for assessing the financial performance and position of a business;

■ explain the significance of the ratios calculated;

■ discuss the limitations of ratios as a tool of financial analysis.

MyAccountingLab Visit www.myaccountinglab.com for practice and revision opportunities

FINANCIAL RATIOS

Financial ratios provide a quick and relatively simple means of assessing the financial health of a business. A ratio simply relates one figure appearing in the financial statements to another figure appearing there (for example operating profit in relation to sales revenue) or, perhaps, to some resource of the business (for example, operating profit per employee).

Ratios can be very helpful when comparing the financial health of different businesses. Differences may exist between businesses in the scale of operations. This means that a direct comparison of, say, the operating profit generated by each business may be misleading. By expressing operating profit in relation to some other measure (for example, capital employed), the problem of scale is eliminated. A business with an operating profit of, say, £10,000 and capital employed of £100,000 can be compared with a much larger business with an operating profit of, say, £80,000 and capital employed of £1,000,000 by the use of a simple ratio. The operating profit to capital employed ratio for the smaller business is 10 per cent (that is, (10,000/100,000) × 100%) and the same ratio for the larger business is 8 per cent (that is, (80,000/1,000,000) × 100%). These ratios can be directly compared, whereas a comparison of the absolute operating profit figures would be much less meaningful. The need to eliminate differences in scale through the use of ratios can also apply when comparing the performance of the same business over time.

By calculating a small number of ratios it is often possible to build up a revealing picture of the position and performance of a business. It is not surprising, therefore, that ratios are widely used by those who have an interest in businesses and business performance. Although ratios are not difficult to calculate, they can be difficult to interpret. It is important to appreciate that they are really only the starting point for further analysis.

Ratios help to highlight the financial strengths and weaknesses of a business, but they cannot, by themselves, explain why those strengths or weaknesses exist or why certain changes have occurred. Only a detailed investigation will reveal these underlying reasons. Ratios tend to enable us to know which questions to ask, rather than provide the answers.

Ratios can be expressed in various forms, for example as a percentage or as a proportion. The way that a particular ratio is presented will depend on the needs of those who will use the information. Although it is possible to calculate a large number of ratios, only a few, based on key relationships, tend to be helpful to a particular user. Many ratios that could be calculated from the financial statements (for example, rent payable in relation to current assets) may not be considered because there is no clear or meaningful relationship between the two items.

There is no generally accepted list of ratios that can be applied to the financial statements, nor is there a standard method of calculating many ratios. Variations in both the choice of ratios and their calculation will be found in practice. However, it is important to be consistent in the way in which ratios are calculated for comparison purposes. The ratios that we shall discuss are very popular – presumably because they are seen as useful for decision-making purposes.

FINANCIAL RATIO CLASSIFICATIONS

Ratios can be grouped into categories, with each category relating to a particular aspect of financial performance or position. The following broad categories provide a useful basis for explaining the nature of the financial ratios to be dealt with. There are five of them:

- *Profitability*. Businesses generally exist with the primary purpose of creating wealth for their owners. Profitability ratios provide insights relating to the degree of success in achieving this purpose. They express the profit made (or figures bearing on profit, such as sales revenue or overheads) in relation to other key figures in the financial statements or to some business resource.
- *Efficiency*. Ratios may be used to measure the efficiency with which particular resources have been used within the business. These ratios are also referred to as *activity* ratios.
- *Liquidity*. It is vital to the survival of a business that there are sufficient liquid resources available to meet maturing obligations (that is, amounts owing that must be paid in the near future). Some liquidity ratios examine the relationship between liquid resources held and amounts due for payment in the near future.
- *Financial gearing*. This is the relationship between the contribution to financing the business made by the owners of the business and the amount contributed by others, in the form of loans. The level of gearing has an important effect on the degree of risk associated with a business, as we shall see. Gearing ratios tend to highlight the extent to which the business uses borrowings.
- *Investment*. Certain ratios are concerned with assessing the returns and performance of shares in a particular business from the perspective of shareholders who are not involved with the management of the business.

These five key aspects of financial health that ratios seek to examine are summarised in Figure 6.1.

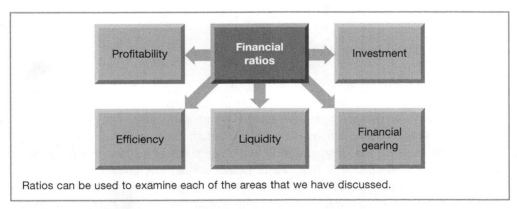

Ratios can be used to examine each of the areas that we have discussed.

Figure 6.1 The key aspects of financial health

The analyst must be clear *who* the target users are and *why* they need the information. Different users of financial information are likely to have different information needs, which will in turn determine the ratios that they find useful. For example, shareholders are likely to be particularly interested in their returns in relation to the level of risk associated with their investment. Profitability, investment and gearing ratios will, therefore, be of particular interest. Long-term lenders are concerned with the long-term viability of the business and, to help them to assess this, the profitability and gearing ratios of the business are also likely to be of particular interest. Short-term lenders, such as suppliers of goods and services on credit, may be interested in the ability of the business to repay the amounts owing in the short term. As a result, the liquidity ratios should be of interest.

THE NEED FOR COMPARISON

Merely calculating a ratio will not tell us very much about the position or performance of a business. For example, if a ratio revealed that a retail business was generating £100 in sales revenue per square metre of floor space, it would not be possible to deduce from this information alone whether this particular level of performance was good, bad or indifferent. It is only when we compare this ratio with some 'benchmark' that the information can be interpreted and evaluated.

Activity 6.1

Can you think of any bases that could be used to compare a ratio that you have calculated from the financial statements of your business for a particular period?
(*Hint*: There are three main possibilities.)

You may have thought of the following bases:

■ past periods for the same business;
■ similar businesses for the same or past periods;
■ planned performance for the business.

We shall now take a closer look at these three in turn.

Past periods

By comparing the ratio that we have calculated with the same ratio, but for a previous period, it is possible to detect whether there has been an improvement or deterioration in performance. Indeed, it is often useful to track particular ratios over time (say, five or ten years) to see whether it is possible to detect trends. The comparison of ratios from different periods brings certain problems, however. In particular, there is always the possibility that trading conditions were quite different in the periods being compared. There is the further problem that, when comparing the performance of a single business over time, operating inefficiencies may not be clearly exposed. For example, the fact that sales revenue per employee has risen by 10 per cent over the previous period may at first sight appear to be satisfactory. This may not be the case, however, if similar businesses have shown an improvement of 50 per cent for the same period or had much better sales revenue per employee ratios to start with. Finally, there is the problem that inflation may have distorted the figures on which the ratios are based. Inflation can lead to an overstatement of profit and an understatement of asset values, as will be discussed later in the chapter.

Similar businesses

In a competitive environment, a business must consider its performance in relation to that of other businesses operating in the same industry. Survival may depend on its ability to achieve comparable levels of performance. A useful basis for comparing a particular ratio, therefore, is the ratio achieved by similar businesses during the same period. This basis is not, however, without its problems. Competitors may have different year ends and so trading conditions may not be identical. They may also have different accounting policies, which can have a significant effect on reported profits and asset values (for example, different methods of calculating depreciation or valuing inventories). Finally, it may be difficult to obtain the financial statements of competitor businesses. Sole proprietorships and partnerships, for example, are not obliged to make their financial statements available to the public. In the case of limited companies, there is a legal obligation to do so. However, a diversified business may not provide a breakdown of activities that is sufficiently detailed to enable analysts to compare the activities with those of other businesses.

Planned performance

Ratios may be compared with the targets that management developed before the start of the period under review. The comparison of planned performance with actual performance may therefore be a useful way of revealing the level of achievement attained. However, the planned levels of performance must be based on realistic assumptions if they are to be useful for comparison purposes.

Planned performance is likely to be the most valuable benchmark against which managers may assess their own business. Businesses tend to develop planned ratios for each aspect of their activities. When formulating its plans, a business may usefully take account of its own past performance and the performance of other businesses. There is no reason, however, why a particular business should seek to achieve either its own previous level of performance or that of other businesses. Neither may be an appropriate target.

Analysts outside the business do not normally have access to the business's plans. For these people, past performance and the performances of other, similar, businesses may provide the only practical benchmarks.

CALCULATING THE RATIOS

Probably the best way to explain financial ratios is through an example. Example 6.1 provides a set of financial statements from which we can calculate important ratios.

Example 6.1

The following financial statements relate to Alexis plc, which operates a wholesale carpet business:

Statements of financial position (balance sheets) as at 31 March

	2011 £m	2012 £m
ASSETS		
Non-current assets		
Property, plant and equipment (at cost less depreciation)		
Land and buildings	381	427
Fixtures and fittings	129	160
	510	587
Current asset		
Inventories	300	406
Trade receivables	240	273
Cash at bank	4	–
	544	679
Total assets	1,054	1,266
EQUITY AND LIABILITIES		
Equity		
£0.50 ordinary shares (Note 1)	300	300
Retained earnings	263	234
	563	534
Non-current liabilities		
Borrowings – 9% loan notes (secured)	200	300
Current liabilities		
Trade payables	261	354
Taxation	30	2
Short-term borrowings (all bank overdraft)	–	76
	291	432
Total equity and liabilities	1,054	1,266

Income statements for the year ended 31 March

	2011 £m	2012 £m
Revenue (Note 2)	2,240	2,681
Cost of sales (Note 3)	(1,745)	(2,272)
Gross profit	495	409
Operating expenses	(252)	(362)
Operating profit	243	47
Interest payable	(18)	(32)
Profit before taxation	225	15
Taxation	(60)	(4)
Profit for the year	165	11

→

Notes

1 The market value of the shares of the business at the end of the reporting period was £2.50 for 2011 and £1.50 for 2012.
2 All sales and purchases are made on credit.
3 The cost of sales figure can be analysed as follows:

	2011	2012
	£m	£m
Opening inventories	241	300
Purchases (Note 2)	1,804	2,378
	2,045	2,678
Closing inventories	(300)	(406)
Cost of sales	1,745	2,272

4 At 31 March 2010, the trade receivables stood at £223 million and the trade payables at £183 million.
5 A dividend of £40 million had been paid to the shareholders in respect of each of the years.
6 The business employed 13,995 staff at 31 March 2011 and 18,623 at 31 March 2012.
7 The business expanded its capacity during 2012 by setting up a new warehouse and distribution centre.
8 At 1 April 2010, the total of equity stood at £438 million and the total of equity and non-current liabilities stood at £638 million.

A BRIEF OVERVIEW

Before we start our detailed look at the ratios for Alexis plc (in Example 6.1), it is helpful to take a quick look at what information is obvious from the financial statements. This will usually pick up some issues that ratios may not be able to identify. It may also highlight some points that could help us in our interpretation of the ratios. Starting at the top of the statement of financial position, the following points can be noted:

■ *Expansion of non-current assets*. These have increased by about 15 per cent (from £510 million to £587 million). Note 7 mentions a new warehouse and distribution centre, which may account for much of the additional investment in non-current assets. We are not told when this new facility was established, but it is quite possible that it was well into the year. This could mean that not much benefit was reflected in terms of additional sales revenue or cost saving during 2012. Sales revenue, in fact, expanded by about 20 per cent (from £2,240 million to £2,681 million); greater than the expansion in non-current assets.
■ *Major expansion in the elements of working capital*. Inventories increased by about 35 per cent, trade receivables by about 14 per cent and trade payables by about 36 per cent between 2011 and 2012. These are major increases, particularly in inventories and payables (which are linked because the inventories are all bought on credit – see Note 2).
■ *Reduction in the cash balance*. The cash balance fell from £4 million (in funds) to a £76 million overdraft, between 2011 and 2012. The bank may be putting the business under pressure to reverse this, which could raise difficulties.

- *Apparent debt capacity*. Comparing the non-current assets with the long-term borrowings implies that the business may well be able to offer security on further borrowing. This is because potential lenders usually look at the value of assets that can be offered as security when assessing loan requests. Lenders seem particularly attracted to land and buildings as security. For example, at 31 March 2012, non-current assets had a carrying amount (the value at which they appeared in the statement of financial position) of £587 million, but long-term borrowing was only £300 million (though there was also an overdraft of £76 million). Carrying amounts are not normally, of course, market values. On the other hand, land and buildings tend to have a market value higher than their value as shown on the statement of financial position due to inflation in property values.
- *Lower operating profit*. Though sales revenue expanded by 20 per cent between 2011 and 2012, both cost of sales and operating expenses rose by a greater percentage, leaving both gross profit and, particularly, operating profit massively reduced. The level of staffing, which increased by about 33 per cent (from 13,995 to 18,623 employees – see Note 6), may have greatly affected the operating expenses. (Without knowing when the additional employees were recruited during 2012, we cannot be sure of the effect on operating expenses.) Increasing staffing by 33 per cent must put an enormous strain on management, at least in the short term. It is not surprising, therefore, that 2012 was not successful for the business – not, at least, in profit terms.

Having had a quick look at what is fairly obvious, without calculating any financial ratios, we shall now go on to calculate and interpret some.

PROFITABILITY

The following ratios may be used to evaluate the profitability of the business:

- return on ordinary shareholders' funds;
- return on capital employed;
- operating profit margin;
- gross profit margin.

We shall now look at each of these in turn.

Return on ordinary shareholders' funds (ROSF)

The **return on ordinary shareholders' funds ratio** compares the amount of profit for the period available to the owners, with the owners' average stake in the business during that same period. The ratio (which is normally expressed in percentage terms) is as follows:

$$ROSF = \frac{\text{Profit for the year (less any preference dividend)}}{\text{Ordinary share capital + Reserves}} \times 100$$

The profit for the year (less any preference dividend) is used in calculating the ratio, as this figure represents the amount of profit that is attributable to the owners.

In the case of Alexis plc, the ratio for the year ended 31 March 2011 is:

$$\text{ROSF} = \frac{165}{(438 + 563)/2} \times 100 = 33.0\%$$

Note that, when calculating the ROSF, the average of the figures for ordinary shareholders' funds as at the beginning and at the end of the year has been used. This is because an average figure is normally more representative. The amount of shareholders' funds was not constant throughout the year, yet we want to compare it with the profit earned during the whole period. We know, from Note 8, that the amount of shareholders' funds at 1 April 2010 was £438 million. By a year later, however, it had risen to £563 million, according to the statement of financial position as at 31 March 2011.

The easiest approach to calculating the average amount of shareholders' funds is to take a simple average based on the opening and closing figures for the year. This is often the only information available, as is the case with Example 6.1. Averaging is normally appropriate for all ratios that combine a figure for a period (such as profit for the year) with one taken at a point in time (such as shareholders' funds).

Where not even the beginning-of-year figure is available, it will be necessary to rely on just the year-end figure. This is not ideal but, if this approach is consistently applied, it can produce ratios that are useful.

Activity 6.2

Calculate the ROSF for Alexis plc for the year to 31 March 2012.

The ratio for 2012 is:

$$\text{ROSF} = \frac{11}{(563 + 534)/2} \times 100 = 2.0\%$$

Broadly, businesses seek to generate as high a value as possible for this ratio. This is provided that it is not achieved at the expense of potential future returns by, for example, taking on more risky activities. In view of this, the 2012 ratio is very poor by any standards; a bank deposit account will normally yield a better return than this. We need to try to find out why things went so badly wrong in 2012. As we look at other ratios, we should find some clues.

Return on capital employed (ROCE)

The **return on capital employed ratio** is a fundamental measure of business performance. This ratio expresses the relationship between the operating profit generated during a period and the average long-term capital invested in the business.

The ratio is expressed in percentage terms and is as follows:

$$\text{ROCE} = \frac{\text{Operating profit}}{\text{Share capital} + \text{Reserves} + \text{Non-current liabilities}} \times 100$$

Note, in this case, that the profit figure used is the operating profit (that is, the profit *before* interest and taxation), because the ratio attempts to measure the returns to all suppliers of long-term finance before any deductions for interest payable on borrowings, or payments of dividends to shareholders, are made.

For the year to 31 March 2011, the ratio for Alexis plc is:

$$\text{ROCE} = \frac{243}{(638 + 763)/2} \times 100 = 34.7\%$$

(The capital employed figure, which is the total equity plus non-current liabilities, at 1 April 2010 is given in Note 8).

ROCE is considered by many to be a primary measure of profitability. It compares inputs (capital invested) with outputs (operating profit). This comparison is vital in assessing the effectiveness with which funds have been deployed. Once again, an average figure for capital employed should be used where the information is available.

Activity 6.3

Calculate the ROCE for Alexis plc for the year to 31 March 2012.

The ratio for 2012 is:

$$\text{ROCE} = \frac{47}{(763 + 834)/2} \times 100 = 5.9\%$$

This ratio tells much the same story as ROSF; namely a poor performance, with the return on the assets being less than the rate that the business has to pay for most of its borrowed funds (that is, 10 per cent for the loan notes).

Real World 6.1 shows how financial ratios are used by businesses as a basis for setting profitability targets.

REAL WORLD 6.1

Targeting profitability

The ROCE ratio is widely used by businesses when establishing targets for profitability. These targets are sometimes made public and here are some examples:

■ Air France-KLM, the world's largest airline (on the basis of sales revenue) has set itself the target of achieving a ROCE of 7 per cent.
■ BMW, the car maker, has a long-term target ROCE in excess of 26 per cent.
■ Marks and Spencer plc, the retailer, announced in June 2011 a target return on capital employed for new capital invested of 12 to 15 per cent over three years.
■ Tesco plc, the supermarket chain, aims to increase ROCE to 14.6 per cent by 2015. So far this has not been achieved and, in 2011, ROCE was 12.9 per cent.
■ EasyJet, the budget airline, has a target ROCE of 12 per cent.

Sources: Information taken from Air France-KLM, press release, 14 February 2008; 'BMW adds to carmakers' gloom', FT.com, 1 August 2008; 'M&S to shake up executive pay to reflect Bolland plan', 8 June 2011, FT.com;. 'Tesco looking afar for growth', 19 April 2011, FT.com; 'Sir Stelios fires warning shot at EasyJet', 4 January 2011, FT.com.

Real World 6.2 provides some indication of the levels of ROCE achieved by UK businesses.

REAL WORLD 6.2

Achieving profitability

ROCE ratios for UK manufacturing and service companies for each of the five years ending in 2010 are shown in Figure 6.2.

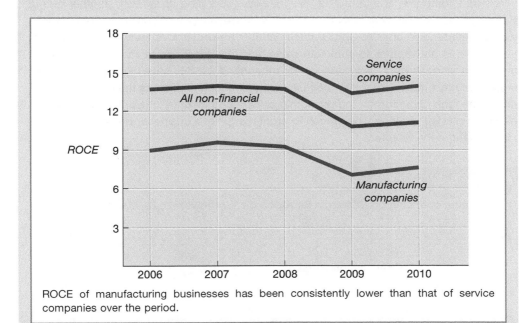

ROCE of manufacturing businesses has been consistently lower than that of service companies over the period.

Figure 6.2 The ROCE of UK companies

According to the Office of National Statistics, the difference in ROCE between the two sectors is accounted for by the higher capital intensity of manufacturing.

Source: Figure compiled from information taken from 'Profitability of UK companies Q1 2011', Office of National Statistics (www.statistics.gov.uk/), 6 July 2011.

Operating profit margin

The **operating profit margin ratio** relates the operating profit for the period to the sales revenue. The ratio is expressed as follows:

$$\text{Operating profit margin} = \frac{\text{Operating profit}}{\text{Sales revenue}} \times 100$$

The operating profit (that is, profit before interest and taxation) is used in this ratio as it represents the profit from trading operations before the interest payable expense is taken into account. This is often regarded as the most appropriate measure of operational performance, when used as a basis of comparison, because differences arising from the way in which the business is financed will not influence the measure.

For the year ended 31 March 2011, Alexis plc's operating profit margin ratio is:

$$\text{Operating profit margin} = \frac{243}{2,240} \times 100 = 10.8\%$$

This ratio compares one output of the business (operating profit) with another output (sales revenue). The ratio can vary considerably between types of business. For example, supermarkets tend to operate on low prices and, therefore, low operating profit margins. This is done in an attempt to stimulate sales and thereby increase the total amount of operating profit generated. Jewellers, on the other hand, tend to have high operating profit margins but have much lower levels of sales volume. Factors such as the degree of competition, the type of customer, the economic climate and industry characteristics (such as the level of risk) will influence the operating profit margin of a business. This point is picked up again later in the chapter.

Activity 6.4

Calculate the operating profit margin for Alexis plc for the year to 31 March 2012.

The ratio for 2012 is:

$$\text{Operating profit margin} = \frac{47}{2,681} \times 100 = 1.8\%$$

Once again, a very weak performance compared with that of 2011. In 2011 for every £1 of sales revenue an average of 10.8p (that is, 10.8 per cent) was left as operating profit, after paying the cost of the carpets sold and other expenses of operating the business. By 2012, however, this had fallen to only 1.8p for every £1. It seems that the reason for the poor ROSF and ROCE ratios was partially, perhaps wholly, a high level of expenses relative to sales revenue. The next ratio should provide us with a clue as to how the sharp decline in this ratio occurred.

Real World 6.3 sets out the target operating profit margins for some well-known car manufacturers.

Gross profit margin

The **gross profit margin ratio** relates the gross profit of the business to the sales revenue generated for the same period. Gross profit represents the difference between sales revenue and the cost of sales. The ratio is therefore a measure of profitability in buying (or producing) and selling goods or services before any other expenses are taken into account. As cost of sales represents a major expense for many businesses, a change in

REAL WORLD 6.3

Profit driven

- BMW has set a target operating profit margin for 2011 of more than 8 per cent.
- Daimler has set a target operating profit margin for its Mercedes unit of 10 per cent to be achieved by the second half of 2012.
- Nissan has a target operating profit margin of 8 per cent and a target global market share of 8 per cent to be achieved by 2017.
- Toyota announced a medium-term target operating profit margin of 5 per cent in March 2011.
- Opel, the European arm of General Motors, aims to achieve an operating profit margin of 4 to 5 per cent by 2013.

Premium car manufacturers, such as BMW and Mercedes, appear to have higher targets for their operating profit margin than mass-market car manufacturers, although the target periods often differ.

Source: 'Emerging markets drive BMW profits', 4 May 2011, FT.com; 'Daimler has grand aims for small cars', 14 June 2010, FT.com; 'Nissan: Ghosn for broke', 28 June 2011, FT.com; 'Nissan: More China please', 27 June 2011, FT.com; 'Opel handed ambitious profit target', 17 December 2009, FT.com.

this ratio can have a significant effect on the 'bottom line' (that is, the profit for the year). The gross profit margin ratio is calculated as follows:

$$\text{Gross profit margin} = \frac{\text{Gross profit}}{\text{Sales revenue}} \times 100$$

For the year to 31 March 2011, the ratio for Alexis plc is:

$$\text{Gross profit margin} = \frac{495}{2,240} \times 100 = 22.1\%$$

Activity 6.5

Calculate the gross profit margin for Alexis plc for the year to 31 March 2012.

The ratio for 2012 is:

$$\text{Gross profit margin} = \frac{409}{2,681} \times 100 = 15.3\%$$

The decline in this ratio means that gross profit was lower *relative* to sales revenue in 2012 than it had been in 2011. Bearing in mind that:

Gross profit = Sales revenue – Cost of sales (or cost of goods sold)

this means that cost of sales was higher *relative* to sales revenue in 2012, than in 2011. This could mean that sales prices were lower and/or that the purchase price of carpets had increased. It is possible that both sales prices and purchase prices had reduced, but the former at a greater rate than the latter. Similarly they may both have increased, but with sales prices having increased at a lesser rate than purchase prices.

Clearly, part of the decline in the operating profit margin ratio is linked to the dramatic decline in the gross profit margin ratio. Whereas, after paying for the carpets sold, for each £1 of sales revenue, 22.1p was left to cover other operating expenses in 2011, this was only 15.3p in 2012.

The profitability ratios for the business over the two years can be set out as follows:

	2011	2012
	%	%
ROSF	33.0	2.0
ROCE	34.7	5.9
Operating profit margin	10.8	1.8
Gross profit margin	22.1	15.3

Activity 6.6

What do you deduce from a comparison of the declines in the operating profit and gross profit margin ratios?

We can see that the decline in the operating profit margin was 9 per cent (that is, 10.8 per cent to 1.8 per cent), whereas that of the gross profit margin was only 6.8 per cent (that is, from 22.1 per cent to 15.3 per cent). This can only mean that operating expenses were greater, compared with sales revenue in 2012, than they had been in 2011. The declines in both ROSF and ROCE were caused partly, therefore, by the business incurring higher inventories' purchasing costs relative to sales revenue and partly through higher operating expenses compared with sales revenue. We should need to compare these ratios with their planned levels before we could usefully assess the business's success.

The analyst must now carry out some investigation to discover what caused the increases in both cost of sales and operating expenses, relative to sales revenue, from 2011 to 2012. This will involve checking on what has happened with sales and inventories prices over the two years. Similarly, it will involve looking at each of the individual areas that make up operating expenses to discover which ones were responsible for the increase, relative to sales revenue. Here, further ratios, for example, staff expenses (wages and salaries) to sales revenue, could be calculated in an attempt to isolate the cause of the change from 2011 to 2012. In fact, as we discussed when we took an overview of the financial statements, the increase in staffing may well account for most of the increase in operating expenses.

Real World 6.4 discusses how high operating costs may adversely affect the future profitability of a leading car maker.

REAL WORLD 6.4

VW accelerates but costs vibrate

Volkswagen's fervent quest to overtake Japanese rival Toyota by 2018 threatens to exacerbate its already high cost structure and to hamper profitability in the coming years, analysts and industry executives have warned. The industry executives and analysts argue that VW's growth initiative – which involves a huge investment of €26.6 billion ($35.7 billion) in the next three years, the €16 billion takeovers of Porsche and its Salzburg dealership and a €1.7 billion stake in Japanese small car specialist Suzuki – will put the carmaker back on a low-(profit)margin track.

So far, Europe's largest carmaker has been one of the most successful during the crisis. The Wolfsburg-based manufacturer posted a €911 million profit after tax and a 1.2 per cent profit margin in 2009 at a time when many others were making losses. VW is now aiming for an industry-leading, pre-tax (profit) margin of more than 8 per cent in 2018, by which time it wants to become the world's leading car producer 'economically as well as ecologically', Martin Winterkorn, VW's chief executive, has said. The carmaker wants to lift its sales from 6.3 milliion cars in the past year to more than 10 million by 2018.

While few dispute that VW could overtake Toyota – which sold almost 9 million cars in 2009 – in terms of sales, the profitability target remains in doubt. 'There should be more doubt in the market about the sustainability of VW's profits,' says Philippe Houchois, analyst at UBS.

In spite of its success, VW's cost structure is still in dire straits, particularly in Germany. With its 370,000 global workforce, the partly state-owned carmaker trails almost all global rivals when it comes to statistics such as revenues or vehicles per employee. 'People forget that despite their large scale, VW has some of the worst cost-structures in the industry. They have abysmal labour productivity and high plant costs,' says Max Warburton, analyst at research firm Sanford Bernstein.

Mr Warburton says high margins have been the exception at VW. '2007 to 2008 represented a brief period of temporary profit maximisation delivered by a [now departed] temporary management team who made temporary, emergency cost cuts,' he says. VW disputes that it has taken its eye off cost-cutting. Hans Dieter Pötsch, the carmaker's chief financial officer, says that 'by optimising our purchasing and increasing productivity . . . we have reached cost cuts of €1 billion throughout 2009'. (In addition) . . . he points to the carmaker's ongoing productivity improvement target of 10 per cent each year.

VW's profit figures for last year paint a dark picture of the carmaker's cost structures. At least three of its nine brands – Seat, Bentley and Lamborghini, and probably also Bugatti whose results are not disclosed – were lossmaking, and are not expected to return to profit this year. VW's light truck operations only posted a profit after a one-off gain from the sale of its Brazil operations. Operating profit at the group's core brand, VW, was crimped by 79 per cent to €561 million, in spite of the marque benefiting hugely from European scrapping incentive programmes.

FT *Source*: Adapted from Schäfer, Daniel, 'Costs vibrate as VW accelerates', FT.com, 29 March 2010.

EFFICIENCY

Efficiency ratios are used to try to assess how successfully the various resources of the business are managed. The following ratios consider some of the more important aspects of resource management:

- average inventories turnover period;
- average settlement period for trade receivables;
- average settlement period for trade payables;
- sales revenue to capital employed;
- sales revenue per employee.

We shall now look at each of these in turn.

Average inventories turnover period

Inventories often represent a significant investment for a business. For some types of business (for example, manufacturers and certain retailers), inventories may account for a substantial proportion of the total assets held. Real World 12.1 on page 437 illustrates this. The **average inventories turnover period ratio** measures the average period for which inventories are being held. The ratio is calculated as follows:

$$\text{Average inventories turnover period} = \frac{\text{Average inventories held}}{\text{Cost of sales}} \times 365$$

The average inventories for the period can be calculated as a simple average of the opening and closing inventories levels for the year. However, in the case of a highly seasonal business, where inventories levels may vary considerably over the year, a monthly average may be more appropriate, should this information be available.

In the case of Alexis plc, the inventories turnover period for the year ended 31 March 2011 is:

$$\text{Average inventories turnover period} = \frac{(241 + 300)/2}{1{,}745} \times 365 = 56.6 \text{ days}$$

(The opening inventories figure was taken from Note 3 to the financial statements.)

This means that, on average, the inventories held are being 'turned over' every 56.6 days. So, a carpet bought by the business on a particular day would, on average, have been sold about eight weeks later. A business will normally prefer a short inventories turnover period to a long one, because holding inventories has costs, for example the opportunity cost of the funds tied up. When judging the amount of inventories to carry, the business must consider such things as the likely demand for them, the possibility of supply shortages, the likelihood of price rises, the amount of storage space available and their perishability/susceptibility to obsolescence.

This ratio is sometimes expressed in terms of weeks or months rather than days: multiplying by 52 or 12, rather than 365, will achieve this.

Activity 6.7

Calculate the average inventories turnover period for Alexis plc for the year ended 31 March 2012.

The ratio for 2012 is:

$$\text{Average inventories turnover period} = \frac{(300 + 406)/2}{2,272} \times 365 = 56.7 \text{ days}$$

The inventories turnover period is virtually the same in both years.

Average settlement period for trade receivables

Selling on credit is the norm for most businesses, except for retailers. Trade receivables are a necessary evil. A business will naturally be concerned with the amount of funds tied up in trade receivables and try to keep this to a minimum. The speed of payment can have a significant effect on the business's cash flow. The **average settlement period for trade receivables ratio** calculates how long, on average, credit customers take to pay the amounts that they owe to the business. The ratio is as follows:

$$\frac{\text{Average settlement period}}{\text{for trade receivables}} = \frac{\text{Average trade receivables}}{\text{Credit sales revenue}} \times 365$$

A business will normally prefer a shorter average settlement period to a longer one as, once again, funds are being tied up that may be used for more profitable purposes. Although this ratio can be useful, it is important to remember that it produces an *average* figure for the number of days for which debts are outstanding. This average may be badly distorted by, for example, a few large customers who are very slow or very fast payers.

Since all sales made by Alexis plc are on credit, the average settlement period for trade receivables for the year ended 31 March 2011 is:

$$\text{Average settlement period for trade receivables} = \frac{(223 + 240)/2}{2,240} \times 365 = 37.7 \text{ days}$$

(The opening trade receivables figure was taken from Note 4 to the financial statements.)

Activity 6.8

Calculate the average settlement period for Alexis plc's trade receivables for the year ended 31 March 2012.

The ratio for 2012 is:

$$\text{Average settlement period for trade receivables} = \frac{(240 + 273)/2}{2,681} \times 365 = 34.9 \text{ days}$$

On the face of it, this reduction in the settlement period is welcome. It means that less cash was tied up in trade receivables for each £1 of sales revenue in 2012 than in 2011. Only if the reduction were achieved at the expense of customer goodwill or a high direct financial cost might the desirability of the reduction be questioned. For example, the reduction may have been due to chasing customers too vigorously or as a result of incurring higher expenses, such as discounts allowed to customers who pay quickly.

Average settlement period for trade payables

The **average settlement period for trade payables ratio** measures how long, on average, the business takes to pay those who have supplied goods and services on credit. The ratio is calculated as follows:

$$\text{Average settlement period for trade payables} = \frac{\text{Average trade payables}}{\text{Credit purchases}} \times 365$$

This ratio provides an average figure, which, like the average settlement period for trade receivables ratio, can be distorted by the payment period for one or two large suppliers.

As trade payables provide a free source of finance for the business, it is perhaps not surprising that some businesses attempt to increase their average settlement period for trade payables. However, such a policy can be taken too far and result in a loss of goodwill of suppliers. We shall return to the issues concerning the management of inventories, trade receivables and trade payables in Chapter 12.

For the year ended 31 March 2011, Alexis plc's average settlement period for trade payables is:

$$\text{Average settlement period for trade payables} = \frac{(183 + 261)/2}{1,804} \times 365 = 44.9 \text{ days}$$

(The opening trade payables figure was taken from Note 4 to the financial statements and the purchases figure from Note 3.)

Activity 6.9

Calculate the average settlement period for trade payables for Alexis plc for the year ended 31 March 2012.

The ratio for 2012 is:

$$\text{Average settlement period for trade payables} = \frac{(261 + 354)/2}{2,378} \times 365 = 47.2 \text{ days}$$

There was an increase, between 2011 and 2012, in the average length of time that elapsed between buying inventories and services and paying for them. On the face of it, this is beneficial because the business is using free finance provided by suppliers. This is not necessarily advantageous, however, if it is leading to a loss of supplier goodwill that could have adverse consequences for Alexis plc.

Real World 6.5 reveals that paying promptly may also be desirable in order to keep small suppliers in business.

REAL WORLD 6.5

Feeling the squeeze

Large companies are increasingly monitoring the credit worthiness of their suppliers for fear that some of the smaller businesses may be at risk of collapse, according to Experian, the credit rating agency. Its claim, based on data and client feedback, suggests that large companies, previously criticised for unfairly squeezing smaller businesses by delaying payment to them, may now be realising that it is in their interests to look after these often vital elements of their supply chain.

This view is backed up by Experian's latest late payment figures, published on Thursday. They show that the time companies took to settle supplier bills in the fourth quarter of 2011 shrank slightly compared with the previous three months despite the economy taking a turn for the worse. On average, companies took 25.84 days beyond the agreed date set out in their terms to pay their suppliers, compared with 26.17 in the third quarter of 2011, with the biggest improvements coming from the largest companies. This runs counter to previous experience, when economic downturns have led to companies stretching out the time they take to pay suppliers in order to preserve some of the cash in their coffers.

Phil McCabe, FPB spokesman, said:

> Perhaps large companies are finally waking up to the fact that paying their suppliers late or imposing unfair changes to payment terms is damaging to their own businesses as well as small firms and the economy. Late payment forces businesses to close. Clearly, a smaller supplier base means less choice for these companies and, ultimately, their customers. Embracing prompt payment is simple commercial common sense.

The improving payment times are not solely down to improved behaviour among large companies, because smaller businesses are also better at getting money owed to them in on time, according to Gareth Rumsey, research director at Experian. 'It is easy to bash the larger businesses that are paying late, but you cannot ignore the need for smaller businesses to get their own house in order,' he said.

 Source: Adapted from Moules, Jonathon, 'Companies monitor companies credit scores', FT.com, 26 January 2012.

Sales revenue to capital employed

The **sales revenue to capital employed ratio** (or net asset turnover ratio) examines how effectively the assets of the business are being used to generate sales revenue. It is calculated as follows:

$$\text{Sales revenue to capital employed ratio} = \frac{\text{Sales revenue}}{\text{Share capital + Reserves + Non-current liabilities}}$$

Generally speaking, a higher sales revenue to capital employed ratio is preferred to a lower one. A higher ratio will normally suggest that assets are being used more productively in the generation of revenue. However, a very high ratio may suggest that the business is 'overtrading on its assets', that is, it has insufficient assets to sustain the level of sales revenue achieved. When comparing this ratio for different businesses, factors such as the age and condition of assets held, the valuation bases for assets and whether assets are leased or owned outright can complicate interpretation.

A variation of this formula is to use the total assets less current liabilities (which is equivalent to long-term capital employed) in the denominator (lower part of the fraction). The identical result is obtained.

For the year ended 31 March 2011 this ratio for Alexis plc is:

$$\text{Sales revenue to capital employed} = \frac{2,240}{(638 + 763)/2} = 3.20 \text{ times}$$

Activity 6.10

Calculate the sales revenue to capital employed ratio for Alexis plc for the year ended 31 March 2012.

The ratio for 2012 is:

$$\text{Sales revenue to capital employed} = \frac{2,681}{(763 + 834)/2} = 3.36 \text{ times}$$

This seems to be an improvement, since in 2012 more sales revenue was being generated for each £1 of capital employed (£3.36) than was the case in 2011 (£3.20). Provided that overtrading is not an issue, and that the additional sales are generating an acceptable profit, this is to be welcomed.

Sales revenue per employee

The **sales revenue per employee ratio** relates sales revenue generated during a reporting period to a particular business resource, that is, labour. It provides a measure of the productivity of the workforce. The ratio is:

$$\textbf{Sales revenue per employee} = \frac{\textbf{Sales revenue}}{\textbf{Number of employees}}$$

Generally, businesses would prefer a high value for this ratio, implying that they are using their staff efficiently.

For the year ended 31 March 2011, the ratio for Alexis plc is:

$$\text{Sales revenue per employee} = \frac{£2,240m}{13,995} = £160,057$$

Activity 6.11

Calculate the sales revenue per employee for Alexis plc for the year ended 31 March 2012.

The ratio for 2012 is:

$$\text{Sales revenue per employee} = \frac{£2,681m}{18,623} = £143,962$$

This represents a fairly significant decline and probably one that merits further investigation. As we discussed previously, the number of employees had increased quite notably (by about 33 per cent) during 2012 and the analyst will probably try to discover why this had not generated sufficient additional sales revenue to maintain the ratio at its 2011 level. It could be that the additional employees were not appointed until late in the year ended 31 March 2012.

The efficiency, or activity, ratios may be summarised as follows:

	2011	2012
Average inventories turnover period	56.6 days	56.7 days
Average settlement period for trade receivables	37.7 days	34.9 days
Average settlement period for trade payables	44.9 days	47.2 days
Sales revenue to capital employed (net asset turnover)	3.20 times	3.36 times
Sales revenue per employee	£160,057	£143,962

Activity 6.12

What do you deduce from a comparison of the efficiency ratios over the two years?

Maintaining the inventories turnover period at the 2011 level might be reasonable, though whether this represents a satisfactory period can probably only be assessed by looking at the business's planned inventories period. The inventories turnover period for other businesses operating in carpet retailing, particularly those regarded as the market leaders, may have been helpful in formulating the plans. On the face of things, a shorter receivables collection period and a longer payables payment period are both desirable. On the other hand, these may have been achieved at the cost of a loss of the goodwill of customers and suppliers, respectively. The increased sales revenue to capital employed ratio seems beneficial, provided that the business can manage this increase. The decline in the sales revenue per employee ratio is undesirable but, as we have already seen, is probably related to the dramatic increase in the level of staffing. As with the inventories turnover period, these other ratios need to be compared with the planned standard of efficiency.

RELATIONSHIP BETWEEN PROFITABILITY AND EFFICIENCY

In our earlier discussions concerning profitability ratios, we saw that return on capital employed (ROCE) is regarded as a key ratio by many businesses. The ratio is:

$$\text{ROCE} = \frac{\text{Operating profit}}{\text{Long-term capital employed}} \times 100$$

where long-term capital comprises share capital plus reserves plus long-term borrowings. This ratio can be broken down into two elements, as shown in Figure 6.3. The first ratio is the operating profit margin ratio and the second is the sales revenue to capital employed (net asset turnover) ratio, both of which we discussed earlier.

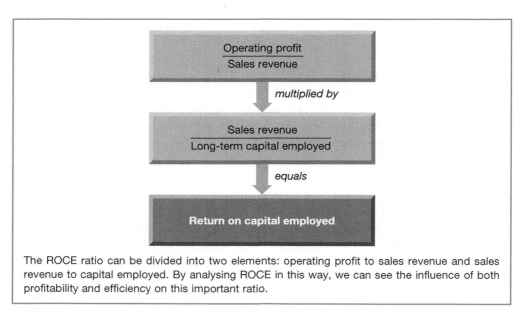

The ROCE ratio can be divided into two elements: operating profit to sales revenue and sales revenue to capital employed. By analysing ROCE in this way, we can see the influence of both profitability and efficiency on this important ratio.

Figure 6.3 The main elements of the ROCE ratio

By breaking down the ROCE ratio in this manner, we highlight the fact that the overall return on funds employed within the business will be determined both by the profitability of sales and by efficiency in the use of capital.

Consider the following information, for last year, concerning two different businesses operating in the same industry:

	Antler plc	Baker plc
	£m	£m
Operating profit	20	15
Average long-term capital employed	100	75
Sales revenue	200	300

The ROCE for each business is identical (20 per cent). However, the manner in which that return was achieved by each business was quite different. In the case of Antler plc, the operating profit margin is 10 per cent and the sales revenue to capital employed ratio is 2 times (so ROCE = 10% × 2 = 20%). In the case of Baker plc, the operating profit margin is 5 per cent and the sales revenue to capital employed ratio is 4 times (and so ROCE = 5% × 4 = 20%).

Example 6.2 demonstrates that a relatively high sales revenue to capital employed ratio can compensate for a relatively low operating profit margin. Similarly, a relatively low sales revenue to capital employed ratio can be overcome by a relatively high operating profit margin. In many areas of retail and distribution (for example, supermarkets and delivery services), operating profit margins are quite low but the ROCE can be high, provided that the assets are used productively (that is, low margin, high sales revenue to capital employed).

Activity 6.13

Show how the ROCE ratio for Alexis plc can be analysed into the two elements for each of the years 2011 and 2012. What conclusions can you draw from your figures?

	ROCE	=	*Operating profit margin*	×	*Sales revenue to capital employed*
2011	34.7%		10.8%		3.20
2012	5.9%		1.8%		3.36

As we can see, the relationship between the three ratios holds for Alexis plc for both years. The small apparent differences arise because the three ratios are stated here only to one or two decimal places.

Although the business was more effective at generating sales revenue (sales revenue to capital employed ratio increased) in 2012 than in 2011, in 2012 it fell well below the level necessary to compensate for the sharp decline in the effectiveness of each sale (operating profit margin). As a result, the 2012 ROCE was well below the 2011 value.

LIQUIDITY

Liquidity ratios are concerned with the ability of the business to meet its short-term financial obligations. The following ratios are widely used:

- current ratio;
- acid test ratio.

These ratios will now be considered.

Current ratio

The **current ratio** compares the 'liquid' assets (that is, cash and those assets held that will soon be turned into cash) of the business with the current liabilities. The ratio is calculated as follows:

$$\text{Current ratio} = \frac{\text{Current assets}}{\text{Current liabilities}}$$

Some people seem to believe that there is an 'ideal' current ratio (usually 2 times or 2:1) for all businesses. However, this fails to take into account the fact that different types of business require different current ratios. For example, a manufacturing business will often have a relatively high current ratio because it has to hold inventories of finished goods, raw materials and work-in-progress. It will also normally sell goods on credit, thereby giving rise to trade receivables. A supermarket chain, on the other hand, will have a relatively low ratio, as it will hold only fast-moving inventories of finished goods and all of its sales will be made for cash (no credit sales). Real World 12.1 on page 437 highlights these differences.

The higher the ratio, the more liquid the business is considered to be. As liquidity is vital to the survival of a business, a higher current ratio might be thought to be preferable to a lower one. If a business has a very high ratio, however, it may be that excessive funds are tied up in cash or other liquid assets and are not, therefore, being used as productively as they might otherwise be.

As at 31 March 2011, the current ratio of Alexis plc is:

$$\text{Current ratio} = \frac{544}{291} = 1.9 \text{ times (or } 1.9{:}1\text{)}$$

Activity 6.14

Calculate the current ratio for Alexis plc as at 31 March 2012.

The ratio as at 31 March 2012 is:

$$\text{Current ratio} = \frac{679}{432} = 1.6 \text{ times (or } 1.6{:}1\text{)}$$

Although this is a decline from 2011 to 2012, it is not necessarily a matter of concern. The next ratio may provide a clue as to whether there seems to be a problem.

Acid test ratio

The **acid test ratio** is very similar to the current ratio, but it represents a more stringent test of liquidity. For many businesses, inventories cannot be converted into cash quickly. (Note that, in the case of Alexis plc, the inventories turnover period was about 57 days in both years (see pages 193–4).) As a result, it may be better to exclude this particular asset from any measure of liquidity.

The minimum level for this ratio is often stated as 1.0 times (or 1:1; that is, current assets (excluding inventories) equal current liabilities). In many highly successful businesses that are regarded as having adequate liquidity, however, it is not unusual for the acid test ratio to be below 1.0 without causing particular liquidity problems.

The acid test ratio is calculated as follows:

$$\text{Acid test ratio} = \frac{\text{Current assets (excluding inventories)}}{\text{Current liabilities}}$$

The acid test ratio for Alexis plc as at 31 March 2011 is:

$$\text{Acid test ratio} = \frac{544 - 300}{291} = 0.8 \text{ times (or } 0.8{:}1)$$

We can see that the 'liquid' current assets do not quite cover the current liabilities, so the business may be experiencing some liquidity problems.

Activity 6.15

Calculate the acid test ratio for Alexis plc as at 31 March 2012.

The ratio as at 31 March 2012 is:

$$\text{Acid test ratio} = \frac{679 - 406}{432} = 0.6 \text{ times}$$

The 2012 ratio is significantly below that for 2011. The 2012 level may well be a cause for concern. The rapid decline in this ratio should lead to steps being taken, at least, to investigate the reason for this and, perhaps, to stop it falling further.

The liquidity ratios for the two-year period may be summarised as follows:

	2011	2012
Current ratio	1.9	1.6
Acid test ratio	0.8	0.6

Activity 6.16

What do you deduce from these liquidity ratios?

Although we cannot make a totally valid judgement without knowing the planned ratios, there appears to have been a worrying decline in liquidity. This is indicated by both of these ratios. The apparent liquidity problem may, however, be planned, short term and linked to the expansion in non-current assets and staffing. It may be that when the benefits of the expansion come on stream, liquidity will improve. On the other hand, short-term claimants may become anxious when they see signs of weak liquidity. This anxiety may lead them to press for payment, which could cause problems for Alexis plc.

FINANCIAL GEARING

Financial gearing occurs when a business is financed, at least in part, by borrowing instead of by finance provided by the owners (the shareholders) as equity. A business's level of gearing (that is, the extent to which it is financed from sources that require a fixed return) is an important factor in assessing risk. Where a business borrows, it takes on a commitment to pay interest charges and make capital repayments. Where the borrowing is heavy, this can be a significant financial burden; it can increase the risk of the business becoming insolvent. Nevertheless, most businesses are geared to some extent. (Costain Group plc, the builders and construction business, is a rare example of a UK business with no borrowings.)

Given the risks involved, we may wonder why a business would want to take on gearing (that is, to borrow). One reason may be that the owners have insufficient funds, so the only way to finance the business adequately is to borrow from others. Another reason is that gearing can be used to increase the returns to owners. This is possible provided that the returns generated from borrowed funds exceed the cost of paying interest. Example 6.3 illustrates this point.

Example 6.3

The long-term capital structures of two new businesses, Lee Ltd and Nova Ltd, are as follows:

	Lee Ltd £	Nova Ltd £
£1 ordinary shares	100,000	200,000
10% loan notes	200,000	100,000
	300,000	300,000

In their first year of operations, they each make an operating profit (that is, profit before interest and taxation) of £50,000. The tax rate is 30 per cent of the profit before taxation but after interest.

Lee Ltd would probably be considered relatively highly geared, as it has a high proportion of borrowed funds in its long-term capital structure. Nova Ltd is much lower geared. The profit available to the shareholders of each business in the first year of operations will be:

	Lee Ltd £	Nova Ltd £
Operating profit	50,000	50,000
Interest payable	(20,000)	(10,000)
Profit before taxation	30,000	40,000
Taxation (30%)	(9,000)	(12,000)
Profit for the year (available to ordinary shareholders)	21,000	28,000

The return on ordinary shareholders' funds (ROSF) for each business will be:

Lee Ltd	Nova Ltd
$\dfrac{21,000}{100,000} \times 100 = 21\%$	$\dfrac{28,000}{200,000} \times 100 = 14\%$

We can see that Lee Ltd, the more highly geared business, has generated a better ROSF than Nova Ltd. This is despite the fact that the ROCE (return on capital employed) is identical for both businesses (that is, (£50,000/£300,000) × 100 = 16.7%).

Note that at the £50,000 level of operating profit, the shareholders of both Lee Ltd and Nova Ltd benefit from gearing. Were the two businesses totally reliant on equity financing, the profit for the year (after taxation profit) would be £35,000 (that is, £50,000 less 30 per cent taxation), giving an ROSF of 11.7 per cent (that is, £35,000/£300,000). Both businesses generate higher ROSFs than this as a result of financial gearing.

An effect of gearing is that returns to shareholders become more sensitive to changes in operating profits. For a highly geared business, a change in operating profits will lead to a proportionately greater change in the ROSF ratio.

Activity 6.17

Assume that the operating profit was 20 per cent higher for each business than stated above (that is, an operating profit of £60,000). What would be the effect of this on ROSF?

The revised profit available to the shareholders of each business in the first year of operations will be:

	Lee Ltd £	Nova Ltd £
Operating profit	60,000	60,000
Interest payable	(20,000)	(10,000)
Profit before taxation	40,000	50,000
Taxation (30%)	(12,000)	(15,000)
Profit for the year (available to ordinary shareholders)	28,000	35,000

The ROSF for each business will now be:

Lee Ltd

$$\frac{28,000}{100,000} \times 100 = 28\%$$

Nova Ltd

$$\frac{35,000}{200,000} \times 100 = 17.5\%$$

We can see that for Lee Ltd, the higher-geared business, the returns to shareholders have increased by one-third (from 21 per cent to 28 per cent), whereas for the lower-geared business, Nova Ltd, the benefits of gearing are less pronounced, increasing by only one-quarter (from 14 per cent to 17.5 per cent). The effect of gearing can, of course, work in both directions. So, for a highly geared business, a small decline in operating profit will bring about a much greater decline in the returns to shareholders.

The reason that gearing tends to be beneficial to shareholders is that interest rates for borrowings are low by comparison with the returns that the typical business can earn. On top of this, interest expenses are tax-deductible, in the way shown in Example 6.3 and Activity 6.17. This makes the effective cost of borrowing quite cheap. It is debatable whether the apparent low interest rates really are beneficial to the shareholders. Some argue that since borrowing increases the risk to shareholders, there is a hidden cost of borrowing. What are not illusory, however, are the benefits to the shareholders of the tax deductibility of interest on borrowings.

The effect of gearing is like that of two intermeshing cogwheels of unequal size (see Figure 6.4). The movement in the larger cog (operating profit) causes a more than propor-tionate movement in the smaller cog (returns to ordinary shareholders). The subject of gearing is discussed further in Chapter 11.

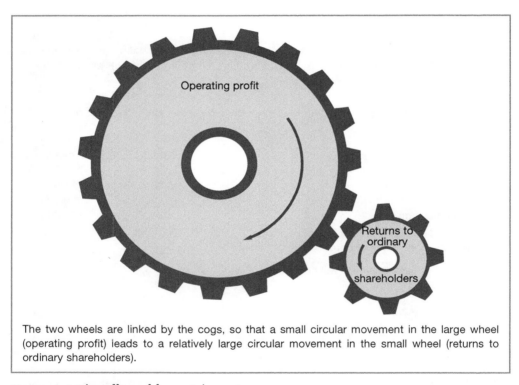

The two wheels are linked by the cogs, so that a small circular movement in the large wheel (operating profit) leads to a relatively large circular movement in the small wheel (returns to ordinary shareholders).

Figure 6.4 The effect of financial gearing

Two ratios are widely used to assess gearing:

■ gearing ratio;
■ interest cover ratio.

Gearing ratio

The **gearing ratio** measures the contribution of long-term lenders to the long-term capital structure of a business:

$$\text{Gearing ratio} = \frac{\text{Long-term (non-current) liabilities}}{\text{Share capital} + \text{Reserves} + \text{Long-term (non-current) liabilities}} \times 100$$

The gearing ratio for Alexis plc, as at 31 March 2011, is:

$$\text{Gearing ratio} = \frac{200}{(563 + 200)} \times 100 = 26.2\%$$

This is a level of gearing that would not normally be considered to be very high.

Activity 6.18

Calculate the gearing ratio of Alexis plc as at 31 March 2012.

The ratio as at 31 March 2012 is:

$$\text{Gearing ratio} = \frac{300}{(534 + 300)} \times 100 = 36.0\%$$

This is a substantial increase in the level of gearing over the year.

Interest cover ratio

The **interest cover ratio** measures the amount of operating profit available to cover interest payable. The ratio may be calculated as follows:

$$\text{Interest cover ratio} = \frac{\text{Operating profit}}{\text{Interest payable}}$$

The ratio for Alexis plc for the year ended 31 March 2011 is:

$$\text{Interest cover ratio} = \frac{243}{18} = 13.5 \text{ times}$$

This ratio shows that the level of operating profit is considerably higher than the level of interest payable. This means that a large fall in operating profit could occur before operating profit levels failed to cover interest payable. The lower the level of operating profit coverage, the greater the risk to lenders that interest payments will not be met, There will also be a greater risk to the shareholders that the lenders will take action against the business to recover the interest due.

Activity 6.19

Calculate the interest cover ratio of Alexis plc for the year ended 31 March 2012.

The ratio for the year ended 31 March 2012 is:

$$\text{Interest cover ratio} = \frac{47}{32} = 1.5 \text{ times}$$

Alexis plc's gearing ratios are:

	2011	2012
Gearing ratio	26.2%	36.0%
Interest cover ratio	13.5 times	1.5 times

Activity 6.20

What do you deduce from a comparison of Alexis plc's gearing ratios over the two years?

The gearing ratio altered significantly. This is mainly due to the substantial increase in the contribution of long-term lenders to the financing of the business.

The interest cover ratio has declined dramatically from a position where operating profit covered interest 13.5 times in 2011, to one where operating profit covered interest only 1.5 times in 2012. This was partly caused by the increase in borrowings in 2012, but mainly caused by the dramatic decline in profitability in that year. The later situation looks hazardous; only a small decline in future profitability would leave the business with insufficient operating profit to cover the interest payments. The gearing ratio at 31 March 2012 would not necessarily be considered to be very high for a business that was trading successfully. It is the low profitability that is the problem.

Without knowing what the business planned these ratios to be, it is not possible to reach a valid conclusion on Alexis plc's gearing.

Real World 6.6 is extracts from an article that discusses the likely lowering of gearing levels in the face of the recession. It explains that many businesses are likely to issue additional ordinary shares (equity) to reduce borrowing as a means of reducing gearing. Note that the gearing ratio mentioned in the article differs slightly from the one discussed above.

REAL WORLD 6.6

Changing gear

With a wave of rights issues and other equity issuance now expected from the UK's non-financial companies – and with funds from these being used to pay down debt – the pendulum is rapidly swinging back in favour of more conservative balance sheet (statement of financial position) management. Gearing levels are set to fall dramatically, analysts say. 'There is going to be an appreciable and material drop in gearing, by about a quarter or a third over the next three years', predicts Mr Siddall, chief executive of the Association of Corporate Treasurers.

Historically, gearing levels – as measured by net debt as a proportion of shareholders funds – have run at an average of about 30 per cent over the past 20 years. Peak levels (around 45 per cent) were reached in the past few years as companies took advantage of cheap credit. Current predictions see it coming down to about 20 per cent – and staying there for a good while to come. Graham Secker, managing director of equity research at Morgan Stanley says: 'This is going to be a relatively long-term phenomenon.'

One of the most immediate concerns to heavily indebted companies is whether, in a recessionary environment, they will be able to generate the profit and cash flows to service their debts.

Gearing levels vary from sector to sector as well. Oil companies prefer low levels given their exposure to the volatility of oil prices. BP's net debt-shareholders' funds ratio of 21 per cent is at the low end of a 20 to 30 per cent range it considers prudent. Miners' gearing is on a clear downward trend already. Xstrata, the mining group, stressed last month that its £4.1 billion rights issue would cut gearing from 40 per cent to less than 30 per cent. A week later, BHP said its $13 billion of first-half cash flows had cut gearing to less than 10 per cent. Rio Tinto, which had gearing of 130 per cent at the last count in August 2008, is desperately trying to cut it by raising fresh equity.

Utilities tend to be highly geared because they can afford to borrow more against their typically reliable cash flows. But even here the trend is downwards. Severn Trent, the UK water group, says its appropriate long-term gearing level is 60 per cent. But 'given ongoing uncertainties . . . it is prudent in the near term to retain as much liquidity and flexibility as possible'. It does not expect to pursue that target until credit markets improve.

Reducing gearing is not easy, especially for the most indebted companies that need to the most: shareholders will be more reluctant to finance replacement equity in companies with highly leveraged balance sheets. The supply of fresh equity will also be constrained, not only by a glut of demand from companies but by the squeeze on investor money from a wave of government bond issuance.

FT *Source*: Grant, Jeremy, 'Gearing levels set to plummet', *The Financial Times*, 10 February 2009.

INVESTMENT RATIOS

There are various ratios available that are designed to help shareholders assess the returns on their investment. The following are widely used:

- dividend payout ratio;
- dividend yield ratio;
- earnings per share;
- price/earnings ratio.

Dividend payout ratio

The **dividend payout ratio** measures the proportion of earnings that a business pays out to shareholders in the form of dividends. The ratio is calculated as follows:

$$\text{Dividend payout ratio} = \frac{\textbf{Dividends announced for the year}}{\textbf{Earning for the year available for dividends}} \times 100$$

In the case of ordinary shares, the earnings available for dividend will normally be the profit for the year (that is, the profit after taxation) less any preference dividends relating to the year. This ratio is normally expressed as a percentage.

The dividend payout ratio for Alexis plc for the year ended 31 March 2011 is:

$$\text{Dividend payout ratio} = \frac{40}{165} \times 100 = 24.2\%$$

The information provided by this ratio is often expressed slightly differently as the **dividend cover ratio**. Here the calculation is:

$$\text{Dividend cover ratio} = \frac{\textbf{Earning for the year available for dividend}}{\textbf{Dividend announced for the year}}$$

In the case of Alexis plc (for 2011) it would be 165/40 = 4.1 times. That is to say, the earnings available for dividend cover the actual dividend paid by just over four times.

Activity 6.21

Calculate the dividend payout ratio of Alexis plc for the year ended 31 March 2012.

The ratio for 2012 is:

$$\text{Dividend payout ratio} = \frac{40}{11} \times 100 = 363.6\%$$

This would normally be considered to be a very alarming increase in the ratio over the two years. Paying a dividend of £40 million in 2012 may be very imprudent.

Dividend yield ratio

The **dividend yield ratio** relates the cash return from a share to its current market value. This can help investors to assess the cash return on their investment in the business. The ratio, expressed as a percentage is:

$$\text{Dividend yield} = \frac{\text{Dividend per share}/(1-t)}{\text{Market value per share}} \times 100$$

where t is the 'dividend tax credit' rate of income tax. This requires an explanation. In the UK, investors who receive a dividend from a business also receive a tax credit. As this tax credit can be offset against any tax liability arising from the dividends received, the dividends are effectively issued net of income tax, at the dividend tax credit rate.

Investors may wish to compare the returns from shares with the returns from other forms of investment. As these other forms of investment are usually quoted on a 'gross' (that is, pre-tax) basis it is useful to 'gross up' the dividend to make comparison easier. We can achieve this by dividing the **dividend per share** by $(1 - t)$, where t is the 'dividend tax credit' rate of income tax.

Using the 2011/12 dividend tax credit rate of 10 per cent, the dividend yield for Alexis plc for the year ended 31 March 2011 is:

$$\text{Dividend yield} = \frac{0.067^*/(1 - 0.10)}{2.50} \times 100 = 3.0\%$$

The share's market value is given in Note 1 to Example 6.1 (page 184).

* Dividend proposed/number of shares = 40/(300 × 2) = £0.067 dividend per share (the 300 is multiplied by 2 because they are £0.50 shares).

Activity 6.22

Calculate the dividend yield for Alexis plc for the year ended 31 March 2012.

The ratio for 2012 is:

$$\text{Dividend yield} = \frac{0.067/(1 - 0.10)}{1.50} \times 100 = 5.0\%$$

Earnings per share

The **earnings per share (EPS)** ratio relates the earnings generated by the business, and available to shareholders, during a period, to the number of shares in issue. For equity (ordinary) shareholders, the amount available is the profit for the year (profit after taxation) less any preference dividend, where applicable. The ratio for equity shareholders is calculated as follows:

$$\text{Earnings per share} = \frac{\text{Earnings available to ordinary shareholders}}{\text{Number of ordinary shares in issue}}$$

In the case of Alexis plc, the earnings per share for the year ended 31 March 2011 is as follows:

$$EPS = \frac{£165m}{600m} = 27.5p$$

Many investment analysts regard the EPS ratio as a fundamental measure of share performance. The trend in earnings per share over time is used to help assess the investment potential of a business's shares. Although it is possible to make total profit rise through ordinary shareholders investing more in the business, this will not necessarily mean that the profitability *per share* will rise as a result.

It is not usually very helpful to compare the EPS of one business with that of another. Differences in financing arrangements (for example, in the nominal value of shares issued) can render any such comparison meaningless. However, it can be very useful to monitor the changes that occur in this ratio for a particular business over time.

Activity 6.23

Calculate the earnings per share of Alexis plc for the year ended 31 March 2012.

The ratio for 2012 is:

$$EPS = \frac{£11m}{600\,m} = 1.8p$$

Price/earnings (P/E) ratio

The **price/earnings ratio** relates the market value of a share to the earnings per share. This ratio can be calculated as follows:

$$P/E\ ratio = \frac{\textbf{Market value per share}}{\textbf{Earnings per share}}$$

The P/E ratio for Alexis plc as at 31 March 2011 is:

$$P/E\ ratio = \frac{£2.50}{27.5p^*} = 9.1\ times$$

*The EPS figure (27.5p) was calculated above.

This ratio indicates that the market value of the share is 9.1 times higher than its current level of earnings. The ratio is a measure of market confidence in the future of a business. The higher the P/E ratio, the greater the confidence in the future earning power of the business and, consequently, the more investors are prepared to pay in relation to the earnings stream of the business.

P/E ratios provide a useful guide to market confidence concerning the future and they can, therefore, be helpful when comparing different businesses. However, differences in accounting policies between businesses can lead to different profit and earnings per share figures. This can distort comparisons.

Activity 6.24

Calculate the P/E ratio of Alexis plc as at 31 March 2012.

The ratio for 2012 is:

$$P/E \text{ ratio} = \frac{£1.50}{1.8p} = 83.3 \text{ times}$$

The investment ratios for Alexis plc over the two-year period are as follows:

	2011	2012
Dividend payout ratio	24.2%	363.6%
Dividend yield ratio	3.0%	5.0%
Earnings per share	27.5p	1.8p
P/E ratio	9.1 times	83.3 times

Activity 6.25

What do you deduce from these investment ratios?
   Can you offer an explanation why the share price has not fallen as much as it might have done, bearing in mind the very poor (relative to 2011) trading performance in 2012?

Although the EPS has fallen dramatically and the dividend payment for 2012 seems very imprudent, the share price seems to have held up remarkably well (fallen from £2.50 to £1.50). This means that dividend yield and P/E value for 2012 look better than those for 2011. This is an anomaly of these two ratios, which stems from using a forward-looking value (the share price) in conjunction with historic data (dividends and earnings). Share prices are based on investors' assessments of the business's future. It seems with Alexis plc that, at the end of 2012, the 'market' was not happy with the business, relative to 2011. This is evidenced by the fact that the share price had fallen by £1 a share. On the other hand, the share price has not fallen as much as profit for the year. It appears that investors believe that the business will perform better in the future than it did in 2012. This may well be because they believe that the large expansion in assets and employee numbers that occurred in 2012 will yield benefits in the future; benefits that the business was not able to generate during 2012.

Real World 6.7 provides information about the share performance of a selection of large, well-known UK businesses. This type of information is provided on a daily basis by several newspapers, notably the *Financial Times*.

REAL WORLD 6.7

Market statistics for some well-known businesses

The following data was extracted from the *Financial Times* of 14 February 2012, relating to the previous day's trading of the shares of some well-known businesses on the London Stock Exchange:

Share	Price	Chng	52 Week		Y'ld	P/E	Volume
			High	Low			000s
Marks and Spencer	348.80	−1.40	411.20	296.20	4.9	9.0	6,362
J D Wetherspoon	410	+1.80	473	370.60	2.9	10.4	92
National Express	227.30	+2.60	272.50	198.90	4.0	11.2	931
Tesco	319.40	−1.25	490.50	280.40	4.6	10.3	35,561
Rolls-Royce	779.50	+7	794	311.06	2.0	17.2	5,279
TUI Travel	207.50	+5.70	266.40	134.10	5.4	8.8	4,125

The column headings are as follows:

Price   Mid-market price in pence (that is, the price midway between buying and selling price) of the shares at the end of trading on 13 February 2012.

Chng   Gain or loss in the mid-market price during 13 February 2012.

High/Low   Highest and lowest prices reached by the share during the 52 weeks ended on 13 February 2012.

Y'ld   Gross dividend yield, based on the most recent year's dividend and the current share price.

P/E   Price/earnings ratio, based on the most recent year's (after-tax) profit for the year and the current share price.

Volume   The number of shares (in thousands) that were bought/sold on 13 February 2012.

So, for example for Marks and Spencer plc, the retail business:

- the shares had a mid-market price of 348.80p each at the close of Stock Exchange trading on 13 February 2012;
- the shares had decreased in price by 1.40p during trading on 13 February 2012;
- the shares had highest and lowest prices during the previous 52 weeks of 411.20p and 296.20p, respectively;
- the shares had a dividend yield, based on the 13 February 2012 price (and the dividend for the most recent year) of 4.9 per cent;
- the shares had a P/E ratio, based on the 13 February 2012 price (and the after-taxation earnings per share for the most recent year) of 9.0;
- during trading on 13 February 2012, 6,362,000 of the business's shares had changed hands between buyers and sellers.

FT   *Source*: Taken from share data in *Financial Times*, 14 February 2012, p. 28.

Real World 6.8 shows how investment ratios can vary between different industry sectors.

REAL WORLD 6.8

Yielding dividends

Investment ratios can vary significantly between businesses and between industries. To give some indication of the range of variations that occur, the average dividend yield ratios and average P/E ratios for listed businesses in twelve different industries are shown in Figures 6.5 and 6.6, respectively.

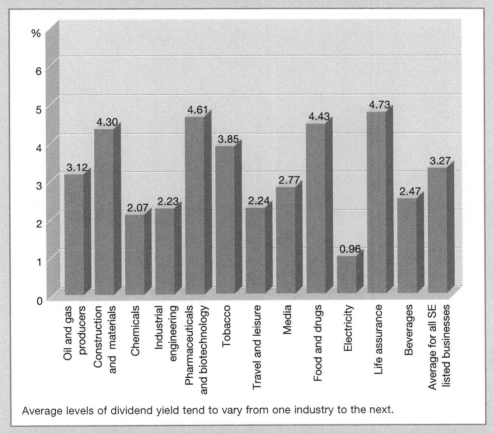

Average levels of dividend yield tend to vary from one industry to the next.

Figure 6.5 Average dividend yield ratios for businesses in a range of industries

These dividend yield ratios are calculated from the current market value of the shares and the most recent year's dividend paid.

Some industries tend to pay out lower dividends than others, leading to lower dividend yield ratios. The average for all Stock Exchange listed businesses was 3.27 per cent (as is shown in Figure 6.5), but there is a wide variation with Electricity at 0.96 per cent and Life Insurance/Assurance at 4.73 per cent.

Some types of businesses tend to invest heavily in developing new products, hence their tendency to pay low dividends compared with their share prices. Some of the inter-industry differences in the dividend yield ratio can be explained by the nature of the calculation of the ratio. The prices of shares at any given moment are based on expectations of their economic futures; dividends are actual past events. A business that had a good trading year recently may have paid a dividend that, in the light of investors' assessment of the business's economic future, may be high (a high dividend yield).

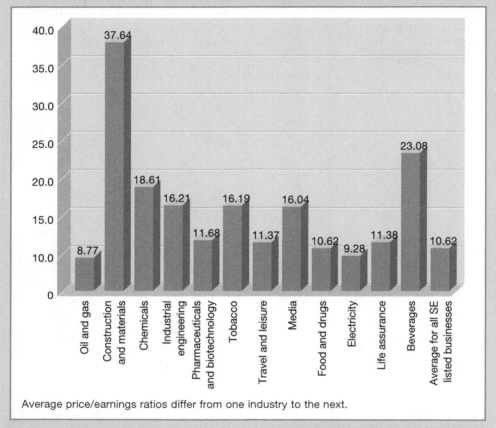

Average price/earnings ratios differ from one industry to the next.

Figure 6.6 Average price/earnings ratios for businesses in a range of industries

These P/E ratios are calculated from the current market value of the shares and the most recent year's earnings per share (EPS).

Businesses that have a high share price relative to their recent historic earnings have high P/E ratios. This may be because their future is regarded as economically bright, which may be the result of investing heavily in the future at the expense of recent profits (earnings). On the other hand, high P/Es also arise where businesses have recent low earnings but investors believe that their future is brighter. The average P/E for all Stock Exchange listed businesses was 10.62 times, but Oil and Gas Producers was as low as 8.77 times and Construction and Materials as high as 37.64 times.

FT   *Source*: Both figures are constructed from share data appearing in the *Financial Times*, 11/12 February 2012, p. 24.

TREND ANALYSIS

It is often helpful to see whether ratios are indicating trends. Key ratios can be plotted on a graph to provide a simple visual display of changes occurring over time. The trends occurring within a business may, for example, be plotted against trends for rival businesses or for the industry as a whole for comparison purposes. An example of trend analysis is shown in **Real World 6.9**.

REAL WORLD 6.9

Trend setting

In Figure 6.7, the current ratio of three of the UK's leading supermarkets is plotted over time. We can see that the current ratios of the three businesses have tended to move closer. Tesco plc was lower than that of its main rivals, until 2005, when it overtook Morrison and 2009, when it overtook Sainsbury. The current ratio of Sainsbury shows a fairly consistent downward path (although in 2010 it increased). With well-managed businesses like Sainsbury and Tesco, it seems highly probable that these changes are the result of deliberate policy.

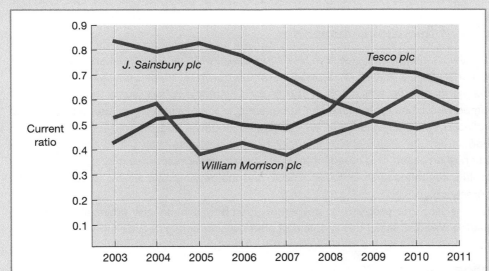

The current ratio for three leading UK supermarkets is plotted for the financial years ended during 2003 to 2011. This enables comparison to be made regarding the ratio, both for each of the three businesses over time and, between the businesses.

Figure 6.7 Graph plotting current ratio against time

Source: Annual reports of the three businesses 2003 to 2011.

USING RATIOS TO PREDICT FINANCIAL FAILURE

Financial ratios, based on current or past performance, have long been used to help predict the future. However, both the choice of ratios and the interpretation of results had normally been dependent on the judgement and opinion of the analyst. Attempts have been made, however, to develop a more rigorous and systematic approach to the use of ratios for prediction purposes. In particular, researchers have investigated the ability of ratios to predict the financial failure of a business. Several methods and models using ratios have been developed that are claimed to predict future financial failure. By financial failure, we mean a business either being forced out of business or being severely affected by an inability to meet its financial obligations. Researchers have also developed ratio-based models with which to assess the vulnerability of a business to takeover by another business. These areas, of course, are likely to be of interest to all those connected with the business.

LIMITATIONS OF RATIO ANALYSIS

Although ratios offer a quick and useful method of analysing the position and performance of a business, they are not without their problems and limitations. We shall now review some of the shortcomings of financial ratio analysis.

Quality of financial statements

It must always be remembered that ratios are based on financial statements. The results of ratio analysis are, therefore, dependent on the quality of these underlying statements. Ratios will inherit the limitations of the financial statements on which they are based. One important limitation of financial statements is their failure to include all resources controlled by the business. Internally generated goodwill and brands, for example, are excluded from the statement of financial position because they fail to meet the strict definition of an asset. This means that, even though these resources may be of considerable value, key ratios such as ROSF, ROCE and the gearing ratio will fail to acknowledge their presence.

There is also the problem of deliberate attempts to make the financial statements misleading. We discussed this problem of *creative accounting* in Chapter 4.

Inflation

A persistent problem, in most countries, is that the financial results of businesses can be distorted as a result of inflation. One effect of inflation is that the reported value of assets held for any length of time may bear little relation to current values. Generally speaking, the reported value of non-current assets will be understated in current terms during a period of inflation as they are usually reported at their original cost (less any amounts written off for depreciation). This means that comparisons, either between businesses or between periods, will be hindered. A difference in, say, ROCE may simply be owing to the fact that assets shown in one of the statements of financial position being compared were acquired more recently (ignoring the effect of depreciation on the asset values). Another effect of inflation is to distort the measurement of profit. In the calculation of profit, sales revenue is often matched with costs incurred at an earlier time. This is because there is often a time lag between acquiring a particular resource and using it to help generate sales revenue. For example, inventories may well be acquired several months before they are sold. During a period of inflation, this will mean that the expense does not reflect prices that are current at the time of the sale. The cost of sales figure is usually based on the historic cost of the inventories concerned. As a result, expenses will be understated in the income statement and this, in turn, means that profit will be overstated. The longer the average inventories turnover period, the greater the distortion. One effect of this will be to distort the profitability ratios discussed earlier.

Over-reliance on ratios

It is important not to rely exclusively on ratios, thereby losing sight of information contained in the underlying financial statements. As we saw earlier in the chapter, some items reported in these statements can be vital in assessing position and performance. For example, the total sales revenue, capital employed and profit figures may be useful in assessing changes in absolute size that occur over time, or in assessing differences in scale between businesses. Ratios do not provide such information. When comparing one figure with another, ratios measure relative performance and position and, therefore, provide only part of the picture. When comparing two businesses, therefore, it will often be useful to assess the absolute size of profits, as well as the relative profitability of each business. For example, Business A may generate £1 million operating profit and have a ROCE of 15 per cent and Business B may generate £100,000 operating profit and have a ROCE of 20 per cent. Although Business B has a higher level of profitability, as measured by ROCE, it generates lower total operating profits. This may well be useful information for the analyst.

The basis for comparison

We saw earlier that if ratios are to be useful, they require a basis for comparison. Moreover, it is important that the analyst compares like with like. Where the comparison is with another business, there can be difficulties. No two businesses are identical: the greater the differences between the businesses being compared, the greater the limitations of ratio analysis. Furthermore, any differences in accounting policies, financing methods (gearing levels) and reporting period ends will add to the problems of making comparisons between businesses.

Statement of financial position ratios

Because the statement of financial position is only a 'snapshot' of the business at a particular moment in time, any ratios based on statement of financial position figures, such as the liquidity ratios, may not be representative of the financial position of the business for the year as a whole. For example, it is common for a seasonal business to have a financial year end that coincides with a low point in business activity. As a result, inventories and trade receivables may be low at the year end. This means that the liquidity ratios may also be low. A more representative picture of liquidity can only really be gained by taking additional measurements at other points in the year.

Real World 6.10 points out another way in which ratios are limited.

REAL WORLD 6.10

Remember, it's people that really count . . .

Lord Weinstock (1924–2002) was an influential industrialist whose management style and philosophy helped to shape management practice in many UK businesses. During his long and successful reign at GEC plc, a major engineering business, Lord Weinstock relied heavily on financial ratios to assess performance and to exercise control. In particular, he relied on ratios relating to sales revenue, expenses, trade receivables, profit margins and inventories turnover. However, he was keenly aware of the limitations of ratios and recognised that, ultimately, people produce profits.

In a memo written to GEC managers he pointed out that ratios are an aid to good management rather than a substitute for it. He wrote:

> The operating ratios are of great value as measures of efficiency but they are only the measures and not efficiency itself. Statistics will not design a product better, make it for a lower cost or increase sales. If ill-used, they may so guide action as to diminish resources for the sake of apparent but false signs of improvement.
>
> Management remains a matter of judgement, of knowledge of products and processes and of understanding and skill in dealing with people. The ratios will indicate how well all these things are being done and will show comparison with how they are done elsewhere.
> But they will tell us nothing about how to do them. That is what you are meant to do.

Source: Extract from Aris, S., *Arnold Weinstock and the Making of GEC* (Aurum Press, 1998), published in *The Sunday Times*, 22 February 1998, p. 3.

? SELF-ASSESSMENT QUESTION 6.1

Both Ali plc and Bhaskar plc operate wholesale electrical stores throughout the UK. The financial statements of each business for the year ended 30 June 2012 are as follows:

Statements of financial position as at 30 June 2012

	Ali plc £m	Bhaskar plc £m
ASSETS		
Non-current assets		
Property, plant and equipment (cost less depreciation)		
Land and buildings	360.0	510.0
Fixtures and fittings	87.0	91.2
	447.0	601.2
Current assets		
Inventories	592.0	403.0
Trade receivables	176.4	321.9
Cash at bank	84.6	91.6
	853.0	816.5
Total assets	1,300.0	1,417.7
EQUITY AND LIABILITIES		
Equity		
£1 ordinary shares	320.0	250.0
Retained earnings	367.6	624.6
	687.6	874.6
Non-current liabilities		
Borrowings – Loan notes	190.0	250.0
Current liabilities		
Trade payables	406.4	275.7
Taxation	16.0	17.4
	422.4	293.1
Total equity and liabilities	1,300.0	1,417.7

Income statements for the year ended 30 June 2012

	Ali plc £m	Bhaskar plc £m
Revenue	1,478.1	1,790.4
Cost of sales	(1,018.3)	(1,214.9)
Gross profit	459.8	575.5
Operating expenses	(308.5)	(408.6)
Operating profit	151.3	166.9
Interest payable	(19.4)	(27.5)
Profit before taxation	131.9	139.4
Taxation	(32.0)	(34.8)
Profit for the year	99.9	104.6

All purchases and sales were on credit. The market values of a share in Ali plc and Bhaskar plc at the end of the year were £6.50 and £8.20 respectively.

Required:

For each business, calculate two ratios that are concerned with each of the following aspects:

- profitability;
- efficiency;
- liquidity;
- gearing;
- investment (ten ratios in total).

What can you conclude from the ratios that you have calculated?

The solution to this question can be found at the back of the book, in Appendix B.

SUMMARY

The main points of this chapter may be summarised as follows.

Ratio analysis

- Compares two related figures, usually both from the same set of financial statements.
- Is an aid to understanding what the financial statements really mean.
- Is an inexact science so results must be interpreted cautiously.
- Past periods, the performance of similar businesses and planned performance are often used to provide benchmark ratios.
- A brief overview of the financial statements can often provide insights that may not be revealed by ratios and/or may help in the interpretation of them.

Profitability ratios

- Profitability ratios are concerned with effectiveness at generating profit.
- The profitability ratios covered are the return on ordinary shareholders' funds (ROSF), return on capital employed (ROCE), operating profit margin and gross profit margin.

Efficiency ratios

- Efficiency ratios are concerned with efficiency of using assets/resources.
- The efficiency ratios covered are the average inventories turnover period, average settlement period for trade receivables, average settlement period for trade payables, sales revenue to capital employed and sales revenue per employee.

Liquidity ratios

- Liquidity ratios are concerned with the ability to meet short-term obligations.
- The liquidity ratios covered are the current ratio and the acid test ratio.

→

Gearing ratios

- Gearing ratios are concerned with relationship between equity and debt financing.
- The gearing ratios covered are the gearing ratio and interest cover ratio.

Investment ratios

- Investment ratios are concerned with returns to shareholders.
- The investment ratios covered are the dividend payout ratio, dividend yield ratio, earnings per share, and price/earnings ratio.

Uses of ratios

- Individual ratios can be tracked to detect trends; for example, plotted on a graph.
- Ratios can be used to help predict the future, particularly financial distress.

Limitations of ratio analysis

- Ratios are only as reliable as the financial statements from which they derive.
- Inflation can distort the information.
- Ratios provide only part of the picture and there should not be over-reliance on them.
- It can be difficult to find a suitable benchmark (for example, another business) to compare with.
- Some ratios could mislead due to the 'snapshot' nature of the statement of financial position.

MyAccountingLab

Go to www.myaccountinglab.com to check your understanding of the chapter, create a personalised study plan, and maximise your revision time

KEY TERMS

FURTHER READING

If you would like to explore the topics covered in this chapter in more depth, try the following books:

Elliott, B. and Elliott, J., *Financial Accounting and Reporting*, 15th edn, Financial Times Prentice Hall, 2012, Chapters 28 and 29.

Fridson, M. and Alvarez, F., *Financial Statement Analysis: A Practitioner's Guide*, 4th edn, Wiley Finance, 2011, Chapters 13 and 14.

Penman, S., *Financial Statement Analysis and Security Valuation*, 3rd edn, McGraw Hill Irwin, 2012, Chapters 7 to 12.

Schoenebeck, K. and Holtzman, M., *Interpreting and Analyzing Financial Statements*, 6th edn, Prentice Hall, 2012, Chapters 2 to 5.

? REVIEW QUESTIONS

Solutions to these questions can be found at the back of the book, in Appendix C.

6.1 Some businesses operate on a low operating profit margin (for example, a supermarket chain). Does this mean that the return on capital employed from the business will also be low?

6.2 What potential problems arise for the external analyst from the use of statement of financial position figures in the calculation of financial ratios?

6.3 Two businesses operate in the same industry. One has an inventories turnover period that is longer than the industry average. The other has an inventories turnover period that is shorter than the industry average. Give three possible explanations for each business's inventories turnover period ratio.

6.4 In the chapter it was mentioned that ratios help to eliminate some of the problems of comparing businesses of different sizes. Does this mean that size is irrelevant when interpreting and analysing the position and performance of different businesses?

✳ EXERCISES

*Exercises 6.1 and 6.2 are basic level, Exercise 6.3 is intermediate level and Exercises 6.4 and 6.5 are advanced level. Those with **coloured numbers** have solutions at the back of the book, in Appendix D.*

If you wish to try more exercises, visit the website at **www.myaccountinglab.com**.

6.1 Set out below are ratios relating to three different businesses. Each business operates within a different industrial sector.

Ratio	A plc	B plc	C plc
Operating profit margin	3.6%	9.7%	6.8%
Sales to capital employed	2.4 times	3.1 times	1.7 times
Average inventories turnover period	18 days	N/A	44 days
Average settlement period for trade receivables	2 days	12 days	26 days
Current ratio	0.8 times	0.6 times	1.5 times

Required:

State, with reasons, which one of the three businesses is:

(a) A holiday tour operator
(b) A supermarket chain
(c) A food manufacturer.

6.2 Amsterdam Ltd and Berlin Ltd are both engaged in retailing, but they seem to take a different approach to it according to the following information:

Ratio	Amsterdam Ltd	Berlin Ltd
Return on capital employed (ROCE)	20%	17%
Return on ordinary shareholders' funds (ROSF)	30%	18%
Average settlement period for trade receivables	63 days	21 days
Average settlement period for trade payables	50 days	45 days
Gross profit margin	40%	15%
Operating profit margin	10%	10%
Average inventories' turnover period	52 days	25 days

Required:

Describe what this information indicates about the differences in approach between the two businesses. If one of them prides itself on personal service and one of them on competitive prices, which do you think is which and why?

6.3 The directors of Helena Beauty Products Ltd have been presented with the following abridged financial statements:

Helena Beauty Products Ltd
Income statement for the year ended 30 September

	2011		2012	
	£000	£000	£000	£000
Sales revenue		3,600		3,840
Cost of sales				
Opening inventories	320		400	
Purchases	2,240		2,350	
	2,560		2,750	
Closing inventories	(400)	(2,160)	(500)	(2,250)
Gross profit		1,440		1,590
Expenses		(1,360)		(1,500)
Profit		80		90

Statement of financial position as at 30 September

	2011	2012
ASSETS	£000	£000
Non-current assets		
Property, plant and equipment	1,900	1,860
Current assets		
Inventories	400	500
Trade receivables	750	960
Cash at bank	8	4
	1,158	1,464
Total assets	3,058	3,324
EQUITY AND LIABILITIES		
Equity		
£1 ordinary shares	1,650	1,766
Retained earnings	1,018	1,108
	2,668	2,874
Current liabilities	390	450
Total equity and liabilities	3,058	3,324

Required:
Using six ratios, comment on the profitability (three ratios) and efficiency (three ratios) of the business. →

6.4 Threads Limited manufactures nuts and bolts, which are sold to industrial users. The abbreviated financial statements for 2011 and 2012 are as follows:

Income statements for the year ended 30 June

	2011	2012
	£000	£000
Revenue	1,180	1,200)
Cost of sales	(680)	(750)
Gross profit	500	450
Operating expenses	(200)	(208)
Depreciation	(66)	(75)
Operating profit	234	167
Interest	(–)	(8)
Profit before taxation	234	159
Taxation	(80)	(48)
Profit for the year	154	111

Statements of financial position as at 30 June

	2011	2012
ASSETS	£000	£000
Non-current assets		
Property, plant and equipment	702	687
Current assets		
Inventories	148	236
Trade receivables	102	156
Cash	3	4
	253	396
Total assets	955	1,083
EQUITY AND LIABILITIES		
Equity		
Ordinary share capital (£1 shares, fully paid)	500	500
Retained earnings	256	295
	756	795
Non-current liabilities		
Borrowings – Bank loan	–	50
Current liabilities		
Trade payables	60	76
Other payables and accruals	18	16
Taxation	40	24
Short-term borrowings (all bank overdraft)	81	122
	199	238
Total equity and liabilities	955	1,083

Dividends were paid on ordinary shares of £70,000 and £72,000 in respect of 2011 and 2012, respectively.

Required:

(a) Calculate the following financial ratios for *both* 2011 and 2012 (using year-end figures for statement of financial position items):
1. return on capital employed
2. operating profit margin
3. gross profit margin
4. current ratio
5. acid test ratio
6. settlement period for trade receivables
7. settlement period for trade payables
8. inventories turnover period.

(b) Comment on the performance of Threads Limited from the viewpoint of a business considering supplying a substantial amount of goods to Threads Limited on usual trade credit terms.

6.5 The financial statements for Harridges Ltd are given below for the two years ended 30 June 2011 and 2012. Harridges Limited operates a department store in the centre of a small town.

Harridges Ltd Income statement for the years ended 30 June

	2011	2012
	£000	£000
Sales revenue	2,600	3,500
Cost of sales	(1,560)	(2,350)
Gross profit	1,040	1,150
Wages and salaries	(320)	(350)
Overheads	(260)	(200)
Depreciation	(150)	(250)
Operating profit	310	350
Interest payable	(50)	(50)
Profit before taxation	260	300
Taxation	(105)	(125)
Profit for the year	155	175 →

Statement of financial position as at 30 June

	2011	2012
ASSETS	£000	£000
Non-current assets		
Property, plant and equipment	1,265	1,525
Current assets		
Inventories	250	400
Trade receivables	105	145
Cash at bank	380	115
	735	660
Total assets	2,000	2,185
EQUITY AND LIABILITIES		
Equity		
Share capital: £1 shares fully paid	490	490
Share premium	260	260
Retained earnings	350	450
	1,100	1,200
Non-current liabilities		
Borrowings – 10% loan notes	500	500
Current liabilities		
Trade payables	300	375
Other payables	100	110
	400	485
Total equity and liabilities	2,000	2,185

Dividends were paid on ordinary shares of £65,000 and £75,000 in respect of 2011 and 2012, respectively.

Required:

(a) Choose and calculate eight ratios that would be helpful in assessing the performance of Harridges Ltd. Use end-of-year values and calculate ratios for both 2011 and 2012.

(b) Using the ratios calculated in (a) and any others you consider helpful, comment on the business's performance from the viewpoint of a prospective purchaser of a majority of shares.

THE RELEVANCE AND BEHAVIOUR OF COSTS

INTRODUCTION

In this chapter, we consider the relevance of costs in making management decisions. Not all costs (and revenues) that appear to be linked to a business decision may actually be relevant to it. It is important to distinguish between costs (and revenues) that are relevant and those that are not. Failure to do this can lead to bad decisions being made.

In this chapter, we also consider the behaviour of cost in the face of changes in activity. Broadly, cost can be analysed between an element that is fixed, relative to the volume of activity, and an element that varies according to the volume of activity. We shall see how knowledge of cost behaviour can be used to make short-term decisions and to assess risk.

The principles outlined here will provide the basis for much of the rest of the book.

Learning outcomes

When you have completed this chapter, you should be able to:

- define and distinguish between relevant costs, outlay costs and opportunity costs;
- distinguish between fixed cost and variable cost and use this distinction to explain the relationship between cost, volume and profit;
- deduce the break-even point for some activity and discuss its usefulness;
- demonstrate the way in which marginal analysis can be used when making short-term decisions.

MyAccountingLab Visit www.myaccountinglab.com for practice and revision opportunities

WHAT IS MEANT BY 'COST'?

Cost represents the amount sacrificed to achieve a particular business objective. Measuring cost may seem, at first sight, to be a straightforward process: it is simply the amount paid for the item of goods being supplied or the service being provided. When measuring cost *for decision-making purposes*, however, things are not quite that simple. The following activity illustrates why this is the case.

Activity 7.1

You own a motor car, for which you paid a purchase price of £5,000 – much below the list price – at a recent car auction. You have just been offered £6,000 for this car.
What is the cost to you of keeping the car for your own use? (*Hint*: Ignore running costs and so on; just consider the 'capital' cost of the car.)

By retaining the car, you are forgoing a cash receipt of £6,000. Thus, the real sacrifice, or cost, incurred by keeping the car for your own use is £6,000.

Any decision that is made with respect to the car's future should logically take account of this figure. This cost is known as the 'opportunity cost' since it is the value of the opportunity forgone in order to pursue the other course of action. (In this case, the other course of action is to retain the car.)

We can see that the cost of retaining the car is not the same as the purchase price. In one sense, of course, the cost of the car in Activity 7.1 is £5,000 because that is how much was paid for it. However, this cost, which for obvious reasons is known as the **historic cost**, is only of academic interest. It cannot logically ever be used to make a decision on the car's future. If we disagree with this point, we should ask ourselves how we should assess an offer of £5,500, from another person, for the car. The answer is that we should compare the offer price of £5,500 with the **opportunity cost** of £6,000. This amount represents the value of being deprived of the next best opportunity by pursuing a particular course of action. By making this comparison, we should reject the offer as it is less than the £6,000 opportunity cost. In these circumstances, it would not be logical to accept the offer of £5,500 on the basis that it was more than the £5,000 that we originally paid. (The only other figure that should concern us is the value to us, in terms of pleasure, usefulness and so on, of retaining the car. If we valued this more highly than the £6,000 opportunity cost, we should reject both offers.)

We may still feel, however, that the £5,000 is relevant here because it will help us in assessing the profitability of the decision. If we sold the car, we should make a profit of either £500 (£5,500 – £5,000) or £1,000 (£6,000 – £5,000) depending on which offer we accept. Since we should seek to make the higher profit, the right decision is to sell the car for £6,000. However, we do not need to know the historic cost of the car to make the right decision. What decision should we make if the car cost us £4,000 to buy? Clearly we should still sell the car for £6,000 rather than for £5,500 as the important comparison is between the offer price and the opportunity cost. We should reach the same conclusion whatever the historic cost of the car.

To emphasise the above point, let us assume that the car cost £10,000. Even in this case the historic cost would still be irrelevant. Had we just bought a car for £10,000 and found that shortly after it is only worth £6,000, we may well be fuming with rage at our mistake, but this does not make the £10,000 a **relevant cost**. The only relevant factors, in a decision on whether to sell the car or to keep it, are the £6,000 opportunity cost and the value of the benefits of keeping it. Thus, the historic cost can never be relevant to a future decision.

To say that historic cost is an **irrelevant cost** is not to say that *the effects of having incurred that cost* are always irrelevant. The fact that we own the car, and are thus in a position to exercise choice as to how to use it, is not irrelevant. It is absolutely relevant.

Opportunity costs are rarely taken into account in financial accounting, as they do not involve any out-of-pocket expenditure. They are normally only calculated where they are relevant to a particular management decision. Historic costs, on the other hand, do involve out-of-pocket expenditure and are recorded. They are used in preparing the annual financial statements, such as the statement of financial position and the income statement. This is logical, however, since these statements are intended to be accounts of what has actually happened and are drawn up after the event.

It might be useful to end this section by stating in formal terms what we mean by cost.

A definition of cost

Cost may be defined as the amount of resources, usually measured in monetary terms, sacrificed to achieve a particular objective. The objective might be to retain a car, to buy a particular house, to make a particular product or to render a particular service.

RELEVANT COSTS: OPPORTUNITY AND OUTLAY COSTS

We have just seen that, when we are making decisions concerning the future, **past costs** (that is, historic costs) are irrelevant. It is future opportunity costs and future **outlay costs** (future amounts spent to achieve an objective) that are of concern. In more formal terms, we can say that, to be relevant to a particular decision, a cost must satisfy all three of the following criteria:

1 *It must relate to the objectives of the business*. Businesses exist primarily to increase their owners' (shareholders) wealth. Thus, to be relevant to a particular decision, a cost must relate to this wealth objective.
2 *It must be a future cost*. Past costs cannot be relevant to decisions being made about the future.
3 *It must vary with the decision*. Only costs (and revenues) that differ between outcomes are relevant. Take, for example, a road haulage business that has decided to buy an additional lorry and the final decision lies between two different models. The load capacity, fuel costs and maintenance costs are different for each lorry. These potential

revenues and costs are all relevant items. The lorry will require a driver, who will need to be employed, but a suitably qualified driver could drive either lorry for the same wage. Thus the cost of employing the driver will be irrelevant to the decision as to which lorry to buy. This is despite the fact that this cost is a future one.

Activity 7.2

Assume that the decision did not concern a choice between two models of lorry but rather whether to operate an additional lorry or not. Would this make a difference to the view taken concerning the cost of employing a driver?

In this case, the cost of employing the additional driver would be relevant. It would now be a cost that would vary with the decision made.

Figure 7.1 shows a decision flow diagram for deciding which costs are relevant.

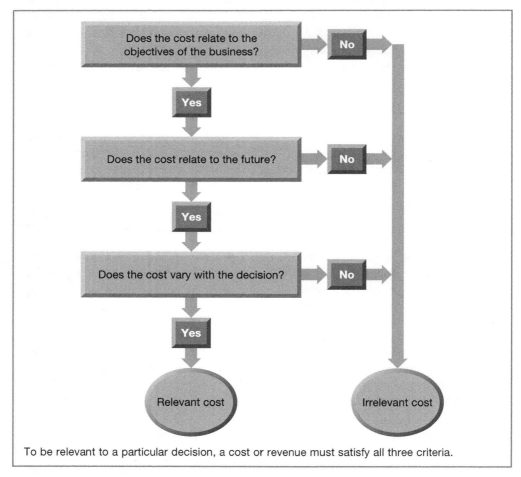

Figure 7.1 Decision flow diagram for identifying relevant costs and revenues

Activity 7.3

A garage business has an old car that it bought several months ago. The car needs a replacement engine before it can be driven. It is possible to buy a reconditioned engine for £300. This would take seven hours to fit by a mechanic who is paid £15 an hour. At present the garage is short of work, but the owners are reluctant to lay off any mechanics or even to cut down their basic working week because skilled labour is difficult to find and an upturn in repair work is expected soon.

The garage paid £3,000 to buy the car. Without the engine it could be sold for an estimated £3,500. What is the minimum price at which the garage should sell the car with a reconditioned engine fitted?

The minimum price is the amount required to cover the relevant costs of the job. At this price, the business will make neither a profit nor a loss. Any price that is lower than this amount will mean that the wealth of the business is reduced. Thus, the minimum price is:

	£
Opportunity cost of the car	3,500
Cost of the reconditioned engine	300
Total	3,800

Note that in Activity 7.3, the original cost of the car is irrelevant for reasons that have already been discussed. It is the opportunity cost of the car that concerns us. The cost of the new engine is relevant because, if the work is done, the garage will have to pay £300 for the engine; but will pay nothing if the job is not done. The £300 is an example of a future outlay cost.

Labour cost is irrelevant because the same cost will be incurred whether the mechanic undertakes the engine-replacement work or not. This is because the mechanic is being paid to do nothing if this job is not undertaken; thus the additional labour cost arising from this job is zero.

It should be emphasised that the garage will not seek to sell the car with its reconditioned engine for £3,800; it will attempt to charge as much as possible for it. However, any price above the £3,800 will make the garage better off financially than it would be by not undertaking the engine replacement.

Activity 7.4

Assume exactly the same circumstances as in Activity 7.3, except that the garage is quite busy at the moment. If a mechanic is to be put on the engine-replacement job, it will mean that other work that the mechanic could have done during the seven hours, all of which could be charged to a customer, will not be undertaken. The garage's labour charge is £60 an hour, though the mechanic is only paid £15 an hour.

What is the minimum price at which the garage should sell the car, with a reconditioned engine fitted, under these altered circumstances?

The minimum price is:

	£
Opportunity cost of the car	3,500
Cost of the reconditioned engine	300
Labour cost (7 × £60)	420
Total	4,220

In Activity 7.4, we can see that the opportunity cost of the car and the cost of the engine are the same as they were in Activity 7.3, but in Activity 7.4 a charge for labour has been added to obtain the minimum price. There, the relevant labour cost is that which the garage will have to sacrifice in making the time available to undertake the engine replacement job. While the mechanic is working on this job, the garage is losing the opportunity to do work for which a customer would pay £420. Note that the £15 an hour mechanic's wage is still not relevant. The mechanic will be paid £15 an hour irrespective of whether it is the engine-replacement work or some other job that is undertaken.

COST BEHAVIOUR

Costs incurred by a business may be classified in various ways and one useful way is according to how they behave in relation to changes in the volume of activity. Costs may be classified according to whether they:

- remain constant (fixed) when changes occur to the volume of activity; or
- vary according to the volume of activity.

These are known as **fixed costs** and **variable costs** respectively. Thus, in the case of a restaurant, part of the manager's salary would normally be a fixed cost of a particular meal while the cost of the unprepared food would be a variable cost.

As we shall see, knowing how much of each type of cost is associated with a particular activity can be of great value to the decision maker.

FIXED COST

The way in which a fixed cost behaves can be shown by preparing a graph that plots the fixed cost of a business against the level of activity, as in Figure 7.2. The distance 0F represents the amount of fixed cost, and this stays the same irrespective of the volume of activity.

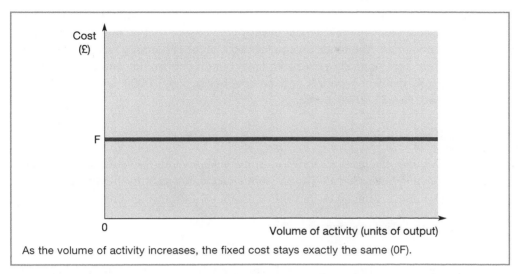

As the volume of activity increases, the fixed cost stays exactly the same (0F).

Figure 7.2 Graph of fixed cost against the volume of activity

Activity 7.5

Can you give some examples of items of cost that are likely to be fixed for a hairdressing business?

We came up with the following:

■ rent
■ insurance
■ cleaning cost
■ staff salaries.

These items of cost are likely to be the same irrespective of the number of customers having their hair cut or styled.

Staff salaries (or wages) are often assumed to be a variable cost but in practice they tend to be fixed. Members of staff are not normally paid according to the volume of output and it is unusual to dismiss staff when there is a short-term downturn in activity. Where there is a long-term downturn, or at least it seems that way to management, redundancies may occur with fixed-cost savings. This, however, is true of all types of fixed cost. For example, management may also decide to close some branches to make rental cost savings.

There are circumstances in which the labour cost is variable (for example, where staff are paid according to how much output they produce), but this is unusual. Whether labour cost is fixed or variable depends on the circumstances in the particular case concerned.

It is important to be clear that 'fixed', in this context, means only that the cost is unaffected by changes in the volume of activity. Fixed cost is likely to be affected by inflation. If rent (a typical fixed cost) goes up because of inflation, a fixed cost will have increased, but not because of a change in the volume of activity.

Similarly, the level of fixed cost does not stay the same, irrespective of the time period involved. Fixed cost elements are almost always *time based*: that is, they vary with the length of time concerned. The rental charge for two months is normally twice that for one month. Thus, fixed cost normally varies with time, but (of course) not with the volume of output. This means that when we talk of fixed cost being, say, £1,000, we must add the period concerned, say, £1,000 a month.

Activity 7.6

Does fixed cost stay the same irrespective of the volume of output, even where there is a massive rise in that volume? Think in terms of the rent cost for the hairdressing business.

No. The fixed cost is likely to increase.

In fact, the rent is only fixed over a particular range (known as the 'relevant' range). If the number of people wanting to have their hair cut by the business increased, and the business wished to meet this increased demand, it would eventually have to expand its physical size. This might be achieved by opening an additional branch, or perhaps by moving the existing business to larger accommodation nearby. It may be possible to cope with relatively minor increases in activity by using existing space more efficiently, or by having longer opening hours. If activity continued to expand, however, increased rent charges would seem inevitable.

In practice, the situation described in Activity 7.6 would look something like Figure 7.3.

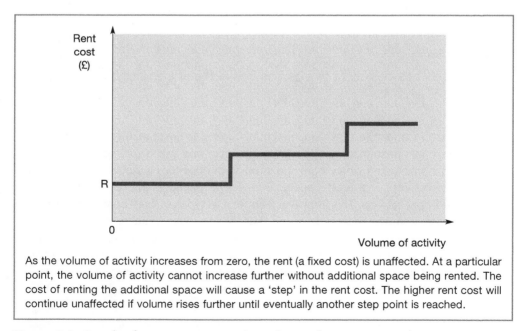

As the volume of activity increases from zero, the rent (a fixed cost) is unaffected. At a particular point, the volume of activity cannot increase further without additional space being rented. The cost of renting the additional space will cause a 'step' in the rent cost. The higher rent cost will continue unaffected if volume rises further until eventually another step point is reached.

Figure 7.3 Graph of rent cost against the volume of activity

At lower volumes of activity, the rent cost shown in Figure 7.3 would be 0R. As the volume of activity expands, the accommodation becomes inadequate and further expansion requires an increase in the size of the accommodation and, therefore, its cost. This higher level of accommodation provision will enable further expansion to take place. Eventually, additional cost will need to be incurred if further expansion is to occur. Elements of fixed cost that behave in this way are often referred to as **stepped fixed costs**.

VARIABLE COST

We saw earlier that variable cost varies with the volume of activity. In a manufacturing business, for example, this would include the cost of raw materials used.

Variable cost can be represented graphically as in Figure 7.4. At zero volume of activity, the variable cost is zero. It then increases in a straight line as activity increases.

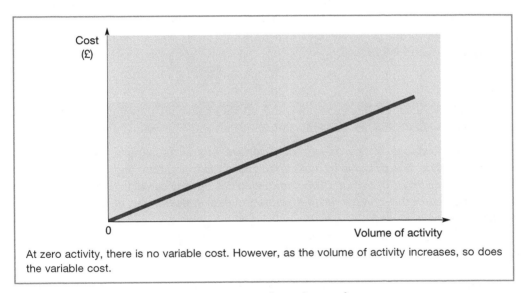

At zero activity, there is no variable cost. However, as the volume of activity increases, so does the variable cost.

Figure 7.4 Graph of variable cost against the volume of activity

Activity 7.7

Can you think of some examples of cost elements that are likely to be variable for a hairdressing business?

We can think of a couple:

■ lotions, sprays and other materials used;
■ laundry cost to wash towels used to dry customers' hair.

You may have thought of some others.

As with many types of business activity, the variable cost incurred by hairdressers tends to be low in comparison with the fixed cost: that is, fixed cost tends to make up the bulk of total cost.

The straight line for variable cost on this graph implies that this type of cost will be the same per unit of activity, irrespective of the volume of activity. We shall consider the practicality of this assumption a little later in this chapter.

SEMI-FIXED (SEMI-VARIABLE) COST

In some cases, a particular cost has an element of both fixed and variable cost. These can be described as **semi-fixed (semi-variable) costs**. An example might be the electricity cost for the hairdressing business. Some of this will be for heating and lighting, and this part is probably fixed, at least until the volume of activity expands to a point where longer opening hours or larger accommodation is necessary. The other part of the cost will vary with the volume of activity. Here we are talking about such things as power for hairdryers.

Analysing semi-fixed (semi-variable) costs into the fixed and variable elements is a relatively easy matter in practice.

FINDING THE BREAK-EVEN POINT

Armed with knowledge of how much each element of cost represents for a particular product or service, it is possible to make predictions regarding total and per-unit cost at various projected levels of output. Such information can be very useful to decision makers. Much of the rest of this chapter will be devoted to seeing how it can be useful, starting with **break-even analysis**.

If, for a particular product or service, we know the fixed cost for a period and the variable cost per unit, we can produce a graph like the one shown in Figure 7.5. This graph shows the total cost over the possible range of volume of activity.

The bottom part of Figure 7.5 shows the fixed cost area. Added to this is the variable cost, the wedge-shaped portion at the top of the graph. The uppermost line represents the total cost over a range of volume of activity. For any particular volume, the total cost can be measured by the vertical distance between the graph's horizontal axis and the relevant point on the uppermost line.

Logically, the total cost at zero activity is the amount of the fixed cost. This is because, even where there is nothing happening, the business will still be paying rent, salaries and so on, at least in the short term. On the other hand, no variable cost will be incurred. As the volume of activity increases from zero, the fixed cost is augmented by the relevant variable cost to give the total cost.

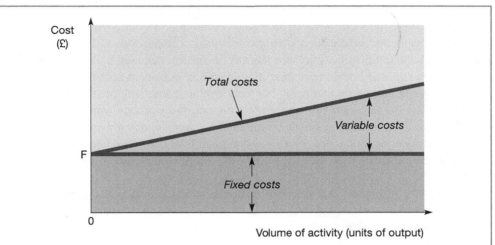

The bottom part of the graph represents the fixed cost element. To this is added the wedge-shaped top portion, which represents the variable cost. The two parts together represent total cost. At zero activity, the variable cost is zero, so total cost equals fixed cost. As activity increases so does total cost, but only because variable cost increases. We are assuming that there are no steps in the fixed cost.

Figure 7.5 Graph of total cost against volume of activity

If we take this total cost graph in Figure 7.5, and superimpose on it a line representing total revenue over the range of volume of activity, we obtain the **break-even chart**. This is shown in Figure 7.6.

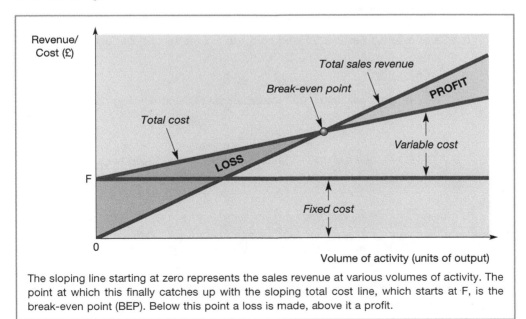

The sloping line starting at zero represents the sales revenue at various volumes of activity. The point at which this finally catches up with the sloping total cost line, which starts at F, is the break-even point (BEP). Below this point a loss is made, above it a profit.

Figure 7.6 Break-even chart

Note in Figure 7.6 that, at zero volume of activity, there is zero sales revenue. The profit (loss), which is the difference between total sales revenue and total cost, for a particular volume of activity, is the vertical distance between the total sales revenue line and the total cost line at that volume of activity. Where there is no vertical distance between these two lines (total sales revenue equals total cost) the volume of activity is at **break-even point (BEP)**. At this point there is neither profit nor loss; that is, the activity *breaks even*. Where the volume of activity is below BEP, a loss will be incurred because total cost exceeds total sales revenue. Where the business operates at a volume of activity above BEP, there will be a profit because total sales revenue will exceed total cost. The further the volume of activity is below BEP, the higher the loss: the further above BEP it is, the higher the profit.

Deducing BEPs graphically is a laborious business. Since, however, the relationships in the graph are all linear (that is, the lines are all straight), it is easy to calculate the BEP.

We know that at BEP (but not at any other volume of activity):

Total sales revenue = Total cost

(At all other volumes of activity except the BEP, either total sales revenue will exceed total cost or the other way round. Only at BEP are they equal.) The above formula can be expanded so that:

Total sales revenue = Fixed cost + Variable cost

If we call the number of units of output at BEP *b*, then

$$b \times \text{Sales revenue per unit} = \text{Fixed cost} + (b \times \text{Variable cost per unit})$$

so:

$$(b \times \text{Sales revenue per unit}) - (b \times \text{Variable cost per unit}) = \text{Fixed cost}$$

and:

$$b \times (\text{Sales revenue per unit} - \text{Variable cost per unit}) = \text{Fixed cost}$$

giving:

$$b = \frac{\text{Fixed cost}}{\text{Sales revenue per unit} - \text{Variable cost per unit}}$$

If we look back at the break-even chart in Figure 7.6, this formula seems logical. The total cost line starts off at point F, higher than the starting point for the total sales revenues line (zero) by amount F (the amount of the fixed cost). Because the sales revenue per unit is greater than the variable cost per unit, the sales revenue line will gradually catch up with the total cost line. The rate at which it will catch up is dependent on the relative steepness of the two lines. Bearing in mind that the slopes of the two lines are the variable cost per unit and the selling price per unit, the above equation for calculating *b* looks perfectly logical.

Though the BEP can be calculated quickly and simply without resorting to graphs, this does not mean that the break-even chart is without value. The chart shows the relationship between cost, volume and profit over a range of activity and in a form that can easily be understood by non-financial managers. The break-even chart can therefore be a useful device for explaining this relationship.

Example 7.1

Cottage Industries Ltd makes baskets. The fixed cost of operating the workshop for a month totals £500. Each basket requires materials that cost £2 and takes one hour to make. The business pays the basket makers £10 an hour. The basket makers are all on contracts such that if they do not work for any reason, they are not paid. The baskets are sold to a wholesaler for £14 each.

What is the BEP for basket making for the business?

Solution

The BEP (in number of baskets) is:

$$BEP = \frac{\text{Fixed cost}}{(\text{Sales revenue per unit} - \text{Variable cost per unit})}$$

$$= \frac{£500}{£14 - (£2 + £10)}$$

$$= 250 \text{ baskets a month}$$

Note that the BEP must be expressed with respect to a period of time.

Real World 7.1 shows information on the BEPs of two well-known businesses.

REAL WORLD 7.1

BE at Ryanair (and BA)

Commercial airlines seem to pay a lot of attention to their BEPs and their 'load factors', that is, their actual level of activity. Figure 7.7 shows the BEPs and load factors for Ryanair, the 'no frills' carrier. We can see that Ryanair made operating profits, in each of the five years considered. This is because the airline's load factor was consistently greater than its BEP.

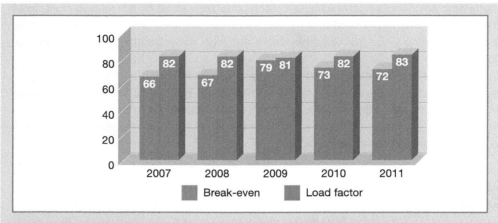

Figure 7.7 Break-even and load factors for Ryanair

Unlike Ryanair, most airlines do not publish their break-even points. British Airways plc (BA) used to do so. In the most recent year that BA disclosed its BEP (2008) it was 64 per cent, with a load factor of 71 per cent. Those figures were quite typical of BA's results during previous recent years.

Source: Based on information contained in the Ryanair Holdings plc Annual Report 2011 and British Airways plc Annual Report 2008.

Activity 7.8

In Real World 7.1, we saw that Ryanair's break-even point varied from one year to the next. It was as low as 66 per cent in 2007, but as high as 79 per cent in 2009. Why was it not roughly the same each year?

Break-even point depends on three broad factors. These are: sales revenue, variable cost and fixed cost. Each of these can vary quite noticeably from one year to another.

Ryanair's sales revenue could be greatly affected by the level of disposable income among the travelling public and/or by levels of competition from other airlines. Costs can vary from one year to another, particularly the cost of aviation fuel. (Interestingly, Ryanair's average fuel cost was 2.351 euros per gallon in 2009, but only 1.515 euros per gallon in 2010.)

Activity 7.9

Can you think of reasons why the managers of a business might find it useful to know the BEP of some activity that they are planning to undertake?

By knowing the BEP, it is possible to compare the expected, or planned, volume of activity with the BEP and so make a judgement about risk. If the volume of activity is expected to be only just above the break-even point, this may suggest that it is a risky venture. Only a small fall from the expected volume of activity could lead to a loss.

Activity 7.10

Cottage Industries Ltd (see Example 7.1) expects to sell 500 baskets a month. The business has the opportunity to rent a basket-making machine. Doing so would increase the total fixed cost of operating the workshop for a month to £3,000. Using the machine would reduce the labour time to half an hour per basket. The basket makers would still be paid £10 an hour.

(a) How much profit would the business make each month from selling baskets
   - without the machine; and
   - with the machine?
(b) What is the BEP if the machine is rented?
(c) What do you notice about the figures that you calculate?

(a) Estimated monthly profit from basket making:

	Without the machine		With the machine	
	£	£	£	£
Sales revenue (500 × £14)		7,000		7,000
Materials (500 × £2)	(1,000)		(1,000)	
Labour (500 × 1 × £10)	(5,000)			
(500 × ½ × £10)			(2,500)	
Fixed cost	(500)		(3,000)	
		(6,500)		(6,500)
Profit		500		500

(b) The BEP (in number of baskets) with the machine:

$$BEP = \frac{Fixed\ cost}{Sales\ revenue\ per\ unit - Variable\ cost\ per\ unit}$$

$$= \frac{£3,000}{£14 - (£2 + £5)}$$

$$= 429\ baskets\ per\ morth$$

The BEP without the machine is 250 baskets per month (see Example 7.1).

(c) There seems to be nothing to choose between the two manufacturing strategies regarding profit, at the expected sales volume. There is, however, a distinct difference between the two strategies regarding the BEP. Without the machine, the actual volume of sales could fall by a half of that which is expected (from 500 to 250) before the business would fail to make a profit. With the machine, however, just a 14 per cent fall (from 500 to 429) would be enough to cause the business to fail to make a profit. On the other hand, for each additional basket sold above the estimated 500, an additional profit of only £2 (that is, £14 – (£2 + £10)) would be made without the machine, whereas £7 (that is, £14 – (£2 + £5)) would be made with the machine. (Note that knowledge of the BEP and the planned volume of activity gives some basis for assessing the riskiness of the activity.)

Real World 7.2 discusses the effect of volume of activity on profit (the 'bottom line') at Halfords' Autocentres, a division of Halfords plc.

REAL WORLD 7.2

Making the fixed costs work

Analysts are relying on Halfords Autocentre division to crank up the company's total profits in 2011. As the spring MOT season looms, all 240 autocentres will have been rebranded with the Halfords name, and a marketing campaign will commence.

'Halfords can drive up customer numbers at Autocentre through national advertising and by leveraging its existing customer database,' said David Jeary, retail analyst at Investec.

'The biggest fixed cost in the Autocentre business is labour, and using that labour more efficiently by increasing customer numbers means the bottom line traction is attractive.'

Source: Adapted from Barrett, Claer, 'Cycle sales push Halfords downhill', FT.com, 13 January 2011.

We shall take a closer look at the relationship between fixed cost, variable cost and profit together with any advice that we might give the management of Cottage Industries Ltd after we have briefly considered the notion of contribution.

CONTRIBUTION

The bottom part of the break-even formula (sales revenue per unit less variable cost per unit) is known as the **contribution per unit**. Thus, for the basket-making activity, without the machine the contribution per unit is £2 and with the machine it is £7. This can be quite a useful figure to know in a decision-making context. It is called 'contribution' because it contributes to meeting the fixed cost and, if there is any excess, it then contributes to profit.

We shall see, a little later in this chapter, how knowing the amount of the contribution generated by a particular activity can be valuable in making short-term decisions of various types, as well as being useful in the BEP calculation.

Contribution margin ratio

The **contribution margin ratio** is the contribution from an activity expressed as a percentage of the sales revenue, thus:

$$\text{Contribution margin ratio} = \frac{\text{Contribution}}{\text{Sales revenue}} \times 100\%$$

Contribution and sales revenue can both be expressed in per-unit or total terms. For Cottage Industries Ltd (Example 7.1 and Activity 7.10), the contribution margin ratios are:

$$\text{Without the machine: } \frac{14-12}{14} \times 100\% = 14\%$$

$$\text{With the machine: } \frac{14-7}{14} \times 100\% = 50\%$$

The ratio can provide an impression of the extent to which sales revenue is eaten away by variable cost.

MARGIN OF SAFETY

The **margin of safety** is the extent to which the planned volume of output or sales lies above the BEP. To illustrate how the margin of safety is calculated, we can use the information in Activity 7.10 relating to each option.

	Without the machine (number of baskets)	With the machine (number of baskets)
(a) Expected volume of sales	500	500
(b) BEP	250	429
Margin of safety (the difference between (a) and (b))	250	71
Expressed as a percentage of expected volume of sales	50%	14%

The margin of safety can be used as a partial measure of risk.

Activity 7.11

What advice would you give Cottage Industries Ltd about renting the machine, on the basis of the values for margin of safety?

It is a matter of personal judgement, which in turn is related to individual attitudes to risk, as to which strategy to adopt. Most people, however, would prefer the strategy of not renting the machine, since the margin of safety between the expected volume of activity and the BEP is much greater. Thus, for the same level of return, the risk will be lower without renting the machine.

The relative margins of safety are directly linked to the relationship between the selling price per basket, the variable cost per basket and the fixed cost per month. Without the machine, the contribution (selling price less variable cost) per basket is £2; with the machine, it is £7. On the other hand, without the machine the fixed cost is £500 a month; with the machine, it is £3,000. This means that, with the machine, the contributions have more fixed cost to 'overcome' before the activity becomes profitable. However, the rate at which the contributions can overcome fixed cost is higher with the machine, because variable cost is lower. Thus, one more, or one fewer, basket sold has a greater impact on profit than it does if the machine is not rented. The contrast between the two scenarios is shown graphically in Figures 7.8(a) and 7.8(b).

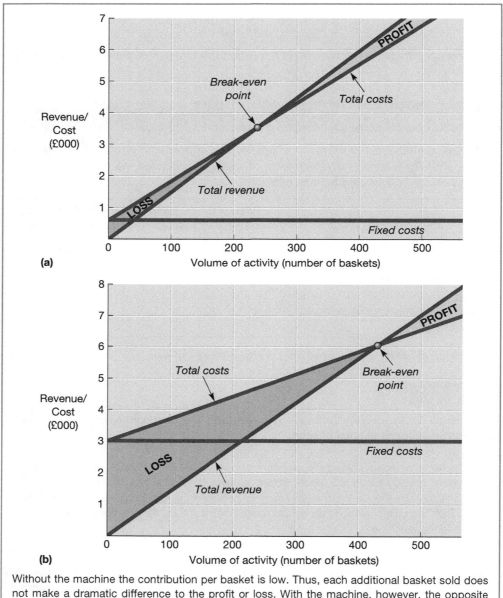

(a)

(b)

Without the machine the contribution per basket is low. Thus, each additional basket sold does not make a dramatic difference to the profit or loss. With the machine, however, the opposite is true; small increases or decreases in the sales volume will have a great effect on the profit or loss.

Figure 7.8 Break-even charts for Cottage Industries' basket-making activities (a) without the machine and (b) with the machine

If we look back to Real World 7.1 (page 242), we can see that Ryanair typically had a much larger margin of safety than BA.

Real World 7.3 goes into more detail on Ryanair's margin of safety and operating profit, over recent years.

REAL WORLD 7.3

Ryanair's margin of safety

As we saw in Real World 7.1, commercial airlines pay a lot of attention to BEPs. They are also interested in their margin of safety (the difference between load factor and BEP).

Figure 7.9 shows Ryanair's margin of safety and its operating profit over a five-year period. Note that in 2009, Ryanair had a load factor that was only just above its break-even point and this led to an unusually small operating profit. In the other years, the load factors were comfortably greater than the BEP. This led to larger operating profits in those years.

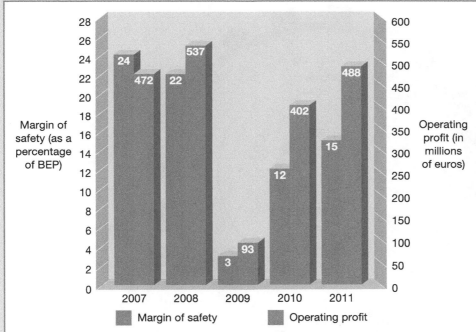

The margin of safety is expressed as the difference between the load factor and the BEP (for each year), expressed as a percentage of the BEP. Generally, the higher the margin of safety, the higher the operating profit.

Figure 7.9 Ryanair's margin of safety

Source: Based on information contained in the Ryanair Holdings plc Annual Report 2011.

OPERATING GEARING

The relationship between contribution and fixed cost is known as **operating gearing** (or operational gearing). An activity with a relatively high fixed cost compared with its total variable cost, at its normal level of activity, is said to have high operating gearing. Thus, Cottage Industries Ltd has higher operating gearing using the machine than it has if not using it. Renting the machine increases the level of operating gearing quite dramatically because it causes an increase in fixed cost, but at the same time it leads to a reduction in variable cost per basket.

Operating gearing and its effect on profit

The reason why the word 'gearing' is used in this context is that, as with intermeshing gear wheels of different circumferences, a movement in one of the factors (volume of output) causes a more-than-proportionate movement in the other (profit) as illustrated by Figure 7.10.

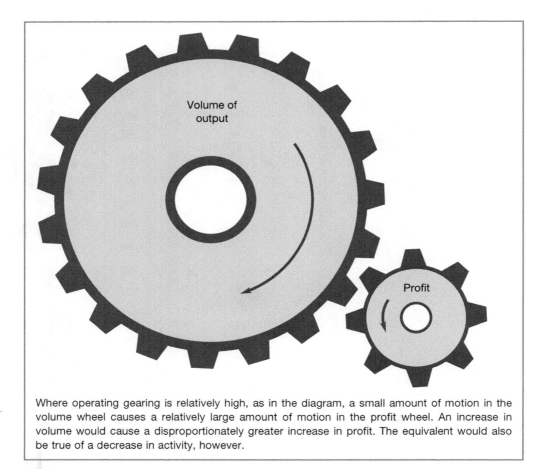

Where operating gearing is relatively high, as in the diagram, a small amount of motion in the volume wheel causes a relatively large amount of motion in the profit wheel. An increase in volume would cause a disproportionately greater increase in profit. The equivalent would also be true of a decrease in activity, however.

Figure 7.10 The effect of operating gearing

Increasing the level of operating gearing makes profit more sensitive to changes in the volume of activity. We can demonstrate operating gearing with Cottage Industries Ltd's basket-making activities as follows:

	Without the machine			With the machine		
Volume (number of baskets)	500	1,000	1,500	500	1,000	1,500
	£	£	£	£	£	£
Contributions*	1,000	2,000	3,000	3,500	7,000	10,500
Fixed cost	(500)	(500)	(500)	(3,000)	(3,000)	(3,000)
Profit	500	1,500	2,500	500	4,000	7,500

* £2 per basket without the machine and £7 per basket with it.

Note that, without the machine (low operating gearing), a doubling of the output from 500 to 1,000 units brings a trebling of the profit. With the machine (high operating gearing), doubling output from 500 units causes profit to rise by eight times. At the same time, reductions in the volume of output tend to have a more damaging effect on profit where the operating gearing is higher.

Activity 7.12

What types of business activity are likely to have high operating gearing? (*Hint*: Cottage Industries Ltd might give you some idea.)

Activities that are capital intensive tend to have high operating gearing. This is because renting or owning capital equipment gives rise to additional fixed cost, but it can also give rise to lower variable cost.

Real World 7.4 shows how a very well-known business has benefited from high operating gearing.

REAL WORLD 7.4

Delivering profit through operating gearing

Domino's Pizza UK and IRL plc, the well-known pizza delivery business, believes that its high level of operating gearing is causing the rate of increases in profits to be greater than the rate of the increase in sales revenue. In its preliminary financial results statement the business said:

> We have had a solid start to 2011, with like-for-like sales for the first seven weeks up 4.7% and are encouraged by the recent strength in like-for-like sales growth. This figure comes against the backdrop of exceptional comparatives from the same period in 2010 and the current difficult economic climate. We are pleased with this performance and we will be benefitting from our accelerated store openings, the recent deal with Moto motorway services, and the operational gearing which will drive our profits going forward.

Domino's is the type of business where quite a lot of its costs are fixed, such as rent, salaries, plant depreciation, motor vehicle running costs, training and advertising.

Source: Domino's Pizza UK and IRL plc, preliminary results for the 52 weeks ended 26 December 2010, 15 February 2011.

FAILING TO BREAK EVEN

Where a business fails to reach its BEP, steps must be taken to remedy the problem: there must be an increase in sales revenue or a reduction in cost, or both. **Real World 7.5** discusses how Tesco plc, the supermarket business, failed to reach its BEP in its stores in China during 2011.

REAL WORLD 7.5

Not breaking China

Tesco has stores in several countries apart from the UK. These include some European countries (particularly Eastern Europe), the United States and Asia. The Chinese stores seem to have proved more difficult for Tesco than was expected. In its preliminary results statement for 2010/11, Tesco said:

> China did not break-even during the second half of the year, which was a consequence of the slower consumer demand growth and our store roll-out being slower than planned.

It went on to say:

> Asian markets offer an exciting long-term growth opportunity and will be a key focus for our future international expansion, both in our established markets and in China. Having continued to invest through the downturn, we are now in an even stronger position as economic recovery continues.

Clearly Tesco expects break-even to be achieved in China before too long, provided that it can add to its portfolio of stores and stimulate faster consumer demand growth.

Source: Extracts from 'Tesco plc Preliminary results 2010/11', Tesco.com, 19 April 2011.

WEAKNESSES OF BREAK-EVEN ANALYSIS

Although break-even analysis can provide useful insights concerning the relationship between cost, volume and profit, it does have its weaknesses. There are three general problems:

1 *Non-linear relationships*. Break-even analysis assumes that total variable cost and total revenue lines are perfectly straight when plotted against volume of output. In real life, this is unlikely to be the case. We shall look at the reason for this in Activity 7.13. Non linearity is probably not a major problem, since, as we have just seen:
   – break-even analysis is normally conducted in advance of the activity actually taking place. Our ability to predict future cost, revenue and so on is limited, so what are probably minor variations from strict linearity are unlikely to be significant, compared with other forecasting errors; and
   – most businesses operate within a narrow range of volume of activity; over short ranges, curved lines tend to be relatively straight.

2 *Stepped fixed cost*. Most types of fixed cost are not fixed over the whole range of activity. They tend to be 'stepped' in the way depicted in Figure 7.3. This means that, in practice, great care must be taken in making assumptions about fixed cost. The problem is heightened because many activities will involve various types of fixed cost (for example rent, supervisory salaries, administration cost), all of which are likely to have steps at different points.

3 *Multi-product businesses*. Most businesses provide more than one product (or service). This can be a problem for break-even analysis since additional sales of one product may affect sales of another of the business's products. There is also the problem of identifying the fixed cost associated with a particular product. Fixed cost may relate to more than one product – for example, work on two products may be carried out in the same rented accommodation. There are ways of dividing the fixed cost between products, but these tend to be arbitrary, which undermines the value of the break-even analysis.

Activity 7.13

We have just seen that, in practice, relationships between costs, revenues and volumes of activity are not necessarily straight-line ones.
  Can you think of at least three reasons, with examples, why this may be the case?

We thought of the following:

■ *Economies of scale with labour*. A business may operate more economically at a higher volume of activity. For example, employees may be able to increase productivity by specialising in particular tasks.

■ *Economies of scale with buying goods or services*. A business may find it cheaper to buy in goods and services where it is buying in bulk, as discounts are often given.

■ *Diseconomies of scale*. This may mean that the per-unit cost of output is higher at higher levels of activity. For example, it may be necessary to pay higher rates of pay to workers to recruit the additional staff needed at higher volumes of activity.

■ *Lower sales prices at high levels of activity*. Some consumers may only be prepared to buy the particular product or service at a lower price. Thus, it may not be possible to achieve high levels of sales activity without lowering the selling price.

Despite some practical problems, break-even analysis seems to be widely used. The media frequently refer to the BEP for businesses and activities. There is seemingly constant discussion, for example, about Eurotunnel's BEP and whether it will ever be reached. Similarly, the number of people regularly needed to pay to watch a football team so that the club breaks even is often mentioned.

Real World 7.6 describes three different situations where breaking even is considered.

REAL WORLD 7.6

Breaking even is breaking out all over

Southern Cross fails to break even

Southern Cross Healthcare Group plc, a business that operated a number of residential care homes for the elderly, found itself in severe financial difficulties in July 2011. This resulted from failing to reach its break-even level of occupancy in its homes. According to the *Financial Times*:

> In the care home business, you can usually break even if 50 to 70 per cent of your beds are occupied. If you pay rent, you only break even when 80 to 85 per cent of your beds are occupied. Southern Cross' occupancy rate fell from 92 per cent in 2006 to 85 per cent in 2010 because it allowed the quality of its homes to deteriorate.

Source: 'Southern Cross run on a failed business model', Sarah O'Connor, FT.com, 30 May 2011.

English universities need to charge £7,000 to break even

Fees will rise a long way at traditional universities, largely because the government is withdrawing teaching subsidies for cheaper courses. The Browne review assumed that institutions would need to charge an average of more than £7,000 to break even. Ministers say universities will need 'exceptional' reasons to want to charge more than £6,000. But top institutions are expected to push to charge nearer the £9,000 barrier. Universities that want to offer accelerated courses, teaching an honours degree within two years, might be able to charge more.

Source: Taken from 'Universities may eye fees near maximum', Chris Cook, FT.com, 3 November 2010.

Not enough coming to see the Cumbrians

The Carlisle United managing director John Nixon said that the attendance at home matches, which averages about 5,200, is well below the figure that enables the club to break even. He went on to say that the club will need to look at its costs and may need to make some cuts. He said that he did not want the club to risk going into administration.

Source: Information taken from 'Carlisle facing budget cuts', www.bbc.co.uk/sport, 25 March 2010.

Real World 7.7 provides evidence concerning the extent to which managers use break-even analysis.

REAL WORLD 7.7

Break-even analysis in practice

A survey of management accounting practice in the United States was conducted in 2003. Nearly 2,000 businesses replied to the survey. These tended to be larger businesses, of which about 40 per cent were manufacturers and about 16 per cent financial services; the remainder were across a range of other industries.

The survey revealed that 62 per cent use break-even analysis extensively, with a further 22 per cent considering using the technique in the future.

Though the survey relates to the US and was undertaken several years ago, in the absence of UK evidence it provides some indication of what is likely also to be current practice in the UK and elsewhere in the developed world.

Source: Taken from the '2003 Survey of Management Accounting' by Ernst and Young, 2003.

USING CONTRIBUTION TO MAKE DECISIONS: MARGINAL ANALYSIS

We saw at the start of this chapter, that when deciding between two or more possible courses of action, *only costs that vary with the decision should be included in the analysis*. This principle can be applied to the consideration of fixed cost.

For many decisions that involve:

■ relatively small variations from existing practice, and/or
■ relatively limited periods of time,

fixed cost is not relevant. This element of cost will be the same irrespective of the decision made. This is because the fixed cost element cannot, or will not, be altered in the short term.

Activity 7.14

Ali plc owns a workshop from which it provides a PC repair and maintenance service. There has recently been a downturn in demand for the service. It would be possible for Ali plc to carry on the business from smaller, cheaper accommodation.

Can you think of any reasons why the business might not immediately move to smaller, cheaper accommodation?

We thought of broadly three reasons:

1 It is not usually possible to find a buyer for the existing accommodation at very short notice and it may be difficult to find an available alternative quickly.
2 It may be difficult to move accommodation quickly where there is, say, delicate equipment to be moved.
3 Management may feel that the downturn might not be permanent, and so would be reluctant to take such a dramatic step and deny itself the opportunity to benefit from a possible revival of trade.

We shall now consider some types of decisions where fixed cost can be regarded as irrelevant. In making these decisions, we should have as our key strategic objective the enhancement of owners' (shareholders') wealth. Since these decisions are short-term in nature, wealth will normally be increased by generating as much net cash inflow as possible.

In **marginal analysis** only costs and revenues that vary with the decision are considered. This usually means that fixed cost can be ignored. This is because marginal analysis is usually applied to minor alterations in the level of activity. It tends to be true, therefore, that the variable cost per unit will be equal to the **marginal cost**, which is the additional cost of producing one more unit of output. Whilst marginal cost normally equals variable cost, there may be times when producing one more unit will involve a step in the fixed cost. If this occurs, the marginal cost is not just the variable cost; it will include the increment, or step, in the fixed cost as well.

Marginal analysis may be used in four key areas of decision making:

- pricing/assessing opportunities to enter contracts;
- determining the most efficient use of scarce resources;
- make-or-buy decisions;
- closing or continuation decisions.

Let us consider each of these areas in turn.

Pricing/assessing opportunities to enter contracts

To understand how marginal analysis may be used in assessing an opportunity, consider the following activity.

Activity 7.15

Cottage Industries Ltd (see Example 7.1, page 242) has spare capacity in that its basket makers have some spare time. An overseas retail chain has offered the business an order for 300 baskets at a price of £13 each.

Without considering any wider issues, should the business accept the order? (Assume that the business does not rent the machine.)

Since the fixed cost will be incurred in any case, it is not relevant to this decision. All we need to do is to see whether the price offered will yield a contribution. If it will, the business will be better off by accepting the contract than by refusing it.

	£
Additional revenue per unit	13
Additional cost per unit	(12)
Additional contribution per unit	1

For 300 units, the additional contribution will be £300 (that is, 300 × £1). Since no fixed cost increase is involved, irrespective of what else is happening to the business, it will be £300 better off by taking this contract than by refusing it.

As ever with decision making, there are other factors that are either difficult or impossible to quantify. These should be taken into account before reaching a final decision. In the case of Cottage Industries Ltd's decision concerning the overseas customer, these could include the following:

- The possibility that spare capacity will have been 'sold off' cheaply when there might be another potential customer who will offer a higher price. There is the danger that, by the time that the higher-priced offer is made, the capacity will be fully committed. It is a matter of commercial judgement as to how likely this will be.
- Selling the same product, but at different prices to different customers, could lead to a loss of customer goodwill. The fact that a different price will be set for customers in different countries (that is, in different markets) may be sufficient to avoid this potential problem.
- If the business is going to suffer continually from being unable to sell its full production potential at the 'usual' price, it might be better, in the long run, to reduce capacity and make fixed-cost savings. Using the spare capacity to produce marginal benefits may lead to the business failing to address this issue.
- On a more positive note, the business may see this as a way of breaking into the overseas market. This is something that might be impossible to achieve if the business charges its usual price.

The most efficient use of scarce resources

Normally, the output of a business is determined by customer demand for the particular goods or services. In some cases, however, output will be restricted by the capacity of the business to supply as much of the product as the customers demand. Limited capacity to supply might stem from a shortage of any factor of production – labour, raw materials, space, machine capacity and so on. Such scarce factors are often known as *key* or *limiting* factors.

Where capacity to supply acts as a brake on output, management must decide on how best to deploy the scarce resource. That is, it must decide which products, from the range available, should be provided and how many of each should be provided. Marginal analysis can be useful to management in such circumstances. The guiding principle is that the most profitable combination of products will occur where the *contribution per unit of the scarce factor* is maximised. Example 7.2 illustrates this point.

Example 7.2

A business provides three different services, the details of which are as follows:

	Service (code name)		
	AX107	AX109	AX220
	£	£	£
Selling price per unit	50	40	65
Variable cost per unit	(25)	(20)	(35)
Contribution per unit	25	20	30
Labour time per unit	5 hours	3 hours	6 hours

Within reason, the market will take as many units of each service as can be provided, but the ability to provide the service is limited by the availability of labour, all of which needs to be skilled. Fixed cost is not affected by the choice of service provided because all three services use the same facilities.

The most profitable service is AX109 because it generates a contribution of £6.67 (£20/3) an hour. The other two generate only £5.00 each an hour (£25/5 and £30/6). So, to maximise profit, priority should be given to the production that maximises the contribution per unit of limiting factor.

Our first reaction might be that the business should provide only service AX220, as this is the one that yields the highest contribution per unit sold. If so, we would have been making the mistake of thinking that it is the ability to sell that is the limiting factor. If the above analysis is not convincing, we can take a random number of available labour hours and ask ourselves what is the maximum contribution (and, therefore, profit) that could be made by providing each service exclusively. Bear in mind that there is no shortage of anything else, including market demand, just a shortage of labour.

Activity 7.16

A business makes three different products, the details of which are as follows:

	Product (code name)		
	B14	B17	B22
Selling price per unit (£)	25	20	23
Variable cost per unit (£)	10	8	12
Weekly demand (units)	25	20	30
Machine time per unit (hours)	4	3	4

Fixed cost is not affected by the choice of product because all three products use the same machine. Machine time is limited to 148 hours a week.

Which combination of products should be manufactured if the business is to produce the highest profit?

	Product (code name)		
	B14	B17	B22
Selling price per unit (£)	25	20	23
Variable cost per unit (£)	(10)	(8)	(12)
Contribution per unit (£)	15	12	11
Machine time per unit (hours)	4	3	4
Contribution per machine hour (£)	3.75	4.00	2.75
Order of priority	2nd	1st	3rd

Therefore produce:

20 units of product B17 using	60 hours
22 units of product B14 using	88 hours
	148 hours

This leaves unsatisfied the market demand for a further 3 units of product B14 and 30 units of product B22.

Activity 7.17

What practical steps could be taken that might lead to a higher level of contribution for the business in Activity 7.16?

The possibilities for improving matters that occurred to us are as follows:

- Consider obtaining additional machine time. This could mean obtaining a new machine, subcontracting the machining to another business or, perhaps, squeezing a few more hours a week out of the business's own machine. Perhaps a combination of two or more of these is a possibility.
- Redesign the products in a way that requires less time per unit on the machine.
- Increase the price per unit of the three products. This might well have the effect of dampening demand, but the existing demand cannot be met at present. It may, therefore, be more profitable, in the long run, to make a greater contribution on each unit sold than to take one of the other courses of action to overcome the problem.

Activity 7.18

Going back to Activity 7.16, what is the maximum price that the business concerned would logically be prepared to pay to have the remaining B14s machined by a subcontractor, assuming that no fixed or variable cost would be saved as a result of not doing the machining itself?

Would there be a different maximum if we were considering the B22s?

If the remaining three B14s were subcontracted at no cost, the business would be able to earn a contribution of £15 a unit, which it would not otherwise be able to gain. Therefore, any price up to £15 a unit would be worth paying to a subcontractor to undertake the machining. Naturally, the business would prefer to pay as little as possible, but anything up to £15 would still make it worthwhile subcontracting the machining.

This would not be true of the B22s because they have a different contribution per unit; £11 would be the relevant figure in their case.

Make-or-buy decisions

Businesses are frequently confronted by the need to decide whether themselves to produce the product or service that they sell, or to buy it in from some other business. Thus, a producer of electrical appliances might decide to subcontract the manufacture of one of its products to another business, perhaps because there is a shortage of production capacity in the producer's own factory. Alternatively, the producer may believe it to be cheaper to subcontract than to make the appliance itself. Obtaining services or products from a subcontractor is often called **outsourcing**.

In many cases whether to outsource or not is a longer term, strategic decision. In that case it needs to be assessed as such. In the present context we are considering more tactical make-or-buy decisions that can be taken quickly for the short term.

Activity 7.19

Shah Ltd needs a component for one of its products. It can subcontract production of the component to a subcontractor who will provide the components for £20 each. Shah Ltd can produce the components internally for a total variable cost of £15 per component. Shah Ltd has spare capacity.

Should the component be subcontracted or produced internally?

The answer is that Shah Ltd should produce the component internally, since the variable cost of subcontracting is greater by £5 (that is, £20 – £15) than the variable cost of internal manufacture.

Activity 7.20

Now assume that Shah Ltd (Activity 7.19) has no spare capacity, so it can only produce the component internally by reducing its output of another of its products. While it is making each component, it will lose contributions of £12 from the other product.

Should the component be subcontracted or produced internally?

The answer is to subcontract. In this case, both the variable cost of production and the opportunity cost of lost contributions must be taken into account.

Thus, the relevant cost of internal production of each component is:

	£
Variable cost of production of the component	15
Opportunity cost of lost production of the other product	12
	27

This is obviously more costly than the £20 per component that will have to be paid to the subcontractor.

Activity 7.21

What factors, other than the immediately financially quantifiable, would you consider when making a make-or-buy decision?

We feel that there are two major factors:

1 The general problems of subcontracting, particularly:
   (a) loss of control of quality;
   (b) potential unreliability of supply.
2 Expertise and specialisation. Generally, businesses should focus on their core competences.

Picking up the second point in Activity 7.21, it is possible for most businesses, with sufficient determination, to do virtually everything in-house. This may, however, require a level of skill and facilities that most businesses neither have nor feel inclined to acquire.

For example, though it is true that most businesses could generate their own electricity, their managements tend to take the view that this is better done by a specialist generator business. Specialists can often do things more cheaply, with less risk of things going wrong.

Closing or continuation decisions

It is quite common for businesses to produce separate financial statements for each department or section, to try to assess their relative performance. Example 7.3 considers how marginal analysis can help decide how to respond where it is found that a particular department underperforms.

Example 7.3

Goodsports Ltd is a retail shop that operates through three departments, all in the same accommodation. The three departments occupy roughly equal-sized areas of the accommodation. The projected trading results for next year are:

	Total £000	Sports equipment £000	Sports clothes £000	General clothes £000
Sales revenue	534	254	183	97
Cost	(482)	(213)	(163)	(106)
Profit/(loss)	52	41	20	(9)

It would appear that if the general clothes department were to close, the business would be more profitable, by £9,000 a year, assuming last year's performance to be a reasonable indication of future performance.

When the cost is analysed between that part that is variable and that part that is fixed, however, the contribution of each department can be deduced and the following results obtained:

	Total £000	Sports equipment £000	Sports clothes £000	General clothes £000
Sales revenue	534	254	183	97
Variable cost	(344)	(167)	(117)	(60)
Contribution	190	87	66	37
Fixed cost (rent and so on)	(138)	(46)	(46)	(46)
Profit/(loss)	52	41	20	(9)

Now it is obvious that closing the general clothes department, without any other developments, would make the business worse off by £37,000 (the department's contribution). The department should not be closed, because it makes a positive contribution. The fixed cost would continue whether the department was closed or not. As can be seen from the above analysis, distinguishing between variable and fixed cost, and deducing the contribution, can make the picture a great deal clearer.

Activity 7.22

In considering Goodsports Ltd (in Example 7.3), we saw that the general clothes department should not be closed 'without any other developments'.

What 'other developments' could affect this decision, making continuation either more attractive or less attractive?

The things that we could think of are as follows:

■ Expansion of the other departments or replacing the general clothes department with a completely new activity. This would make sense only if the space currently occupied by the general clothes department could generate contributions totalling at least £37,000 a year.
■ Subletting the space occupied by the general clothes department. Once again, this would need to generate a net rent greater than £37,000 a year to make it more financially beneficial than keeping the department open.
■ Keeping the department open, even if it generated no contribution whatsoever (assuming that there is no other use for the space), may still be beneficial. If customers are attracted into the shop because it has general clothing, they may then buy something from one of the other departments. In the same way, the activity of a sub-tenant might attract customers into the shop. (On the other hand, it might drive them away!)

Figure 7.11 summarises the four key decision-making areas where marginal analysis tends to be used.

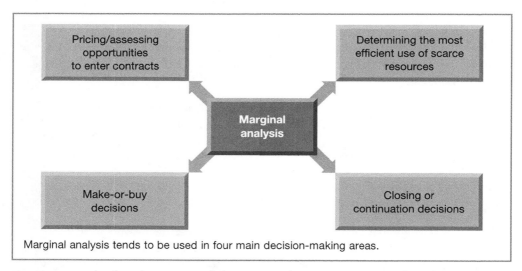

Marginal analysis tends to be used in four main decision-making areas.

Figure 7.11 The four key areas of decision making using marginal analysis

❓ SELF-ASSESSMENT QUESTION 7.1

Khan Ltd can render three different types of service (Alpha, Beta and Gamma) using the same staff. Various estimates for next year have been made as follows:

	Service		
	Alpha	Beta	Gamma
Selling price (£/unit)	30	39	20
Variable material cost (£/unit)	15	18	10
Other variable costs (£/unit)	6	10	5
Share of fixed cost (£/unit)	8	12	4
Staff time required (hours)	2	3	1

Fixed cost for next year is expected to total £40,000.

Required:

(a) If the business were to render only service Alpha next year, how many units of the service would it need to provide in order to break even? (Assume for this part of the question that there is no effective limit to market size and staffing level.)

(b) If the business has limited staff hours available next year, in which order of preference would the three services come?

(c) The maximum market for next year for the three services is as follows:

Alpha	3,000 units
Beta	2,000 units
Gamma	5,000 units

Khan Ltd has a maximum of 10,000 staff hours available next year.
What quantities of each service should the business provide next year and how much profit would this be expected to yield?

The answer to this question can be found at the back of the book, in Appendix B.

SUMMARY

The main points in this chapter may be summarised as follows:

Cost = amount of resources, usually measured in monetary terms, sacrificed to achieve a particular objective

Relevant and irrelevant costs

- Relevant costs must:
  - relate to the objective being pursued by the business;
  - be a future cost;
  - differ from one possible decision outcome to the next.
- Relevant costs therefore include:
  - future opportunity costs;
  - differential future outlay costs.

■ Irrelevant costs therefore include:
  – all past (or sunk) costs;
  – all committed costs;
  – non-differential future outlay costs.

Cost behaviour

■ Fixed cost is independent of the level of activity (for example, rent).

■ Variable cost varies with the level of activity (for example, raw materials).

■ Semi-fixed (semi-variable) cost is a mixture of fixed and variable costs (for example, electricity).

Break-even analysis

■ The break-even point (BEP) is the level of activity (in units of output or sales revenue) at which total cost (fixed + variable) = total sales revenue.

■ Calculation of BEP is as follows:

$$\text{BEP (in units of output)} = \frac{\text{Fixed cost for the period}}{\text{Sales revenue per unit} - \text{variable cost per unit}}$$

■ Knowledge of the BEP for a particular activity can be used to help assess risk.

■ Contribution per unit = sales revenue per unit less variable cost per unit.

■ Contribution margin ratio = contribution/sales revenue ($\times$ 100%).

■ Margin of safety = excess of planned volume (or sales revenue) of activity over volume (or sales revenue) at BEP.

■ Operating gearing is the extent to which the total cost of some activity is fixed rather than variable.

Weaknesses of BE analysis

■ There are non-linear relationships between costs, revenues and volume.

■ There may be stepped fixed costs. Most fixed costs are not fixed over all volumes of activity.

■ Multi-product businesses have problems in allocating fixed costs to particular activities.

Marginal analysis (ignores fixed costs where these are not affected by the decision)

■ Assessing contracts – we consider only the effect on contributions.

■ Using scarce resources – the limiting factor is most effectively used by maximising its contribution per unit.

■ Make-or-buy decisions – we take the action that leads to the highest total contributions.

■ Closing/continuing an activity – should be assessed by net effect on total contributions.

MyAccountingLab

Go to www.myaccountinglab.com to check your understanding of the chapter, create a personalised study plan, and maximise your revision time

KEY TERMS

cost p. 231
historic cost p. 231
opportunity cost p. 231
relevant cost p. 232
irrelevant cost p. 232
past costs p. 232
outlay costs p. 232
fixed costs p. 235
variable costs p. 235
stepped fixed costs p. 238
semi-fixed (semi-variable) costs p. 239

break-even analysis p. 239
break-even chart p. 240
break-even point (BEP) p. 241
contribution per unit p. 245
contribution margin ratio p. 245
margin of safety p. 246
operating gearing p. 249
marginal analysis p. 255
marginal cost p. 255
outsourcing p. 258

FURTHER READING

If you would like to explore the topics covered in this chapter in more depth, we recommend the following books:

Drury, C., *Management and Cost Accounting*, 8th edn, Cengage Learning, 2012, Chapter 8.

Hilton, R., *Managerial Accounting*, 9th edn, McGraw-Hill Higher Education, 2011, Chapter 14.

Horngren, C., Datar, S. and Rajan, M., *Cost Accounting: A Managerial Emphasis*, 14th edn, Prentice Hall International, 2011, Chapter 3.

McWatters, C., Zimmerman, J. and Morse, D., *Management Accounting: Analysis and Interpretation*, Financial Times Prentice Hall, 2008, Chapter 5.

? REVIEW QUESTIONS

Solutions to these questions can be found at the back of the book, in Appendix C.

7.1 Define the terms *fixed cost* and *variable cost*. Explain how an understanding of the distinction between fixed cost and variable cost can be useful to managers.

7.2 What is meant by the *BEP* for an activity? How is the BEP calculated? Why is it useful to know the BEP?

7.3 When we say that some business activity has *high operating gearing*, what do we mean? What are the implications for the business of high operating gearing?

7.4 If there is a scarce resource that is restricting sales, how will the business maximise its profit? Explain the logic of the approach that you have identified for maximising profit.

✳ EXERCISES

*Exercise 7.1 is basic level, exercises 7.2 and 7.3 are intermediate level and exercises 7.4 and 7.5 are advanced level. Those with **coloured numbers** have answers at the back of the book, in Appendix D.*

> **If you wish to try more exercises, visit the website at www.myaccountinglab.com.**

7.1 Lombard Ltd has been offered a contract for which there is available production capacity. The contract is for 20,000 identical items, manufactured by an intricate assembly operation, to be produced and delivered in the next few months at a price of £80 each. The specification for one item is as follows:

Assembly labour	4 hours
Component X	4 units
Component Y	3 units

There would also be the need to hire equipment, for the duration of the contract, at an outlay cost of £200,000.

The assembly is a highly skilled operation and the workforce is currently underutilised. It is the business's policy to retain this workforce on full pay in anticipation of high demand next year, for a new product currently being developed. There is sufficient available skilled labour to undertake the contract now under consideration. Skilled workers are paid £15 an hour.

Component X is used in a number of other sub-assemblies produced by the business. It is readily available. 50,000 units of Component X are currently held in inventories. Component Y was a special purchase in anticipation of an order that did not in the end materialise. It is, therefore, surplus to requirements and the 100,000 units that are currently held may have to be sold at a loss. An estimate of various values for Components X and Y provided by the materials planning department is as follows:

	Component X £/unit	Component Y £/unit
Historic cost	4	10
Replacement cost	5	11
Net realisable value	3	8

It is estimated that any additional relevant costs associated with the contract (beyond the above) will amount to £8 an item.

Required:
Analyse the information and advise Lombard Ltd on the desirability of the contract.

7.2 The management of a business is concerned about its inability to obtain enough fully trained labour to enable it to meet its present budget projection. →

	Service			
	Alpha £000	Beta £000	Gamma £000	Total £000
Variable costs				
Materials	6	4	5	15
Labour	9	6	12	27
Expenses	3	2	2	7
Allocated fixed costs	6	15	12	33
Total cost	24	27	31	82
Profit	15	2	2	19
Sales revenue	39	29	33	101

The amount of labour likely to be available amounts to £20,000. All of the variable labour is paid at the same hourly rate. You have been asked to prepare a statement of plans, ensuring that at least 50 per cent of the budgeted sales revenues are achieved for each service and the balance of labour is used to produce the greatest profit.

Required:

(a) Prepare the statement, with explanations, showing the greatest profit available from the limited amount of skilled labour available, within the constraint stated. *Hint*: Remember that all labour is paid at the same rate.

(b) What steps could the business take in an attempt to improve profitability, in the light of the labour shortage?

7.3 A hotel group prepares financial statements on a quarterly basis. The senior management is reviewing the performance of one hotel and making plans for next year.

The managers have in front of them the results for this year (based on some actual results and some forecasts to the end of this year):

Quarter	Sales revenue £000	Profit/(loss) £000
1	400	(280)
2	1,200	360
3	1,600	680
4	800	40
Total	4,000	800

The total estimated number of guests (guest nights) for this year is 50,000, with each guest night being charged at the same rate. The results follow a regular pattern; there are no unexpected cost fluctuations beyond the seasonal trading pattern shown above.

For next year, management anticipates an increase in unit variable cost of 10 per cent and a profit target for the hotel of £1 million. These will be incorporated into its plans.

Required:

(a) Calculate the total variable and total fixed cost of the hotel for this year. Show the provisional annual results for this year in total, showing variable and fixed cost separately. Show also the revenue and cost per guest.

(b) (i) If there is no increase in guests for next year, what will be the required revenue rate per hotel guest to meet the profit target?

(ii) If the required revenue rate per guest is not raised above this year's level, how many guests will be required to meet the profit target?

(c) Outline and briefly discuss the assumptions, that are made in typical PV or break-even analysis, and assess whether they limit its usefulness.

7.4 A business makes three products, A, B and C. All three products require the use of two types of machine: cutting machines and assembling machines. Estimates for next year include the following:

	Product		
	A	B	C
Selling price (£ per unit)	25	30	18
Sales demand (units)	2,500	3,400	5,100
Material cost (£ per unit)	12	13	10
Variable production cost (£ per unit)	7	4	3
Time required per unit on cutting machines (hours)	1.0	1.0	0.5
Time required per unit on assembling machines (hours)	0.5	1.0	0.5

Fixed cost for next year is expected to total £42,000.

The business has cutting machine capacity of 5,000 hours a year and assembling machine capacity of 8,000 hours a year.

Required:

(a) State, with supporting workings, which products in which quantities the business should plan to make next year on the basis of the above information. *Hint*: First determine which machines will be a limiting factor (scarce resource).

(b) State the maximum price per product that it would be worth the business paying to a subcontractor to carry out that part of the work that could not be done internally.

7.5 Darmor Ltd has three products, which require the same production facilities. Information about the production cost for one unit of its products is as follows:

	Product		
	X	Y	Z
	£	£	£
Labour: Skilled	6	9	3
Unskilled	2	4	10
Materials	12	25	14
Other variable costs	3	7	7
Fixed cost	5	10	10

All labour and materials are variable costs. Skilled labour is paid £12 an hour and unskilled labour is paid £8 an hour. All references to labour cost above are based on basic rates of pay. Skilled labour is scarce, which means that the business could sell more than the maximum that it is able to make of any of the three products.

Product X is sold in a regulated market and the regulators have set a price of £30 per unit for it.

Required:

(a) State, with supporting workings, the price that must be charged for Products Y and Z, such that the business would find it equally profitable to make and sell any of the three products.

(b) State, with supporting workings, the maximum rate of overtime premium that the business would logically be prepared to pay its skilled workers to work beyond the basic time.

FULL COSTING

INTRODUCTION

Full (absorption) costing is a widely used approach that takes account of all of the cost of producing a particular product or service. In this chapter, we shall see how this approach can be used to deduce the cost of some activity, such as making a unit of product (for example, a tin of baked beans), providing a unit of service (for example, a car repair) or creating a facility (for example, building an Olympic athletics stadium).

The full-costing approach is widely used in practice. We shall first take a look at a traditional method of full costing and consider the usefulness of full cost for management purposes. We shall then go on to consider activity-based costing, which represents an alternative to the traditional method.

Learning outcomes

When you have completed this chapter, you should be able to:

■ discuss the usefulness, for decision-making purposes, of deducing the full cost of a unit of output;

■ deduce the full cost of a unit of output both in a single-product environment and in a multi-product environment using the traditional full cost method.

■ discuss the problems of charging full cost to jobs in a multi-product environment;

■ explain the role and nature of activity-based costing.

MyAccountingLab Visit www.myaccountinglab.com for practice and revision opportunities

WHY DO MANAGERS WANT TO KNOW THE FULL COST?

There are broadly four areas where managers use information concerning the full cost of the business's products or services. These are:

- *Pricing and output decisions.* Having full cost information can help managers to make decisions on the price to be charged to customers for the business's products or services. Linked to the pricing decisions are also decisions on the number of units of a product or service that the business should seek to provide to the market.
- *Exercising control.* Managers need information to help them make decisions that seek to ensure that the organisation's plans are met. Budgets are typically expressed in full cost terms. This means that periodic reports that compare actual performance with budgets need to be expressed in the same full cost terms.
- *Assessing relative efficiency.* Full cost information can help managers compare the cost of doing something in a particular way, or particular place, with its cost if done in a different way, or place. For example, a motor car manufacturer may find it useful to compare the cost of building a particular model of car in one of its plants, rather than another. This could help the business decide on where to locate future production.
- *Assessing performance.* The level of profit, or income, generated over a period is an important measure of business performance. To measure profit, or income, we need to compare sales revenue with the associated expenses. Where a business produces a product or renders a service, a major expense will be the cost of making the product or rendering the service. Usually, this expense is based on the full cost of whatever is sold. Measuring income provides managers (and other users) with information that can help them make a whole range of decisions.

Later in the chapter we shall consider some of the issues surrounding these four purposes. Figure 8.1 shows the four uses of full cost information.

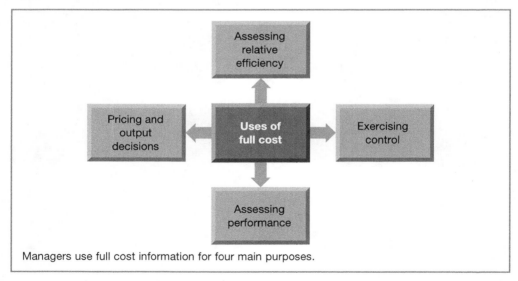

Managers use full cost information for four main purposes.

Figure 8.1 Uses of full cost by managers

Now let us consider **Real World 8.1**.

REAL WORLD 8.1

Operating cost

An interesting example of the use of full cost for pricing decisions occurs in the National Health Service (NHS). In recent years, the funding of hospitals has radically changed. A new system of Payment by Results (PBR) requires the Department of Health to produce a list of prices for an in-patient spell in hospital that covers different types of procedures. This list, which is revised annually, reflects the prices that hospitals will be paid by the government for carrying out the different procedures.

For 2011/12, the price list included the following figures:

- £5,365 for carrying out a hip replacement;
- £5,902 for carrying out a knee replacement.

These figures are based on the full cost of undertaking each type of procedure in 2009/10 (but adjusted for inflation and an efficiency discount). Full cost figures were submitted by all NHS hospitals for that year as part of their annual accounting process and an average for each type of procedure was then calculated. Figures for other procedures on the price list were derived in the same way.

Source: 'Payment by Results, Guidance for 2011/12', Department of Health, 18 February 2011, p. 60.

When considering the information in Real World 8.1, an important question that arises is 'what does the full cost of each type of procedure include?' Does it simply include the cost of the salaries earned by doctors and nurses during the time spent with the patient or does it also include the cost of other items? If the cost of other items is included, how is it determined? Would it include, for example, a charge for:

- the artificial hip and drugs provided for the patient;
- equipment used in the operating theatre;
- administrative and support staff within the hospital;
- heating and lighting;
- maintaining the hospital buildings;
- laundry and cleaning?

If the cost of such items is included, how can an appropriate charge for each procedure be determined? (How, for example, is the cost of heating the hospital included in the cost of a hip replacement?) If, on the other hand, these type of costs are not included, are the figures of £5,365 and £5,902 potentially misleading?

These questions are the subject of this chapter.

WHAT IS FULL COSTING?

Full cost is the total amount of resources, usually measured in monetary terms, sacrificed to achieve a given objective. It takes account of all resources sacrificed to achieve that objective. Thus, if the objective were to supply a customer with a product or service, the cost of all aspects relating to the making of the product or provision of the service would be included as part of the full cost. To derive the full cost figure, we must, therefore, accumulate all elements of cost incurred and then assign them to the particular product or service.

The logic of **full costing** is that the entire cost of running a facility, say an office, is part of the cost of the output of that office. For example, the rent may be a cost that will not alter merely because we provide one more unit of the service. If the office were not rented, however, there would be nowhere for the staff to work, so rent is an important element of the cost of that service. A **cost unit** is one unit of whatever is having its cost determined. This is usually one unit of output of a particular product or service.

In the sections that follow we shall first see how full costing is applied to a single-product business and then to a multi-product one.

SINGLE-PRODUCT BUSINESSES

The simplest case for which to deduce the full cost per unit is where the business has only one product or service, that is, each unit of its production is identical. Here it is simply a question of adding up all of the elements of cost of production incurred in a particular period (materials, labour, rent, fuel, power and so on) and dividing this total by the total number of units of output for that period.

Activity 8.1

Fruitjuice Ltd has just one product, a sparkling orange drink that is marketed as 'Orange Fizz'. During last month the business produced 7,300 litres of the drink. The cost incurred was made up as follows:

	£
Ingredients (oranges and so on)	390
Fuel	85
Rent of accommodation	350
Depreciation of equipment	75
Labour	880

What is the full cost per litre of producing 'Orange Fizz'?

This figure is found simply by adding together all of the elements of cost incurred and then dividing by the number of litres produced:

$$£(390 + 85 + 350 + 75 + 880)/7,300 = £0.24 \text{ per litre}$$

In practice, there can be problems in deciding exactly how much cost was incurred. In the case of Fruitjuice Ltd, for example, how is the cost of depreciation deduced? It is certainly an estimate and so its reliability is open to question. The cost of raw materials may also be a problem. Should we use the 'relevant' cost of the raw materials (in this case, almost certainly the replacement cost), or the actual price paid for it (historic cost)? If the cost per litre is to be used for some decision-making purpose (which it should be), the replacement cost is probably more logical. In practice, however, it seems that historic cost is more often used to deduce full cost. It is not clear why this should be the case.

There can also be problems in deciding precisely how many units of output were produced. If making Orange Fizz is not a very fast process, some of the drink will probably be in the process of being made at any given moment. This, in turn, means that some of the cost incurred last month was for some Orange Fizz that was work in progress at the end of the month, so is not included in last month's output quantity of 7,300 litres. Similarly, part of the 7,300 litres might well have been started and incurred cost in the previous month, yet all of those litres were included in the 7,300 litres that we used in our calculation of the cost per litre. Work in progress is not a serious problem, but some adjustment for the value of opening and closing work in progress for the particular period needs to be made if reliable full cost information is to be obtained.

This approach to full costing, which can be taken where all of the output consists of identical, or near identical items (of goods or services), is often referred to as **process costing**.

MULTI-PRODUCT BUSINESSES

Most businesses produce more than one type of product or service. In this situation, the units of output of the product, or service, will not be identical and so the approach used with litres of 'Orange Fizz' in Activity 8.1 is inappropriate. While it is reasonable to assign an identical cost to units of output that are identical, it is not helpful to do this where the units of output are obviously different. It would be pointless, for example, to assign the same cost to each car repair carried out by a garage, irrespective of the complexity and size of the repair.

Direct and indirect cost

To provide full cost information, we need to have a systematic approach to accumulating the elements of cost and then assigning this total cost to particular cost units on some reasonable basis. Where cost units are not identical, the starting point is to separate cost into two categories: direct cost and indirect cost.

- **Direct cost**. This is the type of cost that can be identified with specific cost units. That is to say, the effect of the cost can be reliably measured in respect of each particular cost unit. The main examples of a direct cost are direct materials and direct labour. Thus, in determining the cost of a motor car repair by a garage, both the cost of spare parts used in the repair and the cost of the mechanic's time would be part of the direct cost of that repair. Collecting elements of direct cost is a simple matter of having a cost-recording system that is capable of capturing the cost of direct materials and direct labour used on each job. The direct labour cost would be based on the hours worked by direct workers and their rate of pay.

■ **Indirect cost** (or **overheads**). This encompasses all other elements of cost, that is, those items that cannot be directly measured in respect of each particular cost unit (job). Thus, the amount paid to rent the garage would be an indirect cost of a motor car repair.

We shall use the terms 'indirect cost' and 'overheads' interchangeably for the remainder of this book. Indirect cost is also sometimes known as **common cost** because it is common to all of the output of the production unit (for example, factory or department) for the period.

Real World 8.2 gives some indication of the relative importance of direct and indirect costs in practice.

REAL WORLD 8.2

Counting the cost

A fairly recent survey of 176 UK businesses operating in various industries, all with annual sales revenue of more than £50 million, was conducted by Al-Omiri and Drury. They discovered that the full cost of the businesses' output on average is split between direct and indirect costs as shown in Figure 8.2:

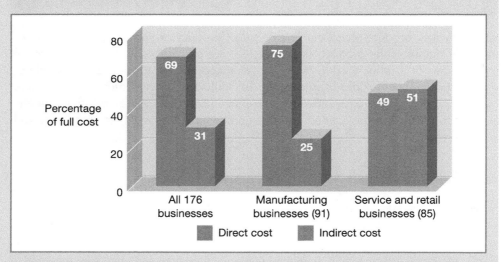

Figure 8.2 Percentage of full cost contributed by direct and indirect cost

For the manufacturers, the 75 per cent direct cost was, on average, made up as follows:

	Per cent
Direct materials	52
Direct labour	14
Other direct costs	9

Source: Al-Omiri, M. and Drury, C., 'A survey of factors influencing the choice of product costing systems in UK organisations', *Management Accounting Research*, December 2007, pp. 399–424.

Activity 8.2

A garage bases its prices on the direct cost of each job (car repair) that it carries out. How could the garage collect the direct cost (labour and materials) information concerning a particular job?

The mechanic doing the job could record the length of time worked on the car by direct workers (that is the mechanic concerned and any colleagues). The stores staff could be required to keep a record of the cost of parts and materials used on each job.

In fact this is the way that job costing tends to operate in businesses like garages. A 'job sheet' will normally be prepared – perhaps on the computer – for each individual job. Staff would need to get into the routine of faithfully recording all elements of direct labour and materials applied to the job.

Job costing

The term **job costing** is used to describe the way in which we identify the full cost per cost unit (unit of output or 'job') where the cost units differ. To deduce the full cost of a particular cost unit, we first identify the direct cost of the cost unit. This, by the definition of direct cost, is fairly straightforward. We then seek to 'charge' each cost unit with a fair share of indirect cost (overheads). Put another way, cost units will absorb overheads. This leads to full costing also being called **absorption costing**. The absorption process is shown graphically in Figure 8.3.

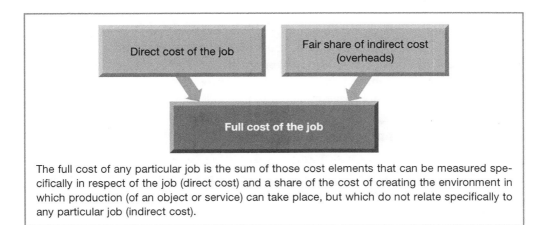

The full cost of any particular job is the sum of those cost elements that can be measured specifically in respect of the job (direct cost) and a share of the cost of creating the environment in which production (of an object or service) can take place, but which do not relate specifically to any particular job (indirect cost).

Figure 8.3 The relationship between direct cost and indirect cost

Activity 8.3

Sparky Ltd is a business that employs a number of electricians. The business undertakes a range of work for its customers, from replacing fuses to installing complete wiring systems in new houses.

In respect of a particular job done by Sparky Ltd, into which category (direct or indirect) would each of the following cost elements fall:

- the wages of the electrician who did the job?
- depreciation of the tools used by the electrician?
- the cost of cable and other materials used on the job?
- rent of the building where Sparky Ltd stores its inventories of cable and other materials?

The electrician's wages earned while working on the particular job and the cost of the materials used on the job are included in direct cost. This is because it is possible to measure how much time was spent on the particular job (and therefore its direct labour cost) and the amount of materials used (and therefore the direct material cost) in the job.

The others are included in the general cost of running the business and, as such, must form part of the indirect cost of doing the job. They cannot be directly measured in respect of the particular job, however.

It is important to note that whether a cost is direct or indirect depends on the item being costed – the cost objective. To refer to indirect cost without identifying the cost objective is incorrect.

Activity 8.4

Into which category, direct or indirect, would each of the elements of cost listed in Activity 8.3 fall, if we were seeking to find the cost of operating the entire business of Sparky Ltd for a month?

All of these costs will form part of the direct cost, since they can all be related to, and measured in respect of, running the business for a month.

Naturally, broader-reaching cost objectives, such as operating Sparky Ltd for a month, tend to include a higher proportion of direct cost than do more limited ones, such as a particular job done by Sparky Ltd. As we shall see shortly, this makes costing broader cost objectives rather more straightforward than costing narrower ones. It is generally the case that elements of direct cost are easier to deal with than indirect cost.

Full (absorption) costing and the behaviour of cost

We saw in Chapter 7 that the full cost of doing something (or total cost, as it is usually known in the context of marginal analysis) can be analysed between the fixed and the variable elements. This is illustrated in Figure 8.4.

The apparent similarity of what is shown in Figure 8.4 to that depicted in Figure 8.3 seems to lead some to believe that variable cost and direct cost are the same, and that fixed cost and indirect cost (overheads) are the same. This is incorrect.

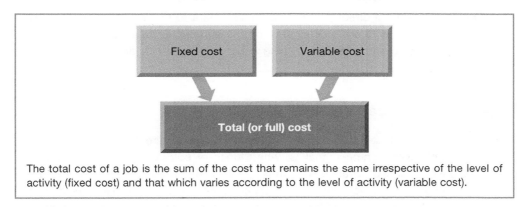

The total cost of a job is the sum of the cost that remains the same irrespective of the level of activity (fixed cost) and that which varies according to the level of activity (variable cost).

Figure 8.4 The relationship between fixed cost, variable cost and total cost

The notions of fixed and variable are concerned with **cost behaviour** in the face of changes in the volume of activity. The notions of direct and indirect, on the other hand, relate to the extent to which cost elements can be measured in respect of particular cost units (jobs). The two sets of notions are entirely different. Though it may be true that there is a tendency for fixed cost elements to be indirect (overheads) and for variable cost elements to be direct, there is no link, and there are many exceptions to this tendency. Most activities, for example, have variable indirect cost. Furthermore, labour is a significant element of direct cost in most types of business activity (14 per cent of the total cost of manufacture – see Real World 8.2) but it is usually a fixed cost.

The relationship between the reaction of cost to volume changes (cost behaviour), on the one hand, and how cost elements need to be gathered to deduce the full cost (cost collection), on the other, in respect of a particular job is shown in Figure 8.5.

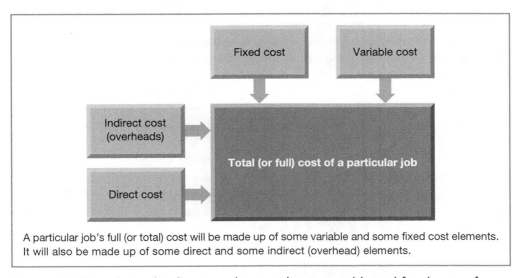

A particular job's full (or total) cost will be made up of some variable and some fixed cost elements. It will also be made up of some direct and some indirect (overhead) elements.

Figure 8.5 The relationship between direct, indirect, variable and fixed costs of a particular job

Total cost is the sum of direct and indirect costs. It is also the sum of fixed and variable costs. These two facts are independent of one another. Thus a particular element of cost may be fixed, but that tells us nothing about whether it is a direct or an indirect cost.

The problem of indirect cost

It is worth emphasising that the distinction between direct and indirect cost is only important in a job-costing environment, that is, where units of output differ. When we were considering costing a litre of 'Orange Fizz' drink in Activity 8.1, whether particular elements of cost were direct or indirect was of no consequence, because all elements of cost were shared equally between the individual litres of 'Orange Fizz'. Where we have units of output that are not identical, however, we have to look more closely at the make-up of the cost to achieve a fair measure of the full cost of a particular job.

Although the indirect cost of any activity must form part of the full cost of each cost unit, it cannot, by definition, be directly related to individual cost units. This raises a major practical issue: how is the indirect cost to be apportioned to individual cost units?

OVERHEADS AS SERVICE RENDERERS

It is reasonable to view the indirect cost (overheads) as rendering a service to the cost units. Take for example a particular legal case, undertaken by a firm of solicitors for a client. This job can be seen as being rendered a service by the office in which the work is done. In this sense, it is reasonable to charge each case (cost unit) with a share of the cost of running the office (rent, lighting, heating, cleaning, building maintenance and so on). It also seems reasonable to relate the charge for the 'use' of the office to the level of service that the particular case has received from the office.

The next step is the difficult one. How might the cost of running the office, which is part of the cost of all of the work done by the firm, be divided between individual cases that differ in size and complexity?

One possibility is sharing this overhead cost equally between each case handled by the firm within the period. This method, however, has little to commend it unless the cases were close to being identical in terms of the extent to which they had 'benefited' from the overheads.

If we are not to propose equal shares, we must identify something observable and measurable about the cases that we feel provides a reasonable basis for distinguishing between one case and the next. In practice, time spent working on each particular cost unit by direct labour is the most popular basis. It must be stressed that this is not the 'correct' way and it certainly is not the only way.

Job costing: a worked example

To see how job costing works, let us consider Example 8.1.

Example 8.1

Johnson Ltd, a business that provides a personal computer maintenance and repair service, has overheads of £10,000 each month. Each month, 1,000 direct labour hours are worked and charged to cost units (jobs carried out by the business). A particular PC repair undertaken by the business used direct materials costing £15. Direct labour worked on the repair was 3 hours and the wage rate is £16 an hour. Johnson Ltd charges overheads to jobs on a direct labour hour basis. What is the full (absorption) cost of the repair?

Solution

First, let us establish the **overhead absorption (recovery) rate**, that is, the rate at which individual jobs will be charged with overheads. This is £10 (that is, £10,000/1,000) per direct labour hour.

Thus, the full cost of the repair is:

	£
Direct materials	15
Direct labour (3 × £16)	48
	63
Overheads (3 × £10)	30
Full cost of the job	93

Note, in Example 8.1, that the number of labour hours (3 hours) appears twice in deducing the full cost: once to deduce the direct labour cost and a second time to deduce the overheads to be charged to the repair. These are really two separate issues, though they are both based on the same number of labour hours.

Note also that, if all the jobs undertaken during the month are assigned overheads in a similar manner, all £10,000 of overheads will be charged to the jobs between them. Jobs that involve a lot of direct labour will be assigned a large share of overheads. Similarly, jobs that involve little direct labour will be assigned a small share of overheads.

Activity 8.5

Can you think of reasons why direct labour hours tend to be regarded as the most logical basis for sharing overheads between cost units?

The reasons that occurred to us are as follows:

- Large jobs should logically attract large amounts of overheads because they are likely to have been rendered more 'service' by the overheads than small ones. The length of time that they are worked on by direct labour may be seen as a rough way of measuring relative size, though other means of doing this may be found – for example, relative physical size, where the cost unit is a physical object, like a manufactured product.

- Most overheads are related to time. Rent, heating, lighting, non-current asset depreciation, supervisors' and managers' salaries, which are all typical overheads, are all more or less time-based. That is to say that the overheads for one week tend to be about half of those for a similar two-week period. Thus, a basis of allotting overheads to jobs that takes account of the length of time that the units of output benefited from the 'service' rendered by the overheads seems logical.
- Direct labour hours are capable of being measured for each job. They will normally be measured to deduce the direct labour element of cost in any case. Thus, a direct labour hour basis of dealing with overheads is practical to apply in the real world.

It cannot be emphasised enough that there is no 'correct' way to allot overheads to jobs. Overheads, by definition, do not naturally relate to individual jobs. If, nevertheless, we wish to take account of the fact that overheads are part of the cost of all jobs, we must find some acceptable way of including a share of the total overheads in each job. If a particular means of doing this is accepted by those who use the full cost deduced, then the method is as good as any other method. Accounting is concerned only with providing useful information to decision makers. In practice, the method that seems to be regarded as being the most useful is the direct labour hour method. Real World 8.4, which we shall consider later in the chapter, provides some evidence of this. Of the businesses surveyed 72 per cent use the direct labour hour basis.

Now let us consider **Real World 8.3**, which gives an example of one well-known organisation that does not use direct labour hours to cost its output.

REAL WORLD 8.3

Operating overheads

As we saw in Real World 8.1, the UK National Health Service (NHS) seeks to ascertain the cost of various medical and surgical procedures that it undertakes for its patients. In determining the costs of a procedure that requires time in hospital as an 'in patient', the NHS identifies the total direct cost of the particular procedure (staff time, medication and so on). To this it adds a share of the hospital overheads. The total overheads are absorbed by individual procedures by taking this overheads total and dividing it by the number of 'bed days' throughout the hospital for the period, to establish a 'bed-day rate'. A bed day is one patient spending one day occupying a bed in the hospital. To ascertain the cost of the procedure for a particular patient, the bed-day rate is included in the cost of the procedure according to how many bed days the particular patient had.

Note that the NHS does not use the direct labour hour basis of absorption. The bed-day rate is, however, an alternative, logical, time-based approach.

Source: NHS Costing Manual 2010/11, Department of Health Gateway, reference 15,969, 3 May 2011.

Activity 8.6

Marine Suppliers Ltd undertakes a range of work, including making sails for small sailing boats on a made-to-measure basis.

The business expects the following to arise during the next month:

Direct labour cost	£60,000
Direct labour time	6,000 hours
Indirect labour cost	£9,000
Depreciation of machinery	£3,000
Rent	£5,000
Heating, lighting and power	£2,000
Machine time	2,000 hours
Indirect materials	£500
Other miscellaneous indirect production cost elements (overheads)	£200
Direct materials cost	£3,000

The business has received an enquiry about a sail. It is estimated that the particular sail will take 12 direct labour hours to make and will require 20 square metres of sailcloth, which costs £2 per square metre.

The business normally uses a direct labour hour basis of charging indirect cost (overheads) to individual jobs.

What is the full (absorption) cost of making the sail?

The direct cost of making the sail can be identified as follows:

	£
Direct materials (20 × £2)	40.00
Direct labour (12 × (£60,000/6,000))	120.00
	160.00

To deduce the indirect cost (overhead) element that must be added to derive the full cost of the sail, we first need to total these cost elements as follows:

	£
Indirect labour	9,000
Depreciation	3,000
Rent	5,000
Heating, lighting and power	2,000
Indirect materials	500
Other miscellaneous indirect production cost (overhead) elements	200
Total indirect cost (overheads)	19,700

Since the business uses a direct labour hour basis of charging indirect cost to jobs, we need to deduce the indirect cost (or overhead) recovery rate per direct labour hour. This is simply:

£19,700/6,000 = £3.28 per direct labour hour

Thus, the full cost of the sail would be expected to be:

	£
Direct materials (20 × £2)	40.00
Direct labour (12 × (£60,000/6,000))	120.00
Indirect cost (12 × £3.28)	39.36
Full cost	199.36

Figure 8.6 shows the process for applying indirect (overhead) and direct costs to the sail that was the subject of Activity 8.6.

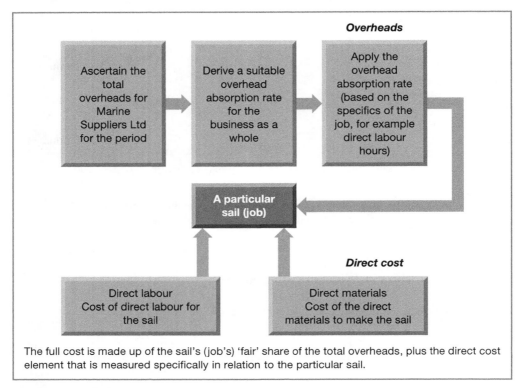

Figure 8.6 How the full cost is derived for the sail by Marine Suppliers Ltd in Activity 8.6

Activity 8.7

Suppose that Marine Suppliers Ltd (see Activity 8.6) used a machine hour basis of charging overheads to jobs. What would be the cost of the job detailed if it was expected to take 5 machine hours (as well as 12 direct labour hours)?

The total overheads of the business will of course be the same irrespective of the method of charging them to jobs. Thus, the overhead recovery rate, on a machine hour basis, will be:

$$£19,700/2,000 = £9.85 \text{ per machine hour}$$

Thus, the full cost of the sail would be expected to be:

	£
Direct materials (20 × £2)	40.00
Direct labour (12 × (£60,000/6,000))	120.00
Indirect cost (5 × £9.85)	49.25
Full cost	209.25

Selecting a basis for charging overheads

We saw earlier that there is no single correct way of charging overheads. The final choice is a matter of judgement. It seems reasonable to say, however, that the nature of the overheads should influence the choice of the basis of charging the overheads to jobs. Where production is capital-intensive and overheads are primarily machine-based (such as depreciation, machine maintenance, power and so on), machine hours might be favoured. Otherwise direct labour hours might be preferred.

It would be irrational to choose one of these bases in preference to the other simply because it apportions either a higher or a lower amount of overheads to a particular job. The total overheads will be the same irrespective of the method of dividing that total between individual jobs and so a method that gives a higher share of overheads to one particular job must give a lower share to the remaining jobs. There is one cake of fixed size: if one person receives a relatively large slice, others must on average receive relatively small slices. To illustrate further this issue of apportioning overheads, consider Example 8.2.

Example 8.2

A business, that provides a service, expects to incur overheads totalling £20,000 next month. The total direct labour time worked is expected to be 1,600 hours and machines are expected to operate for a total of 1,000 hours.

During the next month, the business expects to do just two large jobs. Information concerning each job is as follows:

	Job 1	Job 2
Direct labour hours	800	800
Machine hours	700	300

How much of the total overheads will be charged to each job if overheads are to be charged on:

(a) a direct labour hour basis; and
(b) a machine hour basis?

What do you notice about the two sets of figures that you calculate?

Solution

(a) Direct labour hour basis
Overhead recovery rate = £20,000/1,600 = £12.50 per direct labour hour.

Job 1	£12.50 × 800 = £10,000
Job 2	£12.50 × 800 = £10,000

(b) Machine hour basis
Overhead recovery rate = £20,000/1,000 = £20.00 per machine hour.

Job 1	£20.00 × 700 = £14,000
Job 2	£20.00 × 300 = £6,000

It is clear from these calculations that the total overheads charged to jobs is the same (that is, £20,000) whichever method is used. So, whereas the machine hour basis gives Job 1 a higher share than does the direct labour hour method, the opposite is true for Job 2.

It is not practical to charge overheads on one basis to one job and on the other basis to the other job. This is because either total overheads will not be fully charged to the jobs, or the jobs will be overcharged with overheads. For example, using the direct labour hour method for Job 1 (£10,000) and the machine hour basis for Job 2 (£6,000) will mean that only £16,000 of a total £20,000 of overheads will be charged to jobs. As a result, the objective of full (absorption) costing, which is to charge all of the overheads to the various jobs done during the period, will not be achieved. In this particular case, if selling prices are based on full cost, the business may not charge high enough prices to cover all of its costs.

Figure 8.7 shows the effect of the two different bases of charging overheads to Jobs 1 and 2.

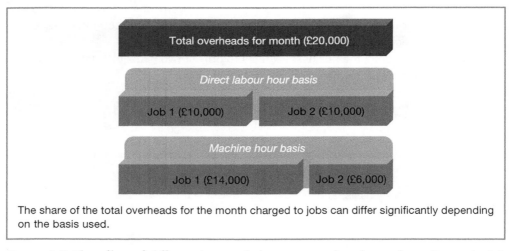

The share of the total overheads for the month charged to jobs can differ significantly depending on the basis used.

Figure 8.7 The effect of different bases of charging overheads to jobs in Example 8.2

Activity 8.8

The point was made above that it would normally be irrational to prefer one basis of charging overheads to jobs simply because it apportions either a higher or a lower amount of overheads to a particular job. This is because the total overheads are the same irrespective of the method of charging the total to individual jobs. Can you think of any circumstances where it would not necessarily be so irrational?

This might apply where, for a particular job, a customer has agreed to pay a price based on full cost plus an agreed fixed percentage for profit. Here it would be beneficial to the producer for the total cost of the job to be as high as possible.

The circumstances outlined in the answer to Activity 8.8 would be relatively unusual, but sometimes public sector organisations, particularly central and local government departments, have entered into contracts to have work done, with the price to be deduced, after the work has been completed, on a cost-plus basis. Such contracts also exist in the private sector. They are pretty rare these days, probably because they are open to abuse in the way described. Usually, contract prices are agreed in advance, typically in conjunction with competitive tendering.

Real World 8.4 provides some insights regarding the basis of overhead recovery in practice.

REAL WORLD 8.4

Overhead recovery rates in practice

A survey of 129 UK manufacturing businesses showed that the direct labour hour basis (or a close approximation to it) of charging indirect cost (overheads) to cost units was overwhelmingly the most popular. It was used by 72 per cent of the respondents to the survey.

15 per cent of respondents used a 'production-time based overhead rate'. This is presumably something like a machine hour rate.

Though this survey applied only to manufacturing businesses, in the absence of other information it provides some impression of what happens in practice.

Source: Based on information taken from Brierley, J., Cowton, C. and Drury, C., 'Product costing practices in different manufacturing industries: A British survey', *International Journal of Management*, December 2007.

Segmenting the overheads

As we have just seen, charging the same overheads to different jobs on different bases is not logical. It is perfectly reasonable, however, to charge one segment of the total overheads on one basis and another segment (or other segments) on another basis (or bases).

Activity 8.9

Taking the same business as in Example 8.2 (page 282), on closer analysis we find that of the overheads totalling £20,000 next month, £8,000 relate to machines (depreciation, maintenance, rent of the space occupied by the machines and so on) and the remaining £12,000 to more general overheads. The other information about the business is exactly as it was before.

How much of the total overheads will be charged to each job if the machine-related overheads are to be charged on a machine hour basis and the remaining overheads are charged on a direct labour hour basis?

Direct labour hour basis

Overhead recovery rate = £12,000/1,600 = £7.50 per direct labour hour

Machine hour basis

Overhead recovery rate = £8,000/1,000 = £8.00 per machine hour

Overheads charged to jobs

	Job 1 £	Job 2 £
Direct labour hour basis:		
£7.50 × 800	6,000	
£7.50 × 800		6,000
Machine hour basis:		
£8.00 × 700	5,600	
£8.00 × 300		2,400
Total	11,600	8,400

Note that, in this answer, the expected overheads of £20,000 are charged in total.

Segmenting the overheads in this way may well be seen as providing a better basis of charging overheads to jobs. This is quite often found in practice, usually by dividing a business into separate 'areas' (cost centres) for costing purposes, charging overheads differently from one area to the next, according to the nature of the work done in each.

Dealing with overheads on a cost centre basis

In practice, all but the smallest businesses are divided into departments. Normally, each department deals with a separate activity. The reasons for dividing a business into departments include the following:

- *Size and complexity*. Many businesses are too large and complex to be managed as a single unit. It is usually more practical to operate each business as a series of relatively independent units with each one having its own manager.
- *Expertise*. Each department normally has its own area of specialism and is managed by a specialist.
- *Accountability*. Each department can have its own accounting records that enable its performance to be assessed. This can lead to greater management control and motivation among the staff.

As is shown in Real World 8.5, which we shall consider shortly, most businesses charge overheads to cost units on a department-by-department basis. They do this because they expect that it will give rise to a more useful way of charging overheads. It is probably only in a minority of cases that it leads to any great improvement in the usefulness of the resulting full cost figures. Though it may not be of enormous benefit in many cases, applying overheads on a departmental basis is probably not an expensive exercise. Since cost elements are collected department by department for other purposes (particularly control), to apply overheads on a department-by-department basis is a relatively simple matter.

We shall now take a look at how the departmental approach to deriving full cost works, in a service-industry context, through Example 8.3.

Example 8.3

Autosparkle Ltd offers a motor vehicle paint-respray service. The jobs that it undertakes range from painting a small part of a saloon car, usually following a minor accident, to a complete respray of a double-decker bus.

Each job starts life in the Preparation Department, where it is prepared for the Paintshop. Here, the job is worked on by direct workers, in most cases taking some direct materials from the stores with which to treat the old paintwork and, generally, to render the vehicle ready for respraying. Thus the job will be charged with direct materials, direct labour and with a share of the Preparation Department's overheads. The job then passes into the Paintshop Department, already valued at the cost that it picked up in the Preparation Department.

In the Paintshop, the staff draw direct materials (mainly paint) from the stores and direct workers spend time respraying the job, using sophisticated spraying apparatus as well as working by hand. So, in the Paintshop, the job is charged with direct materials, direct labour and a share of that department's overheads. The job now passes into the Finishing Department, valued at the cost of the materials, labour and overheads that it accumulated in the first two departments.

In the Finishing Department, jobs are cleaned and polished ready to go back to the customers. Further direct labour and, in some cases, materials are added. All jobs also pick up a share of that department's overheads. The job, now complete, passes back to the customer.

Figure 8.8 shows graphically how this works for a particular job.

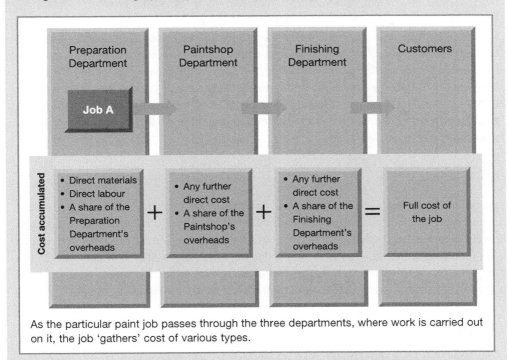

As the particular paint job passes through the three departments, where work is carried out on it, the job 'gathers' cost of various types.

Figure 8.8 A cost unit (Job A) passing through Autosparkle Ltd's process

> The approach to charging overheads to jobs (for example, direct labour hours) might be the same for all three departments, or it might be different from one department to another. It is possible that the cost of running the spraying apparatus dominates the Paintshop overheads. In that case, the Paintshop's overheads might well be charged to jobs on a machine hour basis. The other two departments are probably labour intensive, so that direct labour hours may be seen as being appropriate there.

The passage of a job through the departments, picking up cost as it goes, can be compared to a snowball being rolled across snow: as it rolls, it picks up more and more snow.

Where cost determination is dealt with departmentally, each department is known as a **cost centre**. This can be defined as a particular physical area or some activity or function for which the cost is separately identified. Charging direct cost to jobs, in a departmental system, is exactly the same as where the whole business is one single cost centre. It is simply a matter of keeping a record of:

■ the number of hours of direct labour worked on the particular job and the grade of labour, assuming that there are different grades with different rates of pay;
■ the cost of the direct materials taken from stores and applied to the job; and
■ any other direct cost elements, for example some subcontracted work, associated with the job.

This record keeping will normally be done cost centre by cost centre.

It is obviously necessary to break down the production overheads of the entire business on a cost centre basis. This means that the total overheads of the business must be divided between the cost centres, such that the sum of the overheads of all of the cost centres equals the overheads for the entire business. By charging all of their overheads to jobs, the cost centres will, between them, charge all of the overheads of the business to jobs. **Real World 8.5** provides an indication of the number of different cost centres that businesses tend to use in practice.

Batch costing

The production of many types of goods and services (particularly goods) involves producing in a batch of identical, or nearly identical, units of output, but where each batch is distinctly different from other batches. For example, a theatre may put on a production whose nature (and therefore cost) is very different from that of other productions. On the other hand, ignoring differences in the desirability of the various types of seating, all of the individual units of output (tickets to see the production) are identical.

Cost centres in practice

It is usual for businesses to have several cost centres. A survey of 186 larger UK businesses involved in various activities are shown in Figure 8.9:

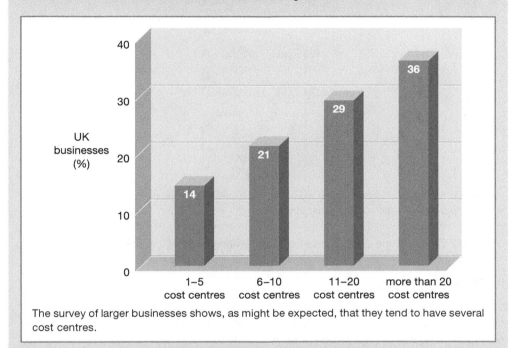

The survey of larger businesses shows, as might be expected, that they tend to have several cost centres.

Figure 8.9 Analysis of the number of cost centres within a business

We can see that 86 per cent of businesses surveyed had six or more cost centres and that 36 per cent of businesses had more than 20 cost centres. Though not shown on the diagram, 3 per cent of businesses surveyed had a single cost centre (that is, there was a business-wide or overall overhead rate used). Clearly, businesses that deal with overheads on a business-wide basis are relatively rare.

Source: Based on information taken from Drury, C. and Tayles, M., 'Profitability analysis in UK organisations', *British Accounting Review*, December 2006.

In these circumstances, the cost per ticket would normally be deduced by:

■ using a job costing approach (taking account of direct and indirect costs and so on) to find the cost of mounting the production; and then

■ dividing the cost of mounting the production by the expected number of tickets to be sold to find the cost per ticket.

This is known as **batch costing**.

Figure 8.10 shows the process for deriving the cost of one cost unit (product) in a batch.

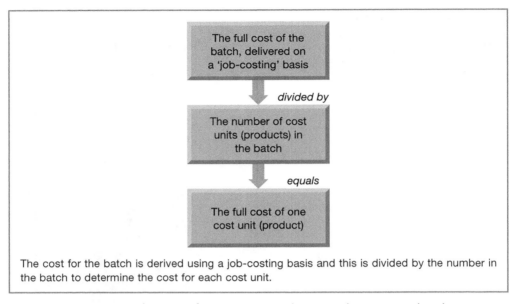

The cost for the batch is derived using a job-costing basis and this is divided by the number in the batch to determine the cost for each cost unit.

Figure 8.10 Deriving the cost of one cost unit where production is in batches

The forward-looking nature of full (absorption) costing

Although deducing full cost can be done after the work has been completed, it is frequently predicted in advance. This is often because an idea of the full cost is needed as a basis for setting a selling price. Predictions, however, rarely turn out to be 100 per cent accurate. Where actual outcomes differ from predicted outcomes an over-recovery or under-recovery of overheads will normally occur.

ACTIVITY-BASED COSTING

We have seen that the traditional approach to job/batch costing involves identifying that part of the cost that can be measured in respect of a particular job/batch (direct cost). Other cost elements (overheads) are thrown into a pool of cost. These are then charged to individual jobs/batches according to some formula, such as the number of direct labour hours worked.

Costing and pricing: the traditional way

The traditional, and still widely used, approach to job costing and product pricing developed when the notion of trying to determine the cost of industrial production first emerged. This was around the time of the UK Industrial Revolution when industry displayed the following characteristics:

- *Direct-labour-intensive and direct-labour-paced production*. Labour was at the heart of production. To the extent that machinery was used, it tended to support the efforts of direct labour and the speed of production was dictated by direct labour.
- *A low level of indirect cost relative to direct cost*. Little was spent on power, personnel services, machinery (leading to low depreciation charges) and other areas typical of the indirect cost (overheads) of modern businesses.
- *A relatively uncompetitive market*. Transport difficulties, limited industrial production worldwide and a lack of knowledge by customers of competitors' prices meant that businesses could prosper without being too scientific in their approach to deriving full costs. Typically they could simply add a margin for profit to arrive at the selling price (cost-plus pricing). Customers would have tended to accept those products that the supplier had to offer, rather than demanding precisely what they wanted.

Since overheads at that time represented a pretty small element of total cost, it was acceptable and practical to deal with them in a fairly arbitrary manner. Not too much effort was devoted to trying to control overheads because the potential rewards of better control were relatively small, certainly when compared with the benefits from firmer control of direct labour and material costs. It was also reasonable to charge overheads to individual jobs on a direct labour hour basis. Most of the overheads were incurred in support of direct labour: providing direct workers with a place to work, heating and lighting the workplace, employing people to supervise the direct workers and so on. Direct workers, perhaps aided by machinery, carried out all production.

At that time, service industries were a relatively unimportant part of the economy and would have largely consisted of self-employed individuals. These individuals would probably have been uninterested in trying to do more than work out a rough hourly/daily rate for their time and to try to base prices on this.

Costing and pricing: the new environment

In recent years, the world of industrial production has fundamentally changed. Most of it is now characterised by:

- *Capital-intensive and machine-paced production*. Machines are at the heart of much production, including both the manufacture of goods and the rendering of services. Most labour supports the efforts of machines, for example, technically maintaining them. Also, machines often dictate the pace of production. According to evidence provided in Real World 8.2 (page 273), direct labour accounts on average for just 14 per cent of manufacturers' total cost.
- *A high level of indirect costs relative to direct costs*. Modern businesses tend to have very high depreciation, servicing and power costs. There are also high costs of personnel and staff welfare, which were scarcely envisaged in the early days of industrial production. At the same time, there are very low (sometimes no) direct labour costs. Although direct material cost often remains an important element of total cost, more efficient production methods lead to less waste and, therefore, to a lower total material cost, again tending to make indirect cost (overheads) more dominant. Again according to

Real World 8.2, overheads account for 25 per cent of manufacturers' total cost and 51 per cent of service sector total cost.

- *A highly competitive international market.* Production, much of it highly sophisticated, is carried out worldwide. Transport, including fast airfreight, is relatively cheap. Fax, telephone and, particularly, the internet ensure that potential customers can quickly and cheaply find the prices of a range of suppliers. Markets now tend to be highly price competitive. Customers increasingly demand products custom made to their own requirements. This means that businesses need to know their product costs with a greater degree of accuracy than historically has been the case. Businesses also need to take a considered and informed approach to pricing their output.

In the UK, as in many developed countries, service industries now dominate the economy, employing the great majority of the workforce and producing most of the value of productive output. Though there are still many self-employed individuals supplying services, many service providers are vast businesses such as banks, insurance companies and cinema operators. For most of these larger service providers, the activities very closely resemble modern manufacturing activity. They too are characterised by high capital intensity, overheads dominating direct costs and a competitive international market.

In the past, the traditional approach to determining product costs has worked reasonably well, mainly because overhead recovery rates (that is, rates at which overheads are absorbed by jobs) were typically of a much lower value for each direct labour hour than the rate paid to direct workers as wages or salaries. It is now, however, becoming increasingly common for overhead recovery rates to be between five and ten times the hourly rate of pay, because overheads are now much more significant. When production is dominated by direct labour paid, say, £8 an hour, it might be reasonable to have an overhead recovery rate of, say, £1 an hour. When, however, direct labour plays a relatively small part in production, to have an overhead recovery rate of, say, £50 for each direct labour hour is likely to lead to very arbitrary product costing. Even a small change in the amount of direct labour worked on a job could massively affect the total cost deduced. This is not because the direct worker is very highly paid, but because of the effect of the direct labour hours on the overhead cost loading. A further problem is that overheads are still typically charged on a direct labour hour basis even though the overheads may not be closely related to direct labour.

Real World 8.6 provides a rather disturbing view of costing and cost control in large banks.

REAL WORLD 8.6

Bank accounts

In a study of the cost structures of 52 international banks, the German consultancy firm, Droege, found that indirect cost (overheads) could represent as much as 85 per cent of total cost. However, whilst direct costs were generally under tight management control, overheads were not. The overheads, which include such items as IT development, risk control, auditing, marketing and public relations, were often not allocated between operating divisions or were allocated in a rather arbitrary manner.

Source: Based on information in Skorecki, A., 'Banks have not tackled indirect costs', FT.com, 7 January 2004.

Taking a closer look

The changes in the competitive environment discussed above have led to much closer attention being paid to the issue of overheads. There has been increasing recognition of the fact that overheads do not just happen; something must be causing them. To illustrate this point, let us consider Example 8.4.

Example 8.4

Modern Producers Ltd has a storage area that is set aside for its inventories of finished goods. The cost of running the stores includes a share of the factory rent and other establishment costs, such as heating and lighting. It also includes the salaries of staff employed to look after the inventories, and the cost of financing the inventories held in the stores.

The business has two product lines: A and B. Product A tends to be made in small batches and low levels of finished inventories are held. The business prides itself on its ability to supply Product B, in relatively large quantities, instantly. As a consequence, most of the space in the finished goods store is filled with finished Product Bs, ready to be despatched immediately an order is received.

Traditionally, the whole cost of operating the stores would have been treated as a part of general overheads and included in the total of overheads charged to jobs, probably on a direct labour hour basis. This means that, when assessing the cost of Products A and B, the cost of operating the stores has fallen on them according to the number of direct labour hours worked on manufacturing each one; a factor that has nothing to do with storage. In fact, most of the stores' cost should be charged to Product B, since this product causes (and benefits from) the stores' cost much more than Product A.

Failure to account more precisely for the cost of running the stores is masking the fact that Product B is not as profitable as it seems to be. It may even be leading to losses as a result of the relatively high stores-operating cost that it causes. However, much of this cost is charged to Product A, without regard to the fact that Product A causes little of it.

Activity-based costing (ABC) aims to overcome the kind of problem just illustrated in Example 8.4, by directly tracing the cost of all support activities (that is, overheads) to particular products or services. For a manufacturing business, these support activities may include materials ordering, materials handling, storage, inspection and so on. The cost of the support activities makes up the total overheads cost. The outcome of this tracing exercise is to provide a more realistic, and more finely measured, account of the overhead cost element for a particular product or service.

To implement a system of ABC, managers must begin by carefully examining the business's operations. They will need to identify:

■ each of the various support activities involved in the process of making products or providing services;

- the costs to be attributed to each support activity; and
- the factors that cause a change in the costs of each support activity, that is the **cost drivers**.

Identifying the cost drivers is a vital element of a successful ABC system. They have a cause-and-effect relationship with activity costs and so are used as a basis for attaching activity costs to a particular product or service. This point is now discussed further.

Attributing overheads

Once the various support activities, their costs and the factors that drive these costs, have been identified, ABC requires:

1 An overhead **cost pool** to be established for each activity. Thus, Modern Producers Ltd, the business in Example 8.4, will create a cost pool for operating the finished goods store. There will be just one cost pool for each separate cost driver.
2 The total cost associated with each support activity to be allocated to the relevant cost pool.
3 The total cost in each pool to then be charged to output (Products A and B, in the case of Example 8.4) using the relevant cost driver.

Step 3 (above) involves dividing the amount in each cost pool by the estimated total usage of the cost driver to derive a cost per unit of the cost driver. This unit cost figure is then multiplied by the number of units of the cost driver used by a particular product, or service, to determine the amount of overhead cost to be attached to it (or absorbed by it).

Example 8.5 should make this last step clear.

Example 8.5

The management accountant at Modern Producers Ltd (see Example 8.4) has estimated that the cost of running the finished goods stores for next year will be £90,000. This will be the amount allocated to the 'finished goods stores cost pool'.

It is estimated that each Product A will spend an average of one week in the stores before being sold. With Product B, the equivalent period is four weeks. Both products are of roughly similar size and have very similar storage needs. It is felt, therefore, that the period spent in the stores ('product weeks') is the cost driver.

Next year, 50,000 Product As and 25,000 Product Bs are expected to pass through the stores. The estimated total usage of the cost driver will be the total number of 'product weeks' that the products will be in store. For next year, this will be:

$$
\begin{array}{lll}
\text{Product A} & 50{,}000 \times 1 \text{ week} & = & 50{,}000 \\
\text{Product B} & 25{,}000 \times 4 \text{ weeks} & = & \underline{100{,}000} \\
& & & 150{,}000
\end{array}
$$

The cost per unit of cost driver is the total cost of the stores divided by the number of 'product weeks', as calculated above. This is:

$$£90{,}000/150{,}000 = £0.60$$

→

To determine the cost to be attached to a particular unit of product, the figure of £0.60 must be multiplied by the number of 'product weeks' that a product stays in the finished goods store. Thus, each unit of Product A will be charged with £0.60 (that is, £0.60 × 1) and each Product B with £2.40 (that is, £0.60 × 4).

Benefits of ABC

Through the direct tracing of overheads to products in the way described, ABC seeks to establish a more accurate cost for each unit of product or service. This should help managers in assessing product profitability and in making decisions concerning pricing and the appropriate product mix. Other benefits, however, may also flow from adopting an ABC approach.

Activity 8.10

Can you think of any other benefits that an ABC approach to costing may provide?

By identifying the various support activities' costs and analysing what causes them to change, managers should gain a better understanding of the business. This, in turn, should help them in controlling overheads and improving efficiency. It should also help them in forward planning. They may, for example, be in a better position to assess the likely effect of new products and processes on activities and costs.

ABC versus the traditional approach

We can see that there is a basic philosophical difference between the traditional and the ABC approaches. The traditional approach views overheads as *rendering a service to cost units*, the cost of which must be charged to those units. ABC, on the other hand, views overheads as being *caused by* activities. Since it is the cost units that cause these activities, it is, therefore, the cost units that must be charged with the costs that they cause.

With the traditional approach, overheads are apportioned to product cost centres. Each product cost centre would then derive an overhead recovery rate, typically overheads per direct labour hour. Overheads would then be applied to units of output according to how many direct labour hours were worked on them.

With ABC, the overheads are analysed into cost pools, with one cost pool for each cost-driving activity. The overheads are then charged to units of output, through activity cost driver rates. These rates are an attempt to represent the extent to which each particular cost unit is believed to cause the particular part of the overheads.

Cost pools are much the same as cost centres, except that each cost pool is linked to a particular *activity* (operating the stores in Examples 8.1 and 8.2), rather than being more general, as is the case with cost centres in traditional job (or product) costing.

The two different approaches are illustrated in Figure 8.11.

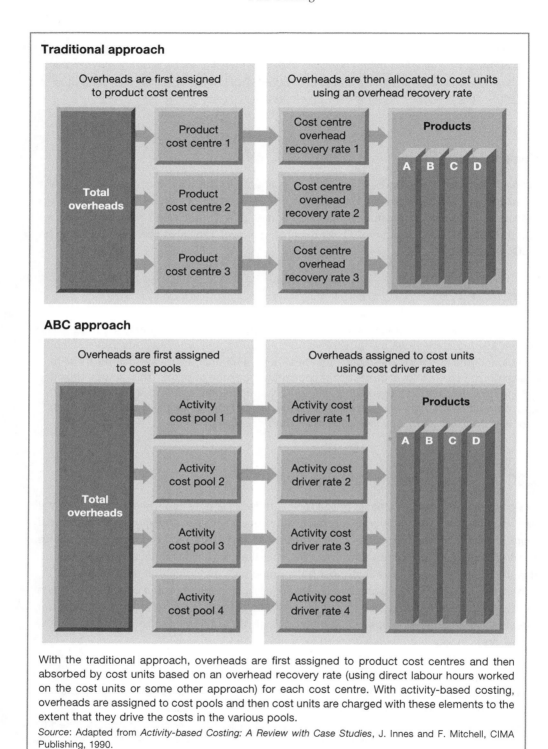

With the traditional approach, overheads are first assigned to product cost centres and then absorbed by cost units based on an overhead recovery rate (using direct labour hours worked on the cost units or some other approach) for each cost centre. With activity-based costing, overheads are assigned to cost pools and then cost units are charged with these elements to the extent that they drive the costs in the various pools.

Source: Adapted from *Activity-based Costing: A Review with Case Studies*, J. Innes and F. Mitchell, CIMA Publishing, 1990.

Figure 8.11 Traditional versus activity-based costing

ABC and service industries

Much of our discussion of ABC has concentrated on the manufacturing industry, perhaps because early users of ABC were manufacturing businesses. In fact, ABC is probably even more relevant to service industries because, in the absence of a direct material element, a service business's total cost is likely to be largely made up of overheads. Real World 8.2 (page 273) shows that, for the businesses included in that survey, overheads represent 51 per cent of total cost for service providers, but only 25 per cent for manufacturers. There is certainly evidence that ABC has been adopted more readily by businesses that sell services rather than products, as we shall see later.

Activity 8.11

What is the difference in the way in which direct costs are accounted for when using ABC, relative to their treatment taking a traditional approach to full costing?

The answer is no difference at all. ABC is concerned only with the way in which overheads are charged to jobs to derive the full cost.

Criticisms of ABC

Critics of ABC argue that analysing overheads in order to identify cost drivers can be time-consuming and costly. The cost of setting up the ABC system, as well as costs of running and updating it, must be incurred. These costs can be very high, particularly where the business's operations are complex and involve a large number of activities and cost drivers. Furthermore, where the products produced are quite similar, the finer measurements provided by ABC may not lead to strikingly different outcomes than under the traditional approach. Supporters of ABC may argue, however, that identifying the activities that cause the costs may still be well worth doing. As mentioned earlier, knowing what drives the costs may make cost control more effective.

ABC is also criticised for the same reason that full costing is generally criticised, which is that it does not provide relevant information for decision-making. This point will be addressed in the following section.

Real World 8.7 shows how ABC came to be used at the Royal Mail.

REAL WORLD 8.7

Delivering ABC

Early in the 2000s the publicly owned Royal Mail adopted ABC and used it to find the cost of making postal deliveries. Royal Mail identified 340 activities that gave rise to costs, created a cost pool and identified a cost driver for each of these.

The Royal Mail continues to use an ABC approach to deriving its costs. The volume of mail is obviously a major driver of costs.

The Royal Mail is a public sector organisation that is subject to supervision by Postcomm, the UK government appointed regulatory body. The government requires the Royal Mail to operate on a commercial basis and to make profits.

Source: Royal Mail Group Ltd, Regulatory Financial Statements 2010/11.

Real World 8.8 provides some indication of the extent to which ABC is used in practice.

REAL WORLD 8.8

ABC in practice

A fairly recent survey of 176 UK businesses operating in various industries, all with annual sales revenue of more than £50 million, was conducted by Al-Omiri and Drury. This indicated that 29 per cent of larger UK businesses use ABC.

The adoption of ABC in the UK varies widely between industries, as is shown in Figure 8.12.

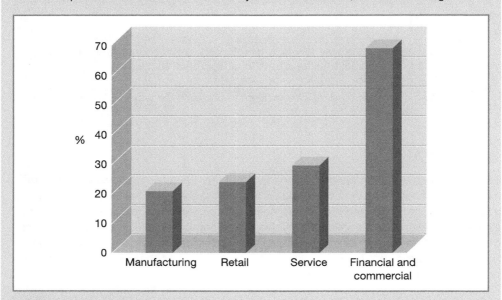

Figure 8.12 ABC in practice

Al-Omiri and Drury took their analysis a step further by looking at the factors that tend to characterise businesses that adopt ABC. They found that businesses that used ABC tended to be:

■ large;
■ sophisticated, in terms of using advanced management accounting techniques generally;
■ in an intensely competitive market for their products;
■ operating in a service industry, particularly in the financial services.

A more recent survey undertaken by the Chartered Institute of Management Accountants (CIMA) – see below – emphatically supported the finding that larger businesses tend to use ABC more than smaller ones. It showed that only 22 per cent of businesses with fewer than 50 employees use ABC, whereas 46 per cent of businesses with more than 10,000 employees use the technique.

All of these findings are broadly in line with other recent research evidence involving businesses from around the world.

Sources: Al-Omiri, M. and Drury, C., 'A survey of factors influencing the choice of product costing systems in UK organisations', *Management Accounting Research*, December 2007; 'Management accounting tools for today and tomorrow', CIMA, 2009, p. 12.

The CIMA survey referred to in Real World 8.8 was conducted in July 2009. Broadly the survey asked management accountants in a wide range of business types and sizes to indicate the extent to which their business used a range of management accounting techniques. A total of 439 management accountants completed the survey. The report on this survey is available online at www.cimaglobal.com/ma. We shall be making reference to this survey on a number of occasions throughout the book. When we do, we shall refer to it as the 'CIMA survey'.

USING FULL (ABSORPTION) COST INFORMATION

Both the traditional and the ABC methods have been criticised because, in practice, they tend to use past (historic) costs. It can be argued that past costs are irrelevant, irrespective of the purpose for which the information is to be used. This is basically because it is not possible to make decisions about the past, only about the future. Advocates of full costing methods would argue, however, that they provide a useful guide to long-run average cost.

Despite the criticisms made of full costing methods, research evidence suggests that their use is widespread, as is indicated in **Real World 8.9**.

REAL WORLD 8.9

The use of full cost information

The businesses surveyed by CIMA derived full cost information to the following extent (see Figure 8.13):

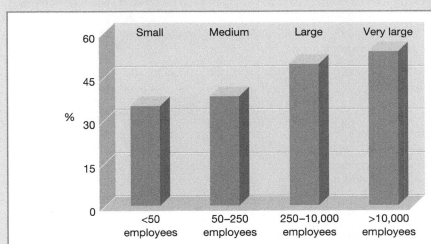

Full cost information is fairly widely used and the size of the business seems to be a factor. It is used by about 45 per cent of all of the businesses surveyed.

Figure 8.13 The use of full cost information

Source: Figure adapted from 'Management accounting tools for today and tomorrow', CIMA, 2009, p. 12.

An International Accounting Standard (IAS 2 *Inventories*) requires that all inventories, including work in progress, be valued at full cost in the published financial reports. This fact demands the use of full costing. As a result, businesses that have work in progress and/or inventories of finished goods at the end of their financial periods apply full costing for profit measurement purposes. (This will include the many service providers that tend to have work in progress.) This requirement alone may explain the widespread use of full costing.

? SELF-ASSESSMENT QUESTION 8.1

Psilis Ltd makes a product in two qualities, called 'Basic' and 'Super'. The business is able to sell these products at a price that gives a standard profit mark-up of 25 per cent of full cost. Full cost is derived using a traditional batch costing approach.

Management is concerned by the lack of profit.

To derive the full cost for each product, overheads are absorbed on the basis of direct labour hours. The costs are as follows:

	Basic £	Super £
Direct labour (all £10 an hour)	40	60
Direct material	15	20

The total annual overheads are £1,000,000.

Based on experience over recent years, in the forthcoming year the business expects to make and sell 40,000 Basics and 10,000 Supers.

Recently, the business's management accountant has undertaken an exercise to try to identify activities and cost drivers in an attempt to be able to deal with the overheads on a more precise basis than had been possible before. This exercise has revealed the following analysis of the annual overheads:

Activity (and cost driver)	Cost £000	Annual number of activities Total	Basic	Super
Number of machine set-ups	280	100	20	80
Number of quality-control inspections	220	2,000	500	1,500
Number of sales orders processed	240	5,000	1,500	3,500
General production (machine hours)	260	500,000	350,000	150,000
Total	1,000			

The management accountant explained the analysis of the £1,000,000 overheads as follows:

■ The two products are made in relatively small batches, so that the amount of the finished product held in inventories is negligible. The Supers are made in particularly small batches because the market demand for this product is relatively low. Each time a new batch is produced, the machines have to be reset by skilled staff. Resetting for Basic production

→

occurs about 20 times a year and for Supers about 80 times: about 100 times in total. The cost of employing the machine-setting staff is about £280,000 a year. It is clear that the more set-ups that occur, the higher the total set-up costs; in other words, the number of set-ups is the factor that drives set-up costs.

- All production has to be inspected for quality and this costs about £220,000 a year. The higher specifications of the Supers mean that there is more chance that there will be quality problems. Thus the Supers are inspected in total 1,500 times annually, whereas the Basics only need about 500 inspections. The number of inspections is the factor that drives these costs.
- Sales order processing (dealing with customers' orders, from receiving the original order to dispatching the products) costs about £240,000 a year. Despite the larger amount of Basic production, there are only 1,500 sales orders each year because the Basics are sold to wholesalers in relatively large-sized orders. The Supers are sold mainly direct to the public by mail order, usually in very small-sized orders. It is believed that the number of orders drives the costs of processing orders.

Required:

(a) Deduce the full cost of each of the two products on the basis used at present and, from these, deduce the current selling price.

(b) Deduce the full cost of each product on an ABC basis, taking account of the management accountant's recent investigations.

(c) What conclusions do you draw? What advice would you offer the management of the business?

The answer to this question can be found at the back of the book, in Appendix B.

SUMMARY

The main points in this chapter may be summarised as follows:

> Full (absorption) cost = the total amount of resources sacrificed to achieve a particular objective.

Uses of full (absorption) cost information

- Pricing and output decisions.
- Exercising control.
- Assessing relative efficiency.
- Profit measurement.

Single-product businesses

- Where all the units of output are identical, the full cost can be calculated as follows:

$$\text{Cost per unit} = \frac{\text{Total cost of output}}{\text{Number of units produced}}$$

Multi-product businesses – job costing

- Where units of output are not identical, it is necessary to divide the cost into two categories: direct cost and indirect cost (overheads).

- Direct cost = cost that can be identified with specific cost units (for example, labour of a garage mechanic, in relation to a particular job).

- Indirect cost (overheads) = cost that cannot be directly measured in respect of a particular job (for example, the rent of a garage).

- Full (absorption) cost = direct cost + indirect cost.

- Direct/indirect cost is not linked to variable/fixed cost.

- Indirect cost is difficult to relate to individual cost units – various bases are used and there is no single correct method.

- Traditionally, indirect cost is seen as the cost of providing a 'service' to cost units.

- Direct labour hour basis of applying indirect cost to cost units is the most popular in practice.

Dealing with indirect cost on a cost centre (departmental) basis

- Indirect cost (overheads) can be segmented – usually on cost centre basis: each product cost centre has its own overhead recovery rate.

- Cost centres are areas, activities or functions for which cost are separately determined.

Batch costing

- A variation of job costing where each job consists of a number of identical (or near identical) cost units:

$$\text{Cost per unit} = \frac{\text{Cost of the batch (direct + indirect)}}{\text{Number of units in the batch}}$$

Activity-based costing

- Activity-based costing is an approach to dealing with overheads (in full costing) that treats all costs as being caused or 'driven' by activities.

- Advocates argue that it is more relevant to the modern commercial environment than is the traditional approach.

- Identification of the cost drivers can lead to more accurate indirect cost treatment in full costing.

- Identification of the cost drivers can also lead to better control of overheads.

- Critics argue that ABC is time-consuming and expensive to apply – not justified by the possible improvement in the quality of information.

- Full cost information is seen by some as not very useful because it can be backward looking: it includes information irrelevant to decision making, but excludes some relevant information.

MyAccountingLab

Go to www.myaccountinglab.com to check your understanding of the chapter, create a personalised study plan, and maximise your revision time

KEY TERMS

full cost p. 270
full costing p. 271
cost unit p. 271
process costing p. 272
direct cost p. 272
indirect cost p. 273
overheads p. 273
common cost p. 273
job costing p. 274

absorption costing p. 274
cost behaviour p. 276
overhead absorption (recovery) rate
  p. 278
cost centre p. 287
batch costing p. 289
activity-based costing (ABC) p. 292
cost drivers p. 293
cost pool p. 293

FURTHER READING

If you would like to explore the topics covered in this chapter in more depth, we recommend the following books:

Atkinson, A., Banker, R., Kaplan, R. and Young, S. M., *Management Accounting*, 6th edn, Prentice Hall, 2011, Chapter 3.

Atrill, P. and McLaney, E., *Management Accounting for Decision Makers*, 7th edn, Financial Times Prentice Hall, 2012, Chapters 4 and 5.

Drury, C., *Management and Cost Accounting*, 8th edn, South Western Cengage Learning, 2012, Chapters 3, 4 and 5.

Horngren, C., Datar, S. and Rajan, M., *Cost Accounting: A Managerial Emphasis*, 14th edn, Prentice Hall International, 2011, Chapter 4.

? REVIEW QUESTIONS

Answers to these questions can be found at the back of the book, in Appendix C.

8.1 What problem does the existence of work in progress cause in process costing?

8.2 What is the point of distinguishing direct cost from indirect cost? Why is this not necessary in process costing environments?

8.3 Are direct cost and variable cost the same thing? Explain your answer.

8.4 How does activity-based costing (ABC) differ from the traditional approach? What is the underlying difference in the philosophy of each of them?

✳ EXERCISES

*Exercises 8.1 and 8.2 are basic level, exercise 8.3 is intermediate level and exercises 8.4 and 8.5 are advanced level. Those with **coloured numbers** have answers at the back of the book, in Appendix D.*

> If you wish to try more exercises, visit the website at **www.myaccountinglab.com**.

8.1 Distinguish between:

- job costing;
- process costing; and
- batch costing.

8.2 Pieman Products Ltd makes road trailers to the precise specifications of individual customers. The following are predicted to occur during the forthcoming year, which is about to start:

Direct materials cost	£50,000
Direct labour cost	£160,000
Direct labour time	16,000 hours
Indirect labour cost	£25,000
Depreciation of machine	£8,000
Rent	£10,000
Heating, lighting and power	£5,000
Indirect materials	£2,000
Other indirect cost (overhead) elements	£1,000
Machine time	3,000 hours

All direct labour is paid at the same hourly rate.

A customer has asked the business to build a trailer for transporting a racing motor-cycle to race meetings. It is estimated that this will require materials and components that will cost £1,150. It will take 250 direct labour hours to do the job, of which 50 will involve the use of machinery.

Required:

Deduce a logical cost for the job and explain the basis of dealing with overheads that you propose.

8.3 Athena Ltd is an engineering business doing work for its customers to their particular requirements and specifications. It determines the full cost of each job taking a 'job costing' approach, accounting for overheads on a cost centre (departmental) basis. It bases its prices to customers on this full cost figure. The business has two departments (both of which are cost centres): a Machining Department, where each job starts, and a Fitting Department, which completes all of the jobs. Machining Department overheads are charged to jobs on a machine hour basis and those of the Fitting Department on a direct labour hour basis. The budgeted information for next year is as follows:

Heating and lighting	£25,000	(allocated equally between the two departments)
Machine power	£10,000	(all allocated to the Machining Department)
Direct labour	£200,000	(£150,000 allocated to the Fitting Department and £50,000 to the Machining Department. All direct workers are paid £10 an hour)
Indirect labour	£50,000	(apportioned to the departments in proportion to the direct labour cost)
Direct materials	£120,000	(all applied to jobs in the Machining Department)
Depreciation	£30,000	(all relates to the Machining Department)
Machine time	20,000 hours	(all worked in the Machining Department)

Required:

(a) Prepare a statement showing the budgeted overheads for next year, analysed between the two cost centres. This should be in the form of three columns: one for the total figure for each type of overhead and one column each for the two cost centres, where each type of overhead is analysed between the two cost centres. Each column should also show the total of overheads for the year.

(b) Derive the appropriate rate for charging the overheads of each cost centre to jobs (that is, a separate rate for each cost centre).

(c) Athena Ltd has been asked by a customer to specify the price that it will charge for a particular job that will, if the job goes ahead, be undertaken early next year. The job is expected to use direct materials costing Athena Ltd £1,200, to need 50 hours of machining time, 10 hours of Machine Department direct labour and 20 hours of Fitting Department direct labour. Athena Ltd charges a profit loading of 20% to the full cost of jobs to determine the selling price.

Show workings to derive the proposed selling price for this job.

8.4 Moleskin Ltd manufactures a range of products used in the building industry. Manufacturing is undertaken using one of two processes: the Alpha Process and the Omega process. All of the products are manufactured in batches. The current pricing policy has been to absorb all overheads using direct labour hours to obtain total cost. Price is then calculated as total cost plus a 35 per cent mark-up.

A recent detailed analysis has examined overhead cost; the results are:

Analysis of overhead costs

	Cost per month £	Monthly volume
Alpha Process cost	96,000	480 hours
Omega Process cost	44,800	1,280 hours
Set-up cost	42,900	260 set-ups
Handling charges	45,600	380 movements
Other overheads	50,700	(see below)
	280,000	

There are 4,000 direct labour hours available each month.

Two of Moleskin's products are a joist (JT101) and a girder (GR27). JT101s are produced by the Alpha Process in a simple operation. GR27s are manufactured by the Omega Process, a more complex operation with more production stages. Both products are sold by the metre.

Details for the two products are:

	JT101	GR27
Monthly volume	1,000 metres	500 metres
Batch size	1,000 metres	50 metres
Processing time per batch		
– Alpha	100 hours	–
– Omega	–	25 hours
Set-ups per batch	1	2
Handling charges per batch	1 movement	5 movements
Materials per metre	£16	£15
Direct labour per metre	1/2 hour	1/2 hour

Direct labour is paid £16 per hour.

Required:

(a) Calculate the price per metre for both JT101s and GR27s detailed above, using traditional absorption costing based on direct labour hours.

(b) Calculate the price per metre for both JT101s and GR27s using activity-based costing. Assume that 'Other overheads' are allocated using direct labour hours.

(c) Outline the points that you would raise with the management of Moleskin in the light of your answers to (a) and (b).

(d) Outline the practical problems that may be encountered in implementing activity-based techniques and comment on how they may be overcome.

8.5 A business manufactures refrigerators for domestic use. There are three models: Lo, Mid and Hi. The models, their quality and their price are aimed at different markets.

Product costs are computed using a blanket (business-wide) overhead-rate. Products absorb overheads on a labour hour basis. Prices as a general rule are set based on cost plus 20 per cent. The following information is provided:

	Lo	Mid	Hi
Material cost (£/unit)	25	62.5	105
Direct labour hours (per unit)	1/2	1	1
Budget production/sales (units)	20,000	1,000	10,000

The budgeted overheads for the business, for the year, amount to £4,410,000. Direct labour is costed at £8 an hour.

The business is currently facing increasing competition, especially from imported goods. As a result, the selling price of Lo has been reduced to a level that produces a very low profit margin. To address this problem, an activity-based costing approach has been suggested. The overheads have been analysed and it has been found that these are grouped around main business activities of machining (£2,780,000), logistics (£590,000) and establishment costs (£1,040,000). It is maintained that these costs could be allocated based respectively on cost drivers of machine hours, material orders and space, to reflect the use of resources in each of these areas. After analysis, the following proportionate statistics are available related to the total volume of products:

Full Costing

	Lo	Mid	Hi
	%	%	%
Machine hours	40	15	45
Material orders	47	6	47
Space	42	18	40

Required:

(a) Calculate for each product the full cost and selling price determined by:
   (i) The original (traditional) costing method.
   (ii) The activity-based costing method.

(b) What are the implications of the two systems of costing in the situation given?

(c) What business/strategic options exist for the business in the light of the new information?

BUDGETING

INTRODUCTION

In its 2010 annual report, BSkyB Group plc, the satellite television broadcaster, stated:

> There is a comprehensive budgeting and forecasting process, and the annual budget, which is regularly reviewed and updated, is approved by the board [of directors].

The practice at BSkyB is typical of businesses of all sizes.

What is a budget? What is it for? How is it prepared? Who prepares it? How is it used? Why does the board regard it as important enough to spend time on? The answers to these questions form the basis of this chapter.

We shall see that budgets set out short-term plans to help managers run the business. They provide the means to assess whether actual performance was as planned and, if not, the reasons for this. Budgets do not exist in a vacuum; they are an integral part of a planning framework adopted by well-run businesses. To understand fully the nature of budgets we must, therefore, understand the planning framework within which they are set.

The chapter begins with a discussion of the budgeting framework and then goes on to consider detailed aspects of the budgeting process. It ends with considering the use of budgets in monitoring performance and exercising control.

Learning outcomes

When you have completed this chapter, you should be able to:

- define a budget and show how budgets, strategic objectives and strategic plans are related;
- explain the budgeting process and the interlinking of the various budgets within the business;
- indicate the uses of budgeting and construct various budgets, including the cash budget, from relevant data;
- show how flexing the budget can be used to exercise control over the business.

MyAccountingLab Visit www.myaccountinglab.com for practice and revision opportunities

HOW BUDGETS LINK WITH STRATEGIC PLANS AND OBJECTIVES

It is vital that businesses develop plans for the future. What a business is trying to achieve is unlikely to come about unless its managers are clear what the future direction of the business is going to be. The development of plans involves five key steps:

1 *Establish mission and objectives*
   The **mission statement** sets out the ultimate purpose of the business. It is a broad statement of intent. Strategic objectives, on the other hand, are more specific and will usually include quantifiable goals.

2 *Undertake a position analysis*
   This involves an assessment of where the business is currently placed in relation to where it wants to be, as set out in its mission and strategic objectives.

3 *Identify and assess the strategic options*
   The business must explore the various ways in which it might move from where it is now (identified in Step 2) to where it wants to be (identified in Step 1).

4 *Select strategic options and formulate plans*
   This involves selecting what seems to be the best of the courses of action or strategies (identified in Step 3) and formulating a long-term strategic plan. This strategic plan is then normally broken down into a series of short-term plans, one for each element of the business. These plans are the budgets. Thus, a **budget** is a business plan for the short term – typically one year – and is expressed mainly in financial terms. Its role is to convert the strategic plans into actionable blueprints for the immediate future. Budgets will define precise targets concerning such things as:
   - Cash receipts and payments
   - Sales volumes and revenues, broken down into amounts and prices for each of the products or services provided by the business
   - Detailed inventories requirements
   - Detailed labour requirements
   - Specific production requirements.

5 *Perform, review and control*
   Here the business pursues the budgets derived in Step 4. By comparing the actual outcome with the budgets, managers can see if things are going according to plan. Action would be taken to exercise control where actual performance appears not to be matching the budgets.

From the above description of the planning process, we can see that the relationship between the mission, strategic objectives, strategic plans and budgets can be summarised as follows:

- the mission sets the overall direction and, once set, is likely to last for quite a long time – perhaps throughout the life of the business;
- the strategic objectives, which are also long-term, will set out how the mission can be achieved;
- the strategic plans identify how each objective will be pursued; and
- the budgets set out, in detail, the short-term plans and targets necessary to fulfil the strategic objectives.

An analogy might be found in terms of a student enrolling on a course of study. His or her mission might be to have a happy and fulfilling life. A key strategic objective flowing from this mission might be to embark on a career that will be rewarding in various ways. He or she might have identified the particular study course as the most effective way to work towards this objective. Successfully completing the course would then be the strategic plan. In working towards this strategic plan, passing a particular stage of the course might be identified as the target for the forthcoming year. This short-term target is analogous to the budget. Having achieved the 'budget' for the first year, the budget for the second year becomes passing the second stage.

Exercising control

However well planned the activities of a business might be, they will come to nothing unless steps are taken to try to achieve them in practice. The process of making planned events actually occur is known as **control**. This is part of Step 5 (above).

Control can be defined as compelling events to conform to plan. This definition is valid in any context. For example, when we talk about controlling a motor car, we mean making the car do what we plan that it should do. In a business context, management accounting is very useful in the control process. This is because it is possible to state many plans in accounting terms (as budgets). Since it is also possible to state *actual* outcomes in the same terms, making comparison between actual and planned outcomes is a relatively simple matter. Where actual outcomes are at variance with budgets, this variance should be highlighted by accounting information. Managers can then take steps to get the business back on track towards the achievement of the budgets. We shall be looking more closely at the control aspect of budgeting later in the chapter.

Figure 9.1 shows the planning and control process in diagrammatic form.

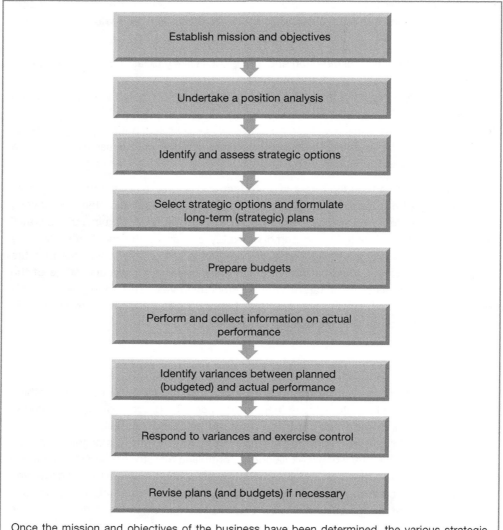

Once the mission and objectives of the business have been determined, the various strategic options available must be considered and evaluated in order to derive a strategic plan. The budget is a short-term financial plan for the business that is prepared within the framework of the strategic plan. Control can be exercised through the comparison of budgeted and actual performance. Where a significant divergence emerges, some form of corrective action should be taken. If the budget figures prove to be based on incorrect assumptions about the future, it might be necessary to revise the budget.

Figure 9.1 The planning and control process

It should be emphasised that planning (including budgeting) is the responsibility of managers rather than accountants. Though accountants should play a role in the planning process, by supplying relevant information to managers and by contributing to decision making as part of the management team, they should not dominate the process. In practice, it seems that the budgeting aspect of planning is often in danger of being dominated

½ parl-

by accountants, perhaps because most budgets are expressed in financial terms. However, managers are failing in their responsibilities if they allow this to happen.

TIME HORIZON OF PLANS AND BUDGETS

Setting strategic plans is a major exercise normally performed every five years or so, and budgets are usually set for the forthcoming year. These planning horizons, however, are not cast in stone. Businesses involved in certain industries – say, information technology – may find that a strategic planning horizon of five years is too long since new developments can, and do, occur virtually overnight. Two or three years may be more feasible. Similarly, a budget need not be set for one year, although this is a widely used time horizon.

One business that keeps its strategic planning under frequent review is J Sainsbury plc, the supermarket business. **Real World 9.1**, which is an extract from the annual report for the business, explains how strategic planning is a regular annual event.

REAL WORLD 9.1

Strategic planning at the supermarket

According to its annual report, Sainsbury's has the following approach to strategic planning:

> The Board continues to focus on strategic matters during the year. We hold a two-day Strategy Conference in the autumn, with the Operating Board Directors in attendance for the first day. This enables the Board to conduct an in-depth review of the market and key opportunities and threats, consider the draft budget and corporate plan and agree the strategic goals for the short-term and longer term perspectives. The Board receives a detailed half-year update on progress against the agreed priorities and then, to complete the cycle, agrees the objectives and principal areas of focus for the next conference.

Source: J Sainsbury plc Annual Report 2011, p. 31.

Activity 9.1

Can you think of any reason why most businesses prepare detailed budgets for the forthcoming year, rather than for a shorter or longer period?

The reason is probably that a year represents a long enough time for the budget preparation exercise to be worthwhile, yet short enough into the future for detailed plans to be capable of being made. The process of formulating budgets can be a time-consuming exercise, but there are economies of scale – for example, preparing the budget for the next year would not normally take twice as much time and effort as preparing the budget for the next six months.

An annual budget sets targets for the forthcoming year for all aspects of the business. It is usually broken down into monthly budgets, which define monthly targets. Indeed, in many instances, the annual budget will be built up from monthly figures. Thus, the sales staff may be required to set sales targets for each month of the budget period. These targets may vary from month to month, perhaps due to variations in seasonal demand.

LIMITING FACTORS

Some aspect of the business will, inevitably, stop it achieving its objectives to the maximum extent. This is often a limited ability of the business to sell its products. Sometimes, however, it is some production shortage (such as labour, materials or plant) that is the **limiting factor**. Production shortages can often be overcome by an increase in funds – for example, more plant can be bought or leased. This is not always a practical solution, however, because no amount of money will buy certain labour skills or increase the world supply of some raw material. As a last resort, it might be necessary to revise the sales budget to a lower level to match the production limitation.

Activity 9.2

Can you think of any ways in which a short-term shortage of production facilities of a manufacturer might be overcome?

We thought of the following:

- Higher production in previous months and increasing inventories ('stockpiling') to meet periods of higher demand
- Increasing production capacity, perhaps by working overtime and/or acquiring (buying or leasing) additional plant
- Subcontracting some production
- Encouraging potential customers to change the timing of their purchases by offering discounts or other special terms during the months that have been identified as quiet.

You might well have thought of other approaches.

While easing an initial limiting factor may be possible, another limiting factor will replace it, though at a higher level of output. In the end, the business will hit a ceiling; some limiting factor will prove impossible to ease.

The limiting factor should try to be identified at the outset. All managers can then be informed and can take it into account when preparing their budgets.

BUDGETS AND FORECASTS

We have seen that a budget is a business plan for the short term, which is mainly expressed in financial terms. Note particularly that a budget is a *plan*, not a forecast. To talk of a plan suggests an intention or determination to achieve the targets; **forecasts** tend to be predictions of the future state of the environment.

Clearly, forecasts are very helpful to the planner/budget setter. If, for example, a reliable forecaster has predicted the number of new cars to be purchased in the UK during next year, it will be valuable for a manager in a car manufacturing business to take account of this information when setting next year's sales budgets. However, a forecast and a budget are distinctly different.

HOW BUDGETS LINK TO ONE ANOTHER

A business will prepare more than one budget for a particular period. Each budget prepared will relate to a specific aspect of the business. Probably, the ideal situation is for there to be a separate operating budget for each manager, no matter how junior. The contents of all of the individual operating budgets will be summarised in **master budgets** consisting of a budgeted income statement and statement of financial position (balance sheet). The cash budget is, however, considered by some to be a third master budget.

Figure 9.2 illustrates the interrelationship and interlinking of individual operating budgets, in this particular case using a manufacturing business as an example.

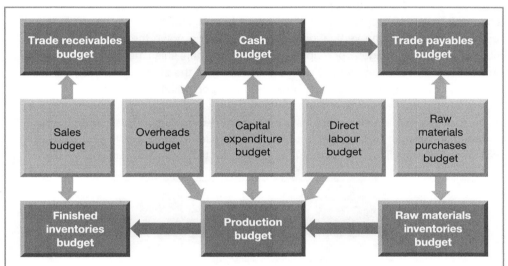

The starting point is usually the sales budget. The expected level of sales normally defines the overall level of activity for the business. The other operating budgets will be drawn up in accordance with this. Thus, the sales budget will largely define the finished inventories requirements and, from this, we can define the production requirements and so on. This shows the interrelationship of operating budgets for a manufacturing business.

Figure 9.2 The interrelationship of operating budgets

The sales budget is usually the first one to be prepared (at the left of Figure 9.2), as the level of sales often determines the overall level of activity for the forthcoming period. This is because it is the most common limiting factor (see page 312). The finished inventories requirement tends to be set by the level of sales, though it would also be dictated by the policy of the business on the level of the finished products inventories. The requirement for finished inventories will define the required production levels, which will, in turn, dictate the requirements of the individual production departments or sections. The demands of manufacturing, in conjunction with the business's policy on how long it holds raw materials before they enter production, define the raw materials inventories budget.

The purchases budget will be dictated by the materials inventories budget, which will, in conjunction with the policy of the business on taking credit from suppliers, dictate the trade payables budget. One of the determinants of the cash budget will be the trade payables budget; another will be the trade receivables budget, which itself derives, through the business's policy on credit periods granted to credit customers, from the sales budget. Cash will also be affected by overheads and direct labour costs (themselves linked to production) and by capital expenditure. Cash will also be affected by new finance and redemption of existing sources. (This is not shown in Figure 9.2 because the diagram focuses only on budgets concerned with operational matters.) The factors that affect policies on matters such as inventories holding and trade receivables collection and trade payables payment periods will be discussed in some detail in Chapter 12.

A manufacturing business has been used as the example in Figure 9.2 simply because it has all of the types of operating budgets found in practice. Service businesses, however, have similar types of budgets, with the exception perhaps of inventories budgets.

There will be the horizontal relationships between budgets, which we have just looked at, but there will usually be vertical ones as well. Breaking down the sales budget into a number of subsidiary budgets, perhaps one for each regional sales manager, is a common approach. The overall sales budget will be a summary of the subsidiary ones. The same may be true of virtually all of the other budgets, most particularly the production budget.

Figure 9.3 shows the vertical relationship of the sales budgets for a business. The business has four geographical sales regions each one the responsibility of a separate manager. Each regional manager is responsible to the overall sales manager of the business. The overall sales budget will be the sum of the budgets for the four sales regions.

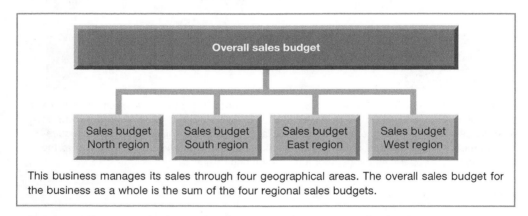

This business manages its sales through four geographical areas. The overall sales budget for the business as a whole is the sum of the four regional sales budgets.

Figure 9.3 The vertical relationship between a business's sales budgets

Although sales are often managed on a geographical basis, they may be managed on some other basis. For example, a business that sells a range of products may employ a specialist manager for each type of product. Thus, an insurance business may have separate sales managers, and so separate sales budgets, for life insurance, household insurance, motor insurance and so on. Large businesses may even have separate product-type managers for each geographical region. Each of these managers would have a separate budget, which would combine to form the overall sales budget for the business as a whole.

All of the operating budgets that we have just reviewed must mesh with the master budgets, that is, the budgeted income statement and statement of financial position.

HOW BUDGETS HELP MANAGERS

Budgets are generally regarded as having five areas of usefulness. These are:

1 *Budgets tend to promote forward thinking and the possible identification of short-term problems*. We saw above that a shortage of production capacity might be identified during the budgeting process. Making this discovery in good time could leave a number of means of overcoming the problem open to exploration. If the potential production problem is picked up early enough, all of the suggestions in the answer to Activity 9.2 and, possibly, other ways of overcoming the problem can be explored. Early identification of the potential problem gives managers time for calm and rational consideration of the best way of overcoming it. The best solution to the potential problem may only be feasible if action can be taken well in advance. This would be true of all of the suggestions made in the answer to Activity 9.2.

2 *Budgets can be used to help co-ordination between the various sections of the business*. It is crucially important that the activities of the various departments and sections of the business are linked so that the activities of one are complementary to those of another. The activities of the purchasing/procurement department of a manufacturing business, for example, should dovetail with the raw materials needs of the production departments. If they do not, production could run out of raw materials, leading to expensive production stoppages. Alternatively, excessive amounts of raw materials could be bought, resulting in large and unnecessary inventories holding costs. We shall see how this co-ordination works in practice later in the chapter.

3 *Budgets can motivate managers to better performance*. Having a stated task can motivate managers in their performance. Simply telling managers to do their best is not very motivating, but to set a required level of achievement can be. It can help them to relate their particular role to the overall objectives of the business. Since budgets are directly derived from strategic objectives, budgeting makes this possible. It is clearly not possible to allow managers to operate in an unconstrained environment. Having to operate in a way that matches the goals of the business is a price of working in an effective business.

4 *Budgets can provide a basis for a system of control*. As we saw earlier in the chapter, control is concerned with ensuring that events conform to plans. If senior management wishes to control and to monitor the performance of more junior staff, it needs some yardstick against which to measure and assess performance. Current performance could possibly be compared with past performance or perhaps with what happens in another business. However, planned performance is usually the most logical yardstick. If there is information available concerning the actual performance for a period, and this can be compared with the planned performance, then a basis for control will have been established. This will enable the use of **management by exception**, a technique where senior managers can spend most of their time dealing with those staff or activities that have failed to achieve the budget (the exceptions). Thus senior managers do not have to spend too much time on those that are performing well. It also allows junior managers to exercise self-control. By knowing what they are expected to do and what they have actually achieved, they can assess how well they are performing and take steps to correct matters where they are failing to achieve.

5 *Budgets can provide a system of authorisation for managers to spend up to a particular limit.* Some activities (for example, staff development and research expenditure) are

315

allocated a fixed amount of funds at the discretion of senior management. This provides the authority to spend.

Figure 9.4 shows in diagrammatic form the benefits of budgets.

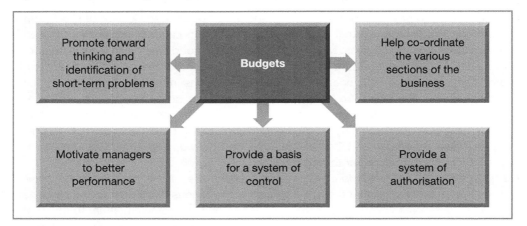

Figure 9.4 Budgets are seen as having five main benefits to the business

The following two activities pick up issues that relate to some of the uses of budgets.

Activity 9.3

The fourth on the above list of the uses of budgets (control) implies that under a 'management by exception' approach, junior managers who are performing well will not attract much attention from their seniors.
   Can you think of any reason why this may not be totally beneficial?

There is the danger that well-performing junior managers may feel undervalued as a result of being ignored. It is probably better if senior managers make clear to these junior managers that their good performance has been noted and is appreciated.

Activity 9.4

The fourth on the above list of the uses of budgets (control) implies that managers are set stated tasks. Do you think there is a danger that requiring managers to work towards such predetermined targets will stifle their skill, flair and enthusiasm?

If the budgets are set in such a way as to offer challenging yet achievable targets, the manager is still required to show skill, flair and enthusiasm. There is the danger, however, that if targets are badly set (either unreasonably demanding or too easy to achieve), they could be demotivating and have a stifling effect.

The five identified uses of budgets can conflict with one another on occasions. Using the budget as a motivational device provides a possible example. Some businesses set budget targets at a more difficult level than managers can be expected to achieve to try to motivate them to strive hard to reach the targets. For control purposes, however, the budget becomes less meaningful as a benchmark against which to compare actual performance. Incidentally, there is good reason to doubt the effectiveness of setting excessive targets as a motivational device, as we shall see later in the chapter.

Conflict between the different uses will mean that managers must decide which particular uses for budgets should be given priority. Managers must be prepared, if necessary, to trade off the benefits resulting from one particular use for the benefits of another.

USING BUDGETS IN PRACTICE

This section provides a flavour of how budgets are used, the extent to which they are used and their level of accuracy.

Real World 9.2 shows how Greene King plc, the UK brewer, pub and hotel operator, undertakes its budgeting process.

REAL WORLD 9.2

Budgeting at Greene King

According to Greene King's annual report:

> The group's comprehensive planning and financial reporting procedures include annual detailed operational budgets and a three year strategic plan, both of which are reviewed and approved by the board. Performance against the budgets is monitored, and relevant action taken, throughout the year, through the periodic reporting of detailed management accounts and key performance indicators. Forecasts are updated during the course of the year.

Source: Greene King plc Annual Report 2011, p. 90.

There is quite a lot of recent survey evidence that shows the extent to which budgeting is used by businesses in practice. **Real World 9.3** reviews some of this evidence, which shows that most businesses prepare and use budgets.

REAL WORLD 9.3

Budgeting in practice

A survey of 41 UK manufacturing businesses found that 40 of the 41 prepared budgets.

Source: Dugdale, D., Jones, C. and Green, S., 'Contemporary management accounting practices in UK manufacturing', CIMA Publication, Elsevier, 2006.

Another survey of UK businesses, but this time businesses involved in the food and drink sector, found that virtually all of them used budgets.

Source: Abdel-Kader, M. and Luther R., 'An empirical investigation of the evolution of management accounting practices', Working paper No. 04/06, University of Essex, October 2004.

A survey of the opinions of senior finance staff at 340 businesses of various sizes and operating in a wide range of industries in North America revealed that 97 per cent of those businesses had a formal budgeting process.

Source: 'Perfect how you project', BPM Forum, 2008.

Though these three surveys relate to UK and North American businesses, they provide some idea of what is likely also to be practice elsewhere in the developed world.

Real World 9.4 gives some insight regarding the accuracy of budgets.

REAL WORLD 9.4

Budget accuracy

The survey of senior finance staff of North American businesses, mentioned in Real World 9.3, asked them to compare the actual revenues with the budgeted revenues for 2007. Figure 9.5 shows the results:

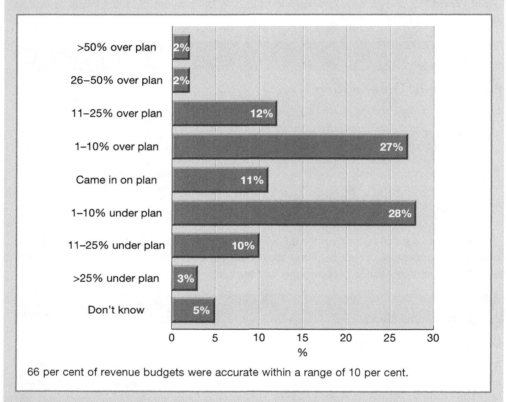

66 per cent of revenue budgets were accurate within a range of 10 per cent.

Figure 9.5 The accuracy of revenue budgets

We can see that only 66 per cent of revenue budgets were accurate within 10 per cent. The survey revealed that budgets for expenses were generally more accurate, with 74 per cent being accurate within 10 per cent.

Source: 'Perfect how you project', BPM Forum, 2008.

PREPARING THE CASH BUDGET

We shall now look in some detail at how the various budgets used by the typical business are prepared, starting with the cash budget. It is helpful for us to start with the cash budget because it is a key budget (some people see it as a 'master budget' along with the budgeted income statement and budgeted statement of financial position). Most economic aspects of a business are reflected in cash sooner or later, so that for a typical business, the cash budget reflects the whole business more comprehensively than any other single budget.

A very small, unsophisticated business (for example, a corner shop) may feel that full-scale budgeting is not appropriate to its needs, but almost certainly it should prepare a cash budget as a minimum.

Since budgets are documents that are to be used only internally by a business, their layout is a question of management choice and will vary from one business to the next. However, as managers, irrespective of the business, are likely to be using budgets for similar purposes, some consistency of approach tends to be found. In most businesses, the cash budget will probably possess the following features:

1 The budget period would be broken down into sub-periods, typically months.
2 The budget would be in columnar form, with one column for each month.
3 Receipts of cash would be identified under various headings and a total for each month's receipts shown.
4 Payments of cash would be identified under various headings and a total for each month's payments shown.
5 The surplus of total cash receipts over payments, or of payments over receipts, for each month would be identified.
6 The running cash balance would be identified. This would be achieved by taking the balance at the end of the previous month and adjusting it for the surplus (or deficit) of receipts over payments for the current month.

Typically, all of the pieces of information in points 3 to 6 in this list would be useful to management for one reason or another.

Probably the best way to deal with this topic is through an example.

Example 9.1

Vierra Popova Ltd is a wholesale business. The budgeted income statements for each of the next six months are as follows:

	Jan £000	Feb £000	Mar £000	Apr £000	May £000	June £000
Sales revenue	52	55	55	60	55	53
Cost of goods sold	(30)	(31)	(31)	(35)	(31)	(32)
Salaries and wages	(10)	(10)	(10)	(10)	(10)	(10)
Electricity	(5)	(5)	(4)	(3)	(3)	(3)
Depreciation	(3)	(3)	(3)	(3)	(3)	(3)
Other overheads	(2)	(2)	(2)	(2)	(2)	(2)
Total expenses	(50)	(51)	(50)	(53)	(49)	(50)
Profit for the month	2	4	5	7	6	3

The business allows all of its customers one month's credit (this means, for example, that cash from January sales will be received in February). Sales revenue during December totalled £60,000.

The business plans to maintain inventories at their existing level until some time in March, when they are to be reduced by £5,000. Inventories will remain at this lower level indefinitely. Inventories purchases are made on one month's credit. December purchases totalled £30,000. Salaries, wages and 'other overheads' are paid in the month concerned. Electricity is paid quarterly in arrears in March and June. The business plans to buy and pay for a new delivery van in March. This will cost a total of £15,000, but an existing van will be traded in for £4,000 as part of the deal.

The business expects to have £12,000 in cash at the beginning of January.

The cash budget for the six months ending in June will look as follows:

	Jan £000	Feb £000	Mar £000	Apr £000	May £000	June £000
Receipts						
Trade receivables (Note 1)	60	52	55	55	60	55
Payments						
Trade payables (Note 2)	(30)	(30)	(31)	(26)	(35)	(31)
Salaries and wages	(10)	(10)	(10)	(10)	(10)	(10)
Electricity			(14)			(9)
Other overheads	(2)	(2)	(2)	(2)	(2)	(2)
Van purchase	–	–	(11)	–	–	–
Total payments	(42)	(42)	(68)	(38)	(47)	(52)
Cash surplus for the month	18	10	(13)	17	13	3
Opening balance (Note 3)	12	30	40	27	44	57
Closing balance	30	40	27	44	57	60

Notes

1 The cash receipts from credit customers (trade receivables) lag a month behind sales because customers are given a month in which to pay for their purchases. So, December sales will be paid for in January and so on.

2 In most months, the purchases of inventories will equal the cost of goods sold. This is because the business maintains a constant level of inventories. For inventories to remain constant at the end of each month, the business must replace exactly the amount that has been used. During March, however, the business plans to reduce its inventories by £5,000. This means that inventories purchases will be lower than inventories usage in that month. The payments for inventories purchases lag a month behind purchases because the business expects to be allowed a month to pay for what it buys.

3 Each month's cash balance is the previous month's figure plus the cash surplus (or minus the cash deficit) for the current month. The balance at the start of January is £12,000 according to the information provided earlier.

4 Depreciation does not give rise to a cash payment. In the context of profit measurement (in the income statement), depreciation is a very important aspect. Here, however, we are interested only in cash.

Activity 9.5

Looking at the cash budget of Vierra Popova Ltd (Example 9.1), what conclusions do you draw and what possible course of action do you recommend regarding the cash balance over the period concerned?

Given the size of the business, there is a fairly large cash balance that seems to be increasing. Management might consider:

- putting some of the cash into an income-yielding deposit;
- increasing the investment in non-current (fixed) assets;
- paying a dividend to the owners;
- repaying borrowings.

Activity 9.6

Vierra Popova Ltd (Example 9.1) now wishes to prepare its cash budget for the second six months of the year. The budgeted income statements for each month of the second half of the year are as follows:

	July £000	Aug £000	Sept £000	Oct £000	Nov £000	Dec £000
Sales revenue	57	59	62	57	53	51
Cost of goods sold	(32)	(33)	(35)	(32)	(30)	(29)
Salaries and wages	(10)	(10)	(10)	(10)	(10)	(10)
Electricity	(3)	(3)	(4)	(5)	(6)	(6)
Depreciation	(3)	(3)	(3)	(3)	(3)	(3)
Other overheads	(2)	(2)	(2)	(2)	(2)	(2)
Total expenses	(50)	(51)	(54)	(52)	(51)	(50)
Profit for the month	7	8	8	5	2	1

The business will continue to allow all of its customers one month's credit.

It plans to increase inventories from the 30 June level by £1,000 each month until, and including, September. During the following three months, inventories levels will be decreased by £1,000 each month.

Inventories purchases, which had been made on one month's credit until the June payment, will, starting with the purchases made in June, be made on two months' credit.

Salaries, wages and 'other overheads' will continue to be paid in the month concerned. Electricity is paid quarterly in arrears in September and December.

At the end of December, the business intends to pay off part of some borrowings. This payment is to be such that it will leave the business with a cash balance of £5,000 with which to start next year.

Prepare the cash budget for the six months ending in December. (Remember that any information you need that relates to the first six months of the year, including the cash balance that is expected to be brought forward on 1 July, is given in Example 9.1.)

The cash budget for the six months ended 31 December is:

	July £000	Aug £000	Sept £000	Oct £000	Nov £000	Dec £000
Receipts						
Trade receivables	53	57	59	62	57	53
Payments						
Trade payables (Note 1)	–	(32)	(33)	(34)	(36)	(31)
Salaries and wages	(10)	(10)	(10)	(10)	(10)	(10)
Electricity	–	–	(10)	–	–	(17)
Other overheads	(2)	(2)	(2)	(2)	(2)	(2)
Borrowings repayment (Note 2)	–	–	–	–	–	(131)
Total payments	(12)	(44)	(55)	(46)	(48)	(191)
Cash surplus for the month	41	13	4	16	9	(138)
Opening balance	60	101	114	118	134	143
Closing balance	101	114	118	134	143	5

Notes

1 There will be no payment to suppliers (trade payables) in July because the June purchases will be made on two months' credit and will therefore be paid in August. The July purchases, which will equal the July cost of sales figure plus the increase in inventories made in July, will be paid for in September and so on.

2 The borrowings repayment is simply the amount that will cause the balance at 31 December to be £5,000.

PREPARING OTHER BUDGETS

Though each one will have its own particular features, other budgets will tend to follow the same sort of pattern as the cash budget, that is, they will show inflows and outflows during each month and the opening and closing balances in each month.

Example 9.2

To illustrate some of the other budgets, we shall continue to use the example of Vierra Popova Ltd that we considered in Example 9.1. To the information given there, we need to add the fact that the inventories balance at 1 January was £30,000.

Trade receivables budget

This would normally show the planned amount owed to the business by credit customers at the beginning and at the end of each month, the planned total credit sales revenue for each month and the planned total cash receipts from credit customers (trade receivables). The layout would be something like this:

	Jan £000	Feb £000	Mar £000	Apr £000	May £000	June £000
Opening balance	60	52	55	55	60	55
Sales revenue	52	55	55	60	55	53
Cash receipts	(60)	(52)	(55)	(55)	(60)	(55)
Closing balance	52	55	55	60	55	53

The opening and closing balances represent the amount that the business plans to be owed (in total) by credit customers (trade receivables) at the beginning and end of each month, respectively.

Trade payables budget
Typically this shows the planned amount owed to suppliers by the business at the beginning and at the end of each month, the planned credit purchases for each month and the planned total cash payments to trade payables. The layout would be something like this:

	Jan £000	Feb £000	Mar £000	Apr £000	May £000	June £000
Opening balance	30	30	31	26	35	31
Purchases	30	31	26	35	31	32
Cash payment	(30)	(30)	(31)	(26)	(35)	(31)
Closing balance	30	31	26	35	31	32

The opening and closing balances represent the amount planned to be owed (in total) by the business to suppliers (trade payables), at the beginning and end of each month respectively.

Inventories budget
This would normally show the planned amount of inventories to be held by the business at the beginning and at the end of each month, the planned total inventories purchases for each month and the planned total monthly inventories usage. The layout would be something like this:

	Jan £000	Feb £000	Mar £000	Apr £000	May £000	June £000
Opening balance	30	30	30	25	25	25
Purchases	30	31	26	35	31	32
Inventories used	(30)	(31)	(31)	(35)	(31)	(32)
Closing balance	30	30	25	25	25	25

The opening and closing balances represent the amount of inventories, at cost, planned to be held by the business at the beginning and end of each month respectively.

A *raw materials inventories budget*, for a manufacturing business, would follow a similar pattern, with the 'inventories usage' being the cost of the inventories put into production. A *finished inventories budget* for a manufacturer would also be similar to the above, except that 'inventories manufactured' would replace 'purchases'.

→

A manufacturing business would normally prepare both a raw materials inventories budget and a finished inventories budget. Each of these would typically be based on the full cost of the inventories (that is, including overheads). There is no reason why the inventories should not be valued on the basis of either variable cost or direct costs, should managers feel that this would provide more useful information.

The inventories budget will normally be expressed in financial terms, but may also be expressed in physical terms (for example, kg or metres) for individual inventories items.

Note how the trade receivables, trade payables and inventories budgets in Example 9.2 link to one another, and to the cash budget, for the same business in Example 9.1. Note particularly that:

- the purchases figures in the trade payables budget and in the inventories budget are identical;
- the cash payments figures in the trade payables budget and in the cash budget are identical;
- the cash receipts figures in the trade receivables budget and in the cash budget are identical.

Other values would link different budgets in a similar way. For example, the row of sales revenue figures in the trade receivables budget would be identical to the sales revenue figures that will be found in the sales budget. This is how the linking (co-ordination), which was discussed earlier in this chapter, is achieved.

Activity 9.7

Have a go at preparing the trade receivables budget for Vierra Popova Ltd for the six months from July to December (see Activity 9.6 and Example 9.2).

The trade receivables budget for the six months ended 31 December is:

	July £000	Aug £000	Sept £000	Oct £000	Nov £000	Dec £000
Opening balance (Note 1)	53	57	59	62	57	53
Sales revenue (Note 2)	57	59	62	57	53	51
Cash receipts (Note 3)	(53)	(57)	(59)	(62)	(57)	(53)
Closing balance (Note 4)	57	59	62	57	53	51

Notes
1 The opening trade receivables figure is the previous month's sales revenue figure (sales are on one month's credit).
2 The sales revenue is the current month's figure.
3 The cash received each month is equal to the previous month's sales revenue figure.
4 The closing balance is equal to the current month's sales revenue figure.

Note that if we knew any three of the four figures each month, we could deduce the fourth.

This budget could be set out in any manner that would have given the sort of information that management would require in respect of planned levels of trade receivables and associated transactions.

Activity 9.8

Have a go at preparing the trade payables budget for Vierra Popova Ltd for the six months from July to December (see Activity 9.6 and Exercise 9.2). (*Hint*: Remember that the trade payables' payment period alters from the June purchases onwards.)

The trade payables budget for the six months ended 31 December is:

	July £000	Aug £000	Sept £000	Oct £000	Nov £000	Dec £000
Opening balance	32	65	67	70	67	60
Purchases	33	34	36	31	29	28
Cash payments	–	(32)	(33)	(34)	(36)	(31)
Closing balance	65	67	70	67	60	57

This, again, could be set out in any manner that would have given the sort of information that management would require in respect of planned levels of trade payables and associated transactions.

NON-FINANCIAL MEASURES IN BUDGETING

The efficiency of internal operations and customer satisfaction levels have become of critical importance to businesses striving to survive in an increasingly competitive environment. Non-financial performance indicators have an important role to play in assessing performance in such key areas as customer/supplier delivery times, set-up times, defect levels and customer satisfaction levels.

There is no reason why budgeting need be confined to financial targets and measures. Non-financial measures can also be used as the basis for targets and these can be brought into the budgeting process and reported alongside the financial targets for the business.

BUDGETING FOR CONTROL

We have seen that budgets provide a useful basis for exercising control over a business as they provide a yardstick against which performance can be assessed. We must, however, measure actual performance in the same terms as those in which the budget is stated. If they are not in the same terms, valid comparison will not be possible.

Exercising control involves finding out where and why things did not go according to plan and then seeking ways to put them right for the future. One reason why things may not have gone according to plan is that the budget targets were unachievable. In this case, it may be necessary to revise the budgets for future periods so that targets become achievable.

This last point should not be taken to mean that budget targets can simply be ignored if the going gets tough; rather that they should be adaptable. Unrealistic budgets cannot form a basis for exercising control and little can be gained by sticking with them. Budgets may become unrealistic for a variety of reasons, including unexpected changes in the commercial environment (for example, an unexpected collapse in demand for services of the type that the business provides).

Real World 9.5 reveals how one important budget had to be revised because it had become so unrealistic.

REAL WORLD 9.5

No medals for budgeting

Organisers of the London 2012 Olympic Games came under renewed pressure on Thursday after the government revealed that the bill for venues is now forecast to be £196 million over budget.

The revised budget for the Olympic stadium, aquatics centre and other venues is now £1.36 billion, compared with the £1.17 billion that the government assigned to venue costs in November 2007.

That means that venue costs have risen a further £97 million since the Department for Culture, Media and Sport (DCMS) last published an update on the Olympic budget in July.

The DCMS sought to offset criticism of the venue costs increase by saying it was forecasting savings of £193 million between now and the end of construction.

Costs for the Olympic stadium have risen by £22 million because of the lack of competition for contract tenders and extra requirements, such as amendments to the roof and the need to erect a perimeter 'wrap'. The velodrome is costing £25 million more because of 'more complex foundations and ground conditions'.

 Source: Extracts from Blitz, R., 'London Olympics venues over budget by £196m', FT.com, 5 February 2009.

We saw earlier that budgets enable a management-by-exception environment to be created where senior management can focus on areas where things are not going according to plan (the exceptions – it is to be hoped). To create this environment, a comparison of the budget and the actual results must be undertaken to see whether any variances between the two exist. We are now going to discuss the way in which this may be done.

MEASURING VARIANCES FROM BUDGET

We saw in Chapter 1 that the key financial objective of a business is to increase the wealth of its owners (shareholders). Since profit is the net increase in wealth from business operations, the most important budget target to meet is the profit target. We shall therefore take this as our starting point when comparing the budget with the actual results. Example 9.3 shows the budgeted and actual income statement for Baxter Ltd for the month of May.

Example 9.3

The following are the budgeted and actual income statements for Baxter Ltd, a manufacturing business, for the month of May:

	Budget	Actual
Output (production and sales)	1,000 units	900 units
	£	£
Sales revenue	100,000	92,000
Direct materials	(40,000) (40,000 metres)	(36,900) (37,000 metres)
Direct labour	(20,000) (2,500 hours)	(17,500) (2,150 hours)
Fixed overheads	(20,000)	(20,700)
Operating profit	20,000	16,900

From these figures it is clear that the budgeted profit was not achieved. As far as May is concerned, this is a matter of history. However, the business (or at least one aspect of it) is out of control. Senior management must discover where things went wrong during May and try to ensure that these mistakes are not repeated in later months. It is not enough to know that things went wrong overall. We need to know where and why. The approach taken is to compare the budgeted and actual figures for the various items (sales revenue, raw materials and so on) in the above statement.

Activity 9.9

Can you see any problems in comparing the various items (sales, direct materials and so on) for the budget and the actual performance of Baxter Ltd in order to draw conclusions as to which aspects were out of control?

The problem is that the actual level of output was not as budgeted. Baxter Ltd's actual level of output for May was 10 per cent less than budget. This means that we cannot, for example, say that there was a labour cost saving of £2,500 (that is, £20,000 – £17,500) and conclude that all is well in that area.

Flexing the budget

One practical way to overcome our difficulty is to 'flex' the budget to what it would have been had the planned level of output been 900 units rather than 1,000 units. **Flexing the budget** simply means revising it, assuming a different volume of output.

To exercise control, the budget is usually flexed to reflect the volume that actually occurred, where this is higher or lower than that originally planned. This means that we need to know which revenues and costs are fixed and which ones are variable, relative to the volume of output. Once we know this, flexing is a simple operation. We shall assume that sales revenue, material cost and labour cost vary strictly with volume. Fixed overheads, by definition, will not. Whether, in real life, labour cost does vary with the volume of output is not so certain, but it will serve well enough as an assumption for our purposes. Where labour costs are actually fixed, we simply take this into account in the flexing process.

On the basis of our assumptions regarding the behaviour of revenues and costs, the flexed budget would be as follows:

	Flexed budget
Output (production and sales)	900 units
	£
Sales revenue	90,000
Direct materials	(36,000) (36,000 metres)
Direct labour	(18,000) (2,250 hours)
Fixed overheads	(20,000)
Operating profit	16,000

This is simply the original budget, with the sales revenue, raw materials and labour cost figures scaled down by 10 per cent (the same factor as the actual output fell short of the budgeted one).

Putting the original budget, the flexed budget and the actual results for May together, we obtain the following:

	Original budget	*Flexed budget*	*Actual*
Output (production and sales)	1,000 units	900 units	900 units
	£	£	£
Sales revenue	100,000	90,000	92,000
Direct materials	(40,000)	(36,000) (36,000m)	(36,900) (37,000m)
Direct labour	(20,000)	(18,000) (2,250 hr)	(17,500) (2,150 hr)
Fixed overheads	(20,000)	(20,000)	(20,700)
Operating profit	20,000	16,000	16,900

Flexible budgets enable us to make a more valid comparison between the budget (using the flexed figures) and the actual results. Key differences, or variances, between budgeted and actual results for each aspect of the business's activities can then be calculated.

It may seem as if we are saying that it does not matter if there are volume shortfalls because we just revise the budget and carry on as if all is well. However, this is not the case, because losing sales means losing profit. The first point that we must pick up therefore is the loss of profit arising from the loss of sales of 100 units.

Activity 9.10

What will be the loss of profit arising from the sales volume shortfall, assuming that everything except sales volume was as planned?

The answer is simply the difference between the original budget and the flexed budget profit figures. The only difference between these two profit figures is the volume of sales; everything else was the same. (That is to say that the flexing was carried out assuming that the per-unit sales revenue, material cost and labour cost were all as originally budgeted.) This means that the figure for the loss of profit due to the volume shortfall, taken alone, is £4,000 (that is, £20,000 – £16,000).

This difference between the two budgeted profit figures is a **variance** (the sales volume variance). A variance is simply the difference between the actual results and the original budget, relating to a particular factor (sales volume, in the case of Activity 9.10).

Where a variance has the effect of making the actual profit lower than the budgeted profit, it is known as an **adverse variance**. The variance arising from the sales volume shortfall is, therefore an adverse variance. Where a variance has the opposite effect, it is known as a **favourable variance**. We can therefore say that a variance is the effect of that factor (taken alone) on the budgeted profit. When looking at some particular aspect, such as sales volume, we assume that all other factors went according to plan. This is shown in Figure 9.6.

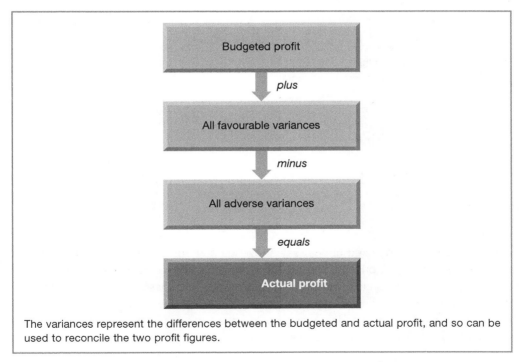

The variances represent the differences between the budgeted and actual profit, and so can be used to reconcile the two profit figures.

Figure 9.6 Relationship between the budgeted and actual profit

For the month of May, we have already identified one of the reasons that the budgeted profit of £20,000 was not achieved and that the actual profit was only £16,900. This was the £4,000 loss of profit (adverse variance) that arose from the sales volume shortfall. Now that the budget is flexed, and the variance arising from the sales volume difference has been stripped out, we can compare like with like and reach further conclusions about May's trading.

The fact that the sales revenue, materials and labour figures differ between the flexed budget and the actual results (see page 328) suggests that the adverse sales volume variance was not the only problem area. To identify the value of the differences that arose from these other three areas (sales revenue, materials and labour), we need to compare the flexed budget and actual values for each of them.

Activity 9.11

Compare the sales revenue, raw materials and labour values between the flexed budget and the actual results and reconcile the original budget and the actual profit for Baxter Ltd. Remember that the sales volume variance is also part of the difference.

This is calculated as follows:

	£
Budgeted profit	20,000
Favourable variances	
Sales price (92,000 – 90,000)	2,000
Direct labour (18,000 – 17,500)	500
Total favourable variances	2,500
Adverse variances	
Sales volume (as above)	(4,000)
Direct materials (36,000 – 36,900)	(900)
Fixed overheads (20,000 – 20,700)	(700)
	(5,600)
Actual profit	16,900

The variance between flexed budget sales revenue and actual sales revenue (£2,000) can only arise from higher prices being charged than were envisaged in the original budget. This is because any variance arising from volume difference has already been isolated in the flexing process. Less was spent on labour than was allowed for a volume of 900 units. More was spent on materials than should have been for an output of 900 units. There was also an overspend on fixed overheads.

Activity 9.12

If you were the chief executive of Baxter Ltd, what attitude would you take to the overall variance between the budgeted profit and the actual one?

How would you react to the five individual variances that are the outcome of the analysis shown in the solution to Activity 9.11?

You would probably be concerned about how large the variances are and their direction (favourable or adverse). In particular you may have thought of the following:

- The overall adverse profit variance is £3,100 (that is £20,000 – £16,900). This represents 15.5 per cent of the budgeted profit (that is £3,100/£20,000 × 100%) and you (as chief executive) would pretty certainly see it as significant and worrying.
- The £4,000 adverse sales volume variance represents 20 per cent of budgeted profit and it too would be a major cause of concern.
- The £2,000 favourable sales price variance represents 10 per cent of budgeted profit. Since this is favourable it might be seen as a cause for celebration rather than concern. On the other hand it means that Baxter's output was, on average, sold at prices 2 per cent above the planned price. This could have been the cause of the worrying adverse sales volume variance. Baxter may have sold fewer units because it charged higher prices.
- The £900 adverse direct materials variance represents 4.5 per cent of budgeted profit. It would be unrealistic to expect the actuals to hit the precise budget figure each month. The question is whether 4.5 per cent for this variance represents a significant amount and a cause for concern.
- The £500 favourable direct labour variance represents 2.5 per cent of budgeted profit. Since this is favourable and relatively small it may be seen as not being a major cause for concern.
- The £700 fixed overhead adverse variance represents 3.5 per cent of budgeted profit. The chief executive may be concerned about this.

The chief executive will now need to ask some questions as to why things went so badly wrong in several areas and what can be done to improve things for the future.

The variance between the actual and flexed figures that has been calculated for both materials and labour overheads can be broken down further. The total direct materials variance (£900) can be analysed to see the extent to which it is caused by a difference (between budget and actual) in the amount of raw material used and by a difference in the prices at which the materials were bought. A similar analysis can be carried out for the total direct labour variance (£500). These further analyses may provide much more helpful information than the broad variances for each of these two areas. Overhead variances can also be broken down further. These further analyses are beyond the scope of this book. If you would like to pursue this topic, the further reading at the end of the chapter provides some appropriate references.

Real World 9.6 shows how two UK-based businesses, Next plc, the retailer, and Tate and Lyle plc, the sugar refiner, use **variance analysis** to exercise control over their operations. Many businesses explain in their annual reports how they operate systems of budgetary control.

REAL WORLD 9.6

Variance analysis in practice

What next?
In its 2011 annual report, Next plc states:

> The Board is responsible for approving semi-annual Group budgets. Performance against budget is reported to the Board monthly and any substantial variances are explained.

Refined controls
Tate and Lyle plc makes it clear that it too uses budgets and variance analysis to help keep control over its activities. The 2011 annual report states:

> There is a comprehensive budgeting and planning system for all items of expenditure with an annual budget approved by the Board. Results are reported against budget on a monthly basis, with significant variances investigated.

> The board of directors of neither of these businesses will seek explanations of variances arising at each branch/department, but they will be looking at figures for the businesses as a whole or the results for major divisions of them.

> Equally certainly, branch/department managers will receive a monthly (or perhaps more frequent) report of variances arising within their area of responsibility alone.

Sources: Next plc Annual Report 2011, p. 25, and Tate and Lyle plc Annual Report 2011, p. 39.

Real World 9.7 gives some indication of the importance of flexible budgeting in practice.

REAL WORLD 9.7

Being flexible about budgeting

A study of the UK food and drink industry by Abdel-Kader and Luther provides some insight as to the importance attached by management accountants to flexible budgeting. The study asked those in charge of the management accounting function to rate the importance of flexible budgeting by selecting one of three possible categories: 'not important', 'moderately important' or 'important'. Figure 9.7 sets out the results, from the sample of 117 respondents.

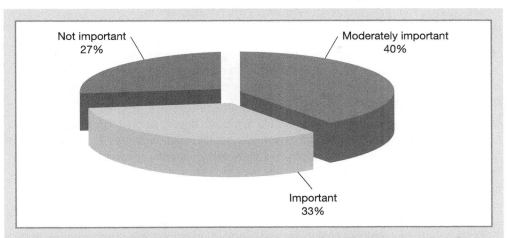

Figure 9.7 Degree of importance attached to flexible budgeting

Respondents were also asked to state the frequency with which flexible budgeting was used within the business, using a five-point scale ranging from 1 (never) through to 5 (very often). Figure 9.8 sets out the results.

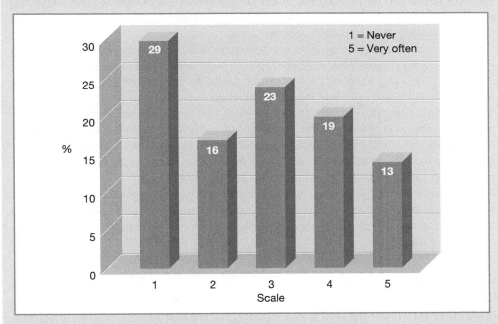

Figure 9.8 Frequency of use of flexible budgets

We can see that although flexible budgeting is regarded as important by a significant proportion of management accountants and is being used in practice, not all businesses use it.

Source: Based on information in Abdel-Kader, M. and Luther, R., 'Management accounting practices in the food and drinks industry', CIMA Research, 2006.

MAKING BUDGETARY CONTROL EFFECTIVE

It should be clear from what we have seen of **budgetary control** that a system, or a set of routines, must be put in place to enable the potential benefits to be gained. Most businesses that operate successful budgetary control systems tend to share some common features. These include the following:

- *A serious attitude taken to the system*. This approach should apply to all levels of management, right from the very top. For example, senior managers need to make clear to junior managers that they take notice of the monthly variance reports and base some of their actions and decisions upon them.
- *Clear demarcation between areas of managerial responsibility*. It needs to be clear which manager is responsible for each business area, so that accountability can more easily be ascribed for any area that seems to be going out of control.
- *Budget targets that are challenging yet achievable*. Setting unachievable targets is likely to have a demotivating effect. There may be a case for getting managers to participate in establishing their own targets to help create a sense of 'ownership'. This, in turn, can increase the managers' commitment and motivation.
- *Established data collection, analysis and reporting routines*. These should take the actual results and the budget figures, and calculate and report the variances. This should be part of the business's regular accounting information system, so that the required reports are automatically produced each month.
- *Reports aimed at individual managers, rather than general-purpose documents*. This avoids managers having to wade through a large report to find the small part that is relevant to them.
- *Fairly short reporting periods*. These would typically be one month long, so that things cannot go too far wrong before they are picked up.
- *Timely variance reports.* Reports should be produced and made available to managers shortly after the end of the relevant reporting period. If it is not until the end of June that a manager is informed that the performance in May was below the budgeted level, it is quite likely that the performance for June will be below target as well. Reports on the performance in May ideally need to emerge in early June.
- *Action being taken to get operations back under control if they are shown to be out of control*. The report will not change things by itself. Managers need to take action to try to ensure that the reporting of significant adverse variances leads to action to put things right for the future.

BEHAVIOURAL ISSUES

Budgets are prepared with the objective of affecting the attitudes and behaviour of managers. We saw earlier that budgets are intended to motivate managers, and research evidence generally shows that budgets can be effective in achieving this. More specifically, the research shows that:

- the existence of budgets generally tends to improve performance;
- demanding, yet achievable, budget targets tend to motivate better than less demanding targets – it seems that setting the most demanding targets that will be accepted by managers is a very effective way to motivate them;

- unrealistically demanding targets tend to have an adverse effect on managers' performance;
- the participation of managers in setting their targets tends to improve motivation and performance. This is probably because those managers feel a sense of commitment to the targets and a moral obligation to achieve them.

It has been suggested that allowing managers to set their own targets will lead to slack (that is, easily achievable targets) being introduced. This would make achievement of the target that much easier. On the other hand, in an effort to impress, a manager may select a target that is not really achievable. These points imply that care must be taken in the extent to which managers have unfettered choice of their own targets.

THE USE OF VARIANCE ANALYSIS

Variance analysis is a very popular management accounting technique. **Real World 9.8** provides some evidence of this.

REAL WORLD 9.8

Using variance analysis

The CIMA survey examined the extent to which the use of variance analysis varies with business size. Figure 9.9 shows the results.

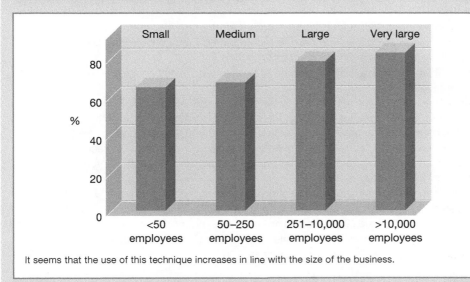

It seems that the use of this technique increases in line with the size of the business.

Figure 9.9 Variance analysis and business size

The survey also indicated that variance analysis was the most widely used of a variety of management accounting tools examined (which included the techniques covered in previous chapters). Overall, more than 70 per cent of respondents used this technique.

Source: Figure adapted from 'Management accounting tools for today and tomorrow', CIMA, 2009, p. 12.

Self-assessment question 9.1 pulls together what we have just seen about preparing budgets.

❓ SELF-ASSESSMENT QUESTION 9.1

Antonio Ltd has planned production and sales for the next nine months as follows:

	Production units	Sales units
May	350	350
June	400	400
July	500	400
August	600	500
September	600	600
October	700	650
November	750	700
December	750	800
January	750	750

During the period, the business plans to advertise so as to generate these increases in sales. Payments for advertising of £1,000 and £1,500 will be made in July and October respectively.

The selling price per unit will be £20 throughout the period. Forty per cent of sales are normally made on two months' credit. The other 60 per cent are settled within the month of the sale.

Raw materials will be held for one month before they are taken into production. Purchases of raw materials will be on one month's credit (buy one month, pay the next). The cost of raw materials is £8 per unit of production.

The direct labour cost will be £6 per unit of production. This is a variable cost. It will be paid in the month concerned.

Various fixed production overheads, which during the period to 30 June had run at £1,800 a month, are expected to rise to £2,000 each month from 1 July to 31 October. These are expected to rise again from 1 November to £2,400 a month and to remain at that level for the foreseeable future. These overheads include a steady £400 each month for depreciation. Overheads are planned to be paid 80 per cent in the month of production and 20 per cent in the following month.

To help to meet the planned increased production, a new item of plant will be bought and delivered in August. The cost of this item is £6,600; the contract with the supplier will specify that this will be paid in three equal amounts in September, October and November.

The business plans to hold raw materials inventories of 500 units on 1 July. The balance at the bank on the same day is planned to be £7,500.

Required:

(a) Draw up the following for the six months ending 31 December:
- (i) A raw materials inventories budget, showing both physical quantities and financial values.
- (ii) A trade payables budget.
- (iii) A cash budget.
- (iv) A budgeted income statement for the month of May.

(b) The cash budget reveals a potential cash deficiency during October and November. Can you suggest any ways in which a modification of plans could overcome this problem?

(c) Calculate the actual profit for May and reconcile it with the budgeted profit for the month calculated in (a)(iv), above. The reconciliation should include the following variances:
  - Sales volume
  - Sales price
  - Direct materials
  - Direct labour
  - Fixed overheads.

The following information is relevant:

■ During May, 360 units were sold for a total of £7,400. The raw material cost was £2,810.
■ The labour cost was £2,250. The fixed production overheads cost was £1,830.

The answer to this question can be found at the back of the book, in Appendix B.

SUMMARY

The main points of this chapter may be summarised as follows:

Budgets

■ A budget is a short-term business plan, mainly expressed in financial terms.

■ Budgets are the short-term means of working towards the business's objectives.

■ They are usually prepared for a one-year period with sub-periods of a month.

■ There is usually a separate budget for each key area.

■ The budgets for each area are summarised in master budgets (budgeted income statement and statement of financial position).

■ Budgets are plans rather than forecasts.

Uses of budgets

■ Promote forward thinking.

■ Help co-ordinate the various aspects of the business.

■ Motivate performance.

■ Provide the basis of a system of control.

■ Provide a system of authorisation.

→

Preparing budgets

- There is no standard style – practicality and usefulness are the key issues.
- They are usually prepared in columnar form, with a column for each month (or similarly short period).
- Each budget must link (co-ordinate) with others.
- Non-financial measures (such as units of output) can be used when budgeting.

Controlling through budgets

- To exercise control, budgets can be flexed to match actual volume of output.
- A variance is an increase (favourable) or decrease (adverse) in profit, relative to the budgeted profit, as a result of some aspect of the business's activities when taken alone.
- Budgeted profit plus all favourable variances less all adverse variances equals actual profit.

Effective budgetary control

- Good budgetary control requires establishing systems and routines to ensure such things as a clear distinction between individual managers' areas of responsibility; prompt, frequent and relevant variance reporting; and senior management commitment.
- There are behavioural aspects of control relating to management style, participation in budget-setting and the failure to meet budget targets that should be taken into account by senior managers.

MyAccountingLab

Go to www.myaccountinglab.com to check your understanding of the chapter, create a personalised study plan, and maximise your revision time

KEY TERMS

FURTHER READING

If you would like to explore the topics covered in this chapter in more depth, we recommend the following books:

Atkinson, A., Banker, R., Kaplan, R. and Young, S. M., *Management Accounting*, 6th edn, Prentice Hall, 2011, Chapter 11.

Atrill, P. and McLaney, E., *Management Accounting for Decision Makers*, 7th edn, Financial Times/Prentice Hall, 2012, Chapters 6 and 7.

Drury, C., *Management and Cost Accounting*, 8th edn, South Western Cengage Learning, 2012, Chapter 15.

Horngren, C., Datar, S. and Rajan, M., *Cost Accounting: A Managerial Emphasis*, 14th edn, Prentice Hall International, 2011, Chapter 6.

? REVIEW QUESTIONS

Answers to these questions can be found at the back of the book, in Appendix C.

9.1 Define a budget. How is a budget different from a forecast?

9.2 What were the five uses of budgets that were identified in the chapter?

9.3 What is meant by a *variance*? What is the point in analysing variances?

9.4 What is the point in flexing the budget in the context of variance analysis? Does flexing imply that differences between budget and actual in the volume of output are ignored in variance analysis?

✳ EXERCISES

*Exercise 9.1 is basic level, exercises 9.2 and 9.3 are intermediate level and exercises 9.4 and 9.5 are advanced level. Those with **coloured numbers** have answers at the back of the book, in Appendix D.*

If you wish to try more exercises, visit the website at **www.myaccountinglab.com**.

9.1 You have overheard the following statements:
   (a) 'A budget is a forecast of what is expected to happen in a business during the next year.'
   (b) 'Monthly budgets must be prepared with a column for each month so that you can see the whole year at a glance, month by month.'
   (c) 'Budgets are OK but they stifle all initiative. No manager worth employing would work for a business that seeks to control through budgets.'
   (d) 'Any sensible person would start with the sales budget and build up the other budgets from there.'

Required:
Critically discuss these statements, explaining any technical terms. →

9.2 A nursing home, which is linked to a large hospital, has been examining its budgetary control procedures, with particular reference to overhead costs. The level of activity in the facility is measured by the number of patients treated in the budget period. For the current year, the budget stands at 6,000 patients and this is expected to be met.

For months 1 to 6 of this year (assume 12 months of equal length), 2,700 patients were treated. The actual variable overhead costs incurred during this six-month period are as follows:

Expense	£
Staffing	59,400
Power	27,000
Supplies	54,000
Other	8,100
Total	148,500

The hospital accountant believes that the variable overhead costs will be incurred at the same rate during months 7 to 12 of the year.

Fixed overheads are budgeted for the whole year as follows:

Expense	£
Supervision	120,000
Depreciation/financing	187,200
Other	64,800
Total	372,000

Required:

(a) Present an overheads budget for months 7 to 12 of the year. You should show each expense, but should not separate individual months. What is the total overheads cost for each patient that would be incorporated into any statistics?

(b) The home actually treated 3,800 patients during months 7 to 12, the actual variable overheads were £203,300 and the fixed overheads were £190,000. In summary form, examine how well the home exercised control over its overheads.

(c) Interpret your analysis and point out any limitations or assumptions.

9.3 Linpet Ltd is to be incorporated on 1 June. The opening statement of financial position (balance sheet) of the business will then be as follows:

Assets	£
Cash at bank	60,000
Share capital	
£1 ordinary shares	60,000

During June, the business intends to make payments of £40,000 for a leasehold property, £10,000 for equipment and £6,000 for a motor vehicle. The business will also purchase initial trading inventories costing £22,000 on credit.

The business has produced the following estimates:

1 Sales revenue for June will be £8,000 and will increase at the rate of £3,000 a month until September. In October, sales revenue will rise to £22,000 and in subsequent months will be maintained at this figure.

2 The gross profit percentage on goods sold will be 25 per cent.

3 There is a risk that supplies of trading inventories will be interrupted towards the end of the accounting year. The business therefore intends to build up its initial level of inventories (£22,000) by purchasing £1,000 of inventories each month in addition to the monthly purchases necessary to satisfy monthly sales requirements. All purchases of inventories (including the initial inventories) will be on one month's credit.

4 Sales revenue will be divided equally between cash and credit sales. Credit customers are expected to pay two months after the sale is agreed.

5 Wages and salaries will be £900 a month. Other overheads will be £500 a month for the first four months and £650 thereafter. Both types of expense will be payable when incurred.

6 80 per cent of sales revenue will be generated by salespeople who will receive 5 per cent commission on sales revenue. The commission is payable one month after the sale is agreed.

7 The business intends to purchase further equipment in November for £7,000 cash.

8 Depreciation will be provided at the rate of 5 per cent a year on property and 20 per cent a year on equipment. (Depreciation has not been included in the overheads mentioned in 5 above.)

Required:

(a) State why a cash budget is required for a business.

(b) Prepare a cash budget for Linpet Ltd for the six-month period to 30 November.

9.4 Newtake Records Ltd owns a small chain of shops selling DVDs and CDs. At the beginning of June the business had an overdraft of £35,000 and the bank had asked for this to be eliminated by the end of November. As a result, the directors have recently decided to review their plans for the next six months.

The following plans were prepared for the business some months earlier:

	May £000	June £000	July £000	Aug £000	Sept £000	Oct £000	Nov £000
Sales revenue	180	230	320	250	140	120	110
Purchases	135	180	142	94	75	66	57
Administration expenses	52	55	56	53	48	46	45
Selling expenses	22	24	28	26	21	19	18
Taxation payment	–	–	–	22	–	–	–
Finance payments	5	5	5	5	5	5	5
Shop refurbishment	–	–	14	18	6	–	–

Notes

1 The inventories level at 1 June was £112,000. The business believes it is preferable to maintain a minimum inventories level of £40,000 over the period to 30 November.

2 Suppliers allow one month's credit.

3 The gross profit margin is 40 per cent.

4 All sales proceeds are received in the month of sale. However, 50 per cent of customers pay with a credit card. The charge made by the credit card business to Newtake Records Ltd is 3 per cent of the sales revenue value. These charges are in addition to the selling expenses identified above. The credit card business pays Newtake Records Ltd in the month of sale.

5 The business has a bank loan, which it is paying off in monthly instalments of £5,000. The interest element represents 20 per cent of each instalment.

6 Administration expenses are paid when incurred. This item includes a charge of £15,000 each month in respect of depreciation.

7 Selling expenses are payable in the following month.

→

341

Required (working to the nearest £1,000):

(a) Prepare an inventories budget for the six months to 30 November also based on the table of plans above.

(b) Prepare a cash budget for the six months ending 30 November which shows the cash balance at the end of each month also based on the plans set out in the table above.

(c) Prepare a budgeted income statement for the whole of the six-month period ending 30 November. (A monthly breakdown of profit is *not* required.)

(d) What problems is Newtake Records Ltd likely to face in the next six months? Can you suggest how the business might deal with these problems?

9.5 Daniel Chu Ltd, a new business, will start production on 1 April, but sales will not start until 1 May. Planned sales for the next nine months are as follows:

	Sales units
May	500
June	600
July	700
August	800
September	900
October	900
November	900
December	800
January	700

The selling price of a unit will be a consistent £100 and all sales will be made on one month's credit. It is planned that sufficient finished goods inventories for each month's sales should be available at the end of the previous month.

Raw materials purchases will be such that there will be sufficient raw materials inventories available at the end of each month precisely to meet the following month's planned production. This planned policy will operate from the end of April. Purchases of raw materials will be on one month's credit. The cost of raw material is £40 a unit of finished product.

The direct labour cost, which is variable with the level of production, is planned to be £20 a unit of finished production. Production overheads are planned to be £20,000 each month, including £3,000 for depreciation. Non-production overheads are planned to be £11,000 a month, of which £1,000 will be depreciation.

Various non-current (fixed) assets costing £250,000 will be bought and paid for during April.

Except where specified, assume that all payments take place in the same month as the cost is incurred.

The business will raise £300,000 in cash from a share issue in April.

Required:

Draw up the following for the six months ending 30 September:

(a) A finished inventories budget, showing just physical quantities.

(b) A raw materials inventories budget showing both physical quantities and financial values.

(c) A trade payables budget.

(d) A trade receivables budget.

(e) A cash budget.

MAKING CAPITAL INVESTMENT DECISIONS

INTRODUCTION

In this chapter we shall look at how businesses can make decisions involving investments in new plant, machinery, buildings and other long-term assets. In making these decisions, businesses should be trying to pursue their key financial objective, which is to enhance the wealth of the owners (shareholders).

Investment appraisal is a very important area for businesses; expensive and far-reaching consequences can flow from bad investment decisions.

This chapter is the first of three dealing with the area generally known as *finance* or *financial management.*

Learning outcomes

When you have completed this chapter, you should be able to:

- explain the nature and importance of investment decision making;
- identify the four main investment appraisal methods found in practice;
- use each method to reach a decision on the particular investment opportunity;
- discuss the attributes of each of the methods.

MyAccountingLab   Visit www.myaccountinglab.com
for practice and revision opportunities

From Chapter 10 of *Accounting and Finance for Non-Specialists*, 8/e. Peter Atrill and Eddie McLaney. © Pearson Education Limited 2013. All rights reserved.

THE NATURE OF INVESTMENT DECISIONS

The essential feature of investment decisions is *time*. Investment involves making an outlay of something of economic value, usually cash, at one (or more) points in time, which is expected to yield economic benefits to the investor at some other points in time. Usually, the outlay precedes the benefits. The outlay is typically a single large amount while the benefits arrive as a series of smaller amounts over a fairly protracted period.

Investment decisions tend to be of profound importance to the business because:

■ *Large amounts of resources are often involved*. Many investments made by businesses involve laying out a significant proportion of their total resources (see Real World 10.2). If mistakes are made with the decision, the effects on the businesses could be significant, if not catastrophic.

■ *It is often difficult and/or expensive to bail out of an investment once it has been undertaken*. Investments made by a business are often specific to its needs. A hotel business, for example, may invest in a new, custom-designed hotel complex. If the business found, after having made the investment, that room occupancy rates were too low, the only course of action might be to sell the complex. The specialist nature of the complex may, however, lead to it having a rather limited resale value. This could mean that the amount recouped from the investment is much less than it had originally cost.

Real World 10.1 gives an illustration of a major investment decision by a well-known airline business.

REAL WORLD 10.1

Plane common sense?

In July 2011, American Airlines announced the purchase of 200 Boeing 737s and 260 Airbus 320 aircraft. This represents the largest order in aviation history and the new aircraft will be delivered to the company over the period 2013 to 2022. Although the precise cost of the new aircraft was not revealed, it has been estimated to be more than £12 billion.

This level of investment is quite extraordinary, even though American Airlines is the fourth largest airline in the world. The business clearly believes that acquiring the new aircraft will be a profitable move, but how would it have reached this conclusion? Presumably, the likely future benefits from passenger fares and likely future operating costs will have been major inputs to the decision.

Source: Based on 'American Airlines announce billion-dollar aircraft order', www.bbc.co.uk, 20 July 2011 and www.telegraph.co.uk, 20 July 2011.

The issues raised by American Airlines' investment will be the main subject of this chapter.

Real World 10.2 indicates the level of annual net investment for a number of randomly selected, well-known UK businesses. We can see that the scale of investment varies from one business to another. (It also tends to vary from one year to the next for a particular business.) In nearly all of these businesses the scale of investment was significant, despite the fact that many businesses were cutting back on investment during the economic recession.

REAL WORLD 10.2

The scale of investment by UK businesses

	Expenditure on additional non-current assets as a percentage of:	
	Annual sales revenue	End-of-year non-current assets
British Sky Broadcasting plc (television)	9.4	20.4
Go-Ahead Group plc (transport)	2.8	11.8
J D Wetherspoon (pub operator)	11.8	13.7
Marks and Spencer plc (stores)	5.1	8.7
Ryanair Holdings plc (airline)	24.7	17.5
Severn Trent Water Ltd (water and sewerage)	24.8	6.2
Vodafone Group plc (telecommunications)	20.4	7.0
Wm Morrison Supermarkets plc (supermarkets)	3.6	7.4

Source: Annual reports of the businesses concerned for the financial year ending in 2011.

Real World 10.2 considers only expenditure on non-current assets, but this type of investment often requires a significant outlay on current assets to support it (additional inventories, for example). This suggests that the real scale of investment is even greater than indicated above.

Activity 10.1

When managers are making decisions involving capital investments, what should the decision seek to achieve?

Investment decisions must be consistent with the objectives of the particular organisation. For a private-sector business, maximising the wealth of the owners (shareholders) is normally assumed to be the key financial objective.

INVESTMENT APPRAISAL METHODS

Given the importance of investment decisions, it is essential that proper screening of investment proposals takes place. An important part of this screening process is to ensure that appropriate methods of evaluation are used.

Research shows that there are basically four methods used by businesses to evaluate investment opportunities. They are:

- accounting rate of return (ARR);
- payback period (PP);
- net present value (NPV);
- internal rate of return (IRR).

It is possible to find businesses that use variants of these four methods. It is also possible to find businesses, particularly smaller ones, that do not use any formal appraisal method but rely instead on the 'gut feeling' of their managers. Most businesses, however, seem to use one (or more) of these four methods.

We are going to assess the effectiveness of each of these methods, but we shall see that only one of them (NPV) is a wholly logical approach. Despite their popularity in practice, the other three all have flaws. To help in examining each of the methods, it might be useful to see how each of them would cope with a particular investment opportunity. Let us consider the following example.

Example 10.1

Billingsgate Battery Company has carried out some research that shows that there is a market for a standard service that it has recently developed.

Provision of the service would require investment in a machine that would cost £100,000, payable immediately. Sales of the service would take place throughout the next five years. At the end of that time, it is estimated that the machine could be sold for £20,000.

Net annual inflows and outflows from sales of the service would be expected to be:

Time		£000
Immediately	Cost of machine	(100)
1 year's time	Operating profit before depreciation	20
2 years' time	Operating profit before depreciation	40
3 years' time	Operating profit before depreciation	60
4 years' time	Operating profit before depreciation	60
5 years' time	Operating profit before depreciation	20
5 years' time	Disposal proceeds from the machine	20

Note that, broadly speaking, the operating profit before deducting depreciation (that is, before non-cash items) equals the net amount of cash flowing into the business. Broadly, apart from depreciation, all of this business's expenses cause cash to flow out of the business. Sales revenues tend to lead to cash flowing in. For the time being, we shall assume that working capital – which is made up of inventories, trade receivables and trade payables – remains constant. This means that operating profit before depreciation will tend to equal the net cash inflow.

To simplify matters, we shall assume that the cash from sales and for the expenses of providing the service are received and paid, respectively, at the end of each year. This is clearly unlikely to be true in real life. Money will have to be paid to employees (for salaries and wages) on a weekly or a monthly basis. Customers will pay within a month or two of buying the service. On the other hand, making the assumption probably does not lead to a serious distortion. It is a simplifying assumption, that is often made in real life, and it will make things more straightforward for us now. We should be clear, however, that there is nothing about any of the four methods that *demands* that this assumption is made.

Having set up the example, we shall now go on to consider how each of the appraisal methods works.

ACCOUNTING RATE OF RETURN (ARR)

The first of the four methods that we shall consider is the **accounting rate of return (ARR)**. This method takes the average accounting operating profit that the investment will generate and expresses it as a percentage of the average investment made over the life of the project. In other words:

$$ARR = \frac{\text{Average annual operating profit}}{\text{Average investment to earn that profit}} \times 100\%$$

We can see from the equation that, to calculate the ARR, we need to deduce two pieces of information about the particular project:

- the annual average operating profit; and
- the average investment.

In our example, the average annual operating profit *before depreciation* over the five years is £40,000 (that is, £000(20 + 40 + 60 + 60 + 20)/5). Assuming 'straight-line' depreciation (that is, equal annual amounts), the annual depreciation charge will be £16,000 (that is, £(100,000 – 20,000)/5). Therefore, the average annual operating profit *after depreciation* is £24,000 (that is, £40,000 – £16,000).

The average investment over the five years can be calculated as follows:

$$\text{Average investment} = \frac{\text{Cost of machine} + \text{Disposal value*}}{2}$$

$$= \frac{£100,000 + £20,000}{2}$$

$$= £60,000$$

* To find the average investment we are simply adding the value of the amount invested at the beginning and end of the investment period together and dividing by two.

The ARR of the investment, therefore, is:

$$ARR = \frac{£24,000}{£60,000} \times 100\% = 40\%$$

The following decision rules apply when using ARR:

- For any project to be acceptable, it must achieve a target ARR as a minimum.
- Where there are competing projects that all seem capable of exceeding this minimum rate (that is, where the business must choose between more than one project), the one with the higher (or highest) ARR should be selected.

To decide whether the 40 per cent return is acceptable, we need to compare this percentage return with the minimum rate required by the business.

Activity 10.2

Chaotic Industries is considering an investment in a fleet of ten delivery vans to take its products to customers. The vans will cost £15,000 each to buy, payable immediately. The annual running costs are expected to total £50,000 for each van (including the driver's salary). The vans are expected to operate successfully for six years, at the end of which period they will all have to be sold, with disposal proceeds expected to be about £3,000 a van. At present, the business outsources transport, for all of its deliveries, to a commercial carrier. It is expected that this carrier will charge a total of £530,000 each year for the next six years to undertake the deliveries.

What is the ARR of buying the vans? (Note that cost savings are as relevant a benefit from an investment as are net cash inflows.)

The vans will save the business £30,000 a year (that is, £530,000 − (£50,000 × 10)), before depreciation, in total. Therefore, the inflows and outflows will be:

Time		£000
Immediately	Cost of vans (10 × £15,000)	(150)
1 year's time	Saving before depreciation	30
2 years' time	Saving before depreciation	30
3 years' time	Saving before depreciation	30
4 years' time	Saving before depreciation	30
5 years' time	Saving before depreciation	30
6 years' time	Saving before depreciation	30
6 years' time	Disposal proceeds from the vans (10 × £3,000)	30

The total annual depreciation expense (assuming a straight-line method) will be £20,000 (that is, (£150,000 − £30,000)/6). Therefore, the average annual saving, *after depreciation*, is £10,000 (that is, £30,000 − £20,000).

The average investment will be:

$$\text{Average investment} = \frac{£150,000 + £30,000}{2}$$

$$= £90,000$$

and the ARR of the investment is:

$$\text{ARR} = \frac{£10,000}{£90,000} \times 100\%$$

$$= 11.1\%$$

ARR and ROCE

In essence, ARR and the return on capital employed (ROCE) ratio take the same approach to measuring business performance. Both relate operating profit to the cost of assets used to generate that profit. ROCE, however, assesses the performance of the overall business *after* it has performed, while ARR assesses the potential performance of a particular investment *before* it has performed.

We saw that investments are required to achieve a minimum target ARR. Given the link between ARR and ROCE, this target could be based on a planned level of ROCE. The planned ROCE might be based on the industry-average ROCE.

The link between ARR and ROCE strengthens the case for adopting ARR as the appropriate method of investment appraisal. ROCE is a widely-used measure of profitability and some businesses express their financial objective in terms of a target ROCE. It therefore seems sensible to use a method of investment appraisal that is consistent with this overall measure of business performance. A secondary point in favour of ARR is that it provides a result expressed in percentage terms, which many managers seem to prefer.

Problems with ARR

Activity 10.3

ARR suffers from a major defect as a means of assessing investment opportunities. Can you reason out what this is? Consider the three competing projects whose profits are shown below. All three involve investment in a machine that is expected to have no residual value at the end of the five years. Note that all of the projects have the same total operating profits after depreciation over the five years.

Time		Project A £000	Project B £000	Project C £000
Immediately	Cost of machine	(160)	(160)	(160)
1 year's time	Operating profit after depreciation	20	10	160
2 years' time	Operating profit after depreciation	40	10	10
3 years' time	Operating profit after depreciation	60	10	10
4 years' time	Operating profit after depreciation	60	10	10
5 years' time	Operating profit after depreciation	20	160	10

(*Hint*: The defect is not concerned with the ability of the decision maker to forecast future events, though this too can be a problem. Try to remember the essential feature of investment decisions, which we identified at the beginning of this chapter.)

The problem with ARR is that it ignores the time factor. In this example, exactly the same ARR would have been computed for each of the three projects.

Since the same total operating profit over the five years (£200,000) arises in all three of the projects in Activity 10.3, and the average investment in each project is £80,000 (that is, £160,000/2), each project will give rise to the same ARR of 50 per cent (that is, £40,000/£80,000).

To maximise the wealth of the owners, a manager faced with a choice between the three projects set out in Activity 10.3 should select Project C. This is because most of the benefits arise within twelve months of making the initial investment. Project A would rank second and Project B would come a poor third. Any appraisal technique that is not capable of distinguishing between these three situations is seriously flawed. We shall look at why timing is so important later in the chapter.

There are further problems associated with the ARR method, which we shall now discuss.

■ *Use of average investment*. Using the average investment in calculating ARR can lead to daft results. Example 10.2 illustrates the kind of problem that can arise.

Example 10.2

George put forward an investment proposal to his boss. The business uses ARR to assess investment proposals using a minimum 'hurdle' rate of 27 per cent. Details of the proposal were:

Cost of equipment	£200,000
Estimated residual value of equipment	£40,000
Average annual operating profit before depreciation	£48,000
Estimated life of project	10 years
Annual straight-line depreciation charge	£16,000 (that is, (£200,000 − £40,000)/10)

The ARR of the project will be:

$$\text{ARR} = \frac{48,000 - 16,000}{(200,000 + 40,000)/2} \times 100\% = 26.7\%$$

The boss rejected George's proposal because it failed to achieve an ARR of at least 27 per cent. Although George was disappointed, he realised that there was still hope. In fact, all that the business had to do was to give away the piece of equipment at the end of its useful life rather than sell it. The residual value of the equipment then became zero and the annual depreciation charge became ([£200,000 − £0]/10) = £20,000 a year. The revised ARR calculation was then:

$$\text{ARR} = \frac{48,000 - 20,000}{(200,000 + 0)/2} \times 100\% = 28\%$$

■ *Use of accounting profit*. We have seen that ARR is based on the use of accounting profit. When measuring performance over the whole life of a project, however, it is cash flows rather than accounting profits that are important. Cash is the ultimate measure of the economic wealth generated by an investment. This is because it is cash that is used to acquire resources and for distribution to owners. Accounting profit is more appropriate for reporting achievement on a periodic basis. It is a useful measure of productive effort for a relatively short period, such as a year or half year. It is really a question of 'horses

·for courses'. Accounting profit is fine for measuring performance over a short period, but cash is the appropriate measure when considering performance over the life of a project.

■ *Competing investments*. The ARR method can create problems when considering competing investments of different size. Consider Activity 10.4.

Activity 10.4

Sinclair Wholesalers plc is currently considering opening a new sales outlet in Coventry. Two possible sites have been identified for the new outlet. Site A has an area of 30,000 sq m. It will require an average investment of £6 million and will produce an average operating profit of £600,000 a year. Site B has an area of 20,000 sq m. It will require an average investment of £4 million and will produce an average operating profit of £500,000 a year.

What is the ARR of each investment opportunity? Which site would you select and why, assuming that the business's main financial objective is to increase its wealth?

The ARR of Site A is £600,000/£6m = 10 per cent. The ARR of Site B is £500,000/£4m = 12.5 per cent. Site B, therefore has the higher ARR. In terms of the absolute operating profit generated, however, Site A is the more attractive. If the ultimate objective is to increase the wealth of the shareholders of Sinclair Wholesalers plc, it would be better to choose Site A even though the percentage return is lower. It is the absolute size of the return rather than the relative (percentage) size that is important.

The point identified in Activity 10.4 is a general problem of using comparative measures, such as percentages, when the objective is measured in absolute terms, like an amount of money.

Real World 10.3 illustrates how using percentage measures can lead to confusion.

REAL WORLD 10.3

Increasing road capacity by sleight of hand

During the 1970s, the Mexican government wanted to increase the capacity of a major four-lane road. It came up with the idea of repainting the lane markings so that there were six narrower lanes occupying the same space as four wider ones had previously done. This increased the capacity of the road by 50 per cent (that is, $^2/_4 \times 100$). A tragic outcome of the narrower lanes was an increase in deaths from road accidents. A year later the Mexican government had the six narrower lanes changed back to the original four wider ones. This reduced the capacity of the road by 33 per cent (that is, $^2/_6 \times 100$). The Mexican government reported that, overall, it had increased the capacity of the road by 17 per cent (that is, 50% – 33%), despite the fact that its real capacity was identical to that which it had been originally. The confusion arose because each of the two percentages (50 per cent and 33 per cent) is based on different bases (four and six).

Source: Gigerenzer G., *Reckoning with Risk*, Penguin, 2002.

PAYBACK PERIOD (PP)

A second approach to appraising possible investments is the **payback period (PP)**. This is the time taken for an initial investment to be repaid out of the net cash inflows from that investment. As the PP method takes time into account, it appears at first glance to overcome a key weakness of the ARR method.

Let us consider PP in the context of the Billingsgate Battery example. We should recall that the project's cash flows are:

Time		£000
Immediately	Cost of machine	(100)
1 year's time	Operating profit before depreciation	20
2 years' time	Operating profit before depreciation	40
3 years' time	Operating profit before depreciation	60
4 years' time	Operating profit before depreciation	60
5 years' time	Operating profit before depreciation	20
5 years' time	Disposal proceeds	20

Note that all of these figures are amounts of cash to be paid or received (we saw earlier that operating profit before depreciation is a rough measure of the cash flows from the project).

We can see that this investment will take three years before the £100,000 outlay is covered by the inflows. (This is still assuming that the cash flows occur at year ends.) Derivation of the payback period can be shown by calculating the cumulative cash flows as follows:

Time		Net cash flows £000	Cumulative cash flows £000	
Immediately	Cost of machine	(100)	(100)	
1 year's time	Operating profit before depreciation	20	(80)	(−100 + 20)
2 years' time	Operating profit before depreciation	40	(40)	(−80 + 40)
3 years' time	Operating profit before depreciation	60	20	(−40 + 60)
4 years' time	Operating profit before depreciation	60	80	(20 + 60)
5 years' time	Operating profit before depreciation	20	100	(80 + 20)
5 years' time	Disposal proceeds	20	120	(100 + 20)

We can see that the cumulative cash flows become positive at the end of the third year. Had we assumed that the cash flows from profit arise evenly over the year, the precise payback period would be:

$$2 \text{ years} + (^{40}/_{60}) \text{ years} = 2^2/_3 \text{ years}$$

where 40 represents the cash flow still required at the beginning of the third year to repay the initial outlay and 60 is the projected cash flow during the third year.

The following decision rules apply when using PP:

■ For a project to be acceptable it should have a payback period no longer than a maximum payback period set by the business.
■ If there were two (or more) competing projects whose payback periods were all shorter than the maximum payback period requirement, the project with the shorter (or shortest) payback period should be selected.

If, for example, Billingsgate Battery had a maximum acceptable payback period of four years, the project would be undertaken. A project with a payback period longer than four years would not be acceptable.

Activity 10.5

What is the payback period of the Chaotic Industries project from Activity 10.2?

The inflows and outflows are expected to be:

Time		Net cash flows £000	Cumulative net cash flows £000	
Immediately	Cost of vans	(150)	(150)	
1 year's time	Saving before depreciation	30	(120)	(−150 + 30)
2 years' time	Saving before depreciation	30	(90)	(−120 + 30)
3 years' time	Saving before depreciation	30	(60)	(−90 + 30)
4 years' time	Saving before depreciation	30	(30)	(−60 + 30)
5 years' time	Saving before depreciation	30	0	(−30 + 30)
6 years' time	Saving before depreciation	30	30	(0 + 30)
6 years' time	Disposal proceeds from the vans	30	60	(30 + 30)

The payback period here is five years; that is, it is not until the end of the fifth year that the vans will pay for themselves out of the savings that they are expected to generate.

The logic of using PP is that projects that can recoup their cost quickly are economically more attractive than those with longer payback periods. In other words, it emphasises liquidity.

The PP method has certain advantages. It is quick and easy to calculate. It can also be easily understood by managers. PP is an improvement on ARR in respect of the timing of the cash flows. It is not, however, a complete answer to the problem.

Problems with PP

Activity 10.6

In what respect is PP not a complete answer as a means of assessing investment opportunities? Consider the cash flows arising from three competing projects:

Time		Project 1 £000	Project 2 £000	Project 3 £000
Immediately	Cost of machine	(200)	(200)	(200)
1 year's time	Operating profit before depreciation	70	20	70
2 years' time	Operating profit before depreciation	60	20	100
3 years' time	Operating profit before depreciation	70	160	30
4 years' time	Operating profit before depreciation	80	30	200
5 years' time	Operating profit before depreciation	50	20	440
5 years' time	Disposal proceeds	40	10	20

(*Hint*: Again, the defect is not concerned with the ability of management to forecast future events. This is a problem, but it is a problem whatever approach we take.)

The PP for each project is three years and so the PP method would regard the projects as being equally acceptable. It cannot distinguish between those projects that pay back a significant amount early within the three-year payback period and those that do not.

In addition, this method ignores cash flows after the payback period. A decision maker concerned with increasing owners' wealth would greatly prefer Project 3 because the cash inflows are received earlier. In fact, most of the initial cost of making the investment has been repaid by the end of the second year. Furthermore, the cash inflows are greater in total.

The cumulative cash flows of each project in Activity 10.6 are set out in Figure 10.1.

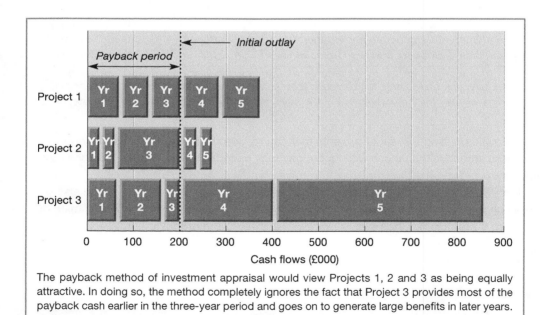

The payback method of investment appraisal would view Projects 1, 2 and 3 as being equally attractive. In doing so, the method completely ignores the fact that Project 3 provides most of the payback cash earlier in the three-year period and goes on to generate large benefits in later years.

Figure 10.1 The cumulative cash flows of each project in Activity 10.6

We shall now consider some additional points concerning the PP method.

- *Relevant information*. We saw earlier that the PP method is simply concerned with how quickly the initial investment can be recouped. Cash flows arising beyond the payback period are ignored. While this neatly avoids the practical problems of forecasting cash flows over a long period, it means that not all relevant information may be taken into account .
- *Risk*. By favouring projects with a short payback period, the PP method appears to provide a means of dealing with the problem of risk. This is, however, a fairly crude approach to the problem. It looks only at the risk that the project will end earlier than expected. This is only one of many risk areas. What, for example, about the risk that the demand for the product may be less than expected? There are more systematic approaches to dealing with risk that can be used.
- *Wealth maximisation*. Although the PP method takes some note of the timing of project costs and benefits, it is not concerned with maximising the wealth of the business owners. Instead, it favours projects that pay for themselves quickly.
- *Required payback period* Managers must select a maximum acceptable payback period. As this cannot be objectively determined, it is really a matter of judgement. This judgement may be difficult to make because there are no reliable guidelines to follow. Managers may simply pick a figure out of the air.

Real World 10.4 looks at a power saving device used by Tesco plc, the supermarket chain, and the payback period involved.

REAL WORLD 10.4

It's payback time at Tesco

Tesco is in the process of installing powerPerfector devices in nearly all of its 2,300 stores and warehouses.The powerPerfector is a device that makes electrically-powered equipment, including lighting, operate more cost effectively. It does this by converting the voltage of mains electricity to the voltage at which the equipment will run at optimum efficiency. Not only does this save electricity, but greatly increases the life of light bulbs and reduces the period between maintenance services for other equipment. It also reduces the noise and heat generated by them. Tesco expects to reduce its electricity cost by 5 to 8 per cent as a result.

Tesco expects to generate a return on investment of about 20 per cent on the cost of installing the powerPerfectors and achieve a payback period of about five years.

Source: Information taken from Jaggi, R.,'Case study: power efficiency', FT.com, 25 November 2009.

NET PRESENT VALUE (NPV)

From what we have seen so far, it seems that to make sensible investment decisions, we need a method of appraisal that both:

- considers *all* of the costs and benefits of each investment opportunity; and
- makes a logical allowance for the *timing* of those costs and benefits.

The third of the four methods of investment appraisal, the **net present value (NPV)** method provides us with this.

Consider the Billingsgate Battery example's cash flows, which we should recall are:

Time		£000
Immediately	Cost of machine	(100)
1 year's time	Operating profit before depreciation	20
2 years' time	Operating profit before depreciation	40
3 years' time	Operating profit before depreciation	60
4 years' time	Operating profit before depreciation	60
5 years' time	Operating profit before depreciation	20
5 years' time	Disposal proceeds	20

Given a financial objective of maximising owners' wealth, it would be easy to assess this investment if all cash inflows and outflows were to occur immediately. It would then simply be a matter of adding up the cash inflows (total £220,000) and comparing them with the cash outflows (£100,000). This would lead us to conclude that the project should go ahead because the owners would be better off by £120,000. Of course, it is not as easy as this because time is involved. The cash outflow will occur immediately, whereas the cash inflows will arise at different times.

Time is an important issue because people do not normally see an amount paid out now as equivalent in value to the same amount being received in a year's time. Therefore, if we were offered £100 in one year's time in exchange for paying out £100 now, we would not be interested, unless we wished to do someone a favour.

Activity 10.7

Why would you see £100 to be received in a year's time as not equal in value to £100 to be paid immediately?

The reason is that, were the investor to have the £100 now, it could be invested so that it would generate income during that year.

Income lost

The income that is foregone represents an *opportunity cost*. As we saw in Chapter 7, an opportunity cost occurs where one course of action deprives us of the opportunity to derive some benefit from an alternative action.

An investment must exceed the opportunity cost of the funds invested if it is to be worthwhile. Therefore, if Billingsgate Battery Company sees investing money elsewhere as the alternative to investment in the machine, the return from investing in the machine must be better than that from the alternative investment. If this is not the case, there is no economic reason to buy the machine.

All investments expose their investors to **risk**. Hence buying a machine, on the strength of estimates made before its purchase, exposes a business to risk. Things may not turn out as expected. We saw in Chapter 1 that people normally expect greater returns in exchange for taking on greater risk. Examples of this in real life are not difficult to find. One such example is that banks tend to charge higher rates of interest to borrowers whom the bank perceives as more risky. Those who can offer good security for a loan and who can point to a regular source of income, tend to be charged lower rates of interest.

Going back to Billingsgate Battery Company's investment opportunity, it is not enough to say that we should buy the machine providing the expected returns are higher than those from an alternative investment. The logical equivalent of investing in the machine would be an investment that is of similar risk. Determining how risky a particular project is and, therefore, how large the **risk premium** should be, is a difficult task.

What will logical investors do?

To summarise, logical investors seeking to increase their wealth will only invest when they believe they will be adequately compensated for the loss of income that the alternative investment will generate. This normally involves checking to see whether the proposed investment will yield a return greater than the basic rate of interest plus an appropriate risk premium.

Let us now return to the Billingsgate Battery Company example. We should recall that the cash flows expected from this investment are:

Time		£000
Immediately	Cost of machine	(100)
1 year's time	Operating profit before depreciation	20
2 years' time	Operating profit before depreciation	40
3 years' time	Operating profit before depreciation	60
4 years' time	Operating profit before depreciation	60
5 years' time	Operating profit before depreciation	20
5 years' time	Disposal proceeds	20

We have already seen that it is not enough simply to compare the basic cash inflows and outflows for the investment. Each of these cash flows must be expressed in similar terms, so that a direct comparison can be made between the sum of the inflows over time and the immediate £100,000 investment. Fortunately, we can do this.

Let us assume that, instead of making this investment, the business could make an alternative investment with similar risk and obtain a return of 20 per cent a year.

Activity 10.8

We know that Billingsgate Battery Company could alternatively invest its money at a rate of 20 per cent a year. How much do you judge the present (immediate) value of the expected first year receipt of £20,000 to be? In other words, if instead of having to wait a year for the £20,000, and being deprived of the opportunity to invest it at 20 per cent, you could have some money now. What sum to be received now would you regard as equivalent to getting £20,000 in one year's time?

We should obviously be happy to accept a lower amount if we could get it immediately than if we had to wait a year. This is because we could invest it at 20 per cent (in the alternative project). Logically, we should be prepared to accept the amount that, with a year's income, will grow to £20,000. If we call this amount PV (for present value) we can say:

$$PV + (PV \times 20\%) = £20,000$$

that is, the amount plus income from investing the amount for the year equals £20,000.

If we rearrange this equation we find:

$$PV \times (1 + 0.2) = £20,000$$

(Note that 0.2 is the same as 20 per cent, but expressed as a decimal.)

Further rearranging gives:

$$PV = £20,000/(1 + 0.2) = £16,667$$

Therefore, logical investors who have the opportunity to invest at 20 per cent a year would not mind whether they have £16,667 now or £20,000 in a year's time. In this sense we can say that, given a 20 per cent alternative investment opportunity, the present value of £20,000 to be received in one year's time is £16,667.

If we derive the present value (PV) of each of the cash flows associated with Billingsgate's machine investment, we could easily make the direct comparison between the cost of making the investment (£100,000) and the various benefits that will derive from it in years 1 to 5.

Using the same logic as was used to derive the PV of a cash flow expected after one year, it can be shown that the PV of a particular cash flow is:

PV of the cash flow of year n = actual cash flow of year n divided by $(1 + r)^n$

where n is the year of the cash flow (that is, how many years into the future) and r is the opportunity financing cost expressed as a decimal (instead of as a percentage).

We have already seen how this works for the £20,000 inflow for year 1 for the Billingsgate project. For year 2 the calculation would be:

$$\text{PV of year 2 cash flow (that is, £40,000)} = £40,000/(1 + 0.2)^2 = £40,000/(1.2)^2$$
$$= £40,000/1.44 = £27,778$$

This means that the present value of the £40,000 to be received in two years' time is £27,778.

Activity 10.9

See if you can show that an investor would find £27,778, receivable now, as equally acceptable to receiving £40,000 in two years' time, assuming that there is a 20 per cent investment opportunity.

The reasoning goes like this:

	£
Amount available for immediate investment	27,778
Income for year 1 (20% × 27,778)	5,556
	33,334
Income for year 2 (20% × 33,334)	6,667
	40,001

(The extra £1 is only a rounding error.)

This is to say that since the investor can turn £27,778 into £40,000 in two years, these amounts are equivalent. We can say that £27,778 is the present value of £40,000 receivable after two years (given a 20 per cent cost of finance).

Now let us calculate the present values of all of the cash flows associated with the Billingsgate machine project and, from them, the *net present value (NPV)* of the project as a whole. The relevant cash flows and calculations are:

Time	Cash flow £000	Calculation of PV	PV £000
Immediately (time 0)	(100)	$(100)/(1 + 0.2)^0$	(100.00)
1 year's time	20	$20/(1 + 0.2)^1$	16.67
2 years' time	40	$40/(1 + 0.2)^2$	27.78
3 years' time	60	$60/(1 + 0.2)^3$	34.72
4 years' time	60	$60/(1 + 0.2)^4$	28.94
5 years' time	20	$20/(1 + 0.2)^5$	8.04
5 years' time	20	$20/(1 + 0.2)^5$	8.04
Net present value (NPV)			24.19

Note that $(1 + 0.2)^0 = 1$.

Once again, we must decide whether the machine project is acceptable to the business. To help us, the following decision rules for NPV should be applied:

- If the NPV is positive the project should be accepted; if it is negative the project should be rejected.
- If there are two (or more) competing projects that have positive NPVs, the project with the higher (or highest) NPV should be selected.

In this case the NPV is positive, so we should accept the project and buy the machine. The reasoning behind this decision rule is quite straightforward. Investing in the machine will make the business, and its owners, £24,190 better off than they would be by taking up the next best available opportunity. The gross benefits from investing in this machine are worth a total of £124,190 today. Since the business can 'buy' these benefits for just £100,000 today, the investment should be made. If, however, the present value of the gross benefits were below £100,000, it would be less than the cost of 'buying' those benefits and the opportunity should, therefore, be rejected.

Activity 10.10

What is the *maximum* the Billingsgate Battery Company would be prepared to pay for the machine, given the potential benefits of owning it?

The business would logically be prepared to pay up to £124,190 since the wealth of the owners of the business would be increased up to this price – although the business would prefer to pay as little as possible.

Using present value tables

To deduce each PV in the Billingsgate Battery Company project, we took the relevant cash flow and multiplied it by $1/(1 + r)^n$. There is a slightly different way to do this. Tables exist that show values of this **discount factor** for a range of values of r and n. Such a table appears in at the end of this book, in Appendix E on page 547. Take a look at it.

Look at the column for 20 per cent and the row for one year. We find that the factor is 0.833. This means that the PV of a cash flow of £1 receivable in one year is £0.833. So the present value of a cash flow of £20,000 receivable in one year's time is £16,660 (that is, 0.833 × £20,000). This is the same result, ignoring rounding errors, as we found earlier by using the equation.

Activity 10.11

What is the NPV of the Chaotic Industries project from Activity 10.2, assuming a 15 per cent opportunity cost of finance (discount rate)? (Use the present value table in Appendix E, page 547.)

Remember that the inflows and outflow are expected to be:

Time		£000
Immediately	Cost of vans	(150)
1 year's time	Saving before depreciation	30
2 years' time	Saving before depreciation	30
3 years' time	Saving before depreciation	30
4 years' time	Saving before depreciation	30
5 years' time	Saving before depreciation	30
6 years' time	Saving before depreciation	30
6 years' time	Disposal proceeds from the vans	30

The calculation of the NPV of the project is as follows:

Time	Cash flows £000	Discount factor (15%)	Present value £000
Immediately	(150)	1.000	(150.00)
1 year's time	30	0.870	26.10
2 years' time	30	0.756	22.68
3 years' time	30	0.658	19.74
4 years' time	30	0.572	17.16
5 years' time	30	0.497	14.91
6 years' time	30	0.432	12.96
6 years' time	30	0.432	12.96
		NPV	(23.49)

Activity 10.12

How would you interpret this result?

The fact that the project has a negative NPV means that the present values of the benefits from the investment are worth less than they cost. Any cost up to £126,510 (the present value of the benefits) would be worth paying, but not £150,000.

The present value table in Appendix E shows how the value of £1 diminishes as its receipt goes further into the future. Assuming an opportunity cost of finance of 20 per cent a year, £1 to be received immediately, obviously, has a present value of £1. However, as the time before it is to be received increases, the present value diminishes significantly, as is shown in Figure 10.2.

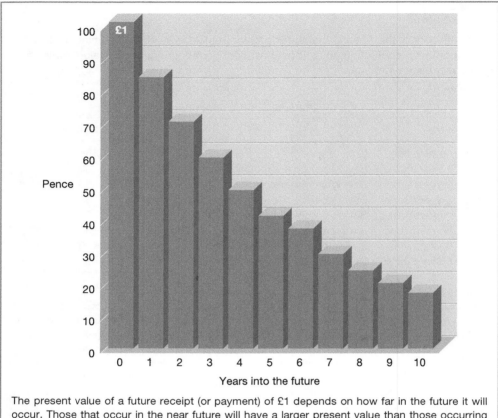

The present value of a future receipt (or payment) of £1 depends on how far in the future it will occur. Those that occur in the near future will have a larger present value than those occurring at a more distant point in time.

Figure 10.2 Present value of £1 receivable at various times in the future, assuming an annual financing cost of 20 per cent

The discount rate and the cost of capital

We have seen that the appropriate discount rate to use in NPV assessments is the opportunity cost of finance. This is, in effect, the cost to the business of the finance needed to fund the investment. It will normally be the cost of a mixture of funds (shareholders' funds and borrowings) employed by the business and is often referred to as the **cost of capital**. We shall refer to it as cost of capital from now on.

WHY NPV IS BETTER

From what we have seen, NPV offers a better approach to appraising investment opportunities than either ARR or PP. This is because it fully takes account of each of the following:

- *The timing of the cash flows.* By discounting the various cash flows associated with each project according to when they are expected to arise, NPV takes account of the time value of money. In other words, as the discounting process incorporates the opportunity cost of capital, the net benefit *after* financing costs have been met is identified (as the NPV of the project).

- *The whole of the relevant cash flows*. NPV includes *all* of the relevant cash flows. They are treated differently according to their date of occurrence, but they are all taken into account. In this way, they all have an influence on the decision.

- *The objectives of the business*. NPV is the only method of appraisal in which the output of the analysis has a direct bearing on the wealth of the owners of the business. Positive NPVs enhance wealth; negative ones reduce it. Since we assume that private sector businesses seek to increase owners' wealth, NPV is superior to the other two methods (ARR and PP) that we have discussed so far.

NPV's wider application

NPV is the most logical approach to making business decisions about investments in productive assets. It also provides the basis for valuing any economic asset, that is, any asset capable of yielding financial benefits. This definition will include such things as equity shares and loans. In fact, when we talk of *economic value*, we mean the value derived by adding together the discounted (present) values of all future cash flows from the asset concerned.

Real World 10.5 is an extract from an article about the lack of success (in terms of NPV) of pharmaceutical research and development expenditure over recent years.

REAL WORLD 10.5

Not taking the medicine

An estimate this month by consultants KPMG suggested that return on investment from R&D among the leading 30 drug companies had halved since 1990, and at 10 per cent last year was barely sufficient to cover their cost of capital. A different calculation in Nature Reviews Drug Discovery two years ago put it at between 7.5 per cent for small, chemical-based molecules, and 13 per cent on biological medicines.

A different analysis in September from Deutsche Bank of the top seven European drugmakers suggests they spent $161 billion in R&D during 2007 to 11 to produce drugs with a net present value of just $86 billion. Only one – Novartis – generated more than it spent, with GlaxoSmithKline and Bayer recovering a significant proportion of their costs. AstraZeneca performed worst.

One industry consultant argues that drug company executives consistently over-estimate not only the chance of their experimental drugs being approved, but the income they will generate at a time of growing scrutiny by healthcare systems and reluctance to pay high prices or purchase in large volumes. 'They have been chronically over-optimistic about payers' willingness to pay,' he says.

 Source: Jack, A., 'Pharmas forced to put squeeze on R&D', FT.com, 16 October 2011.

INTERNAL RATE OF RETURN (IRR)

This is the last of the four major methods of investment appraisal found in practice. It is closely related to the NPV method in that both involve discounting future cash flows. The **internal rate of return (IRR)** of an investment is the discount rate that, when applied to its future cash flows, will produce an NPV of precisely zero. In essence, it represents the yield from an investment opportunity.

Activity 10.13

We should recall that, when we discounted the cash flows of the Billingsgate Battery Company machine project at 20 per cent, we found that the NPV was a positive figure of £24,190 (see page 360). What does the NPV of the machine project tell us about the rate of return that the investment will yield for the business (that is, the project's IRR)?

The fact that the NPV is positive when discounting at 20 per cent implies that the rate of return that the project generates is more than 20 per cent. The fact that the NPV is a pretty large figure implies that the actual rate of return is quite a lot above 20 per cent. We should expect increasing the size of the discount rate to reduce NPV, because a higher discount rate gives a lower discounted figure.

IRR cannot usually be calculated directly. Iteration (trial and error) is the approach normally adopted. Doing this manually, however, is fairly laborious. Fortunately, computer spreadsheet packages can do this with ease.

Despite it being laborious, we shall now go on and derive the IRR for the Billingsgate project manually, to show how it works.

Let us try a higher rate, say 30 per cent and see what happens.

Time	Cash flow £000	Discount factor 30%	PV £000
Immediately (time 0)	(100)	1.000	(100.00)
1 year's time	20	0.769	15.38
2 years' time	40	0.592	23.68
3 years' time	60	0.455	27.30
4 years' time	60	0.350	21.00
5 years' time	20	0.269	5.38
5 years' time	20	0.269	5.38
		NPV	(1.88)

By increasing the discount rate from 20 per cent to 30 per cent, we have reduced the NPV from £24,190 (positive) to £1,880 (negative). Since the IRR is the discount rate that will give us an NPV of exactly zero, we can conclude that the IRR of Billingsgate Battery Company's machine project is very slightly below 30 per cent. Further trials could lead us to the exact rate, but there is probably not much point, given the likely inaccuracy of the cash flow estimates. For most practical purposes, it is good enough to say that the IRR is about 30 per cent.

The relationship between the NPV method discussed earlier and the IRR is shown graphically in Figure 10.3 using the information relating to the Billingsgate Battery Company.

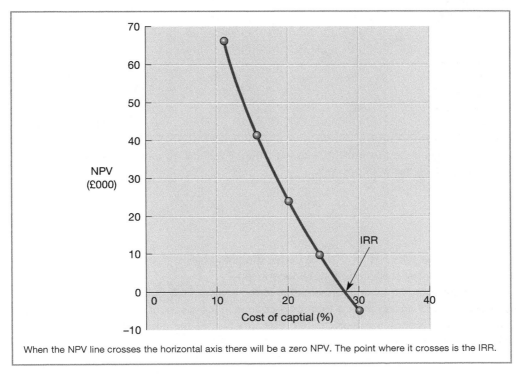

When the NPV line crosses the horizontal axis there will be a zero NPV. The point where it crosses is the IRR.

Figure 10.3 The relationship between the NPV and IRR methods

In Figure 10.3, if the discount rate is equal to zero, the NPV will be the sum of the net cash flows. In other words, no account is taken of the time value of money. However, as the discount rate increases there is a corresponding decrease in the NPV of the project. When the NPV line crosses the horizontal axis there will be a zero NPV. That point represents the IRR.

Activity 10.14

What is the internal rate of return of the Chaotic Industries project from Activity 10.2?

(*Hint*: Remember that you already know the NPV of this project at 15 per cent (from Activity 10.11).)

Since we know that, at a 15 per cent discount rate, the NPV is a relatively large negative figure, our next trial is using a lower discount rate, say 10 per cent:

Time	Cash flows £000	Discount factor (10% – from the table)	Present value £000
Immediately	(150)	1.000	(150.00)
1 year's time	30	0.909	27.27
2 years' time	30	0.826	24.78
3 years' time	30	0.751	22.53
4 years' time	30	0.683	20.49
5 years' time	30	0.621	18.63
6 years' time	30	0.564	16.92
6 years' time	30	0.564	16.92
		NPV	(2.46)

This figure is close to zero NPV. However, the NPV is still negative and so the precise IRR will be a little below 10 per cent.

We could undertake further trials to derive the precise IRR. If, however, we have to do this manually, further trials can be time consuming.

We can get an acceptable approximation to the answer fairly quickly by first calculating the change in NPV arising from a 1 per cent change in the discount rate. This can be done by taking the difference between the two trials (that is, 15 per cent and 10 per cent) that have already been carried out (in Activities 8.12 and 8.15):

Trial	Discount factor %	Net present value £000
1	15	(23.49)
2	10	(2.46)
Difference	5	21.03

The change in NPV for every 1 per cent change in the discount rate will be:

$$(21.03/5) = 4.21$$

The amount by which the IRR would need to fall below the 10% discount rate, in order to achieve a zero NPV would therefore be:

$$[2.46/4.21] \times 1\% = 0.58\%$$

The IRR is therefore:

$$(10.00 - 0.58) = 9.42\%$$

To say that the IRR is about 9 or 10 per cent, however, is near enough for most purposes.

Note that this approach to obtaining a more accurate figure for IRR assumes a straight-line relationship between the discount rate and NPV. We can see from Figure 10.3 that this assumption is not strictly correct. Over a relatively short range, however, this simplifying assumption is not usually a problem and so we can still arrive at a reasonable approximation using the approach that we took.

In practice, businesses have computer software packages that will derive a project's IRR very quickly. It is not usually necessary, therefore, either to make a series of trial discount rates or to make the approximation just described.

The following decision rules are applied when using IRR:

> ■ For any project to be acceptable, it must meet a minimum IRR requirement. Logically, this should be the opportunity cost of capital.
> ■ Where there are competing projects, the one with the higher (or highest) IRR should be selected.

Real World 10.6 describes the evaluation of a mining project that considers the effect of making different assumptions on the prices of gold and silver on the IRR.

REAL WORLD 10.6

Golden opportunity

In a news release, Hochschild Mining plc announced positive results from an independent study of the profitability of its Azuca project in southern Peru. The project involves mining for gold and silver. The business provided calculations based on the most likely outcome (the base case) along with evaluations of the project making other assumptions about gold and silver prices.

The base case is shown in the first column of figures. The other three columns show the position if other assumptions are made about the prices of gold and silver.

The following results were obtained:

Gold price ($ per ounce)	1,000	1,100	1,200	1,300
Silver price ($ per ounce)	17.00	18.70	20.40	21.90
IRR (per cent)	21	30	38	46

Source: Information taken from 'Positive scoping study at 100% owned Azuca project in Peru', News release, Hochschild Mining plc, 30 September 2010 (phx.corporate-ir.net).

Real World 10.7 gives some examples of IRRs sought in practice.

REAL WORLD 10.7

Rates of return

IRRs for investment projects can vary considerably. Here are a few examples of the expected or target returns from investment projects of large businesses.

- GlaxoSmithKline plc, the leading pharmaceuticals business, is aiming to increase its IRR from investments in new products from 11 per cent to 14 per cent.
- Signet Group plc, the jewellery retailer, requires an IRR of 20 per cent over five years when appraising new stores.
- Burberry, the luxury brand business has a 25 per cent IRR hurdle.
- Forth Ports plc, a port operator, concentrates on projects that generate an IRR of at least 15 per cent.
- Marks and Spencer plc, the stores chain, has targeted an IRR of 12 to 15 per cent on a new investment programme.
- Standard Life, the pensions and life assurance business, requires a 15 per cent IRR from new products.

These values seem surprisingly large. A study of returns made by all of the businesses listed on the London Stock Exchange between 1900 and 2010 showed an average annual return of 5.3 per cent. This figure is the *real* return (that is, ignoring inflation). It would probably be fair to add at least 3 per cent to it to compare it with the targets for the businesses listed above. Also, the targets for the five businesses are probably pre-tax (the businesses do not specify). In that case it is probably reasonable to add about a third to the average Stock Exchange returns. This would give us around 12 per cent per year. This would be roughly in line with the GlaxoSmithKline and Marks and Spencer targets. The targets for the other businesses seem rather ambitious, however.

Sources: Doherty, J., 'GSK sales jump in emerging markets', FT.com, 4 February 2010; Signet Group plc, Annual Report 2011, page 72; 'Burberry plans for slump despite results', FT.com, 12 October 2011; FAQs, Forth Ports plc (www.forthports.co.uk), accessed 2 December 2011; Marks and Spencer plc Annual Report 2011, page 34; 'Standard Life flags step up in performance', FT.com, 10 March 2011; Dimson, E., Marsh, P. and Staunton, M. *Credit Suisse Global Investments Returns Sourcebook*, 2011.

Problems with IRR

IRR has certain key attributes in common with NPV. All cash flows are taken into account and their timing is logically handled. The main problem of IRR, however, is that it does not directly address the question of wealth generation. It can therefore lead to the wrong decision being made. This is because the IRR approach will always rank a project with, for example, an IRR of 25 per cent above that of a project with an IRR of 20 per cent. Although accepting the project with the higher percentage return will often generate more wealth, this may not always be the case. This is because IRR completely ignores the *scale of investment*.

With a 15 per cent cost of capital, £15 million invested at 20 per cent for one year, will make us wealthier by £0.75 million (that is, $15 \times (20 - 15)\% = 0.75$). With the same cost of capital, £5 million invested at 25 per cent for one year will make us only £0.5 million (that is, $5 \times (25 - 15)\% = 0.50$). IRR does not recognise this.

Activity 10.15

Which other investment appraisal method ignores the scale of investment?

We saw earlier that the ARR method suffers from this problem.

Competing projects do not usually possess such large differences in scale and so IRR and NPV normally give the same signal. However, as NPV will always give the correct signal, it is difficult to see why any other method should be used.

A further problem with the IRR method is that it has difficulty handling projects with unconventional cash flows. In the examples studied so far, each project has a negative cash flow arising at the start of its life and then positive cash flows thereafter. In practice, however, a project may have both positive and negative cash flows at future points in its life. Such a pattern of cash flows can result in there being more than one IRR, or even no IRR at all. This would make the IRR method difficult to use, although it should be said that this problem is also quite rare in practice. This is never a problem for NPV, however.

SOME PRACTICAL POINTS

When undertaking an investment appraisal, there are several practical points to bear in mind:

- *Relevant costs*. As with all decisions, we should take account only of relevant costs in our analysis. In other words, only costs that vary with the decision should be considered, as we discussed in Chapter 7. Thus, all past and common future costs should be ignored as they cannot vary with the decision. Also, opportunity costs arising from benefits forgone must be taken into account.
- *Taxation*. Owners will be interested in the after-tax returns generated from the business. As a result, taxation will usually be an important consideration when making an investment decision. The profits from the project will be taxed, the capital investment may attract tax relief and so on. Tax is levied on these at significant rates. This means that, in real life, unless tax is formally taken into account, the wrong decision could easily be made. The timing of the tax outflow should also be taken into account when preparing the cash flows for the project.
- *Cash flows not profit flows*. We have seen that for the NPV, IRR and PP methods, it is cash flows rather than profit flows that are relevant to the assessment of investment projects. In an investment appraisal requiring the application of any of these methods, details of the profits for the investment period may be given. These need to be adjusted in order to derive the cash flows. We should remember that the operating profit *before* non-cash items (such as depreciation) is an approximation to the cash flows for the period. We should, therefore, work back to this figure.

  When the data are expressed in profit rather than cash flow terms, an adjustment in respect of working capital may also be necessary. Some adjustment should be made to take account of changes in working capital. For example, launching a new product may give rise to an increase in the net investment made in trade receivables and inventories less trade payables. This working capital investment would normally require an immediate outlay of cash. This outlay for additional working capital should be shown in the NPV calculations as an initial cash outflow. However, at the end of the life of the project, the additional working capital will be released. This divestment results in an effective inflow of cash at the end of the project. It should also be taken into account at the point at which it is received.

■ *Year-end assumption*. In the examples and activities considered so far, we have assumed that cash flows arise at the end of the relevant year. This simplifying assumption is used to make the calculations easier. (It is perfectly possible, however, to deal more precisely with the timing of the cash flows.) As we saw earlier, this assumption is clearly unrealistic, as money will have to be paid to employees on a weekly or monthly basis, credit customers will pay within a month or two of buying the product or service and so on. It is probably not a serious distortion, however. We should be clear that there is nothing about any of the four appraisal methods that demands that this assumption be made.

■ *Interest payments*. When using discounted cash flow techniques (NPV and IRR), interest payments should not be taken into account in deriving cash flows for the period. Discounting already takes account of the costs of financing. To include interest charges in deriving cash flows for the period would therefore be double counting.

■ *Other factors*. Investment decision making must not be viewed as simply a mechanical exercise. The results derived from a particular investment appraisal method will be only one input to the decision-making process. There may be broader issues connected to the decision that have to be taken into account but which may be difficult or impossible to quantify.

The reliability of the forecasts and the validity of the assumptions used in the evaluation will also have a bearing on the final decision.

Activity 10.16

The directors of Manuff (Steel) Ltd are considering closing one of the business's factories. There has been a reduction in the demand for the products made at the factory in recent years. The directors are not optimistic about the long-term prospects for these products. The factory is situated in an area where unemployment is high.

The factory is leased with four years of the lease remaining. The directors are uncertain whether the factory should be closed immediately or at the end of the period of the lease. Another business has offered to sublease the premises from Manuff (Steel) Ltd at a rental of £40,000 a year for the remainder of the lease period.

The machinery and equipment at the factory cost £1,500,000. The value at which they appear in the statement of financial position is £400,000. In the event of immediate closure, the machinery and equipment could be sold for £220,000. The working capital at the factory is £420,000. It could be liquidated for that amount immediately, if required. Alternatively, the working capital can be liquidated in full at the end of the lease period. Immediate closure would result in redundancy payments to employees of £180,000.

If the factory continues in operation until the end of the lease period, the following operating profits (losses) are expected:

	Year 1 £000	Year 2 £000	Year 3 £000	Year 4 £000
Operating profit (loss)	160	(40)	30	20

These figures are derived after deducting a charge of £90,000 a year for depreciation of machinery and equipment. The residual value of the machinery and equipment at the end of the lease period is estimated at £40,000.

Redundancy payments are expected to be £150,000 at the end of the lease period if the factory continues in operation. The business has an annual cost of capital of 12 per cent. Ignore taxation.

Required:

(a) Determine the relevant cash flows arising from a decision to continue operations until the end of the lease period rather than to close immediately.

(b) Calculate the net present value of continuing operations until the end of the lease period, rather than closing immediately.

(c) What other factors might the directors take into account before making a final decision on the timing of the factory closure?

(d) State, with reasons, whether or not the business should continue to operate the factory until the end of the lease period.

Your answer should be:

(a) Relevant cash flows

	Years				
	0	1	2	3	4
	£000	£000	£000	£000	£000
Operating cash flows (Note 1)		250	50	120	110
Sale of machinery (Note 2)	(220)				40
Redundancy costs (Note 3)	180				(150)
Sublease rentals (Note 4)		(40)	(40)	(40)	(40)
Working capital invested (Note 5)	(420)				420
	(460)	210	10	80	380

Notes

1 Each year's operating cash flows are calculated by adding back the depreciation charge for the year to the operating profit for the year. In the case of the operating loss, the depreciation charge is deducted.

2 In the event of closure, machinery could be sold immediately. As a result, an opportunity cost of £220,000 is incurred if operations continue.

3 By continuing operations, there will be a saving in immediate redundancy costs of £180,000. However, redundancy costs of £150,000 will be paid in four years' time.

4 By continuing operations, the opportunity to sublease the factory will be foregone.

5 Immediate closure would mean that working capital could be liquidated. By continuing operations this opportunity is foregone. However, working capital can be liquidated in four years' time.

(b)

	Years				
	0	*1*	*2*	*3*	*4*
Discount factor 12 per cent	1.000	0.893	0.797	0.712	0.636
Present value	(460)	187.5	8.0	57.0	241.7
Net present value	<u>34.2</u>				

(c) Other factors that may influence the decision include:
- *The overall strategy of the business*. The business may need to set the decision within a broader context. It may be necessary to manufacture the products at the factory because they are an integral part of the business's product range. The business may wish to avoid redundancies in an area of high unemployment for as long as possible.
- *Flexibility*. A decision to close the factory is probably irreversible. If the factory continues, however, there may be a chance that the prospects for the factory will brighten in the future.
- *Creditworthiness of sub-lessee*. The business should investigate the creditworthiness of the sub-lessee. Failure to receive the expected sublease payments would make the closure option far less attractive.
- *Accuracy of forecasts*. The forecasts made by the business should be examined carefully. Inaccuracies in the forecasts or any underlying assumptions may change the expected outcomes.

(d) The NPV of the decision to continue operations rather than close immediately is positive. Hence, shareholders would be better off if the directors took this course of action. The factory should therefore continue in operation rather than close down. This decision is likely to be welcomed by employees and would allow the business to maintain its flexibility.

The main methods of investment appraisal are summarised in Figure 10.4.

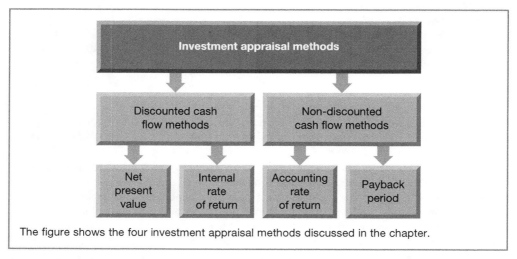

The figure shows the four investment appraisal methods discussed in the chapter.

Figure 10.4 The main investment appraisal methods

INVESTMENT APPRAISAL IN PRACTICE

Many surveys have been conducted in the UK, and elsewhere in the world, into the methods of investment appraisal used by businesses. They have shown the following features:

- Businesses tend to use more than one method to assess each investment decision.
- The discounting methods (NPV and IRR) have become increasingly popular over time. NPV and IRR are now the most popular of the four methods.
- PP continues to be popular and, to a lesser extent, so does ARR. This is despite the theoretical shortcomings of both of these methods.
- Larger businesses tend to rely more heavily on discounting methods than smaller businesses do.

A survey of large businesses in five leading industrialised countries, including the UK, shows considerable support for the NPV and IRR methods. There is less support for the payback method but, nevertheless, it still seems to be fairly widely used. **Real World 10.8** sets out some key findings.

REAL WORLD 10.8

A multinational survey of business practice

A survey of investment and financing practices in five different countries was carried out by Cohen and Yagil. This survey, based on a sample of the largest 300 businesses in each country, revealed the following concerning the popularity of three of the investment appraisal methods discussed in this chapter.

Frequency of the use of investment appraisal techniques

Average	Japan	Canada	Germany	UK	US	
3.93	3.29	4.15	4.08	4.16	4.00	IRR
3.80	3.57	4.09	3.50	4.00	3.88	NPV
3.55	3.52	3.57	3.33	3.89	3.46	Payback period

Response scale 1 = Never   5 = Always

Key findings of the survey include the following:

- IRR is more popular than NPV in all countries, except Japan. The difference between the popularity of the two methods, however, is not statistically significant.
- Managers of UK businesses use investment appraisal techniques the most, while managers of Japanese businesses use them the least. This may be related to business traditions within each country.
- There is a positive relationship between business size and the popularity of the IRR and NPV methods. This may be related to the greater experience and understanding of financial theory of managers of larger businesses.

Source: Cohen, G. and Yagil, J., 'A multinational survey of corporate financial policies', Working Paper, Haifa University, 2007.

Activity 10.17

Earlier in the chapter, we discussed the limitations of the PP method. Can you suggest reasons that might explain why it is still a reasonably popular method of investment appraisal among managers?

There seem to be several possible reasons:

■ PP is easy to understand and use.
■ It can avoid the problems of forecasting far into the future.
■ It gives emphasis to the early cash flows when there is greater certainty concerning the accuracy of their predicted value.
■ It emphasises the importance of liquidity. Where a business has liquidity problems, a short payback period for a project is likely to appear attractive.

The popularity of PP may suggest a lack of sophistication, by managers, concerning investment appraisal. This criticism is most often made against managers of smaller businesses. This point is borne out by the survey discussed in Real World 10.9 which found that smaller businesses are much less likely to use discounted cash flow methods (NPV and IRR) than are larger ones. Other surveys have tended to reach a similar conclusion.

IRR may be popular because it expresses outcomes in percentage terms rather than in absolute terms. This form of expression seems to be preferred by managers, despite the problems of percentage measures that we discussed earlier. This may be because managers are used to using percentage figures as targets (for example, return on capital employed).

Real World 10.9 shows extracts from the 2010 annual report of a well-known business: Rolls-Royce plc, the builder of engines for aircraft and other purposes.

REAL WORLD 10.9

The use of NPV at Rolls-Royce

In its 2010 annual report and accounts, Rolls-Royce plc stated that:

> The Group continues to subject all investments to rigorous examination of risks and future cash flows to ensure that they create shareholder value. All major investments require Board approval.
> The Group has a portfolio of projects at different stages of their life cycles. Discounted cash flow analysis of the remaining life of projects is performed on a regular basis.

Source: Rolls-Royce plc Annual Report 2010, p. 51.

Rolls-Royce makes clear that it uses NPV (the report refers to creating shareholder value and to discounted cash flow, which strongly imply NPV). It is interesting to note that Rolls-Royce not only assesses new projects but also reassesses existing ones. This must be a sensible commercial approach. Businesses should not continue with existing projects unless those projects have a positive NPV based on future cash flows. Just because a project seemed to have a positive NPV before it started does not mean that this will persist, in the light of changing circumstances. Activity 10.16 (pages 371–2) considered a decision to close down a project.

INVESTMENT APPRAISAL AND STRATEGIC PLANNING

So far, we have tended to view investment opportunities as unconnected, independent, events. In practice, however, successful businesses are those that have a clear strategic planning framework within which suitable investment projects are identified.

We saw in Chapter 9 that strategic plans often have a time span of around five years. As part of the planning process managers must ask 'where do we want our business to be in five years' time and how can we get there?' This will help set the appropriate direction in terms of products, markets, financing and so on, so that the business is best placed to generate profitable investment opportunities.

Unless a strategic planning framework is in place, it may be difficult to identify those projects that are likely to generate a positive NPV. The best investment projects are usually those that match the business's internal strengths (for example, skills, experience, access to finance) with the opportunities available. In areas where this match does not exist, other businesses, for which the match does exist, are likely to have a distinct competitive advantage. This means that they will be able to provide the product or service at a better price and/or quality.

Real World 10.10 shows how easyJet made an investment that fitted its strategic objectives.

REAL WORLD 10.10

easyFit

easyJet, the UK budget airline, bought a small rival airline, GB Airways Ltd (GB) in late 2007 for £103 million. According to an article in the *Financial Times*:

> GB is a good strategic fit for easyJet. It operates under a British Airways franchise from Gatwick, which happens to be easyJet's biggest base. The deal makes easyJet the single largest passenger carrier at the UK airport. There is plenty of scope for scale economies in purchasing and back office functions. Moreover, easyJet should be able to boost GB's profitability by switching the carrier to its low-cost business model . . . easyJet makes an estimated £4 a passenger, against GB's £1. Assuming easyJet can drag up GB to its own levels of profitability, the company's value to the low-cost carrier is roughly four times its standalone worth.

The article makes the point that this looks like a good investment for easyJet, because of the strategic fit. For a business other than easyJet, the lack of strategic fit may well have meant that buying GB for exactly the same price of £103 million would not have been a good investment.

Source: Hughes, Chris, 'Easy ride', FT.com, 26 October 2007.

? SELF-ASSESSMENT QUESTION 10.1

Beacon Chemicals plc is considering buying some equipment to produce a chemical named X14. The new equipment's capital cost is estimated at £100 million. If its purchase is approved now, the equipment can be bought and production can commence by the end of this year. £50 million has already been spent on research and development work. Estimates of revenues and costs arising from the operation of the new equipment are:

	Year 1	Year 2	Year 3	Year 4	Year 5
Sales price (£/litre)	100	120	120	100	80
Sales volume (million litres)	0.8	1.0	1.2	1.0	0.8
Variable cost (£/litre)	50	50	40	30	40
Fixed cost (£000)	30	30	30	30	30

If the equipment is bought, sales of some existing products will be lost resulting in a loss of contribution of £15 million a year, over the life of the equipment.

The accountant has informed you that the fixed cost includes depreciation of £20 million a year on the new equipment. It also includes an allocation of £10 million for fixed overheads. A separate study has indicated that if the new equipment were bought, additional overheads, excluding depreciation, arising from producing the chemical would be £8 million a year. Production would require additional working capital of £30 million.

For the purposes of your initial calculations ignore taxation.

Required:
(a) Deduce the relevant annual cash flows associated with buying the equipment.
(b) Deduce the payback period.
(c) Calculate the net present value (as at the date of the purchase of the equipment) using a discount rate of 8 per cent.

(*Hint*: You should deal with the investment in working capital by treating it as a cash outflow at the start of the project and an inflow at the end.)

The solution to this question can be found in at the back of the book, in Appendix B.

SUMMARY

The main points of this chapter may be summarised as follows:

Accounting rate of return

Accounting rate of return (ARR) is the average accounting profit from the project expressed as a percentage of the average investment.

- Decision rule – projects with an ARR above a defined minimum are acceptable; the greater the ARR, the more attractive the project becomes.

- Conclusion on ARR:
  - does not relate directly to shareholders' wealth – can lead to illogical conclusions;
  - takes almost no account of the timing of cash flows;
  - ignores some relevant information and may take account of some irrelevant;
  - relatively simple to use;
  - much inferior to NPV.

Payback period

Payback period (PP) is the length of time that it takes for the cash outflow for the initial investment to be repaid out of resulting cash inflows.

- Decision rule – projects with a PP up to a defined maximum period are acceptable; the shorter the PP, the more attractive the project.

- Conclusion on PP:
  - does not relate to shareholders' wealth;
  - ignores inflows after the payback date;
  - takes little account of the timing of cash flows;
  - ignores much relevant information;
  - does not always provide clear signals and can be impractical to use;
  - much inferior to NPV, but it is easy to understand and can offer a liquidity insight, which might be the reason for its widespread use.

Net present value

Net present value (NPV) is the sum of the discounted values of the net cash flows from the investment.

- Money has a time value.

- Decision rule – all positive NPV investments enhance shareholders' wealth; the greater the NPV, the greater the enhancement and the greater the attractiveness of the project.

- PV of a cash flow = cash flow $\times 1/(1 + r)^n$, assuming a constant discount rate.

- Discounting brings cash flows at different points in time to a common valuation basis (their present value), which enables them to be directly compared.

- Conclusion on NPV:
  - relates directly to shareholders' wealth objective;
  - takes account of the timing of cash flows;
  - takes all relevant information into account;
  - provides clear signals and is practical to use.

Internal rate of return

Internal rate of return (IRR) is the discount rate that, when applied to the cash flows of a project, causes it to have a zero NPV.

- Represents the average percentage return on the investment, taking account of the fact that cash may be flowing in and out of the project at various points in its life.
- Decision rule – projects that have an IRR greater than the cost of capital are acceptable; the greater the IRR, the more attractive the project.
- Cannot normally be calculated directly; a trial and error approach is often necessary.
- Conclusion on IRR:
  - does not relate directly to shareholders' wealth. Usually gives the same signals as NPV but can mislead where there are competing projects of different size;
  - takes account of the timing of cash flows;
  - takes all relevant information into account;
  - problems of multiple IRRs when there are unconventional cash flows;
  - inferior to NPV.

Use of appraisal methods in practice

- All four methods identified are widely used.
- The discounting methods (NPV and IRR) show a steady increase in usage over time.
- Many businesses use more than one method.
- Larger businesses seem to be more sophisticated in their choice and use of appraisal methods than smaller ones.

Investment appraisal and strategic planning

- It is important that businesses invest in a strategic way so as to play to their strengths.

MyAccountingLab

Go to www.myaccountinglab.com to check your understanding of the chapter, create a personalised study plan, and maximise your revision time

KEY TERMS

FURTHER READING

If you would like to explore the topics covered in this chapter in more depth, we recommend the following books:

Arnold, G., *Corporate Financial Management*, 4th edn, Financial Times Prentice Hall, 2009, Chapters 2, 3 and 4.

Drury, C., *Management and Cost Accounting*, 8th edn, South Western Cengage Learning, 2012, Chapters 13 and 14.

McLaney, E., *Business Finance: Theory and practice*, 9th edn, Financial Times Prentice Hall, 2012, Chapters 4, 5 and 6.

Pike, R., Neale, B. and Linsley, P., *Corporate Finance and Investment*, 7th edn, Prentice Hall, 2012, Chapters 3 and 4.

? REVIEW QUESTIONS

Answers to these questions can be found at the back of the book, in Appendix C.

10.1 Why is the net present value method of investment appraisal considered to be theoretically superior to other methods that are found in practice?

10.2 The payback period method has been criticised for not taking the time value of money into account. Could this limitation be overcome? If so, would this method then be preferable to the NPV method?

10.3 Research indicates that the IRR method is extremely popular even though it has shortcomings when compared to the NPV method. Why might managers prefer to use IRR rather than NPV when carrying out discounted cash flow evaluations?

10.4 Why are cash flows rather than profit flows used in the IRR, NPV and PP methods of investment appraisal?

✳ EXERCISES

*Exercise 10.1 is basic level, exercises 10.2 and 10.3 are intermediate level and exercises 10.4 and 10.5 are advanced level. Those with **coloured numbers** have solutions at the back of the book, in Appendix D.*

If you wish to try more exercises, visit the website at **www.myaccountinglab.com**.

10.1 The directors of Mylo Ltd are currently considering two mutually exclusive investment projects. Both projects are concerned with the purchase of new plant. The following data are available for each project:

	Project 1 £000	Project 2 £000
Cost (immediate outlay)	100	60
Expected annual operating profit (loss):		
Year 1	29	18
Year 2	(1)	(2)
Year 3	2	4
Estimated residual value of the plant after 3 years	7	6

The business has an estimated cost of capital of 10 per cent. It uses the straight-line method of depreciation for all non-current (fixed) assets when calculating operating profit. Neither project would increase the working capital of the business. The business has sufficient funds to meet all investment expenditure requirements.

Required:

(a) Calculate for each project:
  (i) The net present value.
  (ii) The approximate internal rate of return.
  (iii) The payback period.

(b) State, with reasons, which, if either, of the two investment projects the directors of Mylo Ltd should accept.

10.2 Newton Electronics Ltd has incurred expenditure of £5 million over the past three years researching and developing a miniature hearing aid. The hearing aid is now fully developed. The directors are considering which of three mutually exclusive options should be taken to exploit the potential of the new product. The options are:

1 The business could manufacture the hearing aid itself. This would be a new departure, since the business has so far concentrated on research and development projects. However, the business has manufacturing space available that it currently rents to another business for £100,000 a year. The business would have to purchase plant and equipment costing £9 million and invest £3 million in working capital immediately for production to begin.

    A market research report, for which the business paid £50,000, indicates that the new product has an expected life of five years. Sales of the product during this period are predicted as:

Predicted sales for the year ended 30 November

	Year 1	Year 2	Year 3	Year 4	Year 5
Number of units (000s)	800	1,400	1,800	1,200	500

    The selling price per unit will be £30 in the first year but will fall to £22 in the following three years. In the final year of the product's life, the selling price will fall to £20. Variable production costs are predicted to be £14 a unit. Fixed production costs (including depreciation) will be £2.4 million a year. Marketing costs will be £2 million a year.

    The business intends to depreciate the plant and equipment using the straight-line method and based on an estimated residual value at the end of the five years of £1 million. The business has a cost of capital of 10 per cent a year.

2 Newton Electronics Ltd could agree to another business manufacturing and marketing the product under licence. A multinational business, Faraday Electricals plc, has offered to undertake the manufacture and marketing of the product. In return it will make a royalty payment to Newton Electronics Ltd of £5 per unit. It has been estimated that the annual number of sales of the hearing aid will be 10 per cent higher if the multinational business, rather than if Newton Electronics Ltd, manufactures and markets the product.

3 Newton Electronics Ltd could sell the patent rights to Faraday Electricals plc for £24 million, payable in two equal instalments. The first instalment would be payable immediately and the second at the end of two years. This option would give Faraday Electricals the exclusive right to manufacture and market the new product.

Ignore taxation.

Required:

(a) Calculate the net present value (as at the beginning of Year 1) of each of the options available to Newton Electronics Ltd.

(b) Identify and discuss any other factors that Newton Electronics Ltd should consider before arriving at a decision.

(c) State, with reasons, what you consider to be the most suitable option.

10.3 Chesterfield Wanderers is a professional football club that has enjoyed some success in recent years. As a result, the club has accumulated £10 million to spend on its further development. The board of directors is currently considering two mutually exclusive options for spending the funds available.

The first option is to acquire another player. The team manager has expressed a keen interest in acquiring Basil ('Bazza') Ramsey, a central defender, who currently plays for a rival club. The rival club has agreed to release the player immediately for £10 million if required. A decision to acquire 'Bazza' Ramsey would mean that the existing central defender, Vinnie Smith, could be sold to another club. Chesterfield Wanderers has recently received an offer of £2.2 million for this player. This offer is still open but will only be accepted if 'Bazza' Ramsey joins Chesterfield Wanderers. If this does not happen, Vinnie Smith will be expected to stay on with the club until the end of his playing career in five years' time. During this period, Vinnie will receive an annual salary of £400,000 and a loyalty bonus of £200,000 at the end of his five-year period with the club.

Assuming 'Bazza' Ramsey is acquired, the team manager estimates that gate receipts will increase by £2.5 million in the first year and £1.3 million in each of the four following years. There will also be an increase in advertising and sponsorship revenues of £1.2 million for each of the next five years if the player is acquired. At the end of five years, the player can be sold to a club in a lower division and Chesterfield Wanderers will expect to receive £1 million as a transfer fee. During his period at the club, 'Bazza' will receive an annual salary of £800,000 and a loyalty bonus of £400,000 after five years.

The second option is for the club to improve its ground facilities. The west stand could be extended and executive boxes could be built for businesses wishing to offer corporate hospitality to clients. These improvements would also cost £10 million and would take one year to complete. During this period, the west stand would be closed, resulting in a reduction of gate receipts of £1.8 million. However, gate receipts for each of the following four years would be £4.4 million higher than current receipts. In five years' time, the club has plans to sell the existing grounds and to move to a new stadium nearby. Improving the ground facilities is not expected to affect the ground's value when it comes to be sold. Payment for the improvements will be made when the work has been completed at the end of the first year. Whichever option is chosen, the board of directors has decided to take on additional ground staff. The additional wages bill is expected to be £350,000 a year over the next five years.

The club has a cost of capital of 10 per cent. Ignore taxation.

Required:

(a) Calculate the incremental cash flows arising from each of the options available to the club.

(b) Calculate the net present value of each of the options.

(c) On the basis of the calculations made in (b) above, which of the two options would you choose and why?

(d) Discuss the validity of using the net present value method in making investment decisions for a professional football club.

10.4 C. George (Controls) Ltd manufactures a thermostat that can be used in a range of kitchen appliances. The manufacturing process is, at present, semi-automated. The equipment used cost £540,000 and has a carrying amount (as shown on the statement of financial position) of £300,000. Demand for the product has been fairly stable at 50,000 units a year in recent years.

The following data, based on the current level of output, have been prepared in respect of the product:

	Per unit	
	£	£
Selling price		12.40
Labour	(3.30)	
Materials	(3.65)	
Overheads: Variable	(1.58)	
Fixed	(1.60)	
		(10.13)
Operating profit		2.27

Although the existing equipment is expected to last for a further four years before it is sold for an estimated £40,000, the business has recently been considering purchasing new equipment that would completely automate much of the production process. The new equipment would cost £670,000 and would have an expected life of four years, at the end of which it would be sold for an estimated £70,000. If the new equipment is purchased, the old equipment could be sold for £150,000 immediately.

The assistant to the business's accountant has prepared a report to help assess the viability of the proposed change, which includes the following data:

	Per unit	
	£	£
Selling price		12.40
Labour	(1.20)	
Materials	(3.20)	
Overheads: Variable	(1.40)	
Fixed	(3.30)	
		(9.10)
Operating profit		3.30

→

Depreciation charges will increase by £85,000 a year as a result of purchasing the new machinery; however, other fixed costs are not expected to change.

In the report the assistant wrote:

> The figures shown above that relate to the proposed change are based on the current level of output and take account of a depreciation charge of £150,000 a year in respect of the new equipment. The effect of purchasing the new equipment will be to increase the operating profit to sales revenue ratio from 18.3 per cent to 26.6 per cent. In addition, the purchase of the new equipment will enable us to reduce our inventories level immediately by £130,000.
> In view of these facts, I recommend purchase of the new equipment.

The business has a cost of capital of 12 per cent. Ignore taxation.

Required:

(a) Prepare a statement of the incremental cash flows arising from the purchase of the new equipment.

(b) Calculate the net present value of the proposed purchase of new equipment.

(c) State, with reasons, whether the business should purchase the new equipment.

(d) Explain why cash flow projections are used rather than profit projections to assess the viability of proposed investment projects.

10.5 The accountant of your business has recently been taken ill through overwork. In his absence his assistant has prepared some calculations of the profitability of a project, which are to be discussed soon at the board meeting of your business. His workings, which are set out below, include some errors of principle. You can assume that there are no arithmetical errors.

Year	0	1	2	3	4	5
	£000	£000	£000	£000	£000	£000
Sales revenue		450	470	470	470	470
Less Costs						
Materials		126	132	132	132	132
Labour		90	94	94	94	94
Overheads		45	47	47	47	47
Depreciation		120	120	120	120	120
Working capital	180					
Interest on working capital		27	27	27	27	27
Write-off of development costs	–	30	30	30	–	–
Total costs	180	438	450	450	420	420
Operating profit/(loss)	(180)	12	20	20	50	50

$$\frac{\text{Total profit (loss)}}{\text{Cost of equipment}} = \frac{(£28,000)}{£600,000} = \text{Return on investment (4.7\%)}$$

You ascertain the following additional information:

1 The cost of equipment includes £100,000, being the carrying value of an old machine. If it were not used for this project it would be scrapped with a zero net realisable value. New equipment costing £500,000 will be purchased on 31 December Year 0. You should assume that all other cash flows occur at the end of the year to which they relate.

2   The development costs of £90,000 have already been spent.

3   Overheads have been charged to the project at 50 per cent of direct labour, which is the business's normal practice. An independent assessment has suggested that incremental overheads are likely to amount to £30,000 a year.

4   The business's cost of capital is 12 per cent.

Ignore taxation in your answer.

Required:

(a) Prepare a corrected statement of the incremental cash flows arising from the project. Where you have altered the assistant's figures you should attach a brief note explaining your alterations.

(b) Calculate:
   (i)   The project's payback period.
   (ii) The project's net present value as at 31 December Year 0.

(c) Write a memo to the board advising on the acceptance or rejection of the project.

Appendix E
PRESENT VALUE TABLE

Present value of £1, that is, $1/(1 + r)^n$

where r = discount rate

n = number of periods until payment

Periods (n)	1%	2%	3%	4%	5%	6%	7%	8%	9%	10%	
1	0.990	0.980	0.971	0.962	0.952	0.943	0.935	0.926	0.917	0.909	1
2	0.980	0.961	0.943	0.925	0.907	0.890	0.873	0.857	0.842	0.826	2
3	0.971	0.942	0.915	0.889	0.864	0.840	0.816	0.794	0.772	0.751	3
4	0.961	0.924	0.888	0.855	0.823	0.792	0.763	0.735	0.708	0.683	4
5	0.951	0.906	0.863	0.822	0.784	0.747	0.713	0.681	0.650	0.621	5
6	0.942	0.888	0.837	0.790	0.746	0.705	0.666	0.630	0.596	0.564	6
7	0.933	0.871	0.813	0.760	0.711	0.665	0.623	0.583	0.547	0.513	7
8	0.923	0.853	0.789	0.731	0.677	0.627	0.582	0.540	0.502	0.467	8
9	0.914	0.837	0.766	0.703	0.645	0.592	0.544	0.500	0.460	0.424	9
10	0.905	0.820	0.744	0.676	0.614	0.558	0.508	0.463	0.422	0.386	10
11	0.896	0.804	0.722	0.650	0.585	0.527	0.475	0.429	0.388	0.350	11
12	0.887	0.788	0.701	0.625	0.557	0.497	0.444	0.397	0.356	0.319	12
13	0.879	0.773	0.681	0.601	0.530	0.469	0.415	0.368	0.326	0.290	13
14	0.870	0.758	0.661	0.577	0.505	0.442	0.388	0.340	0.299	0.263	14
15	0.861	0.743	0.642	0.555	0.481	0.417	0.362	0.315	0.275	0.239	15

Discount rates (r)

Periods (n)	11%	12%	13%	14%	15%	16%	17%	18%	19%	20%	
1	0.901	0.893	0.885	0.877	0.870	0.862	0.855	0.847	0.840	0.833	1
2	0.812	0.797	0.783	0.769	0.756	0.743	0.731	0.718	0.706	0.694	2
3	0.731	0.712	0.693	0.675	0.658	0.641	0.624	0.609	0.593	0.579	3
4	0.659	0.636	0.613	0.592	0.572	0.552	0.534	0.516	0.499	0.482	4
5	0.593	0.567	0.543	0.519	0.497	0.476	0.456	0.437	0.419	0.402	5
6	0.535	0.507	0.480	0.456	0.432	0.410	0.390	0.370	0.352	0.335	6
7	0.482	0.452	0.425	0.400	0.376	0.354	0.333	0.314	0.296	0.279	7
8	0.434	0.404	0.376	0.351	0.327	0.305	0.285	0.266	0.249	0.233	8
9	0.391	0.361	0.333	0.308	0.284	0.263	0.243	0.225	0.209	0.194	9
10	0.352	0.322	0.295	0.270	0.247	0.227	0.208	0.191	0.176	0.162	10
11	0.317	0.287	0.261	0.237	0.215	0.195	0.178	0.162	0.148	0.135	11
12	0.286	0.257	0.231	0.208	0.187	0.168	0.152	0.137	0.124	0.112	12
13	0.258	0.229	0.204	0.182	0.163	0.145	0.130	0.116	0.104	0.093	13
14	0.232	0.205	0.181	0.160	0.141	0.125	0.111	0.099	0.088	0.078	14
15	0.209	0.183	0.160	0.140	0.123	0.108	0.095	0.084	0.074	0.065	15

Appendix E: Present Value Table

Periods (n)	Discount rates (r)										
	21%	22%	23%	24%	25%	26%	27%	28%	29%	30%	
1	0.826	0.820	0.813	0.806	0.800	0.794	0.787	0.781	0.775	0.769	1
2	0.683	0.672	0.661	0.650	0.640	0.630	0.620	0.610	0.601	0.592	2
3	0.564	0.551	0.537	0.524	0.512	0.500	0.488	0.477	0.466	0.455	3
4	0.467	0.451	0.437	0.423	0.410	0.397	0.384	0.373	0.361	0.350	4
5	0.386	0.370	0.355	0.341	0.328	0.315	0.303	0.291	0.280	0.269	5
6	0.319	0.303	0.289	0.275	0.262	0.250	0.238	0.277	0.217	0.207	6
7	0.263	0.249	0.235	0.222	0.210	0.198	0.188	0.178	0.168	0.159	7
8	0.218	0.204	0.191	0.179	0.168	0.157	0.148	0.139	0.130	0.123	8
9	0.180	0.167	0.155	0.144	0.134	0.125	0.116	0.108	0.101	0.094	9
10	0.149	0.137	0.126	0.116	0.107	0.099	0.092	0.085	0.078	0.073	10
11	0.123	0.112	0.103	0.094	0.086	0.079	0.072	0.066	0.061	0.056	11
12	0.102	0.092	0.083	0.076	0.069	0.062	0.057	0.052	0.047	0.043	12
13	0.084	0.075	0.068	0.061	0.055	0.050	0.045	0.040	0.037	0.033	13
14	0.069	0.062	0.055	0.049	0.044	0.039	0.035	0.032	0.028	0.025	14
15	0.057	0.051	0.045	0.040	0.035	0.031	0.028	0.025	0.022	0.020	15

Index